Internationale Politik und Sicherheit

herausgegeben von der
Stiftung Wissenschaft und Politik, Ebenhausen
Redaktion: Dr. Albrecht Zunker

Band 38

Bernard von Plate (Hrsg.)

Europa auf dem Wege zur kollektiven Sicherheit?

Konzeptionelle und organisatorische Entwicklungen der sicherheitspolitischen Institutionen Europas

Nomos Verlagsgesellschaft
Baden-Baden

Die Deutsche Bibliothek – CIP-Einheitsaufnahme

Europa auf dem Wege zur kollektiven Sicherheit?: Konzeptionelle und organisatorische Entwicklungen der sicherheitspolitischen Institutionen Europas / Bernard von Plate (Hrsg.). – 1. Aufl. – Baden-Baden: Nomos Verl.-Ges., 1994
(Internationale Politik und Sicherheit; Bd. 38)
ISBN 3-7890-3239-5
NE: Plate, Bernard von [Hrsg.]; GT

1. Auflage 1994

Inhalt

VORWORT 7

EINLEITUNG 11

1. Ambiguity and Promise. The Security Order in Europe in a Period of Transition: Patterns and Trends 13
   Johan Jørgen Holst

2. The Future of Multinational Security Institutions 29
   Wim F. van Eekelen

3. Overlapping Institutions, Underinsured Security: The Evolution of the Post-Cold War Security Order 49
   James B. Steinberg

4. Ost- und Mittelosteuropa: Eine Herausforderung für KSZE und NATO 71
   Bernard von Plate

5. Die Rolle der KSZE als Einrichtung kooperativer Sicherheit im Rahmen des "interlocking institutions"-Konzepts 95
   Heinz Vetschera

6. Normen- und Institutionenbildung der KSZE im Widerstreit politischer Interessen: Die Durchsetzung des Gewaltverzichts als Prüfstein für die KSZE 155
   Ingo Peters

7. Eine europäische Sicherheitskultur: Aussichten für eine regionalspezifische Normen- und Regimebildung 187
   Michael Staack

8. Die innerstaatliche Funktion der KSZE 209
   Bernard von Plate

9. Adapting the CSCE to Modern Problems: Limits and Opportunities 219
   Anne M. Dixon/Thomas J. Hirschfeld

10. NACC and the CSCE: A Contribution in the Context of the Concept of Interlocking Institutions 249
John Barrett/Hans Jochen Peters

11. Russia's Interests and Approaches towards the System of Interlocking European Institutions 265
Grigoriy J. Chudakov/Dmitriy A. Danilov/ Sergei A. Karaganov/Pavel T. Podlesnyi

12. Das Zusammenwirken multinationaler Institutionen: Neue Optionen für kollektive Verteidigung und internationale Friedensmissionen? 283
Uwe Nerlich

13. Requirements to Coordinate National Security Policies as a Precondition for Effective Multiinstitutional Crisis Management: The Role of Informal Structures 305
Robert D. Blackwill

ANHANG 315

1. Abkürzungen 315

2. Die Autoren 318

Vorwort

Der weltpolitische Umbruch der Jahre 1989 bis 1991 hat die Außen- und Sicherheitspolitik des vereinigten Deutschlands grundlegend verändert. Zwar wurde die Vereinigung im Rahmen der multinationalen Institutionen und Regime vollzogen, in die sich die deutsche Politik schon lange vor dem Umbruch eingegliedert hatte. Aber diese Institutionen und Regime, allen voran die EG und die NATO, müssen sämtlich reformiert bzw. weiterentwickelt werden, um künftigen Aufgaben gewachsen zu sein. Angesichts verbreiteter Trends zur Renationalisierung europäischer Politik erforderte dies von der deutschen Politik ein besonderes Engagement in Richtung internationaler Strukturbildung. Die Gestaltungsaufgaben reichen von der Stabilisierung der Nachfolgestaaten der Sowjetunion über die Neuordnung der europäisch-amerikanischen Beziehungen und der europäischen Gemeinschaftsbildung bis zur Eindämmung der Verbreitung von nuklearen, chemischen und biologischen Waffen. Die Vielfalt ungelöster Probleme im Süden der Welt verschärft diese Lage.

Zielsetzungen, Mittel und Entscheidungsstrukturen deutscher Politik müssen dem erwartbaren Spektrum künftiger Risiken, Konstellationen und Aufgaben angepaßt werden. Zugleich wird die internationale Handlungsfähigkeit Deutschlands mehr als die anderer Demokratien durch innenpolitische Blockaden eingeengt. Es fehlt noch weitgehend ein nationaler Konsens darüber, welche Rolle Deutschland auf längere Sicht international spielen und inwieweit sie Ordnungsmacht werden kann und soll. In der nach dem Umbruch instabilen und fließenden internationalen Umwelt ist dies nicht einfach eine Frage des politischen Willens. Die Grundfrage, ob die deutsche Außen- und Sicherheitspolitik von einem Modell der "Helvetisierung" oder dem Ziel geleitet ist, die internationale Umwelt als kooperierende Ordnungsmacht zu gestalten, ist bis heute nicht wirklich beantwortet. Von außen ist Deutschland trotz verknappter Ressourcen in vielfältiger Weise Gegenstand überzogener Erwartungen und von Ressentiments bestimmten Befürchtungen.

Die außen- und sicherheitspolitische Diskussion in Deutschland hat Mitte 1993 noch keine Orientierung gefunden. In Zeiten solchen Umbruchs kommt dem Diskurs über die künftige Rolle Deutschlands sowie über die Ziele und Instrumente seiner Politik besondere Bedeutung zu. Die Stiftung Wissenschaft und Politik hat frühzeitig begonnen, auf dem Wege der Politikberatung und durch die Beteiligung am allgemeinen außen- und sicherheitspolitischen Diskurs neue Wege aufzuzeigen. Mehrere Sonderforschungsvorhaben für das Bundesministerium der Verteidigung entwickelten hier ein breites Spektrum von Bewertungen und Empfehlungen. Ohne daß das Ministerium oder die Bundesregierung hier festgelegt wurden, führten die erforderlichen Dialoge während der Studienarbeit zu vielen neuen und wertvollen Erkenntnissen.

Die Sonderforschungsvorhaben begannen mit einer Untersuchung des neuen Analysebedarfs der sicherheitspolitischen Entscheidungsträger in der Bundesrepublik Deutschland – bis heute eine weder inhaltlich noch organisatorisch abgeschlossene Aufgabe. In der Zeit zwischen August und November 1991 wurden dann mit einer größeren Projektgruppe und unter Beteiligung zahlreicher externer Experten die neuen sicherheitspolitischen Rahmenbedingungen und möglichen künftigen Konstellationen, die erwartbaren Risiken und Konfliktformen sowie die verfügbaren Instrumente internationaler Sicherheitspolitik untersucht. Diese Studie diente vor allem der konzeptionellen Grundlegung und der Erarbeitung geeigneter methodischer Instrumente.[1]

Darauf aufbauend folgte zwischen April und November 1992 ein weiteres Sonderforschungsvorhaben, das im Februar 1993 zum Abschluß gebracht wurde. Es hatte die doppelte Aufgabe, für die wichtigen Bereiche deutscher Sicherheitspolitik Sachstands- und Trendanalysen zu erarbeiten und Lösungswege für künftige Probleme aufzuzeigen. Diese Studie gliederte sich in *internationale Umfeldanalysen* (zu Konstellationen, Risiken und Instrumentarien für das Krisen- und Konfliktmanagement), *Interessenanalysen* (Sicht Dritter sowie Interessen und Rollen Deutschlands) und *Analysen zu nationalen Planungsaufgaben* (Aufgaben und Struktur der Bundeswehr, Ressourcenstrategie und Organisation nationaler Planungs-, Führungs- und Entscheidungsstrukturen).

Die Leitung der Gesamtstudie lag bei Uwe Nerlich und Wolfgang Heydrich (Stellvertreter). Sie und die für die verschiedenen Teilstudien verantwortlichen Mitarbeiter – Falk Bomsdorf (GUS), Joachim Krause (Nichtverbreitung von Kernwaffen), Winrich Kühne (Völkerrecht und Vereinte Nationen), Jürgen Nötzold (Europäische Integration) und Bernard von Plate (KSZE und NACC) – bildeten die für die Planung und Durchführung der Studie verantwortliche Lenkungsgruppe. Die Projektassistenz lag bei Joachim Rohde und Helga Schubert. An der Gesamtstudie wirkten mehr als 150 Autoren und etliche zusätzliche Berater aus dem In- und Ausland mit, darunter zahlreiche Vertreter aus Rußland, der Ukraine und Mittelosteuropa.

---

1 Größere Teile dieser Untersuchung sind im Bd. 32 dieser Veröffentlichungsreihe zusammengefaßt. Vgl. Wolfgang *Heydrich*/Joachim *Krause*/Uwe *Nerlich*/Jürgen *Nötzold*/Reinhardt *Rummel* (Hrsg.), Sicherheitspolitik Deutschlands: Neue Konstellationen, Risiken, Instrumente, Baden-Baden 1992.

Im vorliegenden Band werden aus diesem Vorhaben die Ergebnisse und Beiträge der vom Herausgeber betreuten Teilstudie über "Möglichkeiten, Erfordernisse und Probleme im Rahmen der KSZE und ergänzender Gremien wie NACC" sowie über "Das Zusammenwirken multinationaler Institutionen" veröffentlicht.[2]

Ebenhausen, August 1993 — Uwe Nerlich

2 Folgende weitere Veröffentlichungen aus diesem Sonderforschungsvorhaben liegen in derselben Schriftenreihe bereits vor oder sind vorläufig beabsichtigt: Joachim *Krause* (Hrsg.), Kernwaffenverbreitung und internationaler Systemwandel – Neue Risiken und Gestaltungsmöglichkeiten, Bd. 36; Jürgen *Nötzold* (Hrsg.), Europäische Konstellationen (Arbeitstitel); Wolfgang *Heydrich*/ Joachim *Rohde* (Hrsg.), Überlegungen zur langfristigen Entwicklung deutscher Streitkräfte und ihrer rüstungswirtschaftlichen Basis (Arbeitstitel); Winrich *Kühne* (Hrsg.), Blauhelme in einer turbulenten Welt. Beiträge internationaler Experten zur Fortentwicklung des Völkerrechts und der Vereinten Nationen, Bd. 37.

Einleitung

Deutschland muß sich der Aufgabe stellen, seine Interessen zu bestimmen und nachdrücklicher zur Geltung zu bringen. Diese Forderung wird seit geraumer Zeit lauter erhoben, als das in den Jahrzehnten zuvor jemals der Fall war. Die Debatte hat gerade erst begonnen, manche harsche Kontroverse steht ihr zweifellos noch bevor. Eines ist jedoch nicht oder allenfalls an den Rändern des politischen Spektrums strittig: Deutschland sollte seinen außen- und sicherheitspolitischen Weg auch in Zukunft nicht alleine gehen. Drei Jahre nach dem weltpolitischen Umbruch herrscht in dieser Frage noch immer ein breiter Konsens. Es kommt nun darauf an, daß dieser Konsens nicht auf dem Seitenpfad einer verfassungsrechtlichen Debatte verlorengeht.

Dies ist der Hintergrund für die im vorliegenden Band zusammengestellten Beiträge. Sie stellen im Hinblick auf die sicherheitspolitischen Institutionen Europas, die in den Jahren des Kalten Krieges und – wie es dann später weniger dramatisch hieß – unter den Bedingungen des Ost-West-Konflikts entstanden und "sozialisiert" worden sind, folgende Frage: Welche Rolle können diese Institutionen jeweils allein und im Zusammenspiel mit anderen in Zukunft wahrnehmen? Es handelt sich also nicht nur um eine Bestandsaufnahme. Den Autoren liegt gleichermaßen an einem Blick nach vorn. Es geht ihnen darum herauszufinden, welchem Veränderungsbedarf die Instrumente europäischer und atlantischer Sicherheitspolitik ausgesetzt sind. Insofern verstehen sich die Beiträge als durchaus praxisorientiert.

Unter den Bedingungen des Ost-West-Gegensatzes war das Verhältnis zwischen *kollektiver Verteidigung* und *kollektiver Sicherheit* irreparabel gestört. Der Ruf nach kollektiver Sicherheit taugte allenfalls für Propagandaschlachten. Schon die bitteren Erfahrungen des Völkerbundes hatten die Ideen und Konzepte kollektiver Sicherheit nachhaltig diskreditiert. Der Antagonismus der Nachkriegsordnung ließ keinen Platz für versöhnlichere Erfahrungen. Mit der Wende in Ost- und Mittelosteuropa zeichnen sich indessen Bedingungen ab, unter denen eine strikte Trennung der beiden sicherheitspolitischen Ordnungsmuster nicht mehr aufrechtzuerhalten ist und das Netz gemeinsamer Sicherheitsstrukturen enger geknüpft werden kann, ohne jedoch die prinzipielle Unterscheidung zwischen den Instrumenten kollektiver Verteidigung und kollektiver Sicherheit bereits im Ansatz aufzuheben. Diese Entwicklung bleibt zweifellos hinter dem zurück, was sich mancher in den euphorischen Wochen der Wende mehr erträumt als mit nüchternem Verstand vorgestellt haben mochte. Doch sie geht weit über das hinaus, was in den Jahren des Ost-West-Konflikts erreichbar war.

Die Mehrheit der Beiträge befaßt sich in der einen oder anderen Weise mit der KSZE. Dieser Akzent ist insofern Programm, als mit ihm noch einmal unterstrichen wird, daß der Raum, in dem am Beginn einer postantagonistischen Ära die Sicherheit zu gestalten ist, im Osten an den Pazifik reicht und im Westen die transatlantischen Staaten USA und Kanada einschließt. Keine andere sicherheitspolitische Einrichtung, sieht man einmal von den Vereinten Nationen ab, umfaßt einen gleich großen, aber auch ähnlich heterogenen Teilnehmerkreis. Dafür hat sich auch kein anderes sicherheitspolitisches Instrument, die Vereinten Nationen eingeschlossen, auf einen ähnlich umfangreichen und ausdifferenzierten Normenkatalog verpflichtet wie die KSZE. Damit ist zugleich das Spannungsfeld abgesteckt, in dem sich die konzeptionellen Überlegungen zur KSZE bewegen.

Die Aufbruchstimmung, von der noch die *Charta von Paris für ein neues Europa* der KSZE getragen war, ist durch die Bilder einer bitteren Realität verdrängt worden. An die Stelle eines beschworenen Zeitalters "der Demokratie, des Friedens und der Einheit" sind vielfach Kriege, "ethnische Säuberungen", Mißtrauen oder unerbittlicher Haß getreten. Gleichwohl, die alte Trennlinie zwischen Ost und West ist hinfällig geworden. So schwer es auch immer sein mag, seine genauen Grenzen festzulegen: Europa ist nicht mehr durch einen ideologischen Limes geteilt. Die gemeinsame Gestaltungsaufgabe betrifft – so mehrheitlich die Perspektive der Autoren – den ganzen Kontinent.

In der einen oder anderen Weise markieren die Beiträge das Stadium einer Debatte, in der die offenen Fragen die gesicherten Antworten an Zahl weit übersteigen. Insofern ist dieser Band auch eine Aufforderung, weiterzudenken und sich der Debatte nicht zu versagen. Über eines sollte dabei jedoch Einigkeit herrschen: An die Stelle des Ost-West-Konflikts und des gesellschaftspolitischen Antagonismus der Nachkriegsjahrzehnte dürfen keine konzeptionellen Glaubenskriege treten.

Ebenhausen, August 1993 Bernard von Plate

1. Ambiguity and Promise. The Security Order in Europe in a Period of Transition: Patterns and Trends*

Johan Jørgen Holst

I. Perspective

The purpose of the present argument is to outline and suggest some salient trajectories which will shape the pattern of security arrangements in Europe. Our purpose is not to present architectural blueprints, such endeavours frequently seem curiously divorced from the contradictory realities of the present order. More often than not they remain silent on the key question of how we get from here to there, on the core issue of what is to be done (Lenin was right in insisting on this constituting the key question in political life). Furthermore, we remain unconvinced that the political order in Europe will ever conform to the abstract logic of neat designs. Our vision is rather one of competing and contradictory trends, of unresolved problems and enduring tensions. The period of transition from the Cold War order, which was in fact less static and frozen than what is commonly postulated in hindsight, is likely to last for quite some time, and the destination will remain largely unknown.

Furthermore, it is our view that institution building does not constitute an abstract political exercise, but rather should reflect responses to the challenges at hand and since the latter will remain multifarious and extremely complex in their interaction and manifestation the institutional framework will be characterized by overlapping jurisdictions, variable geometries, competition for competence, hidden agendas and competing ambitions.

The argument which follows is unashamedly normative in the sense that it takes a stand on controversial issues and recommends specific courses of action. It is focused on the substance of policy rather than on the conditions of policymaking.

II. Core Functions

Let us start the argument by outlining some of the basic security functions as they emerge in the post-Cold War era. At present European security is not threatened by the heavy shadows of hegemonic ambition buttressed by large military forces in a high state of readiness. A clear and present danger of hegemonic drive has been replaced by a general state of uncertainty and ambiguity. Hence, the issue is no longer one of containing of a hegemonic power, but of creating conditions which

---

* The views expressed in this paper are those of the author and should not be construed as the official views of the Norwegian government.

will reduce the chance that a hegemonic power or coalition of powers will re-emerge in the future. Since Russia remains the single largest military power on the Eurasian continent, such preventive construction has to focus on how to integrate Russia into a European political order circumscribed by rules and norms in favour of mutual restraint and community building. Russia has not been part of the European tradition of checks and balances through the classical balance of power system. It has sought security in territorial expansion rather than in the rules of the game. Hence, a major challenge will be that of socializing Russia into the processes of European construction.

It has become commonplace to observe that the Cold War tended to relegate many unresolved issues in Europe to the deep freeze, particularly those which affected the relationship between ethnicity and statehood, between ethnic majorities and minorities. The notion that state borders should coincide with ethnic boundaries is a prescription for perpetual war in Europe in view of the ethnic mosaic which has been shaped by the movements of European history. The idea of nationhood need not, of course, be related solely or even primarily to ethnicity. However, it tends to create a dynamic of us/them which tends towards a reduction to ethnicity. The extreme expression of this dynamics is the notion of ethnic cleansing. Hence, a major challenge is to transcend the logic of the nation-state and to project an integrating alternative to the disintegration of nation-states into smaller (and less viable) units.

It should be interjected at this point that the very term "nation-state" is complicated and misleading. Most of the states in Europe are multinational, spun around different myths other than that of ethnicity. The imagined communities postulate uniqueness and separateness in terms of values, traditions and associations. However, when the uniqueness is challenged and put to a test it tends to beget the notion of ethnic purity. The real constituent element of the state system in Europe in the past was the territorial state and the claim to sovereignty associated with the ability to wield exclusive authority within a clearly delineated and defined area. This construction dominated the European scene since the Peace of Westphalia in 1648. It has become increasingly clear towards the end of the twentieth century that the territorial state is no longer able to provide protection or governance. Nuclear weapons and their long-range delivery means have blown the roofs off the territorial states. No "national" government is able to establish political control over the forces which shape societies in the economic, environmental, technological, informational or cultural domains. The relationship between society and the state has changed. The issue at hand is to recapture lost sovereignty which is not retrievable within the exclusive confines of territorial states, rather only within the broader framework of communities which transcend and comprise the nations of Europe. Hence, a major task is that of taming national sovereignty.

European states have evolved along divergent trajectories. After the end of the Cold War they have started to interact in a manner which poses a challenge to the general stability of the European order. To some extent the process of integration and reconciliation in Western Europe, including the formation and development of the European Community, constituted a response to the challenge from the East, to the stalinist empire which was imposed upon large parts of Central and Eastern Europe. The states which were absorbed into the system of Communist Muscovy had no choice but to submit to an imposed authority which went far beyond the formation of an association of loyal and subservient allies. It imposed a social and political order reflecting the traditions of oriental despotism rather than a liberal order based on the concept of an open society.

Hence, the end of the Cold War inaugurated a process of disintegration in the East at the very moment when Western Europe was moving into a period of expanded and deepened integration. The rising fervour of nationalism tended to link the two processes causing the architects of the European Community, perhaps, to load the train towards an integrated Europe beyond sustainable limits and travel at speeds which the existing rail system could not carry. The states of Central and Eastern Europe sought association with the European Community with an impatience which could bring about economic and social turmoil threatening not only fragile democratic constructions in the East, but also the very process of integration in the West. However, failure to respond adequately to the enormous needs of the states in the East could generate estrangement and new divisions in Europe. Therefore, a principal challenge is that of maintaining and expanding a zone of stability in Europe. The European Community must be at the center of that effort, but it remains clearly inadequate when it comes to the core function of security.

NATO has linked the United States and Canada to the process of maintaining security in Europe during the period of the Cold War. It provided a framework for the containment of Soviet power *and* incentives against nuclear proliferation. Extended deterrence linked the security of North America to that of Western Europe. When the two appeared to separate as when Moscow in the context of strategic parity deployed the SS-20 missile, which could only reach targets in Europe, the Europeans clamoured for additional assurance. (They also tended to back off from implementing the corrective measures once they had persuaded the Americans that they were needed). After the end of the Cold War, the dissolution of the Warsaw Pact, the withdrawal of Soviet forces from Central and Eastern Europe and the break-up of the Soviet Union, questions arise concerning the continued need for NATO, in short about its relevance in the new era.

American decisions will be made in the United States according to an American agenda and perceptions of American interests. However, neither its agenda nor perceptions are beyond European influence. As the military challenge is no longer one of hegemonic proportions, but rather one of local turmoil which could spread and cause broader conflagration, reconstituting the alliance has become a principal task. Peacekeeping and enforcement beyond NATO borders rather than forward defence of those borders has become the first order of business. The tragedy of Yugoslavia has shown that unless the Americans take the lead the Europeans will fail to take sufficient action. NATO was not designed to deal with challenges like the fratricide which is enveloping large portions of former Yugoslavia. However, unless it manages to provide adequate responses to such challenges in the future it will increasingly be viewed as irrelevant and marginal. And unless the Americans take the lead it is unlikely to provide adequate responses. The Yugoslav crisis has its own unique features but it may constitute the prologue to a much broader process of disintegration, to the break-up of the Versailles system in Central and South Eastern Europe. Turmoil could spread to the Carpatians and the plains of Romania. The "Magyar issue" could link disparate regions like Slovakia, Ukraine, Transylvania and Vojvodina. The Balkans could be further ignited by the intervention of outside parties (Albania, Bulgaria, Turkey, Greece) in defence of "their" minorities and interests.

The break-down of the Versailles system will require the constitution of another political order if disorder is to be contained or reversed. NATO could be a key factor in that construction. However, little, if any, thought has gone into designing stabilizing and legitimating arrangments for the soft underbelly of Europe. Attention has been focused rather on orchestrating the interplay of some of the central overlapping institutions of the West. In addition there are the complex processes of dissolution and conflict among and within the successor states of the Soviet Union. They could interact and interlock with the centrifugal forces of Central and South Eastern Europe, and they are likely to pose new problems and questions concerning local balances of power and fears of military dominance like those of Serb dominance in the former Yugoslavia and the Balkan region. Hence, the old tasks of containment and power balancing remain but their context and applications are aimed at smaller regions.

American engagement is needed in order to project relevant power to affect calculations and outcomes in the new era of ambiguity and turmoil. However, it should be recognized that many of the conflicts are beyond rational calculus and the "rules" of deterrence and compellence. In the context of containing the new turmoil it will be necessary also to deter major states from exploiting the weaknesses of regions and smaller states to expand their own spheres of influence by direct or indirect engagement, thereby projecting new threats of hegemonic ambitions. American engagement remains essential, particularly in a period of Russian uncertainty and equivocation in order to constrain a possible return to imperial ambitions.

In the context of increased uncertainty and ambiguity American engagement will also be essential in order to stem impulses and incentives for nuclear proliferation. It has been critical for framing the process of nuclear stabilization in the wake of the break-up of the Soviet Union. All theater nuclear weapons apparently have been moved to Russian territory, but they may still be dispersed to operational units. The disassembly and destruction of the huge nuclear armory will take many years and Russia remains in a volatile stage of political and economic transition. The strategic weapons remain dispersed in four independent states all of which have committed themselves to their dismantlement and to join the Non-proliferation Treaty as non-nuclear weapon states. Ukraine is attempting to use the nuclear weapons on its territory as a means of obtaining security guarantees and economic assistance. All of the states are in the process of grappling with enormous economic, political and social problems. Conflicts between any of them and Russia, particularly Ukraine, could disrupt the process of stabilization and raise the spectre of nuclear proliferation in Europe. It cannot be confidently assumed that if one more state, particularly a turbulent state, should join the nuclear club that the process would end there. Nor can it be assumed that such a line of policy would be uncontested by Russia. In an uncertain period of transition American engagement, including an appropriate nuclear component is essential in contributing to the security arrangements for Western Europe.

We have observed that ethnically or religiously based violence and communal strife may be largely beyond the scope of deterrence. Nuclear weapons served for the five decades of the Cold War to prevent war in Europe. We cannot know what the situation would have been in the absence of nuclear weapons since history is not in the habit of revealing its alternatives, but we can at least establish a correlation between the existence of nuclear weapons and their integration into a strategy of deterrence on the one hand, and the absence of war across the East-West division on the other. It remains a reasonable hypothesis that there is also a causal link here. In any event, that link is widely believed to exist. After the end of the Cold War, hot wars have broken out in Europe. They are largely uncontainable through the system of military strategy and disposition of forces developed for Cold War confrontation. The danger persists that their further prosecution and spread will weaken the mental reservations and lower the political threshold against resorting to war as a means of obtaining possessions and benefits. Such a cultural transformation could impact also on nuclear taboos, thereby also transforming the challenges of nuclear proliferation. American engagement will then remain essential as a stabilizing element in a volatile and fragile European order.

In the context of the Conference on Security and Cooperation in Europe (CSCE), states have codified a set of rules, norms and standards whose observance constitutes a necessary condition for the preservation of minimum order. They apply principally to the conduct of interstate relations. However, increasingly, states have accepted that they are bound also by rules, norms and standards in regard to the conduct of intrastate relations, to the relation between citizens and the state. Traditional international law has focused on protecting the rights of states and consequently on the inviolability of their borders. Since World War II that concern has been supplemented by a focus on protecting rights of individuals and consequently on the inviolability of the individual. States then have duties beyond borders. In the new ethnic conflicts in Europe the agreed rules, norms and standards have been violated in a flagrant manner. Atrocities which most Europeans thought belonged to times long passed have been perpetrated in what used to be Yugoslavia. Acceptance of these atrocities on behalf of the states belonging to the CSCE could amount to erosion of the rules of the game which constitute necessary conditions for the maintenance of minimum order. Without a basic consensus and adherence to the rules of the game security will remain elusive for all states in Europe. States do not only compete and cooperate for purposes of territorial possession, they also have a stake in the basic norms which should govern international behaviour. Hence, it remains a key function of security policy in Europe to socialize the new states of Central and Eastern Europe as well as the successor states of the Soviet Union into the system of rules, norms and standards which has been developed and adopted by the CSCE.

III. Institutional Architecture in the Era of Ambiguity

Having identified some of the key functions to be served by viable security arrangements in Europe we may proceed with some postulates concerning the process of construction in Europe. The basic feature is one of ambiguity and contradictory trends. Clarity is unlikely to replace ambiguity in the foreseeable future and the trends are equally unlikely to conform to consistent patterns. The process of adjustment and adaptation to new circumstances, opportunities and constraints is not susceptible to short term conclusions. Perceptions often lag behind constituted reality. The new reality is understood differently in various regions and countries in Europe and is manifested in different ways throughout Europe. With the end of the Cold War peace no longer seems indivisible and if it is divisible in the turbulent and soft underbelly of Europe it could also become divisible over time in the firmer regions of Europe. Could the end of the Cold War herald a new era of limited wars threatening the security of smaller rimland states? The fact that such questions are posed or suggested explains why some of the smaller states are seeking association with the core political institution of the new Europe, the European Community, in order to prevent their security from being eroded through a process of marginalization and isolation. The volatility and unpredictability of Russia, the heartland power of Europe, add momentum to this desire.

The flora of institutions which are relevant to security in Europe exhibits trends of wasteful duplication, debilitating competition and dubious posturing. Overlapping institutions can add flexibility to the conduct of international relations but they can also lead to new rigidities as jurisdictional battles overshadow basic purpose. Rather than interlocking institutions in a coherent pattern, overlapping ones may produce interblocking institutions, as symbols substitute for substance and as cost-effective solutions become the victims of symbolic demonstration.

IV. Towards a Constructive Interplay

It follows from the preceding argument that NATO constitutes the core institution for the maintenance of peace and security in Europe. Since American engagement is necessary in order to prevent and contain the reemergence of hegemonic powers or coalitions of powers, particularly with Russia as the center of gravity; in order to stem the process of nuclear proliferation; and in order to forge coalitions to enforce and uphold the rules, norms and standards of a minimum order, NATO provides the best framework and machinery for channeling and shaping that engagement. However, the alliance which was forged for purposes of coping with the challenges of the Cold War needs to be transformed and changed to cope with the novel challenges of an era of ambiguity and turmoil.

That transition will require a certain redistribution of roles, risks and responsibilities with Europeans relieving the Americans of some of the burdens of the common defence. But since the concept of a common defence remains essential in order to prevent a return to purely national defence establishments the United States as well as the European allies must remain committed to programs which uphold the notion and substance of a common defence. NATO's very successful infrastructure program is a case in point. It is threatened, however, by US-Congressional insistence on cutting the American share down to levels which are less than fair and European reluctance to assign priority to common funding in a period of budgetary reductions and restructuring of forces.

NATO has been fairly successful in developing new concepts which should govern strategy and force structure in this new era. There is no longer a need to maintain forces at a high state of readiness in forward positions in order to deter the threat of a massive surprise attack across the central front. In fact, there are no more fronts as Soviet (now Russian) troops are withdrawn from their forward positions in Central Europe. Even in the north where there is no territorial buffer, Russian forces are being reduced and restructured to a less offensive posture and they are no longer linked to an offensive war machine pointing at the heart of

Europe. Hence, NATO had to change its military posture in order not to provide obstacles to the political reconstruction of Europe.

A capacity had to be maintained to establish forward presence in any part of the alliance area when needed. The new triad of reaction forces, main defence forces and augmentation forces is designed to provide capabilities for forward presence, territorial defence and reconstitution. However, conceptual clarification must be followed by the restructuring and commitment of forces and here actual implementation is lagging far behind the design. Reaction forces will be expensive and are now receiving maximum attention because they provide vehicles for multinational construction. However, all the attention which is presently devoted to forces for immediate and rapid reaction appears to be drawing attention away from the main defence forces and the need to maintain a capacity to reinforce and relieve reaction forces as well as to reconstitute a major defence capacity in the event of a reversal of present political trends. NATO needs to preserve a balanced defence posture which is directly relevant to protecting its members against armed aggression, however remote that contingency appears today.

Much attention has been focused, and for good reasons, on the need to develop capacities for peacekeeping (Chapter VI) and peace enforcement (Chapter VII). NATO's reaction forces lend themselves to such use, particularly peace enforcement, in addition to their principal task of ensuring the territorial integrity of its member states in a period of no fixed confrontation or front, but with the long-term spectre of local conflicts which may spill over to NATO territory. The residual option may come to dominate the core functions of NATO's reaction forces. Here political tensions may arise as different traditions and perspectives interact. Some NATO countries, most notably the United States and Great Britain, rely on professional soldiers in expeditionary forces while several of the continental European states rely on conscript forces designed and maintained for purposes of defending national territory. Priorities and outlooks could diverge if military engagement beyond NATO territory were to overshadow preparations to defend that territory. On the other hand, in the short-term threats to the security of NATO members are likely to manifest themselves in potentially expanding zones of instability with epicenters in the Balkans and on the southern rim of Russia, necessitating novel concepts of forward defence and flexible response. From the perspective of interlocking institutions it is interesting to note that NATO's engagement in peacekeeping is confined to the CSCE area projecting the possibility that NATO could come to constitute the defence component of the CSCE in the way the Western European Union (WEU) had been projected for the European Community. At present this is but a distant possibility, but urgent requirements and NATO's responses thereto could lend substance to such visions which in turn could help shape NATO's responses in the longer term.

Such developments would necessitate a closer association between NATO and the states in Eastern Europe and in the area of the former Soviet Union. The North Atlantic Cooperation Council (NACC) provides a flexible framework for managing such a process of association. American engagement is necessary in order to maintain the balance required for such association to take place in regard to security arrangements in Europe.

In the short term the NACC constitutes a mechanism for dismantling the vestiges, physical as well as mental, of the military confrontation of the Cold War. Cooperative approaches to such dismantlement, implementation of the START and CFE treaties are the most important aspects, could stimulate a habit of providing mutual reassurance and confidence building. Cooperative undertakings in regard to verification, military exercises, arms exports, nuclear proliferation, conversion, etc could stimulate notions of common security. Equally important, they could serve as means to socialize the Russian military into a cooperative culture, contributing to steering the Russian military establishment towards the path of economic and political reform. Thereby it could be possible to counteract the xenophobic impulses which have strong roots in the Russian military and which could make it into a coalition partner for extremist nationalist forces (the Russian counterpart to the red-brown coalition in Serbia). In this connection NATO countries could be much more responsive than they have been to the need to alleviate a growing social problem by providing housing for Soviet officers in order to prevent their estrangement from the policy of reforms.

Peacekeeping and peace enforcement could provide another area of common endeavour. Here several observations seem necessary. Peacekeeping constitutes a unique way of applying military units in order to generate confidence in the mutual restraint and disengagement of the parties to a conflict. Such operations depend on the consent of those parties and the rules of engagement limit the use of force essentially to self-defence. The authority of peacekeeping forces is a result of their international mandate rather than the power of their weapons. The techniques of peacekeeping must be learned and constitute a subject for potential cooperation between NATO countries and their NACC partners.

Peacekeeping operations now frequently comprise a set of civilian functions like policing and electoral supervision. Increasingly they are likely to extend to protection of humanitarian relief efforts, and in that context the rules of engagement will be stretched to include the use of force if needed to protect such efforts. Finally, there is a new consensus in the Security Council of the United Nations (UN) with the waning of the propensity of great powers to view local conflicts from the perspective of a global contest, as opportunities for the acquisition or denial of clients and proteges in their struggle for power and influence.

From the point of view of European security care should be taken to avoid two different systems of peacekeeping in Europe, one managed by NATO and another by Russia and/or the CIS within the confines of the territory of the former Soviet Union. Even a *de facto* "division of labour" or any such configuration could lead to a reinstitution of the Brezhnev doctrine within the area of the former Soviet Union.

V. The WEU between Promise and Implementation

The West European Union constitutes a double promise: the embodiment of a European pillar within the Atlantic Alliance and the repository of the defence identity of the European Political Union. In many ways it suggests potentiality rather than reality. The two functions could generate tensions and contradictions, particularly if the European defence identity be defined in contrast to the Atlantic Alliance, as a potential substitute or successor, rather than as a complement. At times it may appear to constitute a hedge against the consequences of American withdrawal and a dissolution of NATO, at other times as a means designed to facilitate a French return to collective defence commitments. The problem with the former is that it may generate dispositions which add up to a self-fulfilling prophecy. The latter perspective gives France leverage over the construction which may be at growing variance with notions of equity and equality. In elaborating and defining the European defence identity particular attention should be paid then to the need for transatlantic reassurance in order not to throw Atlantic security out with the European bath water. Tensions exist between the perspectives of the "Europe firsters" and the "Atlantic firsters." However, all members have agreed that "the primary responsibilities of forces answerable to the WEU will remain NATO's collective defence under the Washington Treaty." The danger persists, nevertheless that rhetoric will replace attention to substance, that symbols will replace strategies for coping with real tasks.

Not all of the members of the European Community are full-fledged members of the West European Union. Denmark and Ireland have chosen not to join. Nor are all the European member states of NATO full members of the WEU. Turkey, Iceland and Norway are associate members and Denmark an observer. We discern an emerging pattern of variable geometry in the institutional framework of security in Europe. In the future we may have more members of the EC that are not members of the WEU and members of the WEU who are not members of NATO.

In any event the promise of the WEU will be circumscribed by economic stringency, by the financial need to avoid wasteful duplication at a time when defence budgets are dwindling and forces reduced and restructured. A process of institutional and functional consolidation is underway as the Independent European Program Group (IEPG) is folded into the WEU and the working groups of the Eurogroup transferred thereto. However, such consolidation which makes eminent sense from the point of view of rationalization creates a situation of variable geometry with respect to functional involvement in the WEU as associate members and observers of the WEU will retain full voting rights with respect to matters falling within the purview of the IEPG and the Eurogroup. The earmarking of WEU forces will not generate new forces, but rather suggest alternative frameworks for the commitment of forces already assigned to NATO or in national defence structures. They could add to the flexibility of response, but they could also detract from overall efficiency and clarity with respect to the primary defence functions of NATO, particularly if the integrated defence planning system in NATO were to be scaled down in order to allow allocation of resources to the formation of the planning cell of the WEU. Double and triple hatting could detract from the military cohesion of the Atlantic Alliance.

A major consideration at the present stage of European development is to prevent and constrain tendencies towards a renationalization of defence structures and arrangements. They could give rise to new concerns about internal imbalances in Western Europe and generate competition and uncertainty which could prove detrimental to the process of European integration, both its deepening and widening, as well as to the continued viability of the Atlantic Alliance. At the same time care should be taken not to launch military projects which would move military issues towards the core of the European integration process at a time when priorities should rest with political organization and economic restructuring. Since little substance is likely to be put into the military basket of European construction at this stage, for reasons suggested above, symbolic insistence could generate unnecessary controversy and constrain future options. Emphasis on the creation of multinational formations for peacekeeping and reinforcement in NATO and the WEU should not be confused with a resurrection of the schemes of the 1950s for a European army.

Both the search for a European defence identity and present efforts to restructure NATO defences are based on the notion that defence should constitute a collective undertaking. The salience of that perspective and proposition has been underlined by the unification of Germany and latent fears of internal imbalances and impulses towards *Alleingang* and national assertiveness. Such fears are nurtured also by the potential interplay of militant nationalism in the Eastern parts of Europe and the reemergence of a militant right in the societies of Western Europe, threatening the ethos of integration and internationalism. It is in this perspective, we believe, that we should also view the La Rochelle agreement between Germany and France to expand their military cooperation over and above the existing brigade and to form the nucleus for a European Corps to which forces of other WEU states could be added. It states that "the tasks of the European Corps are part of the perspectives of the European Union." Its tasks are threefold; combat missions, peacekeeping missions, and humanitarian missions tailored to the new era of reduced direct threat against the territorial integrity of the states of Western Europe and increased threat against the conditions for minimum order in Europe.

The European Corps straddles both WEU and NATO, thus contributing to the flexibility as well as the ambiguity of the emerging architecture. It provides a potential vehicle for tying France closer to a collective defence undertaking, and for providing reassurance about German assertiveness. However, it was also viewed as a vehicle for moving Germany away from collective defence commitments in NATO and towards a more Gaullist approach to national defence. Franco-German reconciliation remains at the core of the process of European integration and Germany therefore needs to reconcile her European and Atlantic links. The Joint Committee of the Eurocorps was viewed by some as a trojan horse designed to dismantle the integrated defence organization in NATO. However, the agreements reached between France, Germany and SACEUR on the wartime disposition of the Corps appears to have alleviated many Atlanticist fears of an ugly European duckling.

VI. The CSCE Hat

The CSCE provides a potential mechanism for linking the functions and activities of various regional organizations and groupings in Europe, primarily the core institutions of Western Europe, but also others such as the Commonwealth of Independent States (CIS), the Višegrad group, etc. It is still in an embryonic stage and obviously incapable of replacing the core institutions like NATO, the EC or the WEU. The issue is in fact not one of replacement, but rather linkage, orchestration, rationalization, division of labour and comparative advantage. The CSCE provides a framework for linking other institutions with the broader task of European reconstruction, of reconnecting the eastern part of Europe with its western part. It constitutes a repository of the basic rules, norms and standards which should govern inter-state as well as intra-state relations in a cooperative security order in Europe. Its system of periodic reviews provides an important mechanism for forging, clarifying and legitimating the basic code of conduct.

It was born in the last stage of the Cold War and helped to pave the way to the post-Cold War era. It provided an arena wherein the states of the eastern part of Europe could assume more independent roles, develop international personalities and become socialized into the norms of multilateralism. For some of the states of Central Europe it may appear to be associated with an era of limited sovereignty, as an inadequate substitute for direct association with the core institutions of the West. It is important therefore to develop the CSCE in consonance with the new realities and with a view to dealing with emerging challenges.

During the Cold War era Western states were reluctant to institutionalize the CSCE process beyond the bare minimum in order not to create mechanisms and fora which could weaken or undermine the integrated institutions of the West. Now the challenge is a different one, to relate those integrated institutions to the CSCE in order to enhance the capacity of the latter to function as a regional arrangement in consonance with Chapter VIII of the UN Charter. The CSCE is far from constituting a mechanism for collective security in Europe tending rather in the direction of functioning as a concert of powers. It is an arena for conference diplomacy more than an operational mechanism. It lacks institutional coherence due to the habit of distributing small functional units to various capitals rather than assembling the executive machinery in one location. The Council, the Committee of Senior Officials, the Chairman-in-Office troika and the review conferences are designed to manage a process of consultation and rule-making. For the CSCE to function more effectively as a mechanism for linking existing operational capacities in the strong institutions it is probably necessary to establish an office of secretary general co-located with the Conflict Prevention Center (CPC) and other functional cells.

The new Security Forum which will replace and consolidate negotiating fora for arms control in Europe of the era of confrontation could serve the following functions: generalize the arms control regimes, which have been instituted by the INF and CFE treaties (harmonization); strengthen the non-proliferation regime; elaborate guidelines for the export of arms and dual-use technologies; consolidate and broaden the system of confidence and security building measures; and develop systems of reassurance and restraint in regard to military dispositions and activities in certain border regions in order to avoid offensive concentration and orientation, etc.

The CSCE has put peacekeeping on the agenda. It will not establish its own capacities, but rather draw on those of member states, including the collective capacities of NATO and, possibly, the CIS. It could serve as a mandating institution for peacekeeping operations in Europe. However, in many instances the UN is likely to assume direct responsibility for organizing and implementing peacekeeping and peacemaking operations. The CSCE could alleviate the pressures on the UN by developing its own peacekeeping office in whose absence the mandating function will be purely symbolic. Such an office could be linked to the CPC and concentrate, perhaps, on developing procedures and mechanisms for early warning, fact-finding, observation and preventive deployments.

VII. The Logic of the European Construction: A Summary

The European construction reflects a compelling logic. The European order requires a taming of sovereignty, its transformation by a process of community building, linking local communities in broader associations, breaking the monopoly of the territorial state, making it less sovereign, creating multiple identities also across borders, and transforming relations between societies and states. The states of Europe are multiethnic entities although they pose as nation states. Imagined communities may be forged around other myths than that of ethnicity, myths which may supplement and moderate the ethnic myth. When that is not accomplished states may slide towards fratricidal conflicts. A European community is our best insurance against the balkanization of Europe. The frightening alternative has been written in blood on the walls in what used to be Yugoslavia.

The territorial state no longer wields exclusive authority within its borders. It is no longer sovereign. It has been penetrated by the internationalization of finance, production, distribution, communication, learning, environmental impact, technology, and the power to destroy. The territorial state has lost its power to protect. Functional integration has torn it asunder. Political integration has become necessary in order to recapture lost sovereignty. It is retrievable only within a broader framework than that of the territorial state.

Community building is no simple task. Europe will not constitute a United States of Europe patterned on the American model. The European Community is a construction *sui generis*, without precedents and prior models. Its future shape and structure are obfuscated by contradictory trends and competing ambitions. A balanced construction could easily be jeopardized by competing institutional ambitions within the community, by struggles for jurisdiction and competence which inevitably raise issues concerning democratic accountability and relations between community institutions and national polities.

The European Community runs the danger of creating distance and estrangement in relation to its citizens, appearing to favour centralization rather than diffusion of power. The language of diplomatic compromise and bureaucratic circumspection tends to hamper public comprehension, and the inevitable ambiguity tends to beget suspicion and legitimate even unreasonable interpretation. The problems of the community which have become more visible after the Danish "no" to the union treaty are compounded by the general crisis of confidence permeating industrial societies at present. Frustration and anger, disaffection and discontent, confusion and equivocation flourish in growing opposition to governments which appear to be committed to business as usual, as policies of vision seem to be replaced by politics as management. The European idea, so necessary for Europe's future, seems to be waning because of a lack of credible leadership, leadership which combines inspiration and competence and evokes confidence.

We live in a new world. The Communist menace has been replaced by nationalist perils, a clear and present danger of military attack by unspecified risks, the Soviet threat by uncertainty. How can we motivate open societies to maintain viable defences in such circumstances? We should view defence as prudential insurance. But how high a premium can we expect societies to accept when social needs call out for increased attention and resources? All ministries of defence and defence staffs now devote their full attention to restructuring and reorganization, to how they can increase the productivity of shrinking budgets. Wasteful duplication will have few supporters. It will constrain the development of a European defence identity at this time.

The logic behind the calls for a common defence policy for Europe is compellingly simple. The actual economic integration which has taken place requires a kind of economic and monetary union. Such a union requires in turn a political union in order to preserve political direction, and any political union would have to embrace a common foreign and security policy which in turn necessitates the eventual framing of a common defence policy which in time could lead to a common defence. However, the logic has to be accompanied by a strategy for implementation. A common defence can hardly carry the burden of political reconstruction, it is more a consequence of integration than a vehicle for its promotion. Hence, creating a European defence identity raises issues of timing and priority. In relation to the Atlantic Alliance it raises issues of wasteful duplication, of the need to preserve and not weaken viable arrangements – "If it ain't broke, don't fix it!"

Both the European pillar and the European defence identity should be assessed from five perspectives: equity, efficiency, influence, coherence and organization. Equity relates to the equitable sharing of risks, roles and responsibilities, to the need for the Europeans to carry a larger share of the burden of the common defence. However, the overall level of defence effort is declining, therefore we are talking of relative efforts. Efficiency has to do with coordination and division of labour, with how we get more "bang for the buck." Influence in this context has to do primarily with input on the reconstruction of Europe, particularly in regard to how partly overlapping institutions can interlock and provide mutual support rather than engage in reciprocal emasculation. Organization in regard to defence refers particularly to the question of whether and how to organize defence as a collective responsibility and undertaking, to how to prevent a debilitating and divisive renationalization of defences in Europe.

The classical concepts of security relating to the protection of borders and territory remain at the core of the Atlantic Alliance, but it is now supplemented by protection of the rules, norms and standards needed to maintain minimum order in Europe. In a real sense, of course, absolute protection is impossible since weapons of mass destruction and the means of their speedy delivery over long distances have blown the roofs off the institution of the territorial state. Instead of direct defence of borders, states sought refuge in indirect protection through nuclear deterrence and its extension by guarantees to allies. No state is able any more to provide absolute protection of its citizens and physical values against military attack. They are inevitably and inexorably linked to each other in a condition of mutual interdependence created by mutual vulnerability. Genuine security can only be common security based on the constitution of communities transcending the territorial state, and, perhaps, the eventual and gradual transformation of the system of nuclear deterrence into a system of security cooperation and expanding joint management. Important progress has been made through arms control agreements and extensive systems of verification. NATO has played an essential role in bringing the system into place, and it could not have been achieved without active American participation. NATO and American engagement remain essential to the management and development of a viable arms control regime in Europe and they remain essential to the maintenance of adequate nuclear deterrence in the period of ambiguity. They will be essential also to the successful functioning of the newly created Forum for European Security within the CSCE and the Center for Crisis Prevention.

2. The Future of Multinational Security Institutions*

Wim F. van Eekelen

For forty years NATO has served us well by providing collective defence, extended deterrence and intensive transatlantic consultations on most of the security issues affecting Europe and North America. Its integrated military headquarters worked together day by day to an unprecedented degree, shaping the outlook, approach and routine of thousands of Allied officers. With the threat of massive surprise attack hovering over Europe and the relative weakness of the European members, the defence dimension became so preponderant in transatlantic relations that it overshadowed irritations in other areas, especially trade and monetary matters. Europe accepted US leadership of the Alliance as a natural corollary to the need for nuclear deterrence and American reinforcement capability.

With the end of the Cold War, collective defence appeared just one of the many dimensions of international relations – still important, but no longer an overriding priority. Russia was still the largest military power on the European continent, but was less and less able to wield that power against the West. Its economic problems at home pointed up the need for drastic cuts in military expenditures, while the smaller members of the former Warsaw Pact asserted their independence and progressed along the road to pluralistic democracy and a market economy. At first, when the Soviet Union still held together, they became much to their chagrin, a buffer zone between Western Europe and the USSR. Today their main concern is instability in Eastern Europe in general rather than Russian power which has become more distant. Because of their ambiguous strategic position, they alternated between advocating a Security Council for Europe and membership in NATO or the Western European Union (WEU), or both.

The ending of both Soviet and Russian oppression in Central and Eastern Europe revealed former tensions and conflicts, largely based on ethnic differences. The borders redrawn after the First and Second World Wars were challenged, and Eastern Europe found itself in a phase of disintegration, whereas Western Europe had overcome most of its traditional conflicts and was making great strides towards integration. Eastern Europe apparently needed to reassert national identities first before it could turn its mind to cooperative measures. It looked to the West, but largely along parallel bilateral channels, posing a double problem: the European Community could only be enlarged to include countries with sufficient political and economic maturity; new security arrangements could not entail formal guarantees while the volatile situation was still making it impossible to fathom the extent

* The views expressed in this paper reflect only the personal opinion of the author and do not represent any official position taken by the Western European Union.

and implications of such guarantees. The fact that in several cases former communist leaders managed to remain in power under the cloak of nationalism made the ideal of a "Europe whole and free" increasingly remote. Our hopes for a new peaceful order gave way to disorder, ethnic strife and attempts to change borders and to expel minorities by force. The cherished principles of the Helsinki Final Act of 1975, which had been instrumental in bringing about change in the East, were violated on a frightening scale.

The outcome of all these diverging trends has been an increased sense of uncertainty and instability, a wish to retain the buttresses that have successfully shored up our security, and a groping for ways of isolating and resolving the conflicts erupting so dangerously close to our own borders.

The Atlantic Alliance has defined its core functions, but at the same time has reached out to former adversaries in the East in an effort to respond to their pressure to adhere to Western values and institutions, while at the same time making sure that the Helsinki principles and arms control obligations are respected by all successor states to the Soviet Union. Some have said that NATO would become irrelevant without reaching out to the former Soviet Union. Others have found the claims that the North Atlantic Cooperation Council (NACC) could stabilize the new States somewhat extravagant. In any case, there is still a question mark as to the wisdom of lumping the countries of Central and Eastern Europe together with all the former Soviet republics. The extent to which it is possible or useful to differentiate between the participants is still unclear. Equally, it remains to be seen whether the NACC and the even larger Conference on Security and Cooperation in Europe (CSCE) can usefully co-exist and whether the core functions of NATO will be eroded. For the WEU, the enlargement of these two bodies has increased the desirability of a smaller circle of countries close to us, with the stress on a special relationship in the security field as a corollary to their association with the European Community. The Foreign Ministers of the nine WEU countries, for example, met their counterparts from Hungary, Poland, Czechoslovakia, Bulgaria, Romania and the three Baltic countries on 19 June 1992, near Bonn. The meeting offered those countries an opportunity to talk to the West without their Eastern neighbours being present and enabled WEU Ministers to show their willingness to take the security concerns of the eight countries into consideration when formulating positions or proposals in their international contacts.

I. New Dilemmas and Inconsistencies

One of the most striking of the strange phenomena of the post-Cold War era has been the disinclination to take a comprehensive look at our policy towards the East. The Community is taking a step towards a European Union, which should lead to convergence between economic, foreign and security policy, but the debate has been largely institutional and it has not been possible to bring these strands together to form concrete policies. A case in point is Yugoslavia, where after a first unsuccessful attempt economic leverage was not brought effectively to bear on the belligerents or on neighbouring countries to enforce their compliance with the embargo.

The second element is the reluctance to deploy military capabilities as a means of pressure in support of political objectives. The notion of deterrence has to be reexamined and reintroduced in a comprehensive approach. For more than forty years deterrence was the mainstay of our defence posture vis-à-vis the Warsaw Pact, but, of course, the context was different. Deterrence was directed towards the prevention of major war resulting from Warsaw Pact aggression. On the ground the emphasis was on defending NATO territory, especially the Federal Republic of Germany. Allied solidarity was expressed through forward deployments on friendly lands. Because of the clear demarcation line between the two pacts, the risk of escalation of even minor incidents was high and consequently, the two superpowers behaved very cautiously in their mutual relations. Outside Europe the struggle for influence was far less restrained.

Today, the situation is much more complex. Conflicts in the Third World have lost their East-West context and have a better chance of resolution through impartial efforts of the international community. In Europe the situation is far more fluid. Unfortunately, the political will to deal effectively with a crisis through primarily European action is not strong enough to mobilize military forces for use outside our own borders. Yet, in the Yugoslav crisis it becomes increasingly clear that political actions – mediation, monitoring, peacekeeping – need the backing of military capabilities if they are to be credible in the eyes of the parties to the conflict. In practice, however, it is virtually impossible to show military capability as a sign of readiness to act as soon as political decisions have been taken, thus enhancing the credibility of political negotiations and the role of monitors. It is curious to see the paralysing effect of the question of what to do when deterrence fails and further measures are called for, whereas at the height of the Cold War we had far fewer problems with such measures.

The third problem is the overemphasis on peacekeeping, although in fact there is no peace – just bloody conflict that cannot be contained without some show of force and resolve. This raises the very real problem of the legitimacy of military action. At first the question related to intervention in the internal affairs of a country which had not yet broken up. The Kurdish plight at the end of the war against Iraq seemed to set a precedent for allowing intervention in the internal affairs of another state, but its follow-up is far from clear. It was not until our televisions showed 1,5 million people fleeing and dying on mountain tops that governments were pressured into the initiative to establish "safe havens" for the Kurds and to conduct Operation Provide Comfort. In the case of Yugoslavia, it took longer to cross the threshold of tolerance.

The problem is aggravated by the fact that, except in the Korean War, the United Nations' own actions have never gone beyond peacekeeping in a limited sense, i.e. at the request of the parties, to separate them after some kind of agreement had been established and was appearing to hold. So far, the UN has refused to send its Blue Helmets to potential trouble spots before a crisis erupts. The interesting notion of "preventive deployment" mentioned in the Secretary General's report has not yet been substantiated. Equally, the UN has felt unable to engage in peace enforcement, the (in itself logical) argument being that the Blue Helmets should not themselves become part of the problem. In the Balkans such a policy is unlikely to be sufficient and we shall have to examine what to do when fact-finding, mediation and conciliation are not enough to bridge the gap which exists before peacekeeping can be considered. Unless we do so, the debate as to how we should organize peacekeeping and whether the UN or the CSCE could call on NATO or the WEU to do that job is fairly academic. Even more serious would be the risk of an erosion of public support for defence expenditures, if present plans for reaction forces prove of little practical use. No international organization in the field of defence can exist solely for humanitarian and peacekeeping purposes.

The question of the legitimacy of the use of force outside our own territory is crucial. Everybody would prefer the United Nations to be effective in executing its primary responsibility for peace and security. The problem is, however, what to do when the Security Council is not able to act. This paper argues that in such cases recourse to Article 51 of the UN Charter should be considered. Even then most countries would require legitimation of a wider group to which they belong. Both NATO and the WEU (hopefully responding to a request from the European Union) could provide this on their own if their members provide the necessary consensus.

II. Individual and Collective Self-Defence

The ending of US-Soviet bipolarity was marked by a Soviet withdrawal from most of its commitments in the Third World. Constructive action in the United Nations to deal with most areas of tension in the world therefore received a new impetus. The Kuwait crisis was a most interesting example of the UN Security Council adopting an enabling resolution, so that member nations could use force, without the UN itself having to act in its own right. Only a few years earlier such a resolution would have been most improbable, given the likely opposition from the Soviets, and no doubt the Chinese as well.

New solutions are being tried out, with positive results in cases like Namibia and Cambodia and to some extent Yugoslavia. In the latter case, extensive American diplomacy was needed to keep Russia on board. It is still uncertain, however, to what extent consensus among the permanent members of the Security Council can be reached on cases which have an impact on the direct security interests of both Russia and China. China insists that disputes should be settled by peaceful means through consultation and has not yet indicated what should be done if the consultations remain inconclusive and fighting continues. There is growing unease about the composition of the Security Council and the lack of democratic underpinning of the organization in general. This leads to the conclusion that UN action is still preferable, wherever feasible, but that there will be cases where its effectiveness will be in doubt. For such contingencies, the means provided by the Charter itself should not be underestimated or discarded.

Article 51 states that "nothing in the present Charter shall impair the inherent right of individual or collective self-defence if an armed attack occurs against a Member of the United Nations, until the Security Council has taken the measures necessary to maintain international peace and security." This article was conceived as part of a plan for harmonizing the operation of regional arrangements and agencies with the general provisions of the Charter. More specifically, it aimed at fitting the system of the American republics and the obligations assumed under the Act of Chapultepec of 1945 into the United Nations. In practice, it acquired much wider proportions. Conceptually, there were two avenues of approach.[1] One was to define specifically those acts which are regarded as constituting the unjustifiable use of force. The architects of the Charter decided not to undertake a definition of aggression and to leave it to the Security Council to decide in each case whether a particular act constituted a threat to or violation of the peace. Article 51 took the other approach, i.e. to define the circumstances under which the right of self-defence may be exercised. Presumably it is the right of each member, or members acting jointly, to decide when, and for how long, conditions exist justifying the exercise of this right. Equally, the provisions of Article 51 do not necessarily exclude the right of self-defence in situations not covered by the case of armed attack against the member state. It can be argued that, since the right of self-defence is "inherent," member states retain it subject only to the limitations expressed in the Charter.

Collective action under Article 51 need not be under the terms of a formal agreement or in the context of an international organization containing definite predetermined commitments. It clearly provides the opportunity for countries to act together on an ad hoc basis if the Security Council fails to take the measures

1 Leland Matthew Goodrich and Edward Hambro, *Charter of the United Nations*, 3. and revised edition (New York/London 1969), p. 300.

necessary to maintain or restore peace. Conversely, the power of independent action ceases when the Security Council has taken the necessary measures. As always in international relations, the situation is not clear-cut. It remains difficult to determine where collective defence starts in a justifiable manner. Equally, permanent members could stall in taking measures in the Council, thus allowing the self-defence action to continue even though other members would regard it as inconsistent with the purposes and principles of the UN. Nevertheless, Article 51 remains an important fall-back position in case the Security Council is unable to take action. In the Yugoslav crisis it could have been invoked, especially after the recognition of Croatia and Bosnia.

At the time of the conclusion of the Washington Treaty, the status of the Alliance in relation to the UN caused some headaches. To state explicitly that it would be a regional arrangement within the meaning of Chapter VIII of the UN Charter would imply that no enforcement action is possible without the authorisation of the Security Council. Escott Reid recalled the Canadian line of argument that Article 51 was the governing article, the word "collective" relating in part to regional arrangements. He also gave the text of the understanding formulated at the signature:

> "(7) It is common understanding that the primary purpose of this treaty is to provide for the collective self-defence of the Parties as countries having common interests in the North Atlantic area, while reaffirming their existing obligations for the maintenance of peace and the settlement of disputes among them. It is further understood that the Parties will, in their public statements, stress this primary purpose, recognised and preserved by Art. 51, rather than any specific connections with Chapter VIII or other Articles of the United Nations Charter."[2]

III. Institutional Arrangements

Institutional arrangements should reflect the realities of our time and simultaneously allow evolutionary progress towards interdependence and cooperation. At a time of disintegration in Eastern Europe it is impossible to design architectures which have any likelihood of permanence. We can only emphasize trends which merit being continued, allowing for adaptation while avoiding a relapse into old nationalistic patterns. Our main problem seems to be avoiding analyses according to pre-World War I patterns and maintaining the perspective of integration which has served Western Europe so well.

Of course, tasks and roles are more important than institutions, but in practice, there is no clear division of labour and several institutions contribute to the same tasks. Nevertheless, it is possible to distinguish some major qualities in each of

2 Escott Reid, *Time of Fear and Hope* (Toronto 1977), p. 268.

them. NATO is best suited to the defence of our own territory. Preventive diplomacy can be pursued by UN, CSCE and EC. Peacekeeping used to be primarily a UN task until the EC entered this field in Yugoslavia. Ideally, it should have been carried out by the WEU as the defence and security arm of the Community but in those pre-Maastricht days that road was not yet chosen and the EC undertook both peacekeeping and mediation activities in a twinned operation. Should it come to peace enforcing action, the WEU could do this under the mission specified in the Petersberg Declaration of 19 June 1992 as "the role of combat forces in crisis management, including peacemaking." All organizations aspire to crisis management in one form or another, although in reality there has been very little management in the true sense of the word.

The perspective of a European Union should be maintained, providing for convergence over a period of time of the economic, political, security and defence dimensions. That perspective was confirmed at Maastricht, but was already contained in the Single Act of Luxembourg of 1985. As far as the WEU was concerned the Hague Platform of European security interests of 1987 stated that "the construction of an integrated Europe will remain incomplete as long as it does not include security and defence." That remains as true today as ever, for it is difficult to imagine a European Union – now already 350 million people – without a security and defence dimension. Conversely, if left alone the defence dimension will wither away. It needs the underpinning of common economic and foreign policies, aimed at pushing stability eastwards. After the Danish and French referenda, the future shape and content of the European Union is uncertain; it remains to be seen whether in 1996 important new steps will be taken. Salvaging the essential achievements of the Maastricht Treaty is the immediate priority, and European capitals are unlikely to concentrate on post-1996 perspectives for some time to come. European integration has always been a mixture of community and inter-governmental aspects. We may see a new balance between them in the future, perhaps including new forms of cooperation going across traditional demarcation lines. In the field of security and defence we clearly are in a transitional phase. The Maastricht decision to make use of the WEU for the time being is a case in point. It also underlines the fact that it is not possible to give security and defence a tidy compartment in a European architecture. The present difficulty in ratifying the Maastricht Treaty should not be taken as a vote against Europe. It rather revives the old paradox that in Europe much progress is possible even if there is no agreement on the final destination. Nevertheless, some clarification of objectives seems necessary if Europe is to play a coherent role; it is also necessary to deal with the challenge of enlargement of the Community. So far it has been possible to prevent arrangements of "variable geometry" meaning a long-term arrangement of different groups of participants in specific areas of activity rather than a classic transitional measure with multiple speeds, allowing that some of the partners can catch up in achieving common objectives.

Some variable geometry may be inevitable in dealing with the enlargement of the Community. If neutral countries refuse to participate in a common defence policy and are nevertheless admitted to the EC, the present *de facto* variable geometry of the WEU, with its nucleus of countries willing to include defence and security, will be stressed even more. In determining the compatibility of neutrality with EC membership, defence cooperation does not have to be a decisive factor. The decision at Maastricht to offer the present members of the EC the options of full WEU membership or observer status has already indicated that it does not constitute an obstacle to membership as long as the long-term objective of a common defence policy is accepted. A more important criterion for EC membership seems to be the willingness of neutral countries to engage in an active foreign policy, i.e. a policy which envisages joint action in support of foreign policy objectives. These actions might involve diplomatic démarches, economic sanctions and ultimately, for those who accept them, military measures as well.

The offer made at Maastricht included the option of associate membership in the WEU for the other European members of NATO. All three countries – Iceland, Norway and Turkey – seem willing to take it up, giving the WEU a real chance of becoming the European pillar of NATO. By allowing associate members to participate fully in activities – and by making it clear that, in functions transferred to the WEU from the Independent European Program Group (IEPG) or Eurogroup, there will be complete equality among the countries involved – the WEU could become fully representative of European interests in the Alliance. It could become the focus for introducing common European positions into Alliance consultations. In the field of armaments cooperation it could give European efforts a much needed politico-military impetus and at the same time represent the European end of the "two-way street."

IV. Atlantic Alliance

While the WEU derives its higher profile from recent developments in both European integration and East-West relations, NATO faces a more profound challenge. Not so much to its existence, for even a European Union would still need NATO to balance Russia, the largest military power on our continent. All European allies accept that Europe is more stable and more secure with an American presence. The challenge is not affecting the need for transatlantic consultation on a wide range of politico-military issues in Europe and North America, nor the principle of collective defence, but rather the primacy and high visibility that NATO has enjoyed for more than forty years. NATO will no longer ride high on the priority of defence in transatlantic relations, as other dimensions assume equal importance in that relationship. Defence is no longer the blanket that smothers problems elsewhere, and consequently transatlantic relations will call for even more care than in the past.

In addition, NATO no longer has the monopoly of providing security because security has changed in nature. While it is legally possible to extend its activities beyond the treaty area – nothing in the treaty prevents this if all 16 members agree – it seems politically unrealistic to expect this to happen more than occasionally: NATO's mission during the Cold War was reactive, ready to respond to aggression. Today it does not provide for the necessary convergence between economic, political and security considerations, which need to underpin intervention-oriented actions. Even if, in a practical situation, NATO action becomes possible, it is doubtful whether it will be asked to undertake the whole spectrum of activities, varying from fact-finding, mediation, contribution to peacekeeping and crisis management. The fundamental question, therefore, is whether NATO can survive without assuming new functions and, if so, how the traditional core functions of collective defence and transatlantic consultation could be reorganized for maximum effectiveness. This paper argues that this can be done only on the basis of a two-pillar structure – European and American. Then it would also be possible for NATO when appropriate to undertake intervention-type actions after extensive consultations between Europeans and North Americans in which the European Union assumes its own responsibilities.

NATO suffers from ambiguity in the interpretation of the concept of defence. While the most likely use of military power lies increasingly in the protection of interests wider than territorial integrity and national independence, and is shifting in the direction of intervention, NATO's New Strategic Concept emphasizes that "the primary role of the Alliance military forces remains unchanged" and that "the Alliance is purely defensive in purpose: none of its weapons will ever be used except in self-defence."[3] The Strategic Concept was intended primarily to give a signal to Moscow that the Cold War had truly ended. It provided little guidance to national defence policies and was soon lagging behind new political initiatives such as those giving NATO a role, "by supporting peacekeeping initiatives under the responsibility of CSCE, including by making available Alliance resources and expertise."[4] The Oslo Communiqué also stated that the CSCE should declare itself a regional arrangement under Chapter VIII of the UN Charter and that its means for conflict prevention and crisis management should be strengthened. Subsequently, the

---

3 *The Alliance's New Strategic Concept*, agreed to by the heads of state and government in the meeting of the North Atlantic Council in Rome, November 7-8, 1991, Paragraphs 41 and 36, respectively.

4 *Oslo Communiqué*, North Atlantic Council Meeting, June 4, 1992, Paragraph 11.

Summit Conference at Helsinki on 9 June, made a similar declaration, placing it under Chapter VIII.

The irony of this sequence will not escape the notice of old hands in NATO and UN matters. At its inception, NATO took pains to avoid a close link with Chapter VIII, because it would make any action dependent upon decisions of the Security Council. Now it has not only encouraged the CSCE to become a regional organization under this chapter but also declared itself in support of peacekeeping activities under the responsibility of the CSCE. The WEU followed a similar course in its Petersberg Declaration of 19 June 1992, but also referred to requests by the UN. The obvious risk in these developments is that people may argue that both NATO and the WEU are authorized to take peacekeeping action only if they are requested to do so by the CSCE or directly by the UN, thus losing much of their autonomy of action in peacekeeping and crisis management.

What are the resources which the Alliance could make available? They are considerable and unmatched by any other organization, but some of its claims are exaggerated. Logistics still remains a national responsibility and is not integrated except for the pipeline system (which does not seem relevant to peacekeeping operations). This will have to be reconsidered for the increasing number of multinational units being created over the next 4-5 years, but it remains doubtful whether it will be possible to develop NATO logistics or whether we have to be content with bi- or trilateral logistic arrangements among participating countries for specific units. Only if multinationality becomes a characteristic of peacetime standing forces, is there a chance for integrated logistics. The Franco-German corps might offer an interesting testcase in this context.

Of course, NATO has an integrated air defence system, information and communi-cation system, airborne warning and control aircraft (AWACS) and naval standing forces for the Atlantic and the Mediterranean. Their relevance to peacekeeping is limited, however, and relates more to embargo surveillance or enforcement, as has been the case in the Adriatic. From a purely military point of view, elements of the integrated command structure of NATO could be adapted to missions other than collective defence, even if some Allies decided not to participate. Their capabilities in the field of communications would be particularly valuable assets. Yet peacekeeping implies different requirements in terms of transport, logistic support and training of the personnel from those adduced so far in a collective defence context. For collective defence, all available forces have to be ready as early as possible, but within NATO territory. Peacekeeping and peacemaking require limited forces outside their home countries with different training and equipment. Consequently, there is a need not for large headquarters or a complicated hierarchy of commands, but rather for an advanced, autonomous headquarters able to communicate directly with the political authorities in charge. For this purpose national headquarters, suitably expanded with officers from participating nations, are more likely to be relevant.

A more fundamental question is how to adapt military integration to the new situation. With the increase in warning time, the need for a rapid transition from peacetime postures has diminished, but as long as we perceive a need for collective defence and deterrence, there is a case for integrated headquarters. In addition, the habit of working together daily, with responsibilities assigned to all member countries, has been a crucial element in forging Alliance cohesion. Having admitted that, the question remains as to whether the reorganization of NATO's command structure has gone far enough. In view of the 50% reduction in available combat units, it has been rather modest in scope and conservative as far as the levels of command are concerned. The Commander in Chief Channel Command (CINCCHAN) will disappear, but at the lower levels there are hardly any savings. In Central Europe the Army groups and Allied Tactical Air Forces (ATAFs) are being grouped in Allied Command Land Forces Central Europe (LANDCENT) and Allied Command Air Forces Central Europe (AIRCENT) without merging with Allied Forces Central Europe (AFCENT), primarily because the number of Army corps, though much reduced in size, is unchanged. In view of further expected reductions in several member countries, this structure can be regarded as only transitional. The question of a leaner command structure, which could be aug-mented in times of tension, one that is more European in composition yet emphasizes North American contributions in nuclear deterrence and augmentation, will continue to be with us. Similarly, the force planning system will have to be adjusted. The changed nature of the threat will make it difficult to formulate objective requirements. Renationalization of defence policies and postures has unfortunately progressed much further than commonly perceived. In future, force plans will largely reflect the sum of national intentions. They still make sense where they focus on multinational units constituting useful capabilities, where an element of obligation and commitment can be emphasized.

This brings me back to my favourite idea of concluding a "Euro-Atlantic bargain" or "contract." The name comes from a book by Harlan Cleveland in the 1970s and was recently taken up again by Stan Sloane. So far the bargain has only been implicit. It merits being formalized in a two-pillar structure of the Alliance. In their analysis of possible future missions for their military forces, Europeans and Americans should define the functions they are able and willing to perform and where complementing actions remain essential. Even if the most ambitious schemes are realized, Europe will clearly not be able to match United States capabilities in strategic lift, real-time intelligence and other high-tech aspects of command and control. Equally, the nuclear role of the US will remain essential in balancing other nuclear powers, and US-augmentation capabilities will be an assurance in case things go wrong in Europe. In addition, some combat capability involving land, air and naval forces will be necessary to make the commitment visible, but its size is open to question in an age of increased mobility. Other national US considerations will have an impact on that size, such as the availability of forces closer to potential sources of conflict, especially the Middle East.

The great advantage of a "transatlantic bargain" is that it shifts the debate from the perennial numbers game to a debate over functions and complementing roles. If concluded, either formally or somewhat informally, the bargain would entail an element of obligation and commitment which would underpin defence budgets in national parliaments, stop the slide towards re-nationalization and replace at least part of the "challenge" of the former defence planning cycle, particularly as the content and implementation of the contract would have to be reviewed periodically.

Finally, we have to deal with the question of whether the disappearance of the threat of massive surprise attack affects the application of Article 5 of the Washington Treaty. In the past, there was little difference between NATO taking the "appropriate measures" and the automatic military assistance clause of the WEU, because all Allies had a vital interest in regarding defence and security as indivisible among them. In the future that might be different, even for collective defence, but certainly for actions going beyond it. All member countries will have more choice in determining their actions. The WEU has a military commitment going beyond NATO, but at the same time has been more flexible in its actions and regards it as quite acceptable that only a limited number of partners participate in actual operations after a political consensus on the need for action has been achieved. Would this also apply to NATO or would it undermine the credibility of the Alliance's cohesion in implementing its core function, namely collective defence? The answer may not be entirely conclusive, because hopefully even operations under the WEU would be able to rely on some American support. Yet, the simple answer could be that, if the United States is prepared to be involved substantially (i.e. with ground forces), the operation could be under NATO auspices, if not, the WEU would be the appropriate framework. In the course of consultations, it would become clear which organization regards itself as best placed for action in a concrete situation, without the need for any hierarchy in the decisionmaking process. The WEU does not need a NATO decision to take action but undoubtedly will relate its own activities to the state of NATO consultations. Admittedly, such a pragmatic division of labour would transcend the old burden-sharing debate: Europeans would assume larger responsibilities in a two-pillar Alliance.

V. CSCE

The CSCE was a Soviet initiative turned around to our advantage. It established principles of conduct among states which made human rights a legitimate subject of international consultations, thus becoming an element of pressure in favour of change and a forum for scrutinizing implementation. Without the CSCE process developments in Central and Eastern Europe probably would not have resulted in a virtually bloodless termination of both Soviet and communist domination. With the emergence of the new democracies, the original purpose of the CSCE seemed virtually completed. Although never formally an East-West negotiating forum, in practice it responded to a polarized Europe, with the neutral and non-aligned attempting to act as bridgebuilders of varying utility. The consensus principle was accepted as a fact of life of coexistence, giving rise to occasional nuisance behaviour by certain countries.

Today the consensus principle is an anomaly, restraining CSCE decisionmaking even more than the United Nations. Yet, it remains doubtful whether Russia – and maybe some other countries as well – would be prepared to modify the rules substantially. Anybody present at the Helsinki 1992 Summit would have been struck by the resemblance of the meeting to a UN General Assembly: very few ministers listened to their colleagues' speeches and conducted bi- and multilateral meetings behind the scene. Nothing of substance was negotiated during the summit itself as everything had been agreed beforehand (some issues very shortly before the meeting, which provided the necessary catalyst to reaching agreement).

As far as its membership is concerned, the CSCE adapted quickly to the changes in East-West relations and extended its scope to all republics of the former Soviet Union in order to make sure that the Helsinki principles would apply to them immediately upon assuming independence. Western countries acquiesced in accepting some institutionalization and we saw the creation of a Conflict Prevention Center (CPC), the Committee of Senior Officials and, at the Summit of July 1992, a Security Forum in which it was decided to continue the dialogue and negotiations. A High Commissioner for Minorities will be appointed to deal with this most sensitive issue in post-Cold War Europe.

The main value of the CSCE will continue to lie in providing a forum for dialogue in which the new democracies can find and express their new identity and engage in new forms of cooperation. It will also have important functions in the early stages of developing crises: an early warning function in signalling tensions and inducing partners to accept fact-finding, monitoring, conciliation and mediation. The recent Helsinki decisions provide some additional machinery to make the CSCE more effective. A troïka will alleviate the burden of the Chairman-in-Office, who may also appoint personal representatives. A German proposal was adopted to allow for ad hoc steering groups. All these mechanisms fall short, however, of coercive action. The decision to consider the CSCE a regional organization under Chapter VIII of the UN Charter may facilitate German participation in peacekeeping, but also makes coercion impossible except in pursuance of UN Security Council resolutions. This decision was not essential to provide political legitimacy to peacekeeping operations as the CSCE already possessed this authority de facto beforehand. The debate on modifying the consensus principle so far relates to political actions only and even that becomes less relevant as the membership of the CSCE increases. With 52 members, an odd man out finds it easier to enlist support than when the membership stood at 35.

Over time, the institutional set-up may become clearer. The debate on two or three pillars for the CSCE Forum for Security Cooperation has not been fully resolved. The outcome looks like a dual framework for negotiations, both for classic arms control and a goal-oriented dialogue for security enhancement, governed by a special committee. Apart from it stands the implementing framework in the Crisis Prevention Center directed by a Consultative Committee. The result may not be as bad as it sounds, for member countries will have combined delegations for the two bodies, while there will be common conference services as well.

The main question remains to what extent the CSCE will be able to deal with conflicts erupting or continuing in spite of all preventive efforts. So far the record is not impressive. It is extraordinarily difficult to mobilize the international community, and the extended scope of the CSCE will make this even more difficult. In building collective security, Kissinger's dictum will be hard to beat when he says that if everybody will be allied to everybody else nobody will get real security. In that respect, only collective defence is able to provide collective security. Cooperative structures have their role to play and should be developed. They will make it harder to break the rules commonly agreed to, but in the final analysis the credibility of any international organization will be judged on the effectiveness of its actions. Present arrangements should be tested before further institutional improvements are proposed. The time is not ripe for a European Security Council.

VI. Western European Union

The need for a European defence identity was embodied in the Hague Platform of 1987. After some transatlantic turbulence NATO's Rome Summit of November 1991 confirmed this need and smoothed the road for the Maastricht Summit of the EC to agree on the goal of developing a common defence policy which in time might lead to a common European defence. The WEU could be requested to elaborate and implement decisions in this field. While the WEU was an integral part of the integration process, it would maintain its own autonomy. It would become more operational both on the military and the political side: on the political side by introducing common positions into NATO consultations and on the military side by the creation of a planning cell to develop force packages of units answerable to the WEU. The missions identified in the Petersberg Declaration of 19 June 1992 covered:

- humanitarian missions;
- peacekeeping missions;
- missions of combat forces in crisis management including peacemaking.

All three categories of missions go beyond collective defence. As countries declared themselves willing to make available units from the entire spectrum of their forces, they implied that collective defence action would be undertaken in NATO, while the WEU would primarily deal with cases where NATO action would not be possible or appropriate. It is not possible to have a complete division of labour. It would be odd if the WEU were be able to deal with everything except the most vital defence scenario, i.e. the defence of our own territory. Nevertheless, the Petersberg Declaration went a long way in directing the WEU towards non-NATO scenarios and accepting the notion of "double-hatting" forces for use under both organizations. At the same time, duplication of command functions was avoided. The planning cell will develop arrangements for transport, logistics, communications and command at the level of the force packages. It will not design comprehensive structures for all available forces, which would inevitably duplicate NATO's integrated command structure. On the contrary, it will study the possibility of making use of existing headquarters, either multinational or national, adding to it officers of other nations participating in the specific action. The alternative would be to create an ad hoc headquarters which obviously would be more time-consuming.

The WEU can become properly operational only when its Council and Secretariat move from London to Brussels. Only there will it be possible to have rapid interaction and consultations with NATO and the European institutions. Only there will it be possible to demonstrate that its activities are constructive and add a dimension to both Atlantic and European efforts.

Ultimately, the WEU could merge completely with the European Union. That could be the outcome of the 1996 review but some slippage seems more likely. It will depend on the momentum of European integration, which hopefully will weather the present storms and keep us in the economic and technological competition with the other major players.

VII. The European Union and Its Future Common Foreign and Security Policy (CFSP)

Since the Maastricht Summit scarcely any progress has been made in developing the CFSP. Under the UK Presidency, a working group has been created to report to the Edinburgh Summit on the four areas which have been defined as suitable for common action: arms control, CSCE, non-proliferation and arms transfer. It remains to be seen whether the Danish referendum result will adversely affect the development of the security side of the CFSP. The CSCE has, however, always been one of the most successful areas of European Political Cooperation's (EPC) work. Now the CSCE and Conference on Forces in Europe (CFE) agendas have been merged and the nature of European arms control is likely to shift from the "hard" issues of arms reductions to "soft" issues, like transparency and political dialogue, certainly after the harmonization of verification and the confidence-building measures of the CFE and CSCE have been achieved.

Part of the WEU's "bread and butter" work of the recent past namely politico-military consultations on arms control questions will have to be looked at anew in the light of the CFSP. There are two ways in which the WEU, on the basis of its Maastricht Declaration, can add value to the development of a genuine common European Security Policy. First, both Foreign and Defence Ministries sit around the WEU table: it is therefore well placed to discuss a wide range of security topics with defence implications. Second, the WEU has been accorded a specific role with regard to the Alliance strengthening its European pillar and introducing joint WEU positions into Alliance consultations. Given that NATO will continue to discuss CSCE and other security issues dealt with by the CFSP, it will in practice fall to the WEU in Alliance consultations to present and explain European positions be they formulated in the WEU or CFSP.

The important point to remember will be that the European Union, through its CFSP, and the WEU are working towards the same goal. They should therefore work closely together in developing a coherent European security policy particularly with regard to a strenghtened CSCE. The WEU's move from London to Brussels will assist this process.

Enlargement of the EC automatically entails membership in EPC/CFSP. So far, all the members of the EC have simultaneously been members of NATO as well, Ireland being the only exception. Irish neutrality did not prevent it from accepting the perspective of a European Defence Policy. Indeed, Ireland has no difficulty with the ultimate goal in the context of a final, all-embracing European Union, but rather with the way to achieve it. As it is a problem of a transitional nature, it will be easier to resolve as public opinion gets used to the idea of a defence dimension being indispensable to a true Union. Already, whenever the EPC has touched on politico-military questions, the Irish representatives have not raised strong objections and have acquiesced in silent participation. During the Rome meeting of 16 July 1992 at the level of Political Directors, Ireland indicated its interest in becoming an observer in the WEU.

Will this be a precedent for other new members of the EC, which have so far pursued a policy of neutrality? Their neutrality had a specific significance in the East-West context, but that is now losing its meaning. Neutrality vis-à-vis whom? In fact, in the face of mounting Russian nationalism, countries like Finland or even Sweden may find it attractive to strengthen their security links with the West. In any case, the "Nordic balance" of the past, which was supposed to keep Finland from falling within the Soviet orbit, no longer retains its rationale. Therefore, observer status in the WEU to start with and ultimately full membership might become a real possibility. But it is doubtful whether this would also apply to NATO which continues to be regarded purely as a military alliance. One can, with reason, argue that Article V of the modified Brussels Treaty makes the WEU a military alliance as well. However, as the process of European Union continues uniting the economic, political and security policy areas with the WEU as its defence component, the WEU's Article V can be seen more in terms of the future collective self-defence commitment of the Union.

As a consequence, enlargement of the Community will move us away from the large degree of synchronization of membership in EC/WEU/NATO, which we are about to achieve following the Maastricht decisions. After 1995/6 we may see an enlarged CFSP with several members not belonging to NATO and being only observers in the WEU. If so, we face a new problem of inter-relationships. The emphasis will be on the CFSP as the widest forum compatible with common economic policies, but its development will be flawed. If all new members of the CFSP become full members in the WEU, the discrepancy will be on the side of NATO. Some have argued that accession to the Community should be made conditional on joining NATO according to the 1982 Spanish model of accession. Their main argument is that the automatic defence guarantee to former neutral countries would commit the WEU countries without being covered by the guarantees of NATO. This reasoning assumes that the US and the Alliance would be willing to extend membership to the formal neutrals, which is far from certain. That will also depend on the way the Alliance evolves over the next few years and how the NACC manages to give political content to its cooperation. In any case, integration of these countries into Western defence organizations is more likely to take place through membership in the European institutions than directly through NATO.

VIII. Conclusion

In conclusion I would like to raise two questions. The first concerns the future of both NATO and the WEU. One regards the alleged "indivisibility" of security, especially in situations occurring at the fringe of the NATO area in the absence of any direct threat to the territory of most allies. Under such circumstances, the need for a foreign policy consensus becomes even more important. In that respect a European Union would significantly reinforce the European pillar of the Alliance.

The second question affects most international organizations. It concerns the relationship between machinery and the will to use it. There is a tendency – to quote the *Economist* – to perfect the fire engines, when there is little likelihood of them riding out to quell a fire. The point should not be stretched too far, as clearly military capabilities have to be more flexible and mobile than in the massive surprise attack scenario. In addition, military capabilities, if properly demonstrated, could enhance deterrence and the credibility of political actions. But ultimately, there will have to be some willingness to use them actively in a coherent approach combining foreign policy and economic and security aspects. Otherwise the concept of interlocking institutions becomes a way of shedding responsibility and avoiding action by hiding behind other organizations which are either unable or unwilling to act.

The difference between NATO and the WEU is that the countries participating in integrated military commands made available to the Alliance virtually all their forces. The WEU so far only intends to form force packages covering limited forces for specific missions. Thus it will be possible to limit duplication, although a certain frustration may occur in NATO if the WEU were called to act in the absence of clear collective defence cases or other Alliance-wide contingencies.

The proliferation of new states, many without armed forces to start with, emphasizes the regional character of their security situation. Their immediate neighbours constitute their most pressing problem, especially as many can point to having spread across larger territories some time in the past. The creation of "regional tables" as made possible in the recent Helsinki document seems an obvious remedy.

In restructuring national forces the West can help in advising on the proper role of the military in a democracy. In terms of practical needs, situations vary greatly with the Baltic countries having to start from scratch, their first priority being small arms and ammunition for their new personnel. For all countries, old and new, it will be difficult to quantify the need for military forces and to develop a national strategy. Obviously, it is not possible to match the combined forces of all neighbours, but some threat scenarios may be more likely than others. Or would it suffice to develop a trip-wire strategy, allowing sufficient time for the international community, either world-wide or European, to stop escalation of a conflict? Today our attention is focused less on interstate conflict than on internal strife caused by ethnic or other minority tensions. Overspill of civil war into interstate conflict cannot be excluded, however. That is why it is so important to prevent escalation of the Yugoslav conflicts and the ensuing gross violations of the Helsinki principles.

Satisfactory collective security arrangements are those existing in a transatlantic context or likely to be developed on the Western model. Other organizations will lack the same credibility as long as they do not provide defence arrangements, and – as we have seen – the chances of entering into such commitments are slim in a volatile Eastern Europe. Conceptually, it makes sense to enter into a special relationship with countries which are obtaining the new kind of "European" association treaties with the EC, but even those relations are likely to fall short of a defence guarantee. That will come only as a corollary to full membership in the Community.

The increase of membership in the CSCE raises a multitude of questions, the primary one being how to give substance to the objective of cooperative security. The CSCE will never be able to provide the same kind of collective security, which at present NATO and the WEU offer their members and thus cannot replace collective defence organizations. The guarantee of collective defence is the most far reaching commitment a country can undertake; it will only be given if there is sufficient political maturity and common interest among its members. It is possible to argue that we should encourage a similar process of convergence on a pan-European scale as we saw in the process of Western integration, but, realistically in view of prevailing tensions, it is bound to require a long period of economic and political adaptation.

In the short-term we cannot expect neat solutions. NATO is groping for its new role. The WEU will develop in the perspective of building the European Union. However, should the need arise or the emergency occur, it is very likely that concrete actions will be decided by ad hoc coalitions rather than under the auspices of one or the other available security organization. They will be tools of intergovernmental action. Any attempt to envisage their cooperation and actions according to a rigid, artificial hierarchy between them would only result in costly and politically damaging competition and duplication. It would also entail the risk of wasting considerable time over procedures and conflicts over competence, when swiftness and efficiency are required if crises are to be successfully defused or contained.

3. Overlapping Institutions, Underinsured Security: The Evolution of the Post-Cold War Security Order

James B. Steinberg

Introduction

For the nearly forty years of the Cold War, the European security "architecture" was straightforward: two collective defense alliances, NATO and the Warsaw Pact, froze in place the post-war division of Europe, helped to prevent a massive military confrontation between the two blocs and pacified conflicts among their members. This core arrangement was buttressed by parallel economic and political arrangements within the blocs, such as the Organization of European Economic Cooperation (OEEC)[1] and the European Economic Community (EC) for Western Europe,[2] and the Council on Mutual Economic Assistance (CMEA) for Eastern Europe and the Soviet Union.

The purpose of the two bloc arrangement was straightforward: for the West, it was the keystone of containment and the framework for consolidating democracy and prosperity after the War. For the East, the Warsaw Pact's nominal commitment to mutual self defense served as a convenient fiction for Soviet hegemony over its neighbors, lest they be tempted to slip the hold of communism.

The Western security structure was strongly transatlantic, since the United States' economic strength and military might was essential to balance the perceived threat from the Soviet Union. West European nations made several attempts to develop a stronger European dimension to the transatlantic relationship, first through the proposed European Defense Community, and later through the Western European Union (WEU) and European Political Cooperation (EPC) among the members of the EC, but these activities took place largely on the margins of the central transatlantic framework.

Between the two blocs lay a small number of neutral states, each of which followed a delicate balancing act dictated by geography and history. The world's initial hope for post-War peace, the United Nations, played virtually no role in European security; the mutually blocking vetoes of the Security Council's per-

1 The OEEC was the transatlantic framework for the Marshall plan; once Europe had recovered from war, in 1960 the OEEC was transformed into a broader forum for Western economic co-operation, the Organization for Economic Cooperation and Development (OECD).

2 The European *Economic* Community, created by the Rome Treaty in 1957 and which had its genesis in the European Coal and Steel Community of 1951, is rooted in economic cooperation, but from the beginning it had a political as well as economic dimension; indeed the choice of coal and steel as the first elements of integration was to facilitate West Germany's economic reconstruction without raising fears that Germany might once again pose a military threat to its neighbors.

manent members assured that the world organization would be helpless in the face of crises such as the Berlin blockade, the Soviet invasions of Hungary and Czechoslovakia, and the imposition of martial law in Poland.[3]

At various points during the Cold War, the Soviet Union proposed replacing the two Cold War alliances with a pan-European security organization, an idea which won sympathy from some neutral countries and the left in Western Europe, but which was opposed by Western governments as a transparent Soviet attempt to weaken the anti-Soviet coalition. In its place, the West ultimately agreed to create the Conference on Security and Cooperation in Europe (CSCE), which, in the 1975 Helsinki Final Act, adopted the Soviet Union's proposal committing European states not to alter international borders by force (thus de facto ratifying the post-War division of Europe), in return for Soviet guarantees on human rights. The CSCE had a limited security agenda, primarily focusing on confidence building measures. Although negotiations under the CSCE on confidence-building were conducted outside the Cold War framework (unlike the negotiations on Mutual and Balanced Force Reductions, which were conducted between the two blocs), there was a strong East-West flavor to the negotiations.

With the collapse of the Berlin Wall, and the end of the East-West division of Europe, the rationale for these security arrangements disappeared almost overnight. The Warsaw Pact folded quickly as the Soviet Union was unable to convince its former "allies" that they shared common security interests sufficient to justify a political, much less a military alliance. NATO proved sturdier, as the common bond of values (democracy, human rights, and free markets) continued to bind its members together, but the purpose of the relationship seemed in doubt. Despite dark fears of a "Russian resurgence," few in the West believed seriously in a substantial direct military threat to NATO members' security.

Although the old security threats vanished suddenly, a broad range of new concerns quickly began to surface, many of which lay buried beneath the surface of the deceptive Cold War stability. Nationalism, irredentism, refugee flows, and economic collapse seemed to be the order of the day, rather than massive military confrontation along a well-defined front. Former Warsaw Pact countries sought closer ties with the West and Western institutions, to help ensure their stability during the difficult period of economic and political transition, and to protect them against their erstwhile ally. Europeans, East and West, sought new means to anchor Germany to its neighbors, as the end of the Cold War brought with it the end of Germany's division. Some West Europeans, chafing under the US dominance that flowed from the need for the US military guarantee, hoped that the end of the Cold War would bring greater European independence (or at least a more

3 The exception was Cyprus, where UN peacekeepers have monitored the truce between the Greek and Turkish Cypriot communities since 1974.

equal partnership), while the United States sought to shed some of the financial and military burden of European security in order to tend to pressing domestic needs as well as security problems outside of Europe.

It quickly became clear that the need for new security arrangements in Europe was no abstraction; the violence in Yugoslavia and various parts of the former Soviet Union testify to the reality of conflict in the post-war Europe. Political leaders and analysts alike have offered a variety of proposals for new "architectures," embodying varying mixes of new and old structures. The purpose of this essay is to review the evolution of European security institutions to date, to assess how well the current adaptation meets European needs and to suggest some approaches to a more effective division of roles and responsibilities in the future.

I. Overlapping Institutions: The Struggle to Adapt

As the division of Europe ended, European security institutions sought to adapt to the new circumstances. The pressure of events, and the need to respond to unfolding crises drove what was to a considerable extent an ad hoc process, despite lofty proclamations of new, "comprehensive" security architectures. Several key factors shaped the process.

- The United States, a number of West European allies, and several of the emerging democracies in Eastern Europe emphasized the need to *maintain a significant role for NATO*. For the United States, NATO represented the key channel for US influence in European affairs; for the Europeans, it represented the assurance that the United States would remain involved in Europe.
- German unification, and the prospect of growing German economic and political power provided an added inducement to *deeper EC integration*, while the prospect that the United States would play a more limited security role in the non-Cold War Europe generated momentum for *greater West European security cooperation*. At the same time, the end of the East-West confrontation tended to undercut the significance of political neutrality, opening the way for *enlargement of West European political and security organizations to the Cold War neutrals and former communist countries*.
- Most countries accepted the need for an *enhanced pan-European organization, building on the CSCE*. The rationale was in part symbolic, since a pan-European organization reflected a non-divided Europe. For West Europeans and the United States, the CSCE was something to offer nations of Eastern Europe and the former republics of the Soviet Union, which they were not willing to welcome into existing Western security groupings (NATO, the EC, the WEU). For the Soviet Union (later Russia), the CSCE was a place to participate on an equal footing with the West.

- The emerging sources of conflict fit poorly into models of international relations based on preventing war between nations; there was a need to *develop new norms of conduct designed to address these new sources of conflict, and new mechanisms and tools to prevent and manage crises* stemming from internal ethnic conflict, refugee movements, human and minority rights, and the like.

These four factors were reflected in the four principal dimensions of institutional adaptation in the years following the end of the Cold War:

- NATO adaptation;
- movement toward deepening and enlarging the European Community/ Western European Union, including a possible foreign and defense policy dimension; and
- institutionalization of the CSCE;
- enhanced willingness to intervene collectively in internal affairs, especially under the aegis of the United Nations.

1. NATO Adaptation

As the historic events of 1989 began to unfold, NATO sought to change with the times. Although NATO took some cautious preliminary steps as early as May 1989, the first decisive moves came at a special NATO summit in London in July 1990 when the NATO heads of state and government announced that, in view of the changes taking place in Eastern Europe, "this alliance must and will adapt."[4] Over the next two years, this adaptation took a number of forms. First, NATO reformed its military doctrine, beginning with the London Declaration, in which the NATO leaders pledged to "profoundly alter the way we think about defense."[5] This process resulted in the new "Strategic Concept" approved at the November 1991 Rome summit.[6] Second, NATO reached out to develop institutional ties to its former adversaries. NATO began with a new diplomatic liaison relationship and intensified military contacts with the Soviet Union, Czechoslovakia, Hungary, Poland, and Bulgaria.[7] This ultimately found more formal expression in the North

---

4 *London Declaration on a Transformed North Atlantic Alliance*, July 5-6, 1990.

5 In London, NATO announced a number of new principles, including smaller and restructured active forces, lower readiness levels, a reduced role for theater nuclear weapons, including eliminating nuclear artillery and a declaration that NATO intended to move to a strategy that would "make nuclear forces truly weapons of last resort."

6 The Strategic Concept was designed to replace NATO's prevailing strategy, MC 14/3, which was based on forward defense and flexible response, in favor of an approach based on a smaller, more flexible force posture with greater reliance on multi-national formations. *The Alliance's New Strategic Concept*, Agreed by Heads of State and Government participating in the meeting of the North Atlantic Council in Rome, November 7-8, 1991.

7 *London Declaration*; *Partnership with the Countries of Central and Eastern Europe*, Statement issued by the North Atlantic Council meeting in Ministerial Session in Copenhagen, June 6-7, 1991.

Atlantic Cooperation Council (NACC), also announced at the Rome summit.[8] Third, NATO began to expand the definition of its role from a central focus on collective defense to a broader concept of crisis management,[9] including the use of NATO forces for peacekeeping under the UN or CSCE.[10] More broadly, NATO leaders spoke of enhancing the political component of the Alliance.[11]

This new concept of NATO's role was crystallized in Copenhagen in June 1991, when NATO ministers unveiled what they termed "NATO's Core Security Functions." They insisted that the Alliance's fundamental objective, "to safeguard the freedom and security of its members," remained unchanged.[12] But in outlining the Alliance's tasks, they downplayed collective defense and military balancing (Tasks III and IV) in favor of a broader conception of European security which emphasized NATO as a foundation for a "stable security environment" based on the growth of democratic institutions and peaceful dispute resolution (Task I) and transatlantic consultation (Task II).[13]

At the same time NATO leaders also sought to place NATO in the context of other parallel institutional developments. In Copenhagen, NATO ministers first spoke of developing "a network of interlocking institutions and relationships, constituting a comprehensive architecture in which the Alliance, the process of European integration and the CSCE are the key elements."[14] Rome added the Council of Europe to the list of relevant organizations,[15] while Oslo changed the formula to "interlocking and mutually reinforcing institutions," and acknowledged for the first

---

8 *Rome Declaration on Peace and Cooperation*, Issued by the Heads of State and Government participating in the meeting of the North Atlantic Council, November 7-8, 1991.

9 *Strategic Concept.*

10 NATO leaders first broached the idea of using NATO troops for UN peacekeeping in the Strategic Concept, but were careful to use the ambiguous formulation that the "allies" might contribute forces, rather than the "Alliance" as an institution, out of deference to France's reluctance to expand NATO's military role. However, in the June 1992 Oslo Communique, NATO ministers specifically stated that they were "prepared to support, on a case-by-case basis in accordance with our own procedures, peacekeeping activities under the responsibility of the CSCE, including by making available *Alliance* resources and expertise." *Final Communique*, Ministerial Meeting of the North Atlantic Council in Oslo, Norway, June 4, 1992 (emphasis added).

11 See the *London Declaration.*

12 *NATO's Core Security Functions in the New Europe*, Statement issued by the North Atlantic Council meeting in Ministerial Session in Copenhagen, June 6-7, 1991.

13 They identified three tools needed to perform these tasks: adequate military capability "to prevent war and to provide for effective defense;" crisis management capabilities; and political dialogue, including arms control and disarmament.

14 *Partnership with the Countries of Central and Eastern Europe.* The communique also acknowledged that "emerging frameworks of regional cooperation will also be important."

15 The Council of Europe, created in 1949 is an intergovernmental body with an advisory parliamentary assembly that carries on activities in the areas of economic, social, and cultural cooperation. It is best known for the European Convention for the Protection of Human Rights and Fundamental Freedoms and the associated European Commission and European Court of Human Rights.

time the UN's role in conflict settlement and peacekeeping in the "Euro-Atlantic region."[16]

At Copenhagen, NATO noted that the EC, WEU, and CSCE had roles to play "in accordance with their respective responsibilities and purposes" (but not further specified); they insisted that only NATO could perform all four core security functions.[17]

2. The Evolution of the European Community/WEU

The end of the Cold War also accelerated the EC's efforts to adapt to the new environment. Some key developments, such as the drive to complete the single market and a growing interest in economic and monetary union predated Europe's political changes. But, as noted earlier, the end of the East-West division of Europe transformed the debate over the EC's future.

Beginning in April 1990, German Chancellor Helmut Kohl and French President François Mitterrand proposed new steps to enhance the EC's role in foreign and security policy. Over the following eighteen months, a bipolar debate emerged among the Twelve. While virtually all were prepared to see strengthened foreign policy cooperation (though differing over mechanisms and subjects for action), the atlanticist group of EC nations, led by the United Kingdom, insisted that any deeper European defense cooperation should be supplemental to, rather than in competition with, NATO. This approach, fleshed out in an Anglo-Italian proposal in October 1991, envisioned a strengthened WEU to facilitate European military action out of the NATO area, leaving common defense exclusively to NATO.[18]

In contrast, France and Germany offered a vision of enhanced European defense cooperation designed to culminate in a true military capability for the emerging European Union, which would include defense of EC members' territories as well as other military responsibilities, such as peacekeeping or humanitarian relief out-of-area. As a first step down this road, the French and German leaders proposed establishing a Franco-German corps that would become the nucleus for a standing, integrated European army.[19]

In a series of compromises, the leaders of the WEU agreed to strengthen the organization along the lines suggested by the British, though in partial deference to

16 *Oslo Communique*.

17 *NATO's Core Security Functions*.

18 See *Declaration on European Security and Defense*, Policy Statement 62/91, British Information Service, October 4, 1991.

19 "Union Politique Initiative Franco-Allemande," Lettre adressé par M. le Président de la République et M. le Chancelier Helmut Kohl à M. Ruud Lubbers, Premier Ministre des Pay Bas, Président en exercise du Conseil Européen, Paris and Bonn, October 14, 1991; reprinted in *Le Monde*, October 17, 1991, p. 1.

the "Europeanists" suggested that the WEU would maintain links with NATO, but also with an arguably closer, "organic relationship" with the European Union. They put off the decision whether the WEU should merge with the EC, and limited the EC's role for the time being to greater efforts to adopt joint foreign policies (but with limited majority voting in this area) including "the eventual framing of a common defense policy which might in time lead to a common defense."[20] In the meantime, France and Germany vowed to press ahead with the Franco-German corps, but agreed that the Corps could be put under NATO operational command in appropriate circumstances, and pledged to work with NATO to work out the appropriate modalities of cooperation.[21] France and Germany reached a formal agreement with NATO on the relationship between the corps and NATO commands in January 1993.[22]

At their June 1992 summit, the WEU leaders began to define possible missions, including contributing to the common defense, humanitarian and rescue missions, peacekeeping under the UN or CSCE, and "tasks of combat forces in crisis management, including peacemaking."[23]

The second key development related to the emerging European security architecture was the likely enlargement of the Community. With the Cold War barriers swept away, most of the members of the European Free Trade Association (EFTA) decided to apply for EC membership, although each in their way expressed reservations about how far they would be willing to participate in the possible security dimension of the Community, particularly defense. The former communist states of Eastern Europe also pressed for EC membership, but unlike their EFTA counterparts, they affirmatively sought close association with the security dimension, and began to establish a liaison relationship with the WEU.

As the nine WEU members began to move forward with concrete steps to strengthen the organization, there was growing concern over the status of European countries that belonged to either NATO or the EC, but not the WEU. In an effort to strengthen the linkages, the WEU agreed to offer full membership to any EC member who wished to join, while limiting non-EC, European NATO states

---

20 *Treaty on European Union*, Article J.4 (Maastricht, February 7, 1992). The implementation of these provisions of course depends on the Treaty's ratification; the scope of the Community's role in security policy is one of the many issues which has raised problems over ratification, especially in Denmark.

21 *Report of the German and French Defense Ministers on the Creation of the European Corps,* adopted May 22, 1992 by the German and French Council on Defense and Security, La Rochelle, France.

22 See "Signing of Agreement on the Eurocorps," *Atlantic News*, January 15, 1993.

23 Western European Union Council of Ministers, *Petersberg Declaration,* Bonn, June 19, 1992, II. 4.

(Iceland, Norway, Turkey), "associate membership," although assuring them that they can "participate fully in the activities of the WEU."[24]

3. Institutionalization of the CSCE

The end of the ideological confrontation in Europe naturally focused attention on the CSCE, the only pan-European grouping. The CSCE held particular significance for the countries of Eastern Europe: it had long been the focus of Soviet efforts to diminish NATO's role, and with the impending unification of Germany, the Soviet Union hoped to block Germany's membership in NATO and elevate the CSCE's role. Many of the new democratic leaders of Central/Eastern Europe had personal connections to the CSCE by virtue of their participation in Helsinki human rights monitoring organizations such as Charter 77 in Czechoslovakia; at least in the early days of the post-Communist era, leaders like Czechoslovakia's President Vaclav Havel advocated substituting a collective security arrangement based on the CSCE for the previous collective defense alliances.

While most in the West were more skeptical, there was an early recognition that a stronger CSCE could play a useful role. In November 1990, the 34 CSCE nations signed the Charter of Paris, creating the first formal institutions for the CSCE and built on the substantive provisions of the Helsinki Final Act to provide guarantees for minority groups as well as individual rights.[25] Over the next eighteen months the CSCE agreed to adopt an emergency mechanism to trigger consultation in a crisis,[26] laid the groundwork for further institutional development in the January 1992 "Prague Document," and elaborated the concept of "consensus minus one" to allow for action against the wishes of an individual state.

Finally, at the Helsinki Follow-up Conference in July 1992, the now 52 member states[27] adopted a wide ranging document *The Challenges of Change*, which further strengthened the CSCE's organizational structure;[28] created a new High Commis-

---

24 *Declaration by Belgium, Germany, Spain, France, Italy, Luxembourg, the Netherlands, Portugal and the United Kingdom of Great Britain and Northern Ireland* which are *members of the Western European Union*, Maastricht, December 10, 1991.

25 *The Paris Charter for a New Europe*, November 20, 1990.

26 This step was taken at the first CSCE Council Meeting in Berlin in June 1991, on the eve of the outbreak of fighting in Yugoslavia.

27 In June 1991, Albania was admitted to the CSCE, and in September 1991 the three Baltic states joined at the Moscow CSCE meeting. With the Soviet Union's break-up, the CSCE in January 1992 decided to admit all former republics except Georgia. In March 1992, Georgia, Slovenia, and Croatia became members of the CSCE, followed by Bosnia. At the Helsinki summit, the CSCE voted to suspend Yugoslavia's membership.

28 In addition to those steps taken in the Charter of Paris, the 1992 Helsinki document established review conferences to precede the heads of state and government meetings (held every two years), formalized the role of the CSO and the Chairman-in-Office as well as creating mechan-

sioner for National Minorities charged with providing early warning of potential conflicts and early action to prevent the outbreak of conflict; established a more extensive menu of actions for conflict prevention and crisis management, including fact-finding and rapporteur missions and CSCE peacekeeping (which may draw on the EC, NATO and the WEU, as well as the peacekeeping mechanism of the Commonwealth of Independent States); and agreed to explore further ideas for conciliation and arbitration mechanisms. They also established a new CSCE Forum for Security Cooperation, under which the CSCE states would start new arms control and confidence-building negotiations, as well as continue the ongoing dialogues on military doctrine, force planning, armament programs, and non-proliferation. The Follow-Up Conference also took steps to strengthen the other elements of the Helsinki process, economic cooperation and the human dimension.

4. New Norms and Procedures for Collective Involvement in Internal Conflicts

As the end of the Cold War began to break up the UN Security Council's gridlock, a series of international crisis triggered remarkable innovation in the international community's willingness to intervene in internal conflicts. The Gulf War and its aftermath paved the way; in addition to intrusive measures adopted as a part of the peace imposed on Iraq, Western forces, acting under the color (if not explicit authorization) of UN resolutions intervened in Northern Iraq to guarantee a safe haven for the Kurds and to facilitate the return of Kurdish refugees. Operation Provide Comfort offered an opening wedge in an expanding definition of threats to international peace and security sufficient to justify UN enforcement actions and other forms of collective involvement.

Since 1991, the nature and scope of this involvement has grown to embrace authorizing "all measures necessary" for humanitarian relief in Yugoslavia and Somalia, supervising disarmament and elections in Cambodia, human rights investigations in Yugoslavia and El Salvador, no-fly zones in Bosnia and Iraq, and arms embargoes in Yugoslavia and Liberia. Most of these measures were adopted with the assent of Russia; China and some of the neutral countries invariably abstained, but China declined to exercise its veto power. The EC and CSCE succeeded to some extent in overcoming members distaste for intervention in internal affairs in the case of Yugoslavia, though many were painfully aware of their own ethnic and nationalities' problems at home.

This "droit d'ingérence" for humanitarian as well as security reasons remains an evolving concept. The international lawyers carefully tie the Security Council Resolutions to the formal language of the Chapter VII of the Charter, but the

isms to assist the Chairman: The Troika (preceding, present, and succeeding Chairmen), ad hoc steering groups, and personal representatives.

device is becoming more and more transparent. This evolution will have profound repercussions for European security institutions as well. The Helsinki Final Act was built on a clear principle of non-interference in internal affairs, yet its human rights principles implicitly but no less forcefully undermined that guarantee. In the post-Cold War world, Western publics bridled at the brutality in former Yugoslavia, pushing governments to find a way to act, regardless of the niceties of international law.

II. Problems with the Current Institutional Arrangements

This thumbnail sketch of the institutional developments since 1989 reveals at least three critical questions concerning the respective roles and responsibilities of Europe's security organizations: security relations between the West and Eastern Europe (including the former Soviet Union), the organization of Western military capabilities, and the locus of crisis prevention/crisis management. The lack of a clear definition of responsibilities across the various organizations has already become clear in the first post-Cold War crises, leading in some cases to duplicative efforts as multiple organizations compete for the dominant role, while in other cases there has been inaction, as each of the principal institutions declined to act.

1. Links with Eastern Europe

With the end of the Cold War, there has been growing interest in developing security links across the old East-West boundaries. These have generally fallen into two categories: security guarantees and dialogue (including civil-military relations, force planning, and armaments programs). Several Western institutions have become involved in these efforts. In Copenhagen in June 1991, the NATO Ministers declared that "the consolidation and preservation throughout the continent of democratic societies and their freedom from any form of coercion or intimidation are ... of direct and material concern to us."[29] But they stopped short of explicit security guarantees to the East, and rather identified the CSCE as the framework for building closer links with the states of Central and Eastern Europe. At the same time, NATO leaders pledged to intensify military contacts with the East and adopted a new set of initiatives in the political, scientific and environmental realms, as well as defense.

Six months later, NATO further blurred the line between itself and the CSCE in this respect by the decision to "develop a more institutional relationship of consultation and cooperation on political and security issues" through the new North Atlantic Cooperation Council, embracing the sixteen NATO countries plus former

---

29 *Partnership with the Countries of Central and Eastern Europe.*

members of the Warsaw Pact (including the republics of the former Soviet Union).[30] The NATO leaders stated that the effort would focus on security and related issues, such as defense planning, civil-military relations and defense conversion, as well as scientific and environmental programs. Reflecting an awareness of the obvious overlap, they insisted that "this process will contribute to the achievement of the objectives of the CSCE without prejudice to its competence and mechanisms." As the issue of peacekeeping rose to the top of the European security agenda, NACC ministers began to explore ways in which the NACC could play a coordinating role.

The CSCE of course has since its inception embraced a security component linking East and West as well as the neutral states; until the late 1980s this focused predominately on negotiating confidence-building measures, but has expanded to include activities such as the military doctrine seminars, and is broadened even further in the new Security Forum launched at the Helsinki Follow-up Conference in July 1992. In addition, the Helsinki Final Act contains a political commitment by all states not to use force to alter borders; but there is no enforcement mechanism and at the Follow-up Conference in July 1992, the CSCE leaders were unwilling to go beyond this political commitment to accept France's proposal to establish legally binding negative security guarantees, much less affirmative obligations to aid any CSCE nation that comes under attack.

Although the membership differs slightly (since the CSCE contains the neutral and non-aligned nations) there is obvious duplication between the NACC and the CSCE, particularly in aspects of CSCE confidence-building activities such as the military doctrine seminars and the new Security Forum created at the July 1992 Helsinki Follow-up Conference. There is also overlap between the NACC and the liaison activities established by the WEU with some of the East European states.

The former Warsaw Pact countries have been content to pursue all possible avenues for security links with the West, although over time they have placed particular emphasis on ties to NATO. But some (especially Poland, the Czech Republic, the Slovak Republic, and Hungary) have objected to NACC on the grounds that all former "adversaries" are treated alike, regardless of their degree of democratic development. These countries of Central Europe seek preferential security links to the West. But NATO has been wary of making these distinctions formal (while pointing to the more extensive ties in practice) for fear of offending other NACC countries, particularly Russia.

The result of these developments is that several European security organizations (NATO, WEU, and the CSCE) have taken on aspects of a dialogue relationship with the East, but none has offered explicit security guarantees. This is one of

---

30 *Rome Declaration on Peace and Cooperation.*

the key areas where there is both substantial overlap and a significant gap in the responsibilities of European security organizations.

2. The Organization of Western Security and Military Forces

Throughout the period of adaptation there was struggle to reconcile the political and military roles of NATO and an emerging "European security and defense identity" centering around the EC and the WEU. In part, as noted above, this was a debate among Europeans as much as conflict between the United States and Europe, as many of the "atlanticist" members of the EC and WEU, notably the United Kingdom, Denmark, the Netherlands, and Portugal, favored a division of roles and responsibilities that broadly mirrored the US view. While all NATO members endorsed in principle the idea of a stronger European defense identity, disagreements turned on several issues that presented a danger of at best, overlap; at worst, conflict, including

- the relationship between the WEU and NATO as compared with the relationship between the WEU and the EC;
- whether the European defense identity would have any role in defense of NATO members' territory;
- whether members of the EC (or WEU) should reach a common position on security issues which would be binding on them all in NATO (sometimes referred to as a "European caucus in NATO");
- in the event that both NATO and WEU might choose to act in an given area (e.g., as peacekeepers under the CSCE) which organization should take precedence;
- how "institutionalized" should the European defense identity become, in terms of planning staffs, peacetime headquarters and standing forces, independent of NATO structures and processes.

Among Europeans themselves, there was a further set of issues concerning the potential overlap or conflict between the proposed Eurocorps and the WEU (as well as between the Eurocorps and NATO).

As the Yugoslavia conflict unfolded the twin problems of "overlap" and "undercoverage" became glaring. On the one hand, NATO and the WEU virtually fell over each other for the largely symbolic task of "monitoring" the UN sanctions in the Adriatic (expanded in recent days to include a more active role under the 16 November 1992 Security Council resolution); on the other hand, neither organization was prepared to act in its own capacity to assure the delivery of humanitarian relief to Bosnia (much less intervene to stop the fighting), with WEU and NATO nations making their military contributions under the UN umbrella.

More broadly, much of the transatlantic conflict focused on the potential problem of overlap, duplication and conflict among NATO, WEU, and the Franco-German Corps in defending members' territory, a commitment under both Article 5 of the Washington (NATO) Treaty and Article 5 of Brussels (WEU) treaty, arguably the least likely contingency; while neither NATO nor the WEU have resolved concretely under what circumstances they are prepared to act in the case of conflict out-of-area, the far more probable case, as Yugoslavia has already shown.

3. Crisis Management

As the European security challenge moved away from the danger of massive military confrontation to a more diverse range of potential conflicts, the need to develop tools for crisis management (as opposed to military deterrence) became the new focus for conflict prevention. Initially it seemed that the CSCE was ideally suited for at least the political dimension of crisis management, and one of the first CSCE "institutions" to be established was the Conflict Prevention Center in Vienna, followed shortly by the "emergency mechanism" adopted at the Berlin CSCE Council meeting. But the CSCE's failure to act decisively in Yugoslavia, and the competitive search by other institutions to buttress their raison d'être, led both NATO and the WEU to seek to expand their responsibilities in crisis management. In one respect, there seemed to be a clear division of responsibility emerging: since there was little movement for the CSCE to field its own peacekeeping forces, NATO and the WEU were obvious choices to perform that role (although they are arguably in conflict with each other). But assigning CSCE peacekeeping to either NATO or the WEU would exclude most CSCE countries. This led to considering a further variant: the NACC might provide a broader framework for peacekeeping. But this solution too had a flaw; it led to the curious result that the nations with the greatest experience in peacekeeping, Europe's neutrals, would be left out of European peacekeeping arrangements.[31]

Similar problems plague other aspects of crisis management. NATO's strategic concept speaks explicitly of "the Alliance's political authorities choosing and coordinating appropriate crisis management measures as required from a range of political and other measures." But it is unclear how Alliance decisions would fit into the CSCE framework, or which would take precedence over the other. Should NATO be seen as a transatlantic caucus for crisis management, with final decisions to be taken by the CSCE? Or is NATO an agent of the CSCE? Or finally, might NATO act when no agreement can be reached in the CSCE? At least there is little

31 It should be noted that Finland is an "observer" in the NACC, and it would be possible to increase the number of observers and associate them with NACC peacekeeping activities. At some point however, this process would make the enlarged NACC virtually identical in membership to the CSCE.

danger that the CSCE and NATO would act at cross purposes, since NATO members clearly can block any undesired CSCE action.

III. Design Guidelines for the New European Order

Some overlap in institutional competence is not only inevitable, it is probably desirable: it provides a certain amount of flexibility to accommodate specific circumstances. This can be seen most clearly in the cases of NATO and the WEU. Although the two organizations will undoubtably overlap in mission, resulting inevitably in some duplication, the availability of alternative structures allows for operations with or without US participation, as the case may dictate. The trick is to design the overlap in a way to minimize duplication, and, even more important, reduce the probability of conflict.

While there may be some theoretical desirability to begin afresh with new institutions, in the manner of institution building in the immediate post-Cold War period, the already extensive institutional adaptation to date suggests that, as a practical matter, improvements should begin with the existing array of institutions. Given this approach, there are a number of principles which should guide the future evolution of European security institutions.[32]

1. *Norm setting should be the responsibility of institutions with the greatest legitimacy: the United Nations and the CSCE.* Norm setting is an important, albeit limited component of constructing a stable Europe. Norms are important not only because they constrain actions to some degree in themselves (witness the at least partial efficacy of the Helsinki human rights principles even in the absence of enforcement mechanisms), but because they become the predicate for enforcement in the face of violations.

The norm setting function is particularly important in the new Europe because the problems that may lead to conflict are not well addressed by existing norms of international law, which focus primarily on state-to-state relations, and, to a lesser but growing extent, individual rights. Norms governing national minority rights, internal political conflict, responsibilities toward refugees, and the thorny issue of the right to self-determination (including perhaps the right to secede) are needed to provide an agreed framework for resolving disputes peacefully. Agreeing on applicable principles before conflict breaks out is far more likely to prevent conflict

32 Some of these principles are drawn from a more detailed study of the role of security institutions in the Yugoslavia crisis. See James B. Steinberg, "The Response of International Institutions to the Yugoslavia Conflict: Implications and Lessons," in F. Stephen Larrabee, ed., *Europe's Volatile Powderkeg: Balkan Security after the Cold War*, forthcoming.

in the first place (unlike Yugoslavia, where rules seemed sometimes to be made up almost after the fact to ratify circumstantially dictated decisions).[33]

These issues are controversial, and the larger the institution attempting to articulate the norm, the harder it will be to achieve consensus. Russia's well-founded concern that rules on national minorities could affect its own internal policy could hinder agreement in the CSCE, just as China's fear of international involvement in its internal affairs has proved something of an obstacle in the UN Security Council. But precisely because agreement is hard to reach, once adopted, these principles carry greatest authority.

2. Both *voluntary mediation and mandatory arbitration also require the perception of impartiality and are best carried out by broad-based organizations such as the UN and CSCE. They should be given the means to carry out these functions*. If these organizations are to articulate norms, it is natural that they should apply them to specific cases. The CSCE has cautiously moved in this direction by expanding its fact-finding and good offices role, and has begun to explore formal institutions of arbitration.

But there are several flaws in the current approach. The executive responsibility for many of these tasks lies with the Chairman-in-Office (assisted in some cases by the Troika or by ad hoc steering committees). This poses the problem of rotating leadership, which can be problematic in the middle of a crisis (the EC presidency rotated five days after the Yugoslavia conflict began, and has now changed four times during the efforts to mediate the conflict); and also raises problems which may be associated with the specific identity of the Chair (some suggest that the CSCE's efficacy during the beginning of the Yugoslav conflict was hampered because Germany held the Chair and was not considered impartial by the rump Yugoslavia/Serbia). This suggests the need for a stronger Secretary General and permanent staff. The decision to create a CSCE High Commissioner for National Minorities is a step in this direction, but impartial leadership at the top is necessary. Moving in this direction could also help streamline the bureaucratic proliferation within the CSCE, particularly the overlapping responsibilities of the Conflict Prevention Center and the Committee of Senior Officials, which led to furious commuting between Vienna and Prague during the first months of the Yugoslavia crisis.

33 Thus the EC's announced principle opposing the use of force to change *internal borders* which was used to justify recognizing Slovenia and Croatia under Tito's administrative boundaries could have far ranging repercussions throughout Eastern Europe, depending on which "internal" borders count for the purposes of this doctrine (e.g., in the case of Russia does this apply to the borders of autonomous republics? of oblasts? of rayons?). But assuming that this principle is valid and enunciated before the Yugoslav conflict began with a clear commmitment by the international community to stand behind it, the Yugoslav army might have been deterred from attacking Slovenia, and later Croatia, following their declarations of independence in June 1991.

Second, there is a need for both voluntary and mandatory dispute resolution procedures. The CSCE has taken the first step in this direction by convening negotiations in Geneva. Third, and closely connected, the CSCE mandatory dispute resolution machinery should have as its goal merger with the Council of Europe's Human Rights Court, as a part of a broader merger of the Council of Europe and the CSCE. A major barrier to this development is the US unwillingness to accede to the Convention on Human Rights; but this function fits naturally with other individual and group rights responsibilities of the CSCE, including the Office of Democratic Institutions and Human Rights in Warsaw, and there is no compelling reason to retain both organizations.

3. *The CSCE should be the principal institution for authorizing the use of force in Europe, but nations and alliances must retain the right to act if the CSCE is paralyzed.* With the decision to become a Chapter VIII organization under the UN Charter, the CSCE has taken an important step toward expanding its role in regional security; but under the UN Charter the Security Council still reserves the exclusive right to authorize enforcement under Chapter VII.[34] The current structure thus has the effect of forcing decisionmaking on the UN for key aspects of conflict prevention/crisis management, as became clear in the Yugoslav crisis.

Reliance on the UN has a number of drawbacks, the most serious of which is overburdening the UN machinery. In some cases, the burden is justified because the UN offers corresponding benefits. For conflicts in less developed countries, for example, harnessing the support of economically and politically more powerful actors may justify resorting to a world forum, but this is inapplicable for Europe. For certain kinds of measures, such as economic sanctions or oil embargoes, world-wide scope is needed to ensure their efficacy. But in many cases, as UN Secretary-General Boutros-Ghali has argued, regional organizations, especially European organizations, should shoulder a greater share of the burden.[35]

The most serious drawback to the CSCE exercising this role effectively is the requirement of consensus. The problem has been eased more recently by allowing action based on "consensus minus one," and the CSCE's action in suspending Yugoslavia's membership could provide a precedent for dealing with obstructionist states in the future. Some have advocated creating a CSCE Security Council to facilitate effective enforcement action. But such problems as deciding on the composition of such a council (including the issue of permanent versus rotating membership), whether it would act unanimously, by some form of majority rule, or whether some nations would have veto power raise such difficult questions as to

34 UN Charter, Art. 53 (1).

35 *An Agenda for Peace*, Report of the Secretary-General pursuant to the statement adopted at the Summit Meeting of the Security Council on 31 January 1992.

challenge the plausibility of moving in this direction. Instead, the CSCE should view the availability of the UN Security Council as an argument to help promote decision in the CSCE rather than as an excuse for CSCE inaction, on the ground that for a European problem the CSCE carries greater legitimacy than the UN.

Of course, the possibility of paralysis, particularly in a situation where the Security Council itself may be blocked by veto (as, for example, in a conflict involving Russia) means that European nations cannot be expected to forego entirely the option of resorting to force in cases where substantial interests are threatened. The proposed architecture here may be a step on the road to collective security, but they are not predicated on it. Therefore, there will continue to be a role for collective defense alliances and other forms of security assurances between "European" states (including the United States and Canada).

4. *Arms control, disarmament, and confidence-building should take place under the CSCE framework.* The new CSCE Security Forum, picking up on earlier CSCE efforts in confidence-building and dialogue, is well-suited to the new challenges facing European stability, particularly as it embraces the idea of subregional agreements and discussions. A certain amount of this activity also takes place under the aegis of NACC and the associated Defense Council. While it is understandable that former Warsaw Pact countries like to elaborate as many ties as possible with NATO (if nothing else, to benefit from the penumbra of NATO's security shadow), there is no obvious justification for artificially limiting these discussions and activities to the NATO 16 and former Warsaw Pact countries. Sweden has as much to teach Romania about civil-military relations as Greece; and Croatia needs to learn just as much as Poland.

5. *Operational military coordination should take place primarily through NATO and the WEU, but there should be enhanced opportunities for other CSCE states to work with NATO and WEU military forces and a willingness by NATO in particular to expand its membership.*

Were Europe starting with an institutional blank slate, a strong case could be made for organizing some military forces directly under the control of the CSCE, at least for peacekeeping, crisis management and rapid response. But given the difficulty of gaining consensus to move in that direction, and the existence of organizational and material infrastructure in NATO, and to a growing degree, in the WEU, these organizations seem the appropriate building blocks for developing effective coordination of operational military forces. In Helsinki the CSCE moved in this direction by blessing NATO and WEU involvement in CSCE peacekeeping activities.

But it is unlikely that the non-NATO or non-WEU CSCE states would accept handing over all military responsibilities to these two organizations; and adding

CIS peacekeeping as a third option neither satisfies the nations that are outside all three groupings, nor is likely to prove effective even for CIS members in the long run (even assuming there is a CIS in the long run). Thus, there is a need for NATO and/or the WEU to develop more extensive operational links with the other CSCE states to permit effective, timely joint operations in service of CSCE mandates. Although some activities of this sort are beginning to take place under the aegis of the NACC, there is no justification for limiting the cooperation to former Warsaw Pact states; indeed it would be odd to exclude Europe's premier peacekeepers, such neutral states as Austria, Finland and Sweden, from this effort to coordinate multinational European peacekeeping and peacemaking. Thus, under this approach, NACC should be transformed from a consultation among former adversaries to a framework under which all non-NATO European states could associate with various NATO military activities such as training, joint exercises etc., with the prospect that NACC members who showed a durable commitment to democracy, human rights, and peaceful dispute resolution could ultimately become NATO members.

6. *The WEU should assume primary responsibility for the defense of its members' territory and should continue to deepen its relationship with the European Union.* There is an obvious logic to the WEU assuming responsibility for territorial defense of its members, particularly if the process of European integration through the EC survives its current turmoil and follows something resembling the path set out at Maastricht. During the Cold War, dependence on NATO for this mission followed from the fact that Europe could not be defended without the active military engagement of the United States as a deterrent to potential Soviet aggression. But today it is plausible to assume that a successful trajectory of European integration (including the nuclear dimension) could provide an effective force even if the course of political events in Russia turns unfavorable.

This would, of course, represent a sea change, since NATO continues to insist on its primacy as the military forum for defense of its members' territory. The greatest danger is that giving the territorial defense mission to the WEU would "uncouple" the United States from Europe. But there are alternative ways to secure this coupling more consistent with a more sustainable sharing of financial burdens. If nothing else, the low probability of attack against most NATO members' territory suggests that Article 5 is a weak reed indeed to assure US involvement. In the past, some have also suggested that Europeans would not accept stationed US forces unless they were there to defend the host country. But today, it seems equally plausible to believe that in countries like Germany, the host populations would prefer that the United States forces help play a role in promoting stability on the periphery of NATO territory.

This concept of the WEU fits closely with the idea of the WEU as the defense arm of the European Union. By this logic (accepted by the WEU at Maastricht) all EC members should be eligible to join the WEU. If, over time, the EC expands, more and more countries would benefit from the explicit security guarantees of the Brussels Treaty, which would take on additional credibility because of the close economic and political links among EC members. But the WEU should limit its military liaison to candidate members of the EC; other military links with non-EC states would simply duplicate the function of the reformed NACC proposed above.

7. *NATO should become the principal military component of conflict prevention and crisis management in Europe, as well as a forum for a broader security dialogue among all truly democratic states in the "Euro-atlantic" region. Over time, if the democratic transition proceeds well in the East, the membership of NATO would begin to converge with the CSCE, setting the stage for moving toward a more formal collective security regime.* NATO's existing organizational and military infrastructure makes the ideal candidate for providing the military capabilities for conflict prevention/ crisis management, which will require highly ready and trained forces, intelligence and logistical infrastructure, and experience and training in multinational operations. NATO's capability in this field will be enhanced by expanded links with non-members as suggested in point 5, above. This concept of NATO's role also anchors the United States to the most important dimension of future European stability, and takes advantage of some unique political and technological dimensions of US leadership, including US credibility in Eastern Europe.

This new NATO should be prepared to offer security guarantees to new, full members who meet the test of durable democracy, human rights, and a commitment to act collectively. Countries which associate with NATO would to some extent be in limbo (since the CSCE itself would offer no formal affirmative security guarantees), but would benefit from ongoing association with NATO and would have an incentive to take the political steps needed to become members. This, of course, means an expanded US security commitment in Europe (although one collectively undertaken with European NATO members) and it will be necessary to convince the US public that important US interests are at stake to justify this type of involvement. But this rationale seems more plausible than continuing to argue that the United States must remain in Europe to defend "rich" West Europeans.

8. *US-West European consultation and cooperation should develop a second pillar to complement NATO.* One consequence of this revised concept of NATO will be to transform the Alliance from US-West European consultative forum in favor of a US-democratic European institution. This can be a net gain so long as the special ties between the United States and Western Europe are not lost. Fortunately,

there is an answer to that need: build on the Transatlantic Declaration of November 1990, linking the United States and the EC to a richer partnership in both the political and economic dimension. This means closer links between the United States and the EC common foreign and security policy (should Maastricht proceed as signed) as well as economic, environmental, and other issues of mutual concern. A key to the success of this approach is to introduce into the US-EC dialogue the kind of transparency and comity that characterizes discussions in NATO's North Atlantic Council.

9. *The European Community should take primary responsibility for building political and economic links to the East, assuming responsibility for many of the activities under Basket II of the CSCE.* The EC's experience with administering the G-24 aid to Eastern Europe, coupled with its efforts at negotiating and implementing various forms of association and cooperation agreements with Eastern Europe and the republics of the former Soviet Union makes it ideally suited to serve as the focus for aid, technical assistance, and coordination in the field of economic development. This is not to say that others shouldn't contribute: the reconstruction of Russia, to say nothing of the other CIS states, will take a substantial contribution from other Western countries, notably Japan and the United States. But the EC might consider forming something akin to an economic NACC (open to all CSCE states) to assume the CSCE Basket II responsibilities as well as other ongoing economic development efforts. This will allow taking advantage of the EC Commission's institutional expertise (totally lacking at the CSCE as an institution) and also can allow the cooperation to be structured in a way to facilitate these countries' eventual membership in the EC itself. This is a particularly important goal for long-term European stability. The EC's founders believed that economic integration was essential to prevent future conflict among the Community's members; the same rationale applies to other emerging democracies to the Community's east. Although premature Community membership could undermine the benefits of integration already achieved, it should be a priority of the European architecture to help all European states reach the point where Community membership is appropriate.

Conclusion

These nine principles are by no means exhaustive, nor do they solve all the problems of European stability. Leadership is hard to generate from institutions, yet leadership is clearly a key to galvanize appropriate and timely action to prevent and manage conflict. Difficult large states are harder to manage through institutional mechanisms than smaller ones, although arguably they are even less manageable without institutions. National interests still dominate leaders' calculations;

invoking a just world order is rarely sufficient to convince publics to sacrifice blood or treasure. There are a number of "architectural" problems that stem from the ambiguity of which countries are in Europe: it is unclear whether the EC will ever accept Turkey or Russia as members if they meet all objective criteria. Would a different institutional arrangement have increased the chance that Western nations would act decisively to stop the bloodshed in Bosnia? Will the CSCE take on a powerful Russia that seeks to quell ethnic and national dissent (or even secession) in its midst? Institutions can only partially help solve these dilemmas; but some attempt to see at least more than one step ahead of the next crisis may improve the prospects that appropriate institutions and capabilities will be there when needed.

4. Ost- und Mittelosteuropa: Eine Herausforderung für KSZE und NATO

Bernard von Plate

I. Das Ende des Ost-West-Konflikts: Die KSZE geht weiter

Der Ost-West-Konflikt ist zu Ende; die KSZE geht weiter. Der Sondergipfel von Paris im November 1990 hat die Frage, ob der Ost-West-Konflikt nicht nur die Existenzbedingungen der KSZE geprägt, sondern für ihre Daseinsberechtigung gesorgt hat, eindeutig beantwortet: Die KSZE ist weitgehend unangefochten im Aufgebot für eine europäische Sicherheitsordnung. Die Stimmen, die sie für so tot hielten wie die Weltordnung, in der sie einst entstand, sind – wenn auch nicht völlig verstummt – leiser und weniger geworden. Von welcher sicherheitspolitischen Konstellation auch ausgegangen wird, in jeder hat die KSZE, von einer Ausnahme abgesehen, ihren Platz. Er ist in seiner jeweiligen Ausstattung konstellationsabhängig, jedoch in keinem Fall überzählig. Nur eine Lage völliger Renationalisierung aller Sicherheitsinteressen und jeglicher Sicherheitsvorsorge ist davon zu unterscheiden. In ihr ist der KSZE (aber nicht nur ihr) der Boden entzogen. Nicht um das Ob der KSZE geht es also, sondern um das Wie ihrer weiteren Entwicklung und das Was ihrer Ausgestaltung.

1. Ost- und Ostmitteleuropa – Eine Aufgabe für die NATO und die KSZE

KSZE und NATO sind keine sich wechselseitig ausschließenden Alternativen; sie ergänzen einander. Eine einpolige europäische Sicherheitsordnung ist weder ein realistisches noch ein erstrebenswertes Ziel. Daran wird sich in einer überschaubaren Zukunft nichts ändern. Diese Prämissen sind im allgemeinen nicht kontrovers; auf Widerspruch stoßen sie nur noch selten. Sie werden hier um eine Feststellung ergänzt und präzisiert: Das Verhältnis der KSZE zur NATO – oder auch umgekehrt – wird nur unter besonderer Berücksichtigung des Teils Europas entschieden, in dem nach dem Ende des Ost-West-Gegensatzes ein vielfältiges Konfliktpotential zutage getreten ist und in dem ordnungspolitisch bislang keine dauerhaften Strukturen erkennbar sind. Im Raum des aufgelösten Warschauer Pakts – die neuen Bundesländer allerdings ausgenommen – ist das Nebeneinander, aber auch das Miteinander der KSZE und der NATO zu bestimmen. Oder anders ausgedrückt, mit Blick auf Ost- und Ostmitteleuropa kann über die KSZE und die NATO nicht getrennt nachgedacht werden. Zu einem vollständigen Bild gehören zwar auch die WEU und eine Europäische Union; hier werden sie jedoch in die Betrachtung nicht miteinbezogen. Wenn zunächst nur von der NATO die Rede ist, dann handelt es sich nur um eine Seite der Medaille, auf deren Kehrseite die KSZE abgebildet ist.

2. Ostmitteleuropa - Ein ungeklärtes Verhältnis

Der herausragende Bündniszweck der NATO war und ist die kollektive Verteidigung ihrer Mitglieder. Dies ist jedoch keine endgültige Aussage darüber, wie viele das in Zukunft sein werden bzw. sein sollten. Die NATO hat sich auf ihrer Gipfelkonferenz in London im Juli 1990 ausdrücklich dazu bekannt, sich einer Entwicklung zu stellen, die mit den Veränderungen im Osten ausgelöst wurde.[1] In ihrer Kopenhagener "Erklärung zu Mittel- und Osteuropa" setzte sie den im Jahr zuvor eingeschlagenen Weg fort: "Unsere Sicherheit ist mit der aller anderen europäischen Staaten untrennbar verknüpft."[2] Aus dieser Einsicht wurden bisher einige, letztlich jedoch nur halbherzige Folgerungen gezogen. Sie sind in erster Linie diplomatischer Natur. Den immerhin eingeschlagenen Weg gilt es nun fortzusetzen. An seinem Ende sollte die NATO im eigenen Interesse nicht vor den Staaten Halt machen, die sich zu denselben politischen Werten bekennen wie die bisherigen Unterzeichner des Washingtoner Vertrages, und die dieses Bekenntnis mit konkretem Inhalt füllen. Eine Stabilitätsverpflichtung seitens der Atlantischen Allianz für einzelne Staaten Ostmitteleuropas, auch wenn mit ihr die Schwelle zu einer uneingeschränkten Mitgliedschaft nicht überschritten wird, ist keine Wohltätigkeitsveranstaltung, sondern eine Frage der Glaubwürdigkeit und des politischen Gestaltungswillens. Ein solcher Schritt wäre der sichtbare Ausdruck dessen, was es heißt, "die politische Komponente [der] Allianz ... zu stärken".[3] Ein höherer Verpflichtungsgrad gegenüber Anrainern im Osten und im Süden wird die NATO unmittelbarer an einer Stabilisierungsaufgabe beteiligen, als dies bei einem nur losen diplomatischen Kontakt möglich ist. Die Frage, auf die eine Antwort aussteht, lautet: Wodurch wird den sicherheitspolitischen Anliegen der Allianz besser gedient, durch eine starre Festschreibung ihrer gegenwärtigen Mitgliederzahl und geographischen Ausdehnung oder durch eine konditionierte Ausweitung ihres Verantwortungsbereichs?

An die Stelle des Ost-West-Konflikts und der beiden Allianzen tritt nicht ein System kollektiver Sicherheit, das die vormaligen Gegner unter einem Dach vereint. Die Sicherheitskonstellation verlangt jedoch nach mehr kollektiven Elementen, als dies zuvor möglich und nötig war. Die Berührungsängste, die - in Erinnerung an den gescheiterten Völkerbund - gegenüber Konzepten kollektiver Sicher-

1 Londoner Erklärung. Die Nordatlantische Allianz im Wandel, in: Bulletin des Presse- und Informationsamts der Bundesregierung (Bulletin), (10.7.1990) 90, S. 777.

2 Kommuniqué der Ministertagung des Nordatlantikrats, ebd. (11.6.1991) 66, S. 528.

3 Londoner Erklärung, S. 777.

heitsvorsorge bestehen, scheinen den Blick dafür zu verstellen, daß es eine klinisch saubere Trennung zwischen kollektiver Verteidigung und einem System kollektiver Sicherheit schon gegenwärtig nicht mehr gibt. Wenn die oben zitierte Aussage der Kopenhagener Erklärung mehr ist als inhaltsleere Formelsprache, dann reflektiert sie bereits, daß mit dem Ende des Ost-West-Konflikts eine Entwicklung eingesetzt hat, in deren Verlauf – zumindest an ihren Rändern – die Sicherheitsmodelle zusammenfließen, die bisher deutlich getrennt waren. Es ist schon jetzt überholt, um der Konzeptionen willen Glaubenskriege auszufechten. Vielmehr geht es ganz konkret darum, das Maß zu bestimmen, in dem die NATO ihre Verantwortung erweitert. Ob das Ziel eine erweiterte Mitgliedschaft ist oder (nur) ein vertieftes Engagement, das sich jedoch der formellen Aufnahme weiterer Staaten versagt, in beiden Fällen übernimmt die NATO eine kollektive Stabilitätsverpflichtung, die es als Bündnisaufgabe unter den antagonistischen Ost-West-Bedingungen nicht gab.

Die Gefahr für die NATO-Mitglieder beginnt nicht mit einem Angriff durch Dritte. Ihre Gefährdung beruht – zumindest mit einem hohen Plausibilitätsgrad – auf Entwicklungen *in den Staaten jenseits ihrer Grenzen.* Doch dies ist nur ein mögliches Szenario. Ein anderes ist, daß die ostmitteleuropäischen Staaten Drohungen ausgesetzt sind oder in Konflikte hineingezogen werden, die ihre Ursachen in der ehemaligen Sowjetunion haben. Der Ablauf derartiger Krisen ist in einer Hinsicht voraussehbar: Ein Hilfeersuchen der gefährdeten Staaten geht an den Westen.

Könnte die NATO einen Konflikt zwischen der Russischen Föderation und der Ukraine, der in Polen als Bedrohung wahrgenommen wird oder Polen tatsächlich bedroht, unbeschadet überstehen, wenn sie um Beistand gefragt wird, ohne dem Ersuchen indessen entsprechen zu können? Denn daß die NATO in einem solchen Fall problemlos handlungsfähig wäre, kann nicht als sicher angenommen werden. So paradox es auf den ersten Blick auch erscheinen mag, eine Stabilitätsverpflichtung der NATO für Ostmitteleuropa, die von ihren Widersachern als eine Überlastung der Atlantischen Allianz und als Schritt zu ihrer Erodierung gesehen wird, kann sich letzten Endes als ein notwendiger Beitrag zu ihrer Stabilität herausstellen. Die Begründung sollte nicht lauten: Weil die potentiellen Beitrittskandidaten keiner Bedrohung ausgesetzt sind und auch keine zu erwarten ist, könne ihrer Mitgliedschaft – wenn auch widerwillig – zugestimmt werden. Schlüssig ist vielmehr eine Argumentation, die vom Gegenteil ausgeht. Die mögliche Gefährdung der ostmitteleuropäischen Staaten ist der Grund dafür, das Verhältnis zu ihnen enger zu gestalten.

Die Annäherung der NATO an einzelne Staaten Ostmitteleuropas soll diesen nicht nur ein höheres Maß an äußerer Sicherheit geben. In dieser Hinsicht wäre sie eine ähnliche Maßnahme, wie sie den Visegrad-Staaten in ihren Assoziationsverträgen mit den Europäischen Gemeinschaften durch die Eröffnung einer Beitrittsperspektive zuteil wurde. Die Bereitschaft der NATO, neue Verpflichtungen einzugehen, dient nicht zuletzt auch dem Zweck, einer Destabilisierung des Bündnisses zuvorzukommen. Erst die Kombination beider Aspekte macht aus der weiteren Öffnung gegenüber Ostmitteleuropa ein dringendes Erfordernis. Deutschlands Interesse muß es zudem sein – und das ist keineswegs ein nebensächlicher Gesichtspunkt –, nicht in eine Lage zu geraten, in der es um Unterstützung gebeten wird, ohne daß sich die Anfrage automatisch an alle übrigen Allianzmitglieder richtet. Spanien wurde in die NATO aufgenommen, weil eine Beistandspflicht nur eine theoretische Möglichkeit zu sein schien; ein größeres Engagement der NATO im Osten und im Süden ist angezeigt, weil es dort um Staaten geht, die durchaus in die Lage geraten können, auf Unterstützung angewiesen zu sein.

3. Konditionen erweiterter Verantwortung

Was aber ist damit gemeint, wenn hier von einer konditionierten Ausweitung des NATO-Verantwortungsbereichs geredet wird? Welches könnten die Konditionen sein, die mit einer Stabilitäts- oder sogar Beistandsverpflichtung der NATO gegenüber neuen oder Noch-nicht-Mitgliedstaaten verbunden sind? So unterschiedlich die denkbaren Antworten auch ausfallen mögen, eine Prämisse gilt für sie alle gleichermaßen: Die "politischen, wirtschaftlichen, sozialen und ökologischen Elemente der Sicherheit" können nicht zusätzlich zur "unverzichtbare(n) Verteidigungsdimension"[4] der NATO allein aufgeladen werden. Sie verlangen nach einer multiinstitutionellen Sicherheitsordnung. Das heißt, daß die Stabilitätskandidaten Bedingungen erfüllen müssen, die sie gegenüber anderen Institutionen als der NATO eingegangen sind. In inhaltlicher Hinsicht können die "Beschlüsse der EG-Außenminister zur Anerkennung neuer Staaten"[5] vom November 1991 als Vorbild dienen, gemessen an formalen Kategorien tun sie es jedoch nicht. Ihnen fehlt der Verpflichtungsgrad, auf den sich die anerkennenden Staaten im Bedarfsfall berufen können. Die Zusage, sich dem Grundsatz von "Treu und Glauben" entsprechend zu verhalten, bleibt weit hinter dem zurück, was als Voraussetzung für eine Sicherheitszusage durch die NATO, auch wenn sie nicht mit einer Mitgliedschaft verbunden ist, einzufordern wäre. Das heißt in anderen Worten, die Staaten, denen gegenüber die NATO besondere Verpflichtungen eingeht, müssen sich zu mehr bereit finden als dem allgemeinen Bekenntnis zur VN-Charta, den Dokumenten der KSZE, Rechtsstaatlichkeit, Demokratie und Menschenrechten. An umfangreichen Normenkatalogen mangelt es ebensowenig wie an Zusagen, sich nach ihnen zu richten. Was fehlt, ist ihre operative Umsetzung und Überwachung.

---

4 Kommuniqué der Ministertagung des Nordatlantikrats (Kopenhagen), in: Bulletin, (11.6.1991) 66, S. 525.

5 Bulletin, (19.12.1991) 144, S. 1173.

Die Voraussetzung für eine Verknüpfung der europäischen und atlantischen Institutionen zu einem tragfähigen Sicherheitsnetz muß in und durch seine einzelnen Teile geschaffen werden. Bezogen auf die KSZE ist damit gemeint, daß sie operativ wirksamer wird, was aber nicht notwendigerweise bedeutet, daß ihre Beschlüsse eine rechtliche Qualität erhalten. Das gilt ganz generell für Verabredungen präventiver Diplomatie. Wer sich ihnen versagt oder ihrer Weiterentwicklung im Wege steht, kann nicht – so etwa eine Verknüpfung zwischen der NATO und der KSZE – eine Stabilitätsverpflichtung oder sogar eine Sicherheitsgarantie durch die NATO beanspruchen.[6] Zu einem Anwendungsfall könnte das auf der KSZE-Ratstagung in Stockholm verabschiedete "Übereinkommen über Vergleichs- und Schiedsverfahren innerhalb der KSZE" werden.[7] Seine Akzeptanz und parlamentarische Ratifizierung wäre ebenso eine Kondition in dem hier behandelten Sinne wie die Bereitschaft, sich den ebenfalls in Stockholm beschlossenen "Bestimmungen über einen Vergleich auf Anordnung"[8] im Bedarfsfall nicht zu entziehen.

Bei Übernahme einer sicherheitspolitischen Verantwortung für ostmitteleuropäische Staaten durch die NATO ist unbedingt zu vermeiden, daß sie als Freibrief mißbraucht wird. Spannungen zwischen neuen Allianzmitgliedern und ihren Nachbarn dürfen nicht mutwillig in einen Bündnisfall verkehrt werden. Die potentiellen Konflikte der möglichen Beitrittskandidaten in ihrem Umfeld sind keine unbekannten Größen. Insofern bedarf es in jedem Einzelfall spezifischer Abmachungen, die die NATO davor bewahren, in Konflikte hineingezogen zu werden, die keinen Verteidigungsfall darstellen. Damit wäre dann auch zu erreichen, daß eine wie auch immer geartete Sicherheitsgarantie der NATO für Staaten in Ostmitteleuropa sich für ihre Nachbarn nicht als eine Quelle der Gefahr, sondern als Beitrag auch zu ihrer Sicherheit erweist.

4. Europa jenseits der NATO

Eine Stabilitätsverpflichtung der NATO gegenüber einigen Staaten Ostmitteleuropas löst, solange sie eine singuläre Maßnahme bleibt, die Probleme einer europäischen Sicherheitsordnung natürlich nicht. Sie akzentuiert vielmehr die Lücken, die es zu schließen, aber auch die Möglichkeiten, die es einzulösen gilt. Man muß die potentiellen Beitrittskandidaten nicht mit letzter Bestimmtheit benennen können, will man die aufzählen, die ohne Zweifel nicht dazu gehören. Die Russische Föderation steht in einer entsprechenden Liste ganz obenan, was durchaus ihrem erklärten Interesse entspricht. Aber auch die anderen slawischen Nach-

---

6 Vgl. zu diesen Überlegungen Bernard *von Plate*, Die Neuordnung in der ehemaligen Sowjetunion: Eine Herausforderung für die KSZE, in: Europa-Archiv, 47 (25.5.1992), S. 290ff.

7 Vgl. Bulletin, (8.1.1993) 2, S. 6ff.

8 Ebd., S. 14.

folgestaaten der Sowjetunion werden – allerdings wohl weniger eindeutig freiwillig – gegenüber der NATO unter allen voraussehbaren Umständen einen deutlichen Abstand halten. Die Kernmacht eines zerfallenden Kolonialreiches hat, insoweit Rußland betroffen ist, in einem kollektiven Verteidigungsbündnis keinen Platz. Mit Blick auf ein kollektives Sicherheitssystem wären die Mitgliedsbedingungen nicht günstiger. Auch eine Gesellschaft, die sich in einem tiefgreifenden, und wie sich unschwer vorhersagen läßt, in einem langwierigen Wandel befindet, dessen Richtung noch keineswegs festgeschrieben und gesichert ist, paßt weder in ein kollektives Verteidigungs- noch in ein kollektives Sicherheitssystem.

Eine europäische Sicherheitsordnung muß sich aber insbesondere um die Staaten kümmern, die auf einem großen Risiko- und Konfliktpotential "sitzen". Das trifft für Rußland, aber auch für fast alle anderen Nachfolgestaaten der Sowjetunion zu. Es ist gefährlicher, sie sich selbst zu überlassen, als sie weit über das gegebene Maß hinaus einzubinden. Ein solcher Versuch muß zumindest unternommen werden, wenn die historische Chance zu einer Neuordnung ganz Europas, die sich mit dem Ende des Ost-West-Konflikts aufgetan hat, nicht schon in ihren Anfängen verpaßt werden soll. Das heißt, eine besondere Stabilitätsverpflichtung gegenüber den Staaten Ostmitteleuropas und erst recht ihre Aufnahme in die NATO darf nicht zu einer Maßnahme der Ausgrenzung von Staaten werden, für die kein besonderes Nahverhältnis zur Atlantischen Allianz absehbar ist. Oder umgekehrt formuliert, der Beitritt von Budapest, Prag, Bratislava und Warschau in die NATO, um gemessen an Kriterien einer konditionierten Erweiterungspolitik die wahrscheinlichsten Kandidaten zu nennen, ist nicht darauf zu beschränken, die Grenzen des kollektiven Verteidigungsbündnisses weiter nach Osten und nach Süden zu verschieben. Was sich für wenige – möglicherweise sogar nur dem ersten Anschein nach – als ein Schritt zugunsten größerer Sicherheit darstellt, wird aus der Sicht anderer durchaus als eine Quelle der Gefahr wahrgenommen. Es muß also etwas geschehen, damit für Weißrußland und die Ukraine und abgeschirmt durch diese beiden Staaten auch für Rußland eine unmittelbare Nachbarschaft zur NATO nicht als Verlust an Sicherheit gilt.

Als nach dem Ende des Warschauer Pakts von einigen Staaten deutliche Signale in die Richtung der NATO gesandt wurden, ist diesen mit dem Argument begegnet worden, die Entwicklungen in der damals noch bestehenden Sowjetunion nicht durch Maßnahmen zu belasten, die rückwärtsgewandten oder nationalistisch-chauvinistischen Kräften (oder beiden gemeinsam) Auftrieb bzw. Rückhalt geben könnten. Die Sowjetunion ist mittlerweile auseinandergebrochen. Die politischen Gefährdungen in den Staaten, die ihren Platz eingenommen haben, sind jedoch unverändert aktuell oder sogar noch brisanter geworden. Der Westen kann also nicht umhin, einen größeren Verpflichtungsgrad der NATO gegenüber ostmitteleuropäischen Nachbarstaaten im Verhältnis zu Moskau und anderen Nachfolgestaaten der Sowjetunion auszugleichen.

In einer umfangreichen politikwissenschaftlichen Literatur ist die Korrelation zwischen Gewaltbereitschaft bzw. Gewaltfähigkeit eines Herrschaftssystems und den in ihm gegebenen partizipatorischen Bedingungen aufgezeigt worden. Auch wenn sich diese Erfahrungswerte nicht uneingeschränkt auf zwischenstaatliche Beziehungen übertragen lassen, so geben sie doch zu einer Nachfrage Anlaß: Inwieweit wird durch ein internationales Forum ein für eine europäische Friedensordnung zuträgliches partizipatorisches Verhältnis aller Staaten befördert? In Europa ist die KSZE der einzige Rahmen, in dem dieser Versuch unternommen werden kann. Wird er nicht ausgefüllt, dann blieben in einer europäischen Sicherheitsordnung einige wichtige Rollen unbesetzt. Das wäre um so fataler, wenn sich in den USA Neigungen durchsetzten, mit den vier nuklearen Nachfolgestaaten der Sowjetunion bilateral zu verhandeln, und alles, was unterhalb der atomaren Ebene angesiedelt ist, sich selbst zu überlassen.

Die Alternative ist eine weitaus engere gesamteuropäische Sicherheitskooperation, als sie bislang angestrebt und in die Wege geleitet wurde. Um sie zu erreichen, bedarf es eines Umdenkens und einer Überprüfung bisheriger – wenn auch nicht immer öffentlich artikulierter – Positionen. Nachdrücklich ist der Vorstellung entgegenzutreten, daß KSZE und NATO in einem Konkurrenzverhältnis zueinander stehen. Diese Annahme ist nicht nur unsinnig, sondern auch gegen eine Sicherheitsordnung gerichtet, die möglichst alle europäischen Staaten einzubinden versucht. Der vermeintliche Gegensatz ist ohne jeden Bezugspunkt: Die NATO steht nicht in der Gefahr, gewissermaßen auf einem Schleichweg einem gesamteuropäischen Sicherheitsvertrag geopfert zu werden. NATO wie KSZE verhalten sich nicht wie kommunizierende Röhren zueinander, in denen der Funktionsgewinn der einen automatisch zum Funktionsverlust der anderen Seite führt. Es geht um ein funktionales Wechselverhältnis, nicht um den Transfer von Kompetenzen. Was die NATO nicht kann und auch nicht können sollte, liegt offen zutage. Auch noch nach Jahren werden viele Staaten in Europa nicht in ihren Reihen zu finden sein. Selbst wenn eines Tages, wie in der politischen Debatte mit einem gelegentlich abwertenden Unterton eingewandt wird, z.B. die Ukraine "auf der Matte" steht, ist dies kein Schaden. Ein höherer Verpflichtungsgrad gegenüber ostmitteleuropäischen Staaten löst insbesondere dann keine Kettenreaktion aus, wenn die Bedingungen hierfür unzweideutig vorbestimmt sind. Zudem ist eine Entwicklung, die zu einem größeren kollektiven Sicherheitsraum führt, kein Sakrileg gegen eine europäische Sicherheitsordnung, wenn dabei eine wachsende Zahl von Staaten in ein Netz obligatorischer Verpflichtungen eingebunden werden kann. Schließlich ist davon auszugehen, daß der Drang in die NATO um so geringer ist, je stärker gesamteuropäische Perspektiven eröffnet werden können.

Die Erwartungen, die sich an die KSZE richten, beruhen darauf, daß es für eine große Zahl europäischer Staaten keine institutionelle Alternative gibt. Die KSZE muß deshalb in erster Linie für die Staaten attraktiver und funktionsfähiger werden, deren Entwicklung für die Stabilität in Europa von ausschlaggebender Bedeutung ist. Das trifft vor allem auf die Russische Föderation und in ihrem Gefolge Weißrußland sowie die Ukraine zu. Gerade die politischen Kräfte und Vordenker in Rußland, die sich die Modernisierung ihres Landes nur im Zusammenwirken mit dem Westen vorstellen können, sind es, die zugleich auch die Grenzen einer Annäherung Rußlands an westliche Sicherheitsinstitutionen zur Sprache bringen.[9] Sie setzen auf eine gestärkte KSZE und nennen dafür vor allem drei eng miteinander verbundene Argumente:

- Eine schwache KSZE nimmt Rußland die Möglichkeit, sich an der Lösung europäischer Sicherheitsprobleme zu beteiligen.
- Die KSZE ist eine der wenigen internationalen Einrichtungen, in denen Rußland mit anderen Staaten gleichberechtigt wirken kann, und
- die KSZE ist ein wichtiger Zugang zu westlichen Institutionen wie der NATO und der WEU.[10]

5. Vom Nordatlantischen zum Europäisch-Nordatlantischen Kooperationsrat

Eine attraktivere KSZE ist nicht voraussetzungslos. Sie muß erst noch geschaffen werden, um den russischen Interessen angesichts der bestehenden und letztlich nicht aufhebbaren Distanz Moskaus zu den westlichen Sicherheitsvereinbarungen entgegenzukommen. Wie und wodurch könnte die KSZE an Substanz gewinnen? Es gibt keine für ganz Europa zuständige Sicherheitsinstitution. Die KSZE könnte jedoch dazu werden. Dafür ist eine eindeutige Weichenstellung notwendig. Es bedarf eines Signals, das sich nicht in Feinheiten verliert, sondern gewissermaßen mit einem Paukenschlag darauf aufmerksam macht, daß die sicherheitspolitische Aufgabe in Europa nicht nur die Verteidigung einiger europäischer und atlantischer Staaten betrifft, sondern sich auf den ganzen KSZE-Raum erstreckt. Ein Signal angemessener Größenordnung wäre es, den Nordatlantischen Kooperationsrat (NACC) in den KSZE-Rahmen zu übertragen und gleichzeitig auch seinen Namen um die europäische Dimension zu ergänzen: Europäisch-Nordatlantischer Kooperationsrat (ENACC). Dieser wäre dann keine Parallelveranstaltung zum KSZE-Forum für Sicherheitskooperation, sondern ein Beitrag zu seiner Aufwertung.

Der NACC hat eine Doppelrolle: Er ist Kooperationsangebot und "Distanzwaffe". Er wurde eingerichtet als Brücke zwischen zwei Organisationen, wobei einige

---

9 Vgl. Grigoriy J. *Chudakov u.a.*, Russia's Interests and Approaches towards the System of Interlocking European Institutions, S. 265-281 in diesem Band.

10 Ebd.

seiner Mitglieder mehr auf die NATO, andere mehr auf die KSZE geblickt haben. In dieser unklaren Zwischenstellung kann der NACC zwar überleben, aber wohl kaum eine dauerhafte Bedeutung erlangen. Den ostmitteleuropäischen Interessenten an einer NATO-Mitgliedschaft ist er nicht genug. Dem kuriosen Zustand, daß er sich – ein willkürliches Beispiel – für armenische Sicherheitsprobleme für zuständig hält, für schwedische indessen nicht, kann der NACC in seiner jetzigen Konstruktion nicht abhelfen. Als Beruhigungspolster für Moskau bei einem größeren Verpflichtungsgrad der NATO gegenüber den ostmitteleuropäischen Staaten reicht er nicht aus.

Gibt es Voraussetzungen, unter denen die Beibehaltung des NACC in seiner jetzigen Form gerechtfertigt ist? Das scheint offenbar nur dann der Fall zu sein, wenn die KSZE darauf verzichtet, sich mehr Gehör zu verschaffen und in europäischen Sicherheitsfragen verstärkt zur operativen Drehscheibe zu werden. Dann bliebe die KSZE allenfalls auf dem Stand eines sicherheitspolitischen Diskussionsforums. Ihr wäre damit eine zukunftsweisende Perspektive genommen und der NACC wäre zumindest in einem Teilbereich in die Rolle einer Alternative zur KSZE gedrängt,[11] ohne sie indessen ganz auszufüllen oder die KSZE insgesamt ersetzen zu können. Der NACC ist und bleibt, so nützlich seine Funktion bei der Anpassung des CFE-Vertrages an die veränderten Bedingungen in Europa auch war, ein Kompromiß zwischen den Verfechtern einer sakrosankten NATO und den Befürwortern einer sicherheitspolitischen Verantwortung für ganz Europa. Er hat den Gegensatz zwischen den unterschiedlichen Positionen in einer begrenzten Phase des europäischen Wandels überbrückt, dauerhaft ausgeräumt hat er ihn indessen nicht. Insofern wäre die Eingliederung des NACC in die KSZE auch als ein Akt der konzeptionellen Bereinigung zu verstehen.

Bei Umbenennung und Umwidmung des NACC zu einem Instrument der KSZE sollte jedoch alles vermieden werden, was den Eindruck einer "Luftnummer" erwecken könnte. Handelt es sich nur um eine deklaratorische Maßnahme, dann verfehlt sie ihr Ziel. Die Absicht, den NACC unter das Dach der KSZE zu stellen, ist als politische Initialzündung zu verstehen. Ihre Verwirklichung ist lediglich der Auftakt für eine engere Zusammenarbeit zwischen NATO und KSZE. Substantiell ist mit der Maßnahme allein noch nicht viel erreicht. Die "Aktivitäten", die für den NACC bei seiner Gründung von den NATO-Staaten vorgeschlagen wurden, sind zu bescheiden, um nach ihrer Verlagerung in den Rahmen der KSZE aus dieser eine aufgewertete sicherheitspolitische Institution werden zu lassen. Der "Arbeitsplan für Dialog, Partnerschaft und Zusammenarbeit im Jahre 1993", dem der Nordatlantische Kooperationsrat auf seiner Tagung im Dezember

11 Vgl. zu den alternativen Entwicklungsmöglichkeiten des NACC den Beitrag von John *Barrett*/ Hans Jochen *Peters*, NACC and the CSCE: A Contribution in the Context of the Concept of Interlocking Institutions, S. 249-263 in diesem Band.

1992 zugestimmt hat, verspricht dahingegen, sofern er nicht nur abgehakt, sondern tatsächlich umgesetzt wird, dem NACC einen deutlichen Substanzgewinn einzubringen.[12] Angesichts der hier vorgetragenen konzeptionellen Überlegungen wäre das Programm für 1993 ein Schritt auf dem Wege zu einem ENACC, einem Organ, das es bislang noch nicht gibt: eine immer präsente Einrichtung, in der Europa betreffende Sicherheitsbelange aus eigenem Recht, ohne jede Zeitverzögerung aufgegriffen und verhandelt werden. Je größer das Gewicht eines ENACC ist, desto geringer ist das Risiko, daß eine Einbettung des NACC in den Rahmen der KSZE als Abstufung dieses Gremiums empfunden wird. Diese Sorge ist insbesondere mit Blick auf die Staaten denkbar, denen in der NATO weder ein Platz eingeräumt noch eine erweiterte Sicherheitszusage zuteil wird, und denen über den Umweg des NACC an einer möglichst engen Anlehnung an die NATO gelegen ist.

Nur vor einem so breiten Hintergrund bedeutet eine nach Osten und Süden erweiterte Sicherheitsverantwortung der NATO für Rußland keinen Verlust an Sicherheit. Es würde vielmehr stärker an europäischen Sicherheitsfragen beteiligt, als dies durch einen NACC möglich und in dem Sicherheitsforum der KSZE bisher angelegt ist.

Die größte Hürde, die vor der Einrichtung eines ENACC steht, waren bislang die USA. Das zumindest bestätigten die amerikanische KSZE-Politik und ihr anfänglicher Widerstand gegen jegliche Institutionenbildung im Rahmen der KSZE. Die amerikanische Ablehnung europäischer Sicherheitsinstitutionen beruhte vor allem auf der Sorge, die NATO intakt zu halten. Solange es Stimmen gab, die Allianz in einem gesamteuropäischen Sicherheitsvertrag aufzulösen, war die amerikanische Zurückhaltung begründet. Die Idee, durch einen umfassenden Vertrag nicht nur das Vakuum in Ostmittel- und Osteuropa auszufüllen, sondern auch die NATO zu ersetzen, war jedoch ein Kind der Monate nach der Wende, geboren auf einer Welle der Hoffnungen und der Zuversicht, nach den Jahrzehnten der europäischen Teilung unter *einem* vertraglichen Dach Platz zu finden. Ein ENACC wäre allenfalls noch ein Nachklang der Euphorie von damals. Er würde das sichtbare Ende einer Debatte verkörpern und verstünde sich als eine Ergänzung und Stütze der NATO, nicht als der Anfang von ihrem Ende.

Diese Aussage unterstellt eine wechselseitige Abhängigkeit. Sie geht davon aus, daß institutionell die NATO nicht gefährdet ist. Jede andere Erwartung ist ohne aktuelle und absehbare Bedeutung. Nicht nur die KSZE ist da, wo sie über keine eigenen Möglichkeiten verfügt, auf Mittel der NATO angewiesen. Das gilt allerdings, wie am Schluß näher begründet werden wird, ausschließlich für Optionen unterhalb der Gewaltschwelle. Aber auch die NATO braucht die KSZE und ihren institutionellen Rahmen. Sie vermittelt der Allianz eine Aufgabenperspektive,

12 Vgl. Bulletin, (29.12.1992) 141, S. 1312ff.

ohne sie indessen *vertraglich* in ihrer Entscheidungsautonomie einzuschränken. Einer stärkeren *politischen* Einbindung in eine Sicherheitsverantwortung, die – bezogen auf den KSZE-Raum – nicht an den Grenzen des Bündnisses halt macht, kann sich die NATO auf Dauer wohl kaum versagen. Mit dem Ende des Ost-West-Konflikts und der bündnispolitischen Zweiteilung Europas ist sie zumindest in die Richtung einer Zwitterstellung gerückt, in der sich die Kernaufgabe einer kollektiven Verteidigung ihrer Mitglieder nicht mehr in jedem Fall von einer kollektiven Zuständigkeit in einem weitergesteckten Rahmen trennen läßt. Hier geht es allerdings nicht um einen verkappten Ersatz für ein verlorengegangenes Feindbild, sondern um eine Gestaltungsaufgabe, deren bedrückende Dringlichkeit nicht zu übersehen ist. Ein ENACC demonstriert, von wo aus diese Aufgabe anzugehen ist, von der NATO mit dem verlängerten Arm des NACC oder der KSZE mit einer aufgewerteten institutionellen Kapazität.

II. Die KSZE "operativer und wirksamer"

1. Die Bedarfslage

Der Krieg in den ehemaligen jugoslawischen Teilrepubliken hat allen Beobachtern schonungslos vor Augen geführt, daß sich die Optionen, Spannungsursachen entgegenzutreten und sie abzubauen, drastisch verringern, wenn diese ein Stadium der Gewalt erreicht haben. Es spiegelt eine gewisse Zwangsläufigkeit wider, daß die Diskussion angesichts des Krieges in und um Bosnien-Herzegowina weitgehend auf die Frage zusammengeschrumpft ist, ob und wie militärische Maßnahmen ergriffen werden können. Nichtmilitärische Reaktionsmöglichkeiten spielen allenfalls noch eine Nebenrolle. Sie gewinnen vermutlich erst dann wieder an Bedeutung, wenn eine – in Bosnien offenbar zwei – Konfliktparteien ihre Ziele militärisch durchsetzen konnten. Nach den anfänglichen Versäumnissen war für die Außenwelt in Jugoslawien nur noch eine militärische Antwort übriggeblieben, die so umfänglich ausgelegt wurde, daß sie für niemanden annehmbar war.

Ethno-religiöse Konflikte sind aufgrund ihres hohen Grades an Irrationalität schwer zu beeinflussen. Sie entziehen sich nahezu vollends der Kontrolle, wenn sie gewaltsame Formen angenommen haben. Diese Erfahrung hat, sofern sie überhaupt noch einmal gemacht werden mußte, ein besonderes Gewicht angesichts der mehrheitlich vertretenen Überzeugung, daß den meisten, wenn nicht sogar allen regionalen Krisen ethnische und religiöse Spannungen zugrunde liegen. Die Staatengemeinschaft muß also, will sie von ihren ohnehin nur geringen Handlungsmöglichkeiten Gebrauch machen und alle Chancen der Konfliktprävention ausnutzen, zu einem Zeitpunkt handlungsfähig sein, an dem sie auf ein noch relativ breites Spektrum von Optionen zurückgreifen kann. Wenn es überhaupt eine Chance gibt, Konfliktparteien der genannten Art die Konsequenzen ihres Handelns vorzuführen, dann nur in einer Phase, in der das Pro und Kontra, in der eine Güterabwägung noch durch Signale von außen beeinflußt werden kann. Ein zu spät aufgelegter Maßnahmenkatalog ist nicht nur folgenlos, sondern wirkt möglicherweise sogar konfliktverschärfend. Dafür sind die Vorgänge in Jugoslawien – eine allerdings kontroverse Sicht – beispielhaft.

Der "Fall Jugoslawien" ersetzt abstrakte konzeptionelle Anläufe. Er beschreibt mit dem Elend des Krieges und dem hunderttausendfachen Leid von Menschen die uneingelösten Desiderate einer europäischen Sicherheitsordnung. Wenn die Gefahren in der Instabilität von Gesellschaften, in der Verletzung von Menschen- und Bürgerrechten, in der Mißachtung ethnischer und religiöser Entwicklungsmöglichkeiten, in der sozialen Entwurzelung großer Bevölkerungsgruppen und auch auf den territorialen Ansprüchen alter oder neuer Machteliten beruhen, dann ist es nicht länger eine inhaltsleere Formel, daß die Antwort nur ein "Geflecht ineinandergreifender Institutionen" sein kann, so die Aussage von Rom, in dem die "NATO, die KSZE, die WEU, die Europäische Gemeinschaft und der Europarat einander ergänzen". Die Realität hat mit der Rhetorik jedoch nicht Schritt gehalten. Statt dessen nehmen die Stimmen zu, die in dem Konzept der "interlocking institutions" nur einen Verschiebebahnhof sehen. So ist es zumindest indikativ, daß der institutionelle Ort, an dem die europäisch/atlantischen Organe zusammengebunden werden können, noch nicht einmal ausgemacht ist. Ein kontinuierliches Gespräch findet nicht statt. Ein wechselseitiges Zusammenwirken ist (noch) nicht begonnen worden. Es ist leicht, diese Defizite aufzuzählen; ein Weg, auf dem sich Abhilfe auftut, ist dagegen nur andeutungsweise zu nennen. Es geht um einen Prozeß, der ohne die Lokomotivrolle eines Staates oder der engen Zusammenarbeit mehrerer nicht auskommt.

2. Institutionelle Konsequenzen

Die beiden amerikanischen Autoren Thomas J. Hirschfeld und Anne M. Dixon haben einen Katalog von Maßnahmen und klärungsbedürftigen Punkten zusammengestellt,[13] die das Verhalten der KSZE-Teilnehmer bei einer Verletzung von

---

13 Vgl. Anne M. *Dixon*/Thomas J. *Hirschfeld*, Adopting the CSCE to Modern Problems: Limits and Opportunities, S. 219-247 in diesem Band, hier S. 242f:

(1) Agreeing collectively not to interfere, or on who among them may interfere, and on the type and extent of such interference;

(2) Agreeing to act together to prevent parties outside the area from interfering;

(3) Embargoing goods traffic and weapons deliveries, and freezing the assets of belligerents;

(4) Collectively denying current and future recognition, credits, commerce and other rights of states in the international community until particular conditions are met;

(5) Interfering with external and internal communications with respect to the affected area;

(6) Monitoring individual acts with a view to subsequent trial and punishment;

KSZE-Regeln bestimmen sollten. Bestenfalls wirken sie abschreckend, zumindest aber können sie dazu beitragen, einen Konflikt zu begrenzen. Was durch die Vorschläge aber vor allem dokumentiert wird, ist die Notwendigkeit, daß unterschiedliche Organisationen ihre jeweils spezifischen Handlungsmöglichkeiten in einen zuvor abgestimmten Verhaltenskodex einbringen. Prävention von Konflikten, die nur auf die "Ressourcen" der KSZE in ihrer Ausstattung vom Juli 1992 und die Beschlüsse und Übereinkommen der KSZE-Ratstagung in Stockholm vom Dezember desselben Jahres zurückgreifen kann, bleibt hinter dem Erreichbaren zurück. Vor diesem Hintergrund zeigt sich noch einmal, was mit einem Transfer des NACC in die KSZE erreicht werden muß: eine Initialzündung zugunsten einer institutionellen Verzahnung aller sicherheitsrelevanten Organe und einer institutionellen Bestandsaufnahme der KSZE. Das heißt mit anderen Worten, daß die Zusammenführung der europäischen Institutionen in einen permanenten sicherheitspolitischen Konsultationsprozeß auf der Ebene der bereits bestehenden KSZE-Institutionen eine Entsprechung finden sollte.

So politisch verständlich es war, mit den in der Charta von Paris begründeten Institutionen vor allem die Staaten Ostmitteleuropas zu ehren, die im Prozeß des Wandels eine Schrittmacherrolle übernommen hatten, so nachteilig erweist sich diese Entscheidung aus der Sicht einer funktionsgerechten Handlungsfähigkeit. Am Prestigewert, seit zwei Jahren eine kleine KSZE-Institution zu beherbergen, sollte es dann nicht scheitern, sie in *einem* gemeinsamen institutionellen Rahmen zusammenzuführen, wenn es in der Zielsetzung um eine Aufwertung der KSZE geht. Zu diesem Schritt gibt es keine Alternative, wenn die Einsicht, daß der Gefährdung von Frieden und Sicherheit in Europa ein breites Ursachenspektrum zugrunde liegt, zu wirksamen Konsequenzen verhelfen soll. So gesehen gehören das Büro für Demokratische Institutionen und Menschenrechte und der Hohe Kommissar der KSZE für nationale Minderheiten unter das gleiche Dach wie das Konfliktverhütungszentrum.

a. Ein KSZE-Generalsekretär

Die Wirksamkeit der KSZE ist nicht zuletzt abhängig von ihrer Erreichbarkeit und dem Zeitaufwand, dessen sie bedarf, um auf Anfrage tätig zu werden. Ein ENACC ist im Prozeß von Konfliktverhütung und Krisenbewältigung hilfreich und notwendig; als erster Adressat für einen interessierten Staat genügt er nicht. Es bedarf eines Anlaufpunktes, der sich deutlich von der komplizierten Maschinerie der

---

(7) Agreeing collectively on the conditions under which refugees shall be accepted, on the accounting for refugee expenses and on which of the parties to the conflict is to be held accountable; and

(8) Identifying the facilities for mediation, separation of forces and other good offices which the community might offer the parties to the dispute.

KSZE abhebt. Die konfliktbeladenen Nachfolgestaaten der Sowjetunion wenden sich, so ist wenigstens zu vermuten, vorzugsweise an die Vereinten Nationen, weil diese durch ihren Generalsekretär einen eindeutig identifizierbaren Bezugspunkt bieten, nicht weil die VN wirkungsvoller tätig werden können als die KSZE.

Nun geht es nicht darum, eine europäische Kopie der Vereinten Nationen zu erstellen. Aber wenn es das Ziel ist, die KSZE zu einem wichtigen Akteur im Bereich europäischer Sicherheitsfragen auf- und auszubauen, dann war es notwendig, mit der Einrichtung des Amts eines Generalsekretärs sowohl eine symbolische, aber vor allem eine funktionale Lücke zu schließen. Seine vorrangige Aufgabe muß es sein, eine Kontinuität herzustellen, die ungeachtet der Troika-Regelung durch den jährlichen Wechsel im Vorsitz des KSZE-Rats nur bedingt gegeben ist. Insofern handelt es sich um eine Rolle, die durch den Amtierenden Vorsitzenden des Rats nicht ausgefüllt wird und ausgefüllt werden kann. Ein KSZE-Generalsekretär sollte nicht nur die sichtbare Spitze an dem Ort sein, an dem auch ein ENACC seinen Sitz haben würde, sondern er wäre mit diesem funktional zu verbinden. Für das Amt des Generalsekretärs gilt wie für die bereits bestehenden KSZE-Institutionen, daß ihm ein international anerkannter Status verliehen werden sollte. Ein KSZE-Generalsekretär müßte eines Tages wie sein Kollege bei den Vereinten Nationen auch aus eigenem Recht den Rat und den Ausschuß Hoher Beamter auf friedensgefährdende Entwicklungen aufmerksam machen können.

b. Ein KSZE-Sicherheitsrat

Ein herausragendes Strukturproblem der KSZE ist das Verhältnis zwischen ihren Institutionen und die mühselige Entscheidungsfindung. Kann und soll die dominierende Rolle des KSZE-Rats und des Ausschusses Hoher Beamter, der dessen jährliche Sitzungen vorbereitet, beibehalten werden? Das Gewicht beider Institutionen ist ursächlich für die Schwerfälligkeit der KSZE. Es steht aber auch – und das muß im selben Atemzug miterwähnt werden – für den nur durch vage Formulierungen eingeschränkten Grundsatz der Einstimmigkeit, der den KSZE-Prozeß bislang geprägt hat. Deshalb klingt, auch wenn vordergründig nur von einer institutionellen Reform der KSZE geredet wird, immer die Frage mit, ob noch einmal der Versuch gemacht werden soll, die Konsensregel über das gegebene Maß hinaus aufzubrechen.

An Vorschlägen, von den geltenden Regelungen abzugehen, fehlt es nicht. Sie orientieren sich – zumindest bei der Wahl der Begriffe wie schon beim Amt eines KSZE-Generalsekretärs – am Vorbild der Vereinten Nationen. Von einem KSZE-Sicherheitsrat ist die Rede, dem ständige und nichtständige Mitglieder angehören sollen, aber in Abweichung von den Vereinten Nationen keine Vetomächte. Da sich jedoch auch an den VN-Sicherheitsrat Reformerwartungen richten, gibt es zwischen beiden Debatten aufschlußreiche Parallelen und Abweichungen.

Der VN-Sicherheitsrat spiegelt eine einmalige historische Situation wider. Jeder Versuch, Anpassungen an eine völlig veränderte internationale Lage vorzunehmen, wird mit einiger Wahrscheinlichkeit nicht in einer Reform enden, bei der wichtige Konstitutionsprinzipien bewahrt bleiben, sondern in einer grundlegenden Verwandlung des Sicherheitsrats. Diese Erwartung macht ihn vermutlich gegen allzu umfassend angelegte Veränderungsvorstellungen weitgehend resistent. Die Vorschläge, die für eine Leistungssteigerung der KSZE-Entscheidungsinstanzen auf ihrer obersten Ebene gemacht wurden, liegen gewissermaßen auf Gegenkurs. Sie beabsichtigen keine Öffnung überholter Strukturen, sondern die Kanalisierung eines breiten Abstimmungsstromes. Gegen diese Absicht haben sich insbesondere Staaten gewandt, die nicht damit rechnen, dauerhaft an einem kleineren Entscheidungsgremium der KSZE beteiligt zu sein und folglich von einer Hierarchisierung der KSZE-Teilnehmer oder sogar Diskriminierung einzelner Staaten sprechen.

Wichtiger als das Problem einer Statusdifferenz ist indessen die Frage, ob es der richtige Weg ist, die Konsensregel institutionell durch eine Entscheidungsspitze einzuschränken. Die Alternative ist, die Konsensregel *fallbezogen* zu umgehen. Das setzt allerdings voraus, die Kriterien deutlich zu bestimmen, wann von einer nicht hinnehmbaren Verletzung von KSZE-Verpflichtungen und einer Gefahr für den Frieden auszugehen ist. Mit anderen Worten, ein (oder mehrere) Teilnehmerstaaten der KSZE stellen sich gewissermaßen selbst außerhalb des Konsenses aller übrigen Staaten, indem sie gegen zentrale Elemente der breiten KSZE-Normenbasis, ein Katalog, der schrittweise erweitert werden könnte, verstoßen. Dies festzustellen muß mehr und mehr nur noch zu einer Formsache werden. Angesichts von zuvor vereinbarten Toleranzgrenzen sollte es jeder Teilnehmerstaat der KSZE weitgehend selbst in der Hand haben, ob und wann sich die Konsens-minus-eins-Regel – die Frage, ob dieser bescheidene Differenzbetrag genügt, bleibt hier außer Betracht – gegen ihn selbst richtet. Ohne dieses Maß an Selbstverantwortlichkeit zu überschätzen: Es kann ein Minimum an präventiver Wirkung entfalten.

Gegen solche Überlegungen wird vorgebracht werden, daß sie den Versuch beschreiben, dieses Mal allerdings vor einem breiteren Hintergrund, noch einmal zu wiederholen, was bereits im Bezug auf eine generell akzeptierte Definition, wann eine Angriffshandlung vorliegt, nicht erfolgreich war. So bedenkenswert die Einwände sind, bei denen die Erfahrungen des Völkerbundes und die Bemühungen der Vereinten Nationen Pate stehen, nie zuvor haben sich Staaten auf einen ähnlich ausdifferenzierten Normenkodex eingelassen wie die KSZE-Teilnehmer. Aus ihm einige wenige unverwechselbare Kategorien herauszukristallisieren, die nicht Gefahr laufen, strittig zu sein, ist eine der dringlichsten Zukunftsaufgaben der KSZE. Durch einen KSZE-Sicherheitsrat würde sie nicht hinfällig werden.

Ebenso wichtig wie der Versuch, die Konsens-minus-eins-Regel in einem vorweggenommenen Konsens, der sich gegen jeden Teilnehmerstaat richten kann, strikter zu formulieren, ist eine Antwort auf die Frage, wer einen Fall "eindeutiger" Verletzungen von KSZE-Normen feststellen darf. Hirschfeld/Dixon schlagen vor, das Konfliktverhütungszentrum mit dem Recht auszustatten, sich in "dringlichen Situationen" an den Ausschuß Hoher Beamter zu wenden.[14] Es bedarf keiner detaillierten Ausführungen, daß das KVZ in seiner gegenwärtigen Ausstattung dazu nicht in der Lage ist. Das KVZ ist mit einer Analysekomponente auszustatten, die dem – wiederholt genannten – Sachverhalt Rechnung trägt, daß die große Mehrheit regionaler Krisen die Folge innerstaatlicher Spannungen ist.

Der im Juni 1991 vereinbarte "Mechanismus für Konsultation und Zusammenarbeit in dringlichen Situationen" legt fest, welche Möglichkeiten ein *Teilnehmerstaat* hat. Im Interesse einer schnellen Reaktionsfähigkeit der KSZE läge es, wenn sie mit *eigenen* Mitteln einen Konfliktgegenstand auf die Tagesordnung der Teilnehmerstaaten setzen könnte, ohne die Initiative eines Teilnehmers abwarten zu müssen. Auch hier geht es, wie schon in anderen Zusammenhängen zuvor, um die Bestallung von KSZE-Institutionen mit originären Zuständigkeiten.

c. KSZE-Botschafter

Die KSZE ist eine Serie von Konferenzen, keine Rechtspersönlichkeit. In ihrem Rahmen werden völkerrechtliche Verträge ausgehandelt; sie ist selbst jedoch "ein Forum für Dialog, Verhandlung und Zusammenarbeit, das der Gestaltung des neuen Europa Richtung und Impulse gibt", wie es in der Helsinki-Erklärung von 1992 heißt. Diesem Selbstverständnis, das seine Geschichte im Ost-West-Konflikt hat, steht nicht entgegen, daß die KSZE-Staaten bestehende institutionelle Einrichtungen oder zusätzliche Organe rechtlich so ausstatten, daß sie gegenüber Dritten im Rahmen ihres Mandats vertragsfähig sind. Von dieser Prämisse gehen die Überlegungen aus, Repräsentanten der KSZE zu schaffen, die einen Botschafterstatus haben.[15] Die Ausführungen berufen sich auf die große Rolle innerstaatlicher Konfliktursachen für die Sicherheit in Europa, worauf bereits in anderem Zusammenhang hingewiesen wurde.

Eine ganze Reihe von KSZE-Staaten ist noch weit davon entfernt, das einhalten zu können, was sie anläßlich ihres Beitritts feierlich gelobt haben. Von dieser wenig originellen Beobachtung bis zur Einsicht, daß es eines langen Sozialisationsprozesses bedarf, bis sich möglichst alle KSZE-Teilnehmer einem normativen Konsens auch in ihrer politischen Praxis angenähert haben, ist es nur ein kleiner Schritt. Kann die KSZE zu diesem Prozeß etwas beitragen? Kann sie anknüpfen

---

14 Ebd.

15 Vgl. Bernard *von Plate*, Die innerstaatliche Funktion der KSZE, S. 209-217 in diesem Band.

an eine Rolle, die ihr Renommee unter den Bedingungen des Ost-West-Konflikts begründet hat, nämlich Berufungsgrundlage für die Kräfte des Wandels und der Demokratie zu sein? Die Voraussetzungen, unter denen die KSZE im postantagonistischen Zeitalter wirksam werden kann, sind ungleich günstiger, als sie es zuvor jemals waren. Auch die Notwendigkeit, in die Staaten hineinwirken zu können, ist dringender als in den Jahren zuvor geworden. Der große Ost-West-Konflikt ist beseitigt. Gleichzeitig ist aber seine pazifizierende Nebenwirkung hinfällig geworden. Die KSZE kann die entstandene Lücke nicht ausfüllen. Sie kann aber einen Beitrag leisten, sie zu schließen, indem sie die KSZE-Normen und Prinzipien institutionell und personell sichtbar in den Hauptstädten ihrer Teilnehmerstaaten zur Geltung bringt. Nur eine KSZE-Instanz, die völkerrechtlich dazu befugt ist, kann diese "Emissäre für Demokratie, Menschenrechte und Grundfreiheiten" entsenden. Konfliktprävention der KSZE ist vor allem eine Aufgabe *in* den Staaten.

III. Eine Regionalisierung der KSZE

Die KSZE umfaßt nicht nur geographisch einen riesigen Raum, sondern repräsentiert auch eine beeindruckende kulturelle und ethnische Vielfalt. Zwar hat sich die KSZE zu einer "regionalen Abmachung" im Sinne von Kapitel VIII der Charta der Vereinten Nationen erklärt, gemessen an der Dichte regionaler Vernetzung und einer wechselseitigen – positiven wie negativen – Interessenverflechtung, die nicht zuletzt auf einer räumlichen Nähe beruht, bestehen nur in wenigen Bereichen Gemeinsamkeiten, die dem KSZE-Gebiet in seiner Gesamtheit den Charakter einer Region verleihen. Zu ihnen gehören an vorderster Stelle – der Name sagt es bereits – transnationale Umweltprobleme. Auch angesichts des Umfangs der zwischen ihren Teilnehmerstaaten vereinbarten Normen kann die KSZE als eine besondere Region gelten. Fragt man jedoch nach den Aussichten, daß der erreichte Standard auch eingehalten oder von anderen Teilnehmerstaaten notfalls sogar gewaltsam eingefordert wird, dann zeichnet sich die KSZE zwar durch eine besondere Regelungs-, nicht aber Handlungsdichte aus.

Von einigen wenigen Ausnahmen abgesehen, erfüllt ein Raum, der Wladiwostok ebenso einschließt wie Vancouver, nicht die Bedingungen einer Region. Die KSZE ist räumlich wie sachlich vielfach untergliedert. Die muslimischen Nachfolgestaaten der Sowjetunion oder Anrainer der Ostsee, um nur zwei Beispiele zu nennen, sind den Problemen ihres jeweiligen Umfeldes in jeder Hinsicht näher als die meisten Staaten Westeuropas oder die beiden transatlantischen KSZE-Teilnehmer, die USA und Kanada.

Aber nicht nur politisch-kulturelle Trennlinien durchschneiden die KSZE. Zwischen der westlichen und der östlichen Hälfte Europas besteht ein Ungleichgewicht. In grober, aber wohl zulässiger Vereinfachung trifft es zu, daß eine Seite –

die westliche – über eine institutionelle Dichte und prinzipiell einsatzfähige Organe verfügt, während sich auf der Gegenseite – der östlichen – ein Risiko- und Konfliktpotential anhäuft bzw. bereits angesammelt hat. Die politische Brisanz dieses Sachverhalts ist offensichtlich und hat zwei Aspekte. Einer – auf ihn wird in dem hier behandelten Kontext nicht weiter eingegangen – betrifft bündnisinterne Probleme der NATO und der WEU und bezieht sich auf die Bedingungen, unter denen die beiden Allianzen außerhalb ihres jeweiligen Vertragsgebietes einsetzbar sind. Für die KSZE ist vor allem von Bedeutung, daß in ihr zumindest solange ein einseitiger Handlungsdruck besteht, wie sich der Westen einer Vielfalt ungeklärter ordnungspolitischer Probleme im Osten gegenübersieht.

Der Einsatz der NATO jenseits ihrer Bündnisgrenzen hat, auch wenn es sich um die Wahrnehmung friedenserhaltender Aufgaben unterhalb der Schwelle von Gewaltanwendungen handelt, eine doppelte Blockierung zu überwinden, die beide Male politischer Natur ist: Die NATO ist – und das macht sie für gesamteuropäische Friedensaufgaben nicht von vornherein geeignet – ein Instrument, auf das nur einige KSZE-Teilnehmer Einfluß ausüben können. Dabei ist es nach nahezu 40jähriger Propaganda vermutlich im Bewußtsein der Menschen in Osteuropa kaum von Belang, daß der Bündnisfall nur nach einem Angriff von außen gegeben ist. Aus der Sicht der ostmitteleuropäischen Staaten, die der NATO beitreten würden, hätten sie dazu die Gelegenheit, ist die Atlantische Allianz nicht mehr der potentiell feindliche Gegenspieler. Für zumindest einige Nachfolgestaaten der Sowjetunion kann das jedoch nicht mit der gleichen Selbstverständlichkeit vorausgesetzt werden. So ist immerhin einzurechnen, daß ihre Distanz zur NATO in dem Maße wächst, wie nationale oder sogar nationalistisch-chauvinistische Kräfte an Boden gewinnen, wofür es insbesondere in der Russischen Föderation eine Reihe von Gründen gibt, zu denen nicht zuletzt die tiefe sozioökonomische Krise des Landes zählt. Auf jeden Fall ist die Sympathie, die der NATO gelegentlich aus Moskau entgegengebracht wird, kein gesichertes Gut und keine Stimmungslage, auf die dauerhaft gebaut werden kann.

Aber auch aus westlicher Sicht steht jeglicher Einsatz der NATO in den konfliktbeladenen Gebieten Europas vor einer hohen politischen Hürde. Dabei kann der politische Widerstand Frankreichs sogar als eine zusätzliche Sondererscheinung betrachtet werden. Unter den Gründen, die einen Staat dazu bewegen, sich an friedensbewahrenden Maßnahmen zu beteiligen, hat das Eigeninteresse einen hohen Stellenwert. Dies gilt in einem noch verstärkten Maße, wenn es darum geht, einen Konflikt mit gewaltsamen Mitteln zu beenden. Die amerikanische Intervention in Somalia scheint dem zu widersprechen. Sie erfolgt nicht vor einem klar identifizierbaren nationalem Interessenhintergrund. Ob mit diesem Beispiel allerdings die Weichen zugunsten humanitärer Interventionsgründe gestellt werden, die regional und nationalstaatlich gebundene Interessen zwar nicht ersetzen, aber immerhin entscheidend ergänzen, ist zweifelhaft. Das Problem humanitärer Intervention ist völkerrechtlich und politisch zu kontrovers, um eine verläßliche Handlungsgrundlage zu sein.[16] Politisch-kulturelle Unterschiede, die ethno-religiöse Vielfalt und das Spannungsverhältnis divergierender politischer Interessen sind der Hintergrund, vor dem sich das Problem einer Regionalisierung der KSZE, aber auch die Frage nach ihrer Entwicklung mit unterschiedlichen Geschwindigkeiten stellt. Kann die KSZE etwas dazu beitragen, um in den Regionen wirkungsvoller zu werden, die nicht nur von den prinzipiell handlungsfähigen Institutionen weit entfernt, sondern von ihnen vor allem auch durch eine tiefe Kluft des Desinteresses getrennt sind? Wo liegen die Fußangeln einer Regionalisierung, und wie sind sie zu umgehen?

1. Der russische Unsicherheitsfaktor

Die KSZE zu regionalisieren heißt, Zuständigkeiten, nicht notwendigerweise Verantwortlichkeiten, an räumlich begrenzte Vereinbarungen zu übertragen. Die Ausgangslage ist, daß das, was die im Helsinki-Dokument von 1992 als Organisatoren von friedenserhaltenden Aktivitäten ausdrücklich aufgeführten Staaten der GUS in dem weiten Bereich der Konfliktprävention und der Wahrnehmung gemeinsamer Sicherheitsinteressen unter sich ausmachen, von der Gesamtheit der KSZE-Teilnehmer mehr oder weniger nur zur Kenntnis genommen, nicht jedoch beeinflußt werden kann. Wäre gesichert, daß sich alle regionalen und bilateralen Aktivitäten an die Vorgaben der KSZE-Dokumente halten, stünde einer Dezentralisierung von KSZE-Aufgaben nichts im Wege. Ihr Daseinszweck wäre dann in kleineren Einheiten gegenstandsnäher und dort voraussichtlich wirkungsvoller aufgehoben. Vorbehaltlos kann von dieser Erwartung allerdings nicht ausgegangen werden. Deshalb handelt es sich auch nicht darum, sich zwischen einer Alleinzuständigkeit der KSZE in ihrer Gesamtheit und regionalen Strukturen im Sinne eines Entweder-Oder zu entscheiden.

Für ein Mischungsverhältnis zwischen friedenserhaltenden Aktivitäten auf regionaler Ebene und der gemeinsamen Zuständigkeit aller KSZE-Teilnehmer spricht insbesondere die mittlerweile zwei Jahre alt gewordene Erfahrung, daß in den Nachfolgestaaten der Sowjetunion nach dem Ende des Ost-West-Gegensatzes ein Konfliktpotential von ungeheurer Brisanz zutage getreten ist. Dabei hat sich gezeigt, daß in nahezu allen aktuellen Konflikten – in zukünftigen Fällen wird es nicht anders sein – die Russische Föderation durch eigene Interessen involviert ist. Diese pauschale Feststellung läßt sich belegen. Rußland ist bislang an der Be-

16 Vgl. Winrich *Kühne*, Völkerrecht und Friedenssicherung in einer turbulenten Welt: Eine analytische Zusammenfassung der Grundprobleme und Entwicklungsperspektiven, in: *ders.* (Hrsg.), Blauhelme in einer turbulenten Welt. Beiträge internationaler Experten zur Fortentwicklung des Völkerrechts und der Vereinten Nationen, Baden-Baden 1993, S. 17-100.

friedung von vier Konflikten unmittelbar beteiligt: in Südossetien, in Transnistrien bzw. der selbsterklärten Dnestr-Republik, in Tadschikistan und Georgien. In allen vier Gebieten sind, vor allem vermittelt über die in ihnen lebenden ethnischen Russen, Interessen Moskaus im Spiel. Im Konflikt um Nagornyj-Karabach ist ihr zahlenmäßiger Umfang offenbar eine vernachlässigbare Größe, was eine Involvierung Rußlands auch in diesem Konflikt aus anderen Gründen natürlich nicht ausschließt. Allerdings haben sich weder Rußland allein noch kollektive Verteidigungstruppen der Gemeinschaft Unabhängiger Staaten (GUS) bereit gefunden, in den Konflikt befriedend einzugreifen.[17] Der Sachverhalt des involvierten Eigeninteresses erfüllt zwar einerseits eine wichtige Bedingung, um sich an präventiven bzw. friedenserhaltenden Aktionen zu beteiligen. Aus der Sicht einer neutralen Konfliktregelung ist er jedoch Anlaß zu vorsichtiger Zurückhaltung. Von einer Reihe der Konfliktschauplätze in der ehemaligen Sowjetunion sind Stimmen zu hören, die Moskau unterstellen, im Zuge von friedenserhaltenden Maßnahmen, die diesen Namen dann allerdings nicht mehr verdienten, den Versuch zu unternehmen, verlorene Einflußmöglichkeiten zurückzugewinnen oder Entwicklungen zu seinen Gunsten zu befördern. Nicht zuletzt die Ereignisse in und um Abchasien liegen offenbar im Bereich einer solchen Interessengrauzone.

Ohnehin läßt sich vermutlich nur schwer ausmachen, wann Rußland Spannungen schürt, um sie anschließend wieder zu beheben. Beide Beteiligungsformen werden nur selten säuberlich voneinander zu trennen sein, zumal das, was in Moskau entschieden wird, auf lokaler politischer wie militärischer Ebene bei der gegebenen Erosion zentraler Einflußmöglichkeiten nicht selten in sein Gegenteil verkehrt werden wird. Es besteht also ein dringender Bedarf, eine Gesamtverantwortung der KSZE zu bewahren und institutionell zu stützen, um die Konfliktrisiken durch eine Dezentralisierung von friedensbewahrenden Maßnahmen nicht noch zu vergrößern.

Die Doppelgesichtigkeit von Interessen ist prinzipiell nicht aufhebbar. Da, wo sie die Bereitschaft begründen, sich an friedenserhaltenden Maßnahmen zu beteiligen, kann der Verdacht, daß sie nicht nur friedlichen Zwecken dienen, nur selten ganz ausgeräumt werden. Ungeachtet dieser Unsicherheit ist es notwendig, regionale Konfliktlösungskapazitäten nicht nur zuzulassen, sondern nach Möglichkeit sogar zu begünstigen. Eine Regionalisierung muß jedoch dort halt machen, wo sie eine Gesamtzuständigkeit der KSZE nicht mehr zuläßt. Voneinander getrennte Zonen der Verantwortung, die dazu führen könnten, daß Rußland und die GUS in jeder Hinsicht für die Osthälfte und die NATO und die WEU für die Westhälfte

---

17 Vgl. auch Suzanne *Crow*, Peace-keeping in the CIS: An Instrument of Russian Hegemonic Desires?, in: *Kühne*, Blauhelme in einer turbulenten Welt, S. 351-375.

der KSZE zuständig sind,[18] bedeuten den Anfang vom Ende der KSZE in ihrer jetzigen Größe.

2. Ein "Code-of-conduct for peace-keeping operations"

Die KSZE muß sich davor hüten, nur als Schirm benutzt zu werden, den die Staaten bei Bedarf aufspannen, um unter ihm Schutz zu suchen, dem sie aber eine dauerhafte und eigenständige Funktion nicht zugestehen. Mit anderen Worten, Regionalisierung ist nicht der Anfang einer Entwicklung, an dessen Ende die stillschweigende Verabschiedung der KSZE aus der gemeinsamen Verantwortung aller Teilnehmerstaaten steht. Sie ist, wobei Subsidiaritätsüberlegungen der Europäischen Gemeinschaft hilfreich sein können, gemeint als eine Maßnahme, die KSZE wirksamer zu machen. Dazu bedarf es institutioneller, rechtlicher wie prozeduraler Vorkehrungen, die als Zielgröße sicherstellen, daß auch regionale Organe nur als Mandatare aller KSZE-Teilnehmerstaaten handeln können.

Artikel 53 der Charta der Vereinten Nationen legt fest, daß sich ihr Sicherheitsrat vorbehält, "regionale Abmachungen" gemäß Artikel 52 der Charta zur Anwendung von Zwangsmaßnahmen zu ermächtigen.[19] Ist ein analoges Verhältnis eines KSZE-Sicherheitsorgans zu regionalen Ad-hoc-Verabredungen oder vertraglichen Vereinbarungen ein erstrebenswertes Modell, um den angesprochenen Ambivalenzen und Gefährdungen zu begegnen? Sollte, um zwei Beispiele anzuführen, der "Vertrag von Taschkent über kollektive Sicherheit"[20] oder die Vereinbarung der GUS, Gruppen militärischer Beobachter und gemeinsame "Peace-keeping"-Verbände aufzustellen,[21] in eine verpflichtende Verbindung zur KSZE gebracht werden? Die KSZE hat keine Gewaltberechtigung und – dies sei hier im Vorgriff vermerkt – sollte auch keine anstreben.[22] Es kann sich im Verhältnis der KSZE zu sicherheitspolitischen Übereinkommen zwischen einigen der Teilnehmerstaaten also nicht darum handeln, ein entsprechendes Vorrecht zu schützen. Im Interesse eines gemeinsamen Sicherheitsraumes aller KSZE-Staaten läge es jedoch, wenn sie sich auf Regeln einigten, die zusammen einen *Code-of-conduct for peace-keeping operations* bilden. Dazu würde an erster Stelle eine Meldeverpflichtung gegenüber einem rechtlich aufgewerteten und in seinen Kompetenzen erweiterten ENACC zählen. Sie sollte in jedem Fall dem Beginn friedenserhaltender Maßnahmen vorausgehen. Der ENACC wäre zu autorisieren, automatisch Beobachterdelegationen zu entsenden, die in ihren Möglichkeiten nicht hinter den Kompeten-

---

18 Vgl. *Chudakov u.a.*, Russia's Interests.

19 Vgl. *Kühne*, Völkerrecht und Friedenssicherung.

20 Abgedruckt in: *Bundespresseamt*, Fernseh-/Hörfunkspiegel Ausland, (27.5.1992) 101, Anhang S. 1ff.

21 Vgl. *Crow*, Peace-keeping in the CIS.

22 Vgl. *Kühne*, Völkerrecht und Friedenssicherung.

zen des Hohen Kommissars für nationale Minderheiten zurückbleiben sollten. Vor der Einleitung regionaler friedensbewahrender Maßnahmen ist der Versuch zu unternehmen, die Beteiligung dritter Staaten zu erreichen, die vor allem aufgrund ihrer räumlichen Distanz nicht in Verdacht stehen, eigennützigen Zielen zu dienen. Der sozialisierenden Rolle der KSZE, das heißt die gemeinsame Einübung in eine multilaterale Sicherheitsvorsorge, wäre sicherlich gut entsprochen, wenn es auf dem Feld friedensbewahrender Maßnahmen zu Kooperationsbeziehungen kommt, die nicht vor den Grenzen von Regionen haltmachen.

3. Eine "géométrie variable" für die KSZE

Wo auch immer friedenserhaltende Maßnahmen im KSZE-Raum ergriffen werden, sie sollten auf der Grundlage eines für alle Staaten und Regionen gleichermaßen gültigen Verfahrenskodex erfolgen. Heißt das aber, daß die KSZE in jedem Fall nur nach dem Grundsatz des "Alles-oder-nichts" in Aktion treten darf? Sind Maßnahmen, wie sie von Hirschfeld/Dixon angeregt wurden, nur dann anwendbar, wenn sie zuvor die Zustimmung aller KSZE-Teilnehmerstaaten gefunden haben? Ein solcher Rigorismus würde die KSZE blockieren und ihre "sozialisierenden" Möglichkeiten beschneiden. Staaten, die sich nicht dazu bereit finden, einem Verhaltenskatalog zuzustimmen, werden nicht dadurch gewonnen, daß auch die übrigen KSZE-Teilnehmer auf seine Anwendung verzichten. Wichtig ist jedoch, daß hinter einem Maßnahmenkatalog eine ausreichend große Gruppe von Staaten steht, von der ein politischer Beteiligungsdruck auf die Staaten ausgeht, die zunächst abseits stehen. Eine "géométrie variable" wäre also auch für die KSZE ein zuträgliches Entwicklungsmodell.

Die KSZE darf sich durch eine größere Anwendungsflexibilität ihrer Verabredungen jedoch nicht in einen Zustand völliger Beliebigkeit auflösen. Es muß den Staaten, die sich in einem Konfliktfall oder generell Verhaltensmaßnahmen nicht anschließen wollen, im voraus bewußt sein, selber zum Ziel von Gegenmaßnahmen werden zu können. Es würde das Prinzip der KSZE, ein größtmögliches Maß an Flexibilität zu bewahren, ad absurdum führen, wenn ein vereinbarter Verhaltenskodex ohne jede Konsequenzen bliebe.

IV. Das Verhältnis der KSZE zu den Vereinten Nationen

Die Erklärung der KSZE zu einer "regionalen Abmachung" im Sinne der Charta der Vereinten Nationen autorisiert sie nicht zur Anwendung von Gewalt. Zwangsmaßnahmen bleiben in der Zuständigkeit des Sicherheitsrats. Dieser kann jedoch "regionale Abmachungen" auch für ihre Durchführung in Anspruch nehmen.[23]

---

23 Vgl. *Kühne*, Völkerrecht und Friedenssicherung.

Über diesen völkerrechtlichen Sachstand gibt es eine zunehmend lebhafte politische Diskussion. Sie dreht sich vor allem um die Frage, ob und inwieweit sich regionale Einrichtungen von den Unwägbarkeiten des Entscheidungsablaufs im Sicherheitsrat abhängig machen sollen. Dahinter steht die Annahme, auf regionaler Ebene entscheidungsfähiger zu sein, als dies in einem Sicherheitsrat wechselnder Zusammensetzung und in der Abhängigkeit von fünf Vetomächten der Fall sei. Hier soll das Problem allerdings nicht in erster Linie aus der Sicht der Vereinten Nationen, sondern mit einigen wenigen Bemerkungen von einem Standpunkt aus angesprochen werden, der vor allem die KSZE im Auge hat.

In der Debatte, was die KSZE könne und was bei den Vereinten Nationen bleiben sollte, wird mitunter übersehen, daß im muslimischen Teil der ehemaligen Sowjetunion – nicht nur an sozialen und ökonomischen Indikatoren gemessen – Staaten der Dritten Welt entstanden sind. Sie finden ihre Interessenpartner gerade auch dann, wenn es um die Behandlung von Konflikten in ihren Reihen geht, mehrheitlich unter dem Dach der Vereinten Nationen und nur in zweiter Linie im Rahmen der KSZE. Das geringe Interesse, das Europa den Vorgängen in Tadschikistan – immerhin einem Teilnehmerstaat an der KSZE – entgegenbringt, spricht für diese Beobachtung. Die Feststellung ist kein verstecktes Plädoyer dafür, die mittelasiatischen und möglicherweise auch einige der transkaukasischen Staaten aus der Verantwortung der KSZE wieder herauszudrängen. Der Hinweis auf die Vereinten Nationen ist auch nicht als willkommene Entlastung von den Folgen des Schritts gemeint, alle Nachfolgestaaten der Sowjetunion an der KSZE zu beteiligen. Am Beispiel der KSZE-Staaten Mittelasiens wird jedoch zweierlei sichtbar: Die KSZE ist auch da, wo sie auf der Grundlage von Artikel 52 der Charta der Vereinten Nationen als regionale Abmachung handelt, in Sonderheit für einige Staaten keine jederzeit gleichwertige Alternative zu den Vereinten Nationen. An den geographischen Rändern der KSZE in Mittelasien wird zudem deutlich, daß in das Zusammenwirken sicherheitsrelevanter Institutionen die Vereinten Nationen von vornherein und dauerhaft einzubeziehen sind.

Immer häufiger taucht die Formulierung auf – und damit ist ein weiterer Aspekt im Verhältnis von KSZE und Vereinten Nationen angesprochen –, daß die NATO und/oder WEU zu Kampfeinsätzen zur Verfügung stehen, wenn sie dazu entweder von den Vereinten Nationen oder von der KSZE das Mandat erhalten. Eine Vorbedingung ist zumindest bislang, sofern von der KSZE geredet wird, daß sie ihrerseits, wie eingangs bereits vermerkt, zuvor vom Sicherheitsrat der Vereinten Nationen zur Ausübung von Gewalt ermächtigt wird. Ist dieser formale Ablauf jedoch die einzige Schwierigkeit, vor die die KSZE gestellt ist? Soll die KSZE überhaupt, sozusagen als "sub-globale Vereinte Nationen" die – wenn auch abgeleitete – Kompetenz anstreben, andere Institutionen zum Einsatz von Gewaltmitteln legitimieren zu können?

Eine zustimmende Antwort müßte erläutern können, warum es der KSZE als Zwischenstück zwischen den Vereinten Nationen und der NATO/WEU bedarf. Doch darum scheint es letzten Endes nicht zu gehen. Der Bezug auf die Vereinten Nationen *oder* die KSZE ist nur dann logisch nachvollziehbar, wenn es das Ziel ist, die KSZE mit einem originären Gewaltrecht auszustatten, das nicht der Rückversicherung durch die Vereinten Nationen bedarf. Nur vor diesem Hintergrund wäre die allerdings keineswegs gesicherte Aussage bedenkenswert, daß sich die KSZE als entscheidungsfähiger erweisen könnte, als es möglicherweise die Vereinten Nationen sind. Nichts spricht jedoch dafür, daß die Diskussion über ein "Gewaltmonopol" in eine Richtung geht, in deren Verlauf die KSZE eine Gewaltzuständigkeit erhielte. Eine zusätzliche Variante in diesem Wechselverhältnis ist allenfalls, daß sich die KSZE zu Gewaltmaßnahmen entschließt und erst in einem zweiten Schritt die Zustimmung der Vereinten Nationen einholt. Diese Abfolge würde jedoch nur einen Unterschied von marginaler Bedeutung ausmachen. Ein bemerkenswerter Entscheidungsvorteil zugunsten der KSZE ergibt sich daraus nicht. Auf diesen Vorteil käme es ohnehin nicht an, wenn es zu einer dauerhaften Zusammenarbeit zwischen den Vereinten Nationen und der KSZE kommt. Nicht zuletzt die Gewaltproblematik ist ein guter Grund dafür.

Ein letzter Aspekt zu diesem Thema betrifft nur die KSZE. Die Annahme ist nicht unplausibel, daß die Aussichten präventiver Diplomatie und friedensbewahrender Maßnahmen erfolgversprechender sind, wenn im Bedarfsfall auch Gewaltmittel eingesetzt werden können. So zutreffend dieses Prinzip generell auch ist, es versagt, will man es zu einem Grundsatz der KSZE machen. Eine Politik der kooperativen Konfliktvermeidung und eine jederzeit aktivierbare Gewaltkompetenz passen nicht zusammen. Es ist schwer vorstellbar, daß es auch dann eine KSZE von der gegebenen Größenordnung und ethnisch-kulturellen Vielfalt gibt, wenn sie sich von einer kooperativen Sicherheitspolitik[24] verabschiedet. Ein "Opting-out" einzelner Mitglieder kann die KSZE ertragen, solange es letzten Endes jedem Staat selbst überlassen bleibt, sich der Mehrheit anzuschließen. Der Einsatz von Gewaltmitteln in der Verantwortung der KSZE würde sie zerreißen. In dieser Hinsicht ist sie keine "sub-globale VN".

---

24 Vgl. Heinz *Vetschera*, Die Rolle der KSZE als Einrichtung kooperativer Sicherheit im Rahmen des "interlocking institutions"-Konzepts, S. 95-154 in diesem Band.

5. Die Rolle der KSZE als Einrichtung kooperativer Sicherheit im Rahmen des "interlocking institutions"-Konzepts*

Heinz Vetschera

Vorbemerkung

Anläßlich des Helsinki-Nachfolgetreffens deklarierten die Teilnehmerstaaten der Konferenz über Sicherheit und Zusammenarbeit in Europa (KSZE) in den Helsinki-Beschlüssen am 10. Juli 1992 die KSZE als "regionale Abmachung" im Sinne des Kapitels VIII der Charta der Vereinten Nationen.[1] Sowohl NATO als auch WEU erklärten ihre Bereitschaft, der KSZE für friedenserhaltende Operationen ihre Kapazitäten zur Verfügung zu stellen. Daraus müßte sich in der Folge eine Struktur ergeben, die dem Konzept der "interlocking" oder "mutually re-inforcing institutions" im Rahmen der europäischen Sicherheitspolitik entspräche. Während aber über die Rolle der Vereinten Nationen wie auch von NATO und WEU einigermaßen konkrete Vorstellungen existieren, besteht hinsichtlich der KSZE und ihrer sicherheitspolitischen Rolle vielfach ein Informationsdefizit, das oftmals durch Analogieschlüsse überbrückt wird, die von bekannten Einrichtungen ausgehen. Da die Analogien zumeist nur bedingt zutreffen, entstehen falsche Vorstellungen über die Rolle der KSZE und verfehlte Erwartungen an ihre Möglichkeiten. Ziel der nachfolgenden Untersuchung ist daher,

- die charakteristischen Wesensmerkmale der KSZE sowie ihre Entwicklung und die Struktur ihrer Institutionen,
- ihre operativen Möglichkeiten als Einrichtung "kooperativer Sicherheit" sowie ihre Krisenmechanismen und Ansätze zur Konfliktverhütung einschließlich der Praxis der präventiven Diplomatie darzustellen, und
- die Möglichkeiten der arbeitsteiligen Kooperation mit den Vereinten Nationen sowie NATO und WEU aufzuzeigen.

I. Die Konferenz über Sicherheit und Zusammenarbeit in Europa (KSZE)

1. Grundlagen

Die KSZE unterscheidet sich maßgeblich von anderen sicherheitspolitischen Institutionen in Europa, wie etwa EG, WEU oder NATO. Vor allem wurde sie nicht als internationale Organisation nach Völkerrecht gegründet. Sie besteht vielmehr im Kern aus einer Serie von Konferenzen und Treffen, die sich aus der eigentli-

---

* Dieser Aufsatz beruht auf einem Beitrag über die sicherheitspolitische Rolle der KSZE zum Österreichischen Jahrbuch für Internationale Politik 1992, Wien 1993.

1 KSZE-Helsinki-Dokument 1992, Beschlüsse von Helsinki, Kap. IV, Pkt. 2.

chen Konferenz über Sicherheit und Zusammenarbeit in Europa (1973-1975) ableiten.[2] Durch die Nachfolgetreffen in Belgrad (1977-1978),[3] Madrid (1980-1983),[4] Wien (1986-1989)[5] und Helsinki (1992) und die verschiedenen Spezialkonferenzen (über Sicherheitspolitik einschließlich militärischer Vertrauens- und Sicherheitsbildung, Menschenrechte, Wirtschaft, Kultur, Mittelmeerraum etc.) entwickelte sich ein dichtes Geflecht von Konferenzen, so daß der resultierende KSZE-Prozeß bereits vor der Schaffung von eigentlichen Institutionen eine quasi-permanente Komponente der gesamteuropäischen Politik wurde.[6]

Die KSZE war von Anfang an breit angelegt. Ihr Aufgabenspektrum reichte von der Frage grundlegender sicherheitspolitischer Prinzipien und Verhaltensregeln für den militärischen Bereich (Vertrauensbildende Maßnahmen, VBM) im "ersten Korb" über Fragen der Wirtschaftsbeziehungen (zweiter Korb) zur humanitären Dimension (dritter Korb).[7] Sie war das einzige Forum, das sich ausdrücklich der europäischen Sicherheit widmete. Weiters war und ist sie das einzige wirklich gesamteuropäische Gremium, an welchem von Anfang an nicht nur praktisch alle europäischen, sondern auch relevante außereuropäische Staaten teilnahmen. Schließlich stand sie während der Phase der Ost-West-Polarisierung als einziges Forum auch solchen Staaten offen, die keiner der beiden Allianzen angehörten.

Als Konferenz unterscheidet sich die KSZE in einigen Punkten maßgeblich von internationalen Organisationen. Da sie formal keine Organisation ist, hat sie auch

---

2 Zur Vorgeschichte vgl. Friedrich-Karl *Schramm*/Wolfgang-Georg *Riggert*/Alois *Friedel* (Hrsg.), Sicherheitskonferenz in Europa, Dokumentation 1954-1973, Frankfurt a.M.: Metzner Verlag 1972; sowie weiters zur Vorgeschichte und zum Verlauf der KSZE Heinz *Vetschera*, Sicherheit und Truppenabbau - Die Konferenzen, Wien 1976 (Studien und Berichte); als Dokumentation Hans-Adolf *Jacobsen*/Wolfgang *Mallmann*/Christian *Meier* (Hrsg.), Sicherheit und Zusammenarbeit in Europa, Analyse und Dokumentation, Dokumente zur Außenpolitik, Bd. II (Entwicklung 1966-1972) und Bd. II/2 (Entwicklung 1973-1978), Bonn: Verlag Wissenschaft und Politik 1973/1978; zur Chronologie des folgenden KSZE-Prozesses vgl. *Auswärtiges Amt*, Sicherheit und Zusammenarbeit in Europa. Dokumentation zum KSZE-Prozeß, 7. Aufl., Bonn 1990, S. 475ff.

3 Zum Belgrader Nachfolgetreffen vgl. Hermann *Volle*/Wolfgang *Wagner* (Hrsg.), Das Belgrader KSZE-Folgetreffen, Bonn: Verlag für Internationale Politik 1978.

4 Zum Madrider Nachfolgetreffen vgl. Hermann *Volle*/Wolfgang *Wagner* (Hrsg.), Das Madrider KSZE-Folgetreffen, Bonn: Verlag für Internationale Politik 1984.

5 Hierzu ausführlich Hans-Heinrich *Wrede*, KSZE in Wien - Kursbestimmung für Europas Zukunft, Köln: Verlag Wissenschaft und Politik 1990.

6 Vgl. Victor-Yves *Ghebali*, The Institutionalization of the CSCE Process: Toward an Instrument for the "Greater Europe"?, in: Kate *Holder*/Robert E. *Hunter*/Paavo *Lipponen* (Hrsg.), Conference on Security and Cooperation in Europe: The Next Phase, Washington, D.C. 1991 (CSIS Significant Issues Series, XIII, 7), S. 50-54.

7 Die Einteilung in "Körbe" beruht auf der Struktur der prozeduralen "Schlußempfehlungen der Helsinki-Konsultationen" vor dem Beginn der eigentlichen KSZE, die der künftigen Konferenz die verschiedenen Aufgabenbereiche zuordnete ("erster Korb", Pkt. 13-24; "zweiter Korb", Pkt. 25-41; "dritter Korb", Pkt. 42-52; darüber hinaus wurde als potentieller "vierter Korb" auch über die Folgen der Konferenz [einschließlich einer allfälligen Schaffung von Institutionen] verhandelt, Pkt. 53).

keine Mitglieder, es gibt lediglich Teilnehmerstaaten. Inhaltlich verfolgt die KSZE, wie andere Konferenzen auch, vor allem langfristige Perspektiven. Wie bereits auf der eigentlichen KSZE festgestellt werden konnte, widmete sie sich vor allem der Aufstellung von Regeln, die das friedliche Zusammenleben in Europa ermöglichen sollten, vermied es aber weitgehend, sich mit der Lösung aktueller Konflikte[8] zu befassen. Weiters ergibt sich aus der Eigenschaft als Konferenz, daß sie um allgemeiner Akzeptanz willen ein Maximum an Konsens herbeizuführen versucht. Hier wäre jede Majorisierung abträglich. Eine Konferenz kann daher – im Gegensatz zu einer Organisation – kaum ohne Konsensregel auskommen. Schließlich ist zu bedenken, daß multilaterale Konferenzen im Regelfalle selbst kein Akteur der internationalen Beziehungen sind. Sie stellen üblicherweise eher die Bühne für Initiativen ihrer Teilnehmer dar. Konferenzen machen keine Politik – sie *sind* Politik.

2. Institutionen[9] und weitere Entwicklung der KSZE

Nach dem Zusammenbruch der kommunistischen Diktaturen in Osteuropa beschlossen die KSZE-Staaten auf Einladung Frankreichs ein Gipfeltreffen, auf dem die Grundlagen für ein neues Europa kodifiziert werden sollten.[10] Es erarbeitete

---

8 Wie etwa die 1974 akut gewordene Zypernkrise.

9 Die Struktur der Institutionen folgt im wesentlichen den Vorgaben des Londoner NATO-Gipfels vom 5. bis 6. Juli 1990, auf dem unter Punkt 22 folgende Elemente zur Institutionalisierung der KSZE vorgeschlagen worden waren:

- "... regular consultations among member governments at the Heads of State and Government or Ministerial level, at least once each year, with other periodic meetings of officials to prepare for and follow up on these consultations;
- a schedule of CSCE review conferences once every two years to assess progress toward a Europe whole and free;
- a small CSCE secretariat to coordinate these meetings and conferences;
- a CSCE mechanism to monitor elections in all CSCE countries, on the basis of the Copenhagen Document;
- a CSCE Centre for the Prevention of Conflicts that might serve as a forum for exchanges of military information, discussion of unusual activities, and the conciliation of disputes involving CSCE member states; and
- a CSCE parliamentary body, the Assembly of Europe, to be based on the existing parliamentary assembly of the Council of Europe, in Strasbourg, and include representatives of all CSCE member states".

London Declaration on a Transformed North Atlantic Alliance, issued by the Heads of State and Government participating in the meeting of the North Atlantic Council in London on 5th and 6th July, 1990, Brüssel: NATO Information Service, Juli 1990. Beachtlich erscheint dabei die Verwendung des Begriffs "member states" anstelle der KSZE-üblichen Terminologie, die von "participating states" spricht.

10 Zu den Vorbereitungen durch einen in Wien ab 10. Juli 1990 tagenden Ausschuß vgl. Simon *Palmisano*, KSZE/VVSBM, Das Wiener Dokument 1990, Chronik, Wien: Landesverteidigungsakademie 1991, S. 35, und John *Borawski*, Security for a New Europe, The Vienna Negotiations on Confidence- and Security Building Measures, London/Washington/New York 1992, S. 106.

jene Beschlüsse, die dann auf dem Gipfel[11] als "Charta von Paris für ein neues Europa" von den Teilnehmerstaaten angenommen wurden.

a. Die Schaffung der KSZE-Institutionen

Während bis zur Charta von Paris die jeweiligen Konferenzen und Treffen im KSZE-Rahmen ihr Mandat von einem der Folgetreffen erhalten hatten, wurden nunmehr folgende regelmäßige Treffen verabredet sowie feste Gremien und Institutionen[12] geschaffen:

an regelmäßigen Treffen:

- die Folgetreffen der KSZE, an denen auch die Staats- und Regierungschefs der KSZE Staaten zusammentreten werden; diese Folgetreffen werden in der Regel alle zwei Jahre stattfinden;

an regelmäßig zusammentretenden Gremien:

- regelmäßige Treffen der Außenminister als Rat, mindestens einmal jährlich;
- der Ausschuß Hoher Beamter (AHB) zur Vorbereitung der Treffen des Rates (der Außenminister); der Ausschuß kann auch zusätzliche Treffen der Vertreter der Teilnehmerstaaten vereinbaren; des weiteren sieht die Charta von Paris vor, daß der Rat "die Erarbeitung von Bestimmungen prüfen [wird], die die Einberufung von Treffen des Ausschusses Hoher Beamter in dringlichen Situationen vorsehen";[13]

an ständigen Institutionen:

- ein Sekretariat in Prag zur administrativen Unterstützung "dieser Konsultationen" (nämlich des Rates und des Ausschusses Hoher Beamter);
- ein Konfliktverhütungszentrum (KVZ) in Wien, das den Rat beim Abbau der Gefahren von Konflikten unterstützen soll;
- ein Büro für freie Wahlen in Warschau, um Kontakte und den Informationsaustausch im Zusammenhang mit Wahlen in den Teilnehmerstaaten zu erleichtern.

Weiters spricht sich die Charta für eine stärkere Einbeziehung der Parlamentsarbeit in die KSZE aus, insbesondere durch die Schaffung einer parlamentarischen Versammlung der KSZE unter Beteiligung von Parlamentsmitgliedern aus allen Teilnehmerstaaten.[14] Das KVZ verfügt als einzige der drei Einrichtungen mit dem Konsultativausschuß über ein eigenes repräsentatives Organ der Teilnehmerstaaten und wurde deshalb nicht dem AHB, sondern dem Rat direkt untergeordnet.

---

11 Der Gipfel tagte vom 19. bis zum 21. November 1990, die Charta datiert vom 21. November.

12 Charta, S. 10f.

13 Ebd.

14 Dieser Strang der Institutionalisierung wird im Rahmen dieser Arbeit nicht weiter verfolgt, da sie sich vorwiegend der sicherheitspolitischen Funktion der KSZE widmet.

b. Die weitere Entwicklung

Die weiteren Entwicklungsschritte der KSZE als Rahmeninstitution der europäischen Sicherheit erfolgten auf den Sitzungen des Rates in Berlin (19.-20.6.1991), Prag (30.-31.1.1991) sowie Stockholm (14.-15.12.1992) und auf dem Helsinki-Nachfolgetreffen im Jahre 1992 (24.3.-10.7.).

Das Berliner Ratstreffen

Der Rat beschloß die Annahme eines Mechanismus für Konsultation und Zusammenarbeit in dringlichen Situationen,[15] der Krisensitzungen des AHB auslöst.

Das Prager Ratstreffen

Der Rat stärkte die Rolle des AHB[16] und erweiterte das bisherige "Büro für Freie Wahlen" zu einem "Büro für Demokratische Institutionen und Menschenrechte" (BDIMR).[17] Zudem wurde beschlossen, daß in Fällen eindeutiger, grober und nicht behobener Verletzungen einschlägiger KSZE-Verpflichtungen angemessene Maßnahmen durch den Rat bzw. den AHB getroffen werden können, "erforderlichenfalls auch ohne Zustimmung des betroffenen Staates".[18] Dies bedeutet die Abkehr vom bisher geltenden Konsensprinzip (Konsens minus eins).

Das Helsinki-Nachfolgetreffen

Entsprechend den Bestimmungen des Schlußdokuments des Wiener Nachfolgetreffens[19] der KSZE wurde das vierte Nachfolgetreffen 1992 in Helsinki abgehalten. Es begann am 24. März und schloß mit einem Gipfeltreffen am 9. und 10. Juli, auf dem das Helsinki-Dokument verabschiedet wurde. Das Dokument enthält zwei Hauptteile: die (vorwiegend deklaratorische) Gipfelerklärung und die (materiellen) Beschlüsse.

Die Teilnehmerstaaten erklärten, "daß sie sich einig sind, daß die KSZE eine regionale Abmachung im Sinne von Kapitel VIII der Charta der Vereinten Nationen ist und als solche ein wichtiges Bindeglied zwischen europäischer und globaler

---

15 Berliner Treffen des Rates der KSZE, 19.-20.6.1991, Zusammenfassung der Schlußfolgerungen, Kap. II, Pkt. 6.

16 Prager Dokument über die weitere Entwicklung der KSZE-Institutionen und -Strukturen, Kap. I, Pkt. 2.

17 Ebd., Kap. III, Pkt. 9.

18 Ebd., Kap. IV, Pkt. 16.

19 Abschließendes Dokument des Wiener Treffens 1986 der Vertreter der Teilnehmerstaaten der Konferenz über Sicherheit und Zusammenarbeit in Europa, Wien, 15. Januar 1989, Kapitel "Folgen der Konferenz".

Sicherheit darstellt".[20] Die Helsinki-Beschlüsse sehen weiters die Einrichtung eines Hohen Kommissars für nationale Minderheiten vor, dessen Aufgabe in der "Frühwarnung" und gegebenenfalls in "Frühmaßnahmen" besteht, und zwar "im Hinblick auf Spannungen bezüglich Fragen nationaler Minderheiten, die sich noch nicht über ein Frühwarnstadium hinaus entwickelt haben, die jedoch nach Einschätzung des Hohen Kommissars das Potential in sich bergen, sich im KSZE-Gebiet zu einem den Frieden, die Stabilität und die Beziehungen zwischen Teilnehmerstaaten beeinträchtigenden Konflikt zu entwickeln,[21] der die Aufmerksamkeit oder das Eingreifen des Rates oder des AHB erfordert."[22]

Die Helsinki-Beschlüsse begründen ferner das KSZE-Forum für Sicherheitskooperation,[23] "mit einem gestärkten Konfliktverhütungszentrum, als integralen Bestandteil der Konferenz über Sicherheit und Zusammenarbeit in Europa".[24] Das Forum weist zwei Erscheinungsformen auf. Einerseits tritt es als "Besonderer Ausschuß" (Special Committee) zusammen, entweder

- zu Verhandlungen über Rüstungskontrolle, Abrüstung und Vertrauens- und Sicherheitsbildung, oder
- zur Erörterung von, zu einem zielgerichteten Dialog über und gegebenenfalls zur Erarbeitung oder Verhandlung von Vorschlägen zur Stärkung der Sicherheit und Zusammenarbeit.[25]

Andererseits tritt es als Konsultativausschuß zusammen, der sich mit bestehenden und künftigen Aufgaben des KVZ befaßt.[26] Kapitel III der Helsinki-Beschlüsse widmet sich der Frühwarnung, der Konfliktverhütung und der Krisenbewältigung sowie der friedlichen Beilegung von Streitfällen. Frühwarnung soll durch das BDIMR und das KVZ erfolgen,[27] innerhalb der Konsultationen der Teilnehmerstaaten.[28] Hinsichtlich der Instrumente für Konfliktverhütung und Krisenbewältigung sehen die Helsinki-Beschlüsse vor, daß der AHB oder der Konsultativausschuß durch Konsens über die Durchführung von Erkundungs- und Berichterstattermissionen entscheiden können.[29] Das Schwergewicht der Helsinki-Beschlüsse liegt dagegen bei den friedenserhaltenden Operationen.

---

20 KSZE, Helsinki-Dokument 1992, Beschlüsse von Helsinki, 10.7.1992, Kap. IV, Pkt. 2.

21 Ebd., Kap. I, Pkt. 23.

22 Ebd., Kap. II, Pkt. 3.

23 Ebd., Kap. V.

24 Ebd., Pkt. 9.

25 Ebd., Pkt. 30.

26 Ebd., Pkt. 31. Die gewählte Formulierung könnte allerdings auch so verstanden werden, daß der Konsultativausschuß neben dem Forum existiere. Aus den vorherigen Bestimmungen kann aber abgeleitet werden, daß er als Erscheinungsform des Forums zu gelten hat.

27 Ebd., Kap. III, Pkt. 2.

28 Ebd., Pkt. 3.

29 Ebd., Pkt. 12 und 13.

Der Rat beschloß die Weiterentwicklung von KSZE-Strukturen und -Institutionen,[30] darunter die Einrichtung des Amtes eines Generalsekretärs, regelmäßige Zusammenkünfte von Vertretern der Teilnehmerstaaten in Wien zwischen den AHB-Sitzungen "Wiener AHB-Gruppe) sowie die Einrichtung einer einzigen organisatorischen Struktur für die Sekretariate in Prag und Wien unter der Leitung des Generalsekretärs. Weiters beauftragten die Minister das KVZ, rasche Schritte zur Stärkung seiner Fähigkeit einzuleiten, vorbeugende diplomatische Missionen und friedenserhaltende Aktivitäten der KSZE operativ zu unterstützen.[31]

Der Generalsekretär,[32] der höchste administrative Beamte der KSZE, wird unter Anleitung des amtierenden Vorsitzenden[33] und als sein Vertreter handeln und ihn bei allen auf die Erfüllung der Ziele der KSZE ausgerichteten Aktivitäten unterstützen; er wird auf Empfehlung des AHB und des amtierenden Vorsitzenden vom Rat per Konsens für drei Jahre ernannt.[34] Der Generalsekretär wird den amtierenden Vorsitzenden darin unterstützen, die KSZE-Maßnahmen und -Praktiken international bekanntzumachen, und dem Rat einen Jahresbericht vorlegen.

Schließlich beschloß das Ratstreffen die Verbesserung der Zusammenarbeit und der Kontakte mit internationalen Organisationen, insbesondere mit den Vereinten Nationen.[35] Die Minister wiesen die amtierende Vorsitzende[36] des AHB an, unverzüglich regelmäßige Kontakte mit dem Generalsekretär der Vereinten Nationen aufzunehmen, um zu gewährleisten, daß sowohl die Vereinten Nationen als auch die KSZE-Teilnehmerstaaten über die jeweiligen Aktivitäten auf dem laufenden gehalten werden, insbesondere im Bereich der Frühwarnung, der Konfliktverhütung, der Bewältigung und Lösung von Konflikten sowie der Förderung von demokratischen Werten und Menschenrechten.

---

30 Beschlüsse des Stockholmer Ratstreffens, Pkt. 7.

31 Tatsächlich hatte das KVZ bereits seit Beginn der beiden Missionen vorbeugender Diplomatie im früheren Jugoslawien, also seit September 1992, entsprechende Unterstützung geleistet, obwohl zu diesem Zeitpunkt keine formale Kompetenz dazu bestanden hatte. Da diese Missionen vom AHB beschlossen worden waren, wurde zeitweise die Meinung vertreten, daß sie auch vom KSZE-Sekretariat in administrativen, finanziellen und logistischen Fragen zu betreuen wären. In der Zwischenzeit hatte sich aber die Unterstützung der Missionen durch das KVZ bewährt. Die Aufforderung der Minister stellt damit den formalisierten Nachvollzug dieser faktischen Entwicklung dar.

32 Beschlüsse des Stockholmer Ratstreffens, Anhang 1, Pkt. 1 sowie 5 (Mandat).

33 Der Vorsitz im AHB wird bis zum nächsten Ratstreffen vom Vorsitzenden des abgelaufenen Ratstreffens wahrgenommen.

34 In der Folge wurde Dr. Wilhelm Höynck (Deutschland) zum Generalsekretär der KSZE ernannt.

35 Beschlüsse des Stockholmer Ratstreffens, Pkt. 8.

36 Die schwedische Außenministerin Margaretha af Ugglas.

II. Die KSZE als Einrichtung "kooperativer" Sicherheitspolitik

Die KSZE unterscheidet sich nicht nur hinsichtlich ihrer Entwicklungsgeschichte von anderen sicherheitspolitischen Institutionen in Europa, sondern auch durch ihre spezifische Befassung mit der europäischen Sicherheit, die sich in ihrer Struktur und in ihren Instrumenten niederschlägt. Da sie auf die Bereitschaft der Teilnehmerstaaten zur Kooperation angewiesen ist, stellt sie typischerweise eine Einrichtung der "kooperativen Sicherheit" dar. Dies drückt sich zunächst im Namen aus, der nicht nur zum Ausdruck bringt, daß Stabilität in Europa sowohl Sicherheit (im traditionellen Sinne) als auch Zusammenarbeit verlangt. Es zeigt sich auch in den sicherheitspolitischen Instrumenten, die allesamt der "kooperativen Sicherheitspolitik" zuzurechnen sind.

1. "Konfrontative" und "kooperative" Sicherheitspolitik

Im Bereich der internationalen Sicherheit wird Sicherheitspolitik üblicherweise als Politik der Friedenssicherung und Kriegsverhütung definiert. Dabei sind ein "konfrontativer" sowie ein "kooperativer" Ansatz zu unterscheiden.[37] Innerhalb des konfrontativen Ansatzes nimmt das Instrument der individuellen oder kollektiven Selbstverteidigung[38] die ursprünglichste Funktion ein. Es richtet sich gegen einen von außen kommenden, oftmals mehr oder weniger bekannten potentiellen[39] Gegner. Es kann sich in der Form der Verteidigungspolitik im engeren Sinne oder in der Strategie der Abschreckung ausdrücken. Demgegenüber richtet sich das Instrument der "kollektiven Sicherheit", wie es etwa im Völkerbund oder in den Vereinten Nationen[40] postuliert wurde, nicht mehr gegen einen von außen kommenden, mehr oder weniger feststehenden Gegner, sondern gegen jeden potentiellen Friedensbrecher innerhalb des Systems.[41] Er soll durch die zusammengefaßte Macht der anderen Teilnehmer des Systems von der Aggression abgehalten werden. Solche Systeme benötigen daher auch Entscheidungsorgane, die – wenn er-

---

37 Diese Unterscheidung entspricht in etwa der Unterscheidung zwischen "Machtlösungen" und "Vertrauenslösungen" bei Daniel *Frei*, Sicherheit – Grundfragen der Weltpolitik, Stuttgart/Berlin/Köln/Mainz: Kohlhammer 1977, S. 23ff.

38 Vgl. Artikel 51 der Charta der Vereinten Nationen. Hierzu ausführlich Hanspeter *Neuhold*, Internationale Konflikte – Verbotene und erlaubte Mittel ihrer Austragung, Wien/New York: Springer 1977 (Forschungen aus Staat und Recht, Bd. 37), S. 135ff; vgl. zu Artikel 51 auch Albrecht *Randelzhofer*, Kommentar zu Artikel 51 der Satzung der Vereinten Nationen, in: Bruno *Simma u.a.* (Hrsg.), Charta der Vereinten Nationen. Kommentar, München 1991, S. 617-635.

39 Wie etwa der Sowjetunion und ihren Verbündeten in den ursprünglichen Bedrohungsvorstellungen der westlichen Allianz.

40 Vgl. Artikel 1 der Charta der Vereinten Nationen: "wirksame Kollektivmaßnahmen zu treffen, um Bedrohungen des Friedens zu verhüten und zu beseitigen, Angriffshandlungen und andere Friedensbrüche zu unterdrücken".

41 Vgl. *Neuhold*, Internationale Konflikte, S. 110ff.

forderlich – Zwangsmaßnahmen verhängen können.[42] Wenngleich diese Komponente ausdrücklich konfrontativ ist, geht es solchen Systemen der kollektiven Sicherheit darüber hinaus zumeist auch um die Förderung friedlicher Beziehungen sowie die friedliche Streitbeilegung zwischen ihren Mitgliedern.[43] Sie enthalten damit auch ein kooperatives Element.[44]

Kooperative Sicherheit im eigentlichen Sinn verzichtet dagegen völlig auf Zwangsdurchsetzung und damit auf Konfrontation. Sie zielt in erster Linie auf die Förderung der Zusammenarbeit, um so das Entstehen von Konflikten zu minimieren oder zumindest zu verhindern, daß aus politischen Spannungen militärische Auseinandersetzungen werden.[45] Der Akzent kooperativer Sicherheit liegt auf der Verbesserung der Vorhersehbarkeit von Konflikten, des Abbaus von Mißverständnissen sowie auf der Konfliktverhütung durch Verhandlung und Konsultation.[46] Da mit ihnen keine Anwendung von Zwang verbunden ist, benötigen Einrichtungen der kooperativen Sicherheit zumeist auch keine besonderen Vorkehrungen oder Verfahrensregeln zur Überstimmung einzelner Teilnehmer oder Mitglieder.

Konfrontative und kooperative Sicherheitspolitik stehen in einer komplementären Beziehung zueinander. Konfrontative Sicherheitspolitik ist ihrem Wesen nach repressiv, sie droht Zwangs- und Strafmaßnahmen für den Friedensbruch an.[47] Sie kann damit zwar zur Friedenserhaltung und Kriegsverhütung beitragen, aber nur über den Umweg der angedrohten Nachteile, die der Friedensbrecher erwarten muß.[48] Wenngleich Einrichtungen der kollektiven Verteidigung oder kollektiven Sicherheit geeignet erscheinen, eine kalkulierte Aggression abzuschrecken, können sie dort versagen, wo Kriege oder andere bewaffnete Konflikte aus Mißdeutung, Fehlbeurteilungen der Lage oder ähnlichen Ursachen entstehen.

---

42 So etwa der Sicherheitsrat der Vereinten Nationen, Kap. V der VN-Charta.

43 Vgl. die "kooperative" Komponente in der Bestimmung des Artikels 1 Absatz 1 der Charta der Vereinten Nationen: "internationale Streitigkeiten oder Situationen, die zu einem Friedensbruch führen könnten, durch friedliche Mittel nach den Grundsätzen der Gerechtigkeit und des Völkerrechts zu bereinigen oder beizulegen".

44 Vgl. *Neuhold*, Internationale Konflikte, S. 393ff.

45 Im militärischen Bereich entspricht diese Definition dem ursprünglichen Begriff der Rüstungskontrolle. "A nation's military force, while opposing the military force of potentially hostile nations, is also bound to *collaborate*, implicitly if not explicitly, in avoiding the kinds of crises in which withdrawal is intolerable for both sides, in avoiding false alarms and mistaken intentions, and in providing reassurance that restraint on the part of the potential enemies would be matched by restraint on one's own side" (Thomas C. *Schelling*/Morton H. *Halperin*, Strategy and Arms Control, 1961; Reprint 1985, McLean, VA, S. 1).

46 Vgl. Gert *Krell*, Die Entwicklung des Sicherheitsbegriffs, in: Beiträge zur Konfliktforschung, 10 (1980) 3, S. 33-57.

47 Vgl. Kap. VII der Charta der Vereinten Nationen.

48 Zur Frage "repressiver" und "präventiver" Instrumente vgl. Heinz *Vetschera*, International Law and International Security: The Case of Force Control; in: Jost *Delbrück* (Hrsg.), German Yearbook of International Law (Berlin), 24 (1981), S. 144-165 (151f).

Demgegenüber richtet sich kooperative Sicherheitspolitik gerade an die Verhütung solcher Konflikte, indem sie Mißverständnisse und Fehldeutungen vermeiden hilft. Sie ist ihrem Wesen nach unmittelbar präventiv, indem sie die Zusammenarbeit auch zwischen potentiellen Gegnern sicherstellen möchte, um so den Frieden zu erhalten. Damit ist kooperative Sicherheitspolitik aber an den Willen aller Beteiligten zur Zusammenarbeit gebunden. Sie wäre demzufolge ungeeignet, kalkulierte Aggressionen abzuschrecken, da sie auf Kooperation angewiesen ist, die ein planender Aggressor kaum einzugehen bereit sein wird. Konfrontative und kooperative Sicherheit können damit jeweils nur einen Teilbereich des sicherheitspolitischen Spektrums abdecken. Sie können einander ergänzen, aber nicht ersetzen.

2. Die sicherheitspolitischen Ziele und Mittel der KSZE

Der "erste Korb" definiert einerseits die sicherheitspolitischen Ziele, die sich die Teilnehmerstaaten setzen, und enthält andererseits die Instrumente, mit denen sie erreicht werden sollen, wobei zunächst die Sicherheit in militärischen Fragen im Vordergrund stand.

Wenngleich die Schlußakte den Begriff der europäischen Sicherheit nicht definiert, läßt sich eine Definition doch aus den Präambeln zum ersten Hauptdokument ("Fragen der Sicherheit in Europa") sowie zu den beiden darin enthaltenen Dokumenten ("Erklärung über die Prinzipien, die die Beziehungen der Teilnehmerstaaten leiten" und "Dokument über vertrauensbildende Maßnahmen und bestimmte Aspekte der Sicherheit und Abrüstung") erschließen.[49]

Im ersten Absatz der Präambel zum ersten Hauptdokument bekräftigen die Teilnehmerstaaten ihr Ziel, "Bedingungen zu gewährleisten, unter denen ihre Völker in echtem und dauerhaftem Frieden, frei von jeglicher Bedrohung oder Beeinträchtigung ihrer Sicherheit leben können". Im letzten Absatz wird die enge Verbindung von "Frieden und Sicherheit in Europa und in der ganzen Welt" anerkannt und von den Teilnehmern gefordert, daß "jeder von ihnen seinen Beitrag zur Festigung des Friedens und der Sicherheit in der Welt" leisten solle. Gleichermaßen werden "Frieden" und "Sicherheit" im dritten Absatz der Präambel verbunden. Auch im ersten Absatz der Präambel zum zweiten Dokument werden beide Begriffe gemeinsam genannt, wogegen der zweite Absatz "Sicherheit" mit dem Begriff der "Stabilität" verbindet ("zur Erhöhung der Stabilität und Sicherheit").

Der Begriff der "europäischen Sicherheit" im Sinne der Schlußakte scheint damit deckungsgleich mit dem Begriff der "Sicherheit" in der Charta der Vereinten Nationen. In beiden Fällen wird er mit dem Begriff des "Friedens" verbunden und

---

49 Die nachfolgenden Ausführungen beruhen auf Heinz *Vetschera*, Effects of Basket I: Security and Confidence-Building, in: Hanspeter *Neuhold* (Hrsg.), CSCE: N+N Perspectives, Wien 1987 (*Österreichisches Institut für Internationale Politik [ÖIIP]*, Laxenburg Paper No. 8), S. 101-125 (102f).

bezeichnet somit die relative Abwesenheit der Gefahr der Anwendung oder Androhung von bewaffneter Gewalt.[50] "Sicherheit" führt also zum "Frieden". Diese Interpretation deckt sich mit der Bezugnahme auf die "Androhung oder Anwendung von Gewalt" sowohl im operativen Teil des ersten Dokuments (Prinzip II) als auch in der angeschlossenen Deklaration über "Fragen der Verwirklichung einiger der vorstehenden Prinzipien", die im zweiten und dritten Absatz die Staaten an ihre Pflicht erinnert, "sich der Androhung oder Anwendung von Gewalt in ihren Beziehungen zueinander zu enthalten".[51]

a. Die Prinzipienerklärung der KSZE

Die in der Schlußakte enthaltene "Erklärung über die Prinzipien, die die Beziehungen der Teilnehmerstaaten leiten" weist als weiteres Element den Begriff "Gerechtigkeit" auf, der gleichfalls eng mit den Begriffen der "Sicherheit" und des "Friedens" verbunden ist. Formal wird "Gerechtigkeit" im ersten und dritten Absatz der Präambel zum ersten Dokument den beiden genannten Begriffen gleichgestellt ("Frieden, Sicherheit und Gerechtigkeit"). Inhaltlich ergibt sich die Einbeziehung der "Gerechtigkeit" aus dem Katalog der zehn Prinzipien im ersten Dokument, die nicht nur die klassischen Prinzipien der Sicherheit enthalten (Gewaltverbot [II], Unverletzlichkeit der Grenzen [III], Territoriale Integrität [IV], Nichteinmischung in innere Angelegenheiten [VI]), sondern auch die "Achtung der Menschenrechte und Grundfreiheiten" (VII), die "Gleichberechtigung und [das] Selbstbestimmungsrecht der Völker" (VIII) als Ausdruck der Gerechtigkeit innerhalb der Staaten sowie die Verpflichtung zur Achtung der souveränen Gleichheit (I) und zur Erfüllung völkerrechtlicher Verpflichtungen nach Treu und Glauben (X) als Ausdruck der Gerechtigkeit zwischen den Staaten. Damit enthält der Prinzipienkatalog nicht nur die traditionellen "prohibitiven" Grundsätze der internationalen Sicherheit, sondern auch "vorwirkende" Prinzipien der Sicherheit, die bei den möglichen Ursachen künftiger Bedrohungen der Sicherheit ansetzen. Schließlich findet sich im Prinzipienkatalog auch noch der Hinweis auf Alternativen zum Gewaltgebrauch, nämlich die friedliche Austragung von Streitfällen (V) und die Zusammenarbeit zwischen den Staaten, insbesondere zur Förderung von internationalem Frieden, internationaler Sicherheit und Gerechtigkeit (IX/2).

50 Vgl. Stephan *Verosta*, Der Begriff "Internationale Sicherheit" in der Satzung der Vereinten Nationen, in: Internationale Festschrift für Alfred Verdross, München 1971, S. 533-547 (533).

51 Schlußakte von Helsinki, Prinzipienerklärung, Kap. (b), Pkt. (i).

"Frieden", "Sicherheit" und "Gerechtigkeit" sowie die zehn Prinzipien des ersten Dokuments lassen sich in folgender Übersicht darstellen:

SICHERHEIT	FRIEDEN	GERECHTIGKEIT zwischen den Staaten	innerhalb der Staaten
Enthaltung von der Androhung oder Anwendung von Gewalt (II)	Friedliche Regelung von Streitfällen (V)	Gleichheit (I)	Souveräne Achtung der Menschenrechte und Grundfreiheiten einschl. der Gedanken-, Gewissens- oder Überzeugungsfreiheit (VII)
Unverletzlichkeit der Grenzen (III)		Erfüllung völkerrechtlicher Verpflichtungen nach Treu und Glauben (X)	
Territoriale Integrität der Staaten (IV)	Zusammenarbeit zwischen den Staaten (IX)		Gleichberechtigung und Selbstbestimmungsrecht der Völker (VIII)
Nichteinmischung in innere Angelegenheiten (VI)			

b. Die sicherheitspolitischen Instrumente der KSZE: Vertrauens- und sicherheitsbildende Maßnahmen, Krisenmechanismen, Friedliche Streitbeilegung, Friedenserhaltende Operationen und präventive Diplomatie

Die sicherheitspolitischen Instrumente im Rahmen der KSZE entwickelten sich graduell von den vertrauensbildenden Maßnahmen im militärischen Bereich über Krisenmechanismen im militärischen und zivilen Bereich bis zu friedenserhaltenden Operationen und präventiver Diplomatie, wobei sich jeweils ein Instrument aus dem anderen ableiten ließ. Daneben stand von Anfang an die Idee der friedlichen Beilegung von Streitigkeiten, die bereits in der Prinzipienerklärung verankert worden war, aber erst spät einen operativen Rahmen erhielt.

(1) Die Entwicklung der vertrauens- und sicherheitsbildenden Maßnahmen

Das erste sicherheitspolitische Instrument, das im Rahmen der KSZE entwickelt wurde, waren die vertrauensbildenden Maßnahmen (VBM) im militärischen Bereich.[52] Wie sich aus der Schlußakte ableiten läßt, besteht das vorrangige Ziel der

52 Zum Thema VBM vgl. folgende Sammelbände: Jonathan *Alford* (Hrsg.), The Future of Arms Control, Part III: Confidence Building Measures, London 1979 (*IISS*, Adelphi Papers No. 149); Karl *Birnbaum* (Hrsg.), Confidence-Building Measures and East-West Relations, Wien 1983 (*ÖIIP*, Laxenburg Paper No. 5); F. Stephen *Larrabee*/Dietrich *Stobbe* (Hrsg.), Confidence-Building Measures in Europe, New York 1983 (*Institute for East-West Security Studies*, East-

VBM in der "Verminderung der Gefahr von bewaffneten Konflikten und von Mißverständnissen oder Fehleinschätzungen militärischer Tätigkeiten ... insbesondere in einer Situation, in der den Teilnehmerstaaten klare und rechtzeitige Informationen über den Charakter solcher Tätigkeiten fehlen".[53] Diese Bestimmung definiert über den eigentlichen Anlaßfall hinaus den Begriff "Konflikt", wie er in der späteren Folge im KSZE-Kontext zunächst auch für die Bezeichnung des "Konfliktverhütungszentrums" relevant blieb, nämlich als bewaffneter, das heißt mit militärischen Mitteln geführter Konflikt zwischen Staaten. Sie definiert weiterhin die grundlegende Funktion von VBM, durch wechselseitige Information die Eskalation von angespannten Situationen zu friedensbedrohenden Konflikten zu verhindern. Dieser Ansatz reflektiert das kooperative Element in der Sicherheitspolitik im Rahmen der KSZE. Sicherheit resultiert aus Vorhersehbarkeit, die durch Offenheit und Transparenz erhöht werden soll.

Der Katalog der vertrauensbildenden Maßnahmen in der Schlußakte war zunächst relativ eng begrenzt und umfaßte

- die vorherige Ankündigung größerer militärischer Manöver;
- die vorherige Ankündigung anderer militärischer Manöver;
- den Austausch von Beobachtern;
- die vorherige Ankündigung größerer militärischer Bewegungen;
- die Förderung des Austausches von militärischem Personal auf Einladung einschließlich des Besuches von Militärdelegationen.[54]

Das KSZE-Nachfolgetreffen von Madrid gab dann das Mandat für die Konferenz über Vertrauens- und Sicherheitsbildende Maßnahmen und Abrüstung in Europa (KVAE),[55] die von 1984 bis 1986 dauerte und vor Beginn des Wiener Nach-

---

West Monograph No. 1); Karl *Kaiser* (Hrsg.), Confidence-Building Measures, Bonn 1983 (*Deutsche Gesellschaft für Außenpolitik*, Arbeitspapiere zur internationalen Politik, Bd. 28); R. B. *Byers*/F. Stephen *Larrabee*/Allen *Lynch* (Hrsg.), Confidence-Building Measures and International Security, New York 1987 (*Institute for East-West Security Studies*, East-West Monograph Series No. 4), sowie folgende Monographien: Hans-J. *Schütz*, Militärische Vertrauensbildende Maßnahmen aus völkerrechtlicher Sicht, Berlin 1984; Michael *Zielinski*, Vertrauensbildende Maßnahmen, Frankfurt a.M. 1985; Heinz *Vetschera*, Confidence-Building Measures (CBMs) and European Security, Wien 1986 (Studien und Berichte). Zu dieser Ableitung und zu ihrer Erweiterung zu einem allgemeinen Konzept der VBM vgl. Heinz *Vetschera*, Vertrauensbildende Maßnahmen – Ein sicherheitspolitisches Instrument, in: Österreichische Militärische Zeitschrift (ÖMZ), 15 (1977) 1, S. 23-27.

53 Schlußakte von Helsinki, Präambel zum Dokument über Vertrauensbildende Maßnahmen und bestimmte Aspekte der Abrüstung.

54 Die letzte Maßnahme wird freilich im Dokument nicht explizit aufgeführt, sondern beispielhaft angegeben unter dem Titel "andere Vertrauensbildende Maßnahmen".

55 Gemäß diesem Mandat sollte es das Ziel der Verhandlungen sein, neue wirksame und konkrete Schritte zu unternehmen, die darauf gerichtet sind, Fortschritte bei der Festigung des Vertrauens und der Sicherheit und bei der Verwirklichung der Abrüstung zu erzielen, um der Pflicht der Staaten, sich der Androhung oder Anwendung von Gewalt in ihren gegenseitigen Beziehungen zu enthalten, Wirkung und Ausdruck zu verleihen. Die Maßnahmen sollten ganz Europa sowie das angrenzende Seegebiet und den angrenzenden Luftraum umfassen; sie sollten militä-

folgetreffens (1986-1989) mit einem umfassenden Dokument abgeschlossen werden konnte.[56]

Es enthielt weitgehende Verbesserungen bei der Ankündigung militärischer Aktivitäten und bei deren Beobachtung, die Verpflichtung zur Abgabe eines Jahreskalenders geplanter Aktivitäten sowie erstmals in der Geschichte der Rüstungskontrolle Vorkehrungen zur Inspektion an Ort und Stelle.[57] In der Folge erteilte das Wiener Nachfolgetreffen der KSZE[58] das Mandat für zwei Rüstungskontrollkonferenzen,[59] nämlich einerseits für die Verhandlungen über konventionelle Streitkräfte in Europa (VKSE/CFE), die de facto die seit 1973 ergebnislos verlaufenen Wiener Truppenabbauverhandlungen (Mutual Reduction of Forces and Armaments and Associated Measures in Central Europe, MURFAAMCE) ersetzten, und andererseits für die Verhandlungen über Vertrauens- und Sicherheitsbildende Maßnahmen (VVSBM), "um auf den bereits bei der Stockholmer Konferenz erzielten Ergebnissen aufzubauen und sie zu erweitern, mit dem Ziel, einen neuen Satz einander ergänzender Vertrauens- und Sicherheitsbildender Maßnahmen auszuarbeiten und anzunehmen, die darauf gerichtet sind, die Gefahr einer militärischen Konfrontation in Europa zu vermindern".[60]

Die VVSBM wurden am 6. März 1989 in Wien eröffnet. Am 17. November 1990 wurde als erster Schritt das Wiener Dokument 1990 angenommen.[61] Es enthielt neben der Bestätigung und Verbesserung der in Stockholm vereinbarten Maßnahmen eine Reihe zusätzlicher Maßnahmen, wie die Verpflichtung zum Aus-

---

risch bedeutsam und politisch verbindlich sein und von angemessenen Formen der Verifikation begleitet werden, die ihrem Inhalt entsprechen. Siehe Abschließendes Dokument des Madrider Treffens 1980, Madrid, 6. September 1983, Kapitel Fragen der Sicherheit in Europa, Konferenz über Vertrauens- und Sicherheitsbildende Maßnahmen und Abrüstung in Europa. Zum Mandat vgl. *Vetschera*, Confidence-Building Measures, S. 86ff; zur Stockholmer Konferenz umfassend John *Borawski*, From the Atlantic to the Urals. Negotiating Arms Control at the Stockholm Conference, Washington/New York/London/Oxford: Pergamon-Brassey's 1988.

56 Dokument der Stockholmer Konferenz über Vertrauens- und Sicherheitsbildende Maßnahmen, Stockholm, 19. September 1986; zum Inhalt vgl. *Borawski*, From the Atlantic to the Urals, S. 102ff.

57 Artikel 63-96; vgl. *Borawski*, From the Atlantic to the Urals, S. 106f.

58 Abschließendes Dokument des Wiener Treffens 1986 der Vertreter der Teilnehmerstaaten der Konferenz über Sicherheit und Zusammenarbeit in Europa, Wien, 15. Januar 1989.

59 Der Begriff der Rüstungskontrolle wird hier entsprechend der eingangs erwähnten weiten Definition von *Schelling/Halperin*, Strategy, verwendet und umfaßt damit auch den Bereich der Vertrauens- und Sicherheitsbildenden Maßnahmen.

60 Abschließendes Dokument, S. 12.

61 Zum Ablauf der Verhandlungen und zum Ergebnis vgl. *Borawski*, Security for a New Europe; Günther *Joetze*, Verhandlungen über Vertrauens- und Sicherheitsbildende Maßnahmen in Wien und das "Wiener Dokument 1990", in: Europa-Archiv, 46 (1991) 14, S. 422-428, und *Palmisano*, KSZE/VVSBM. Die Verhandlungen wurden in der Folge fortgesetzt und schließlich mit dem Wiener Dokument 1992 abgeschlossen; vgl. Simon *Palmisano*, Vom Wiener Dokument 1990 zum Wiener Dokument 1992 (Chronik), Wien: Landesverteidigungsakademie 1992.

tausch "*statischer*" Information[62] über die Streitkräfte der Teilnehmerstaaten (Maßnahme I), die durch Überprüfung verifiziert werden kann, Verbesserung der Kontakte einschließlich des Besuchs von Militärflugplätzen (Maßnahme III), ein jährliches Treffen der Teilnehmerstaaten zur Überprüfung (Maßnahme X), aber auch "Verminderung der Risiken" (Maßnahme II) durch geeignete Konsultationsmechanismen und "Kommunikation" (Maßnahme IX) über ein eigens dafür eingerichtetes Datennetz.[63] Während die Verfeinerung der in Stockholm beschlossenen Maßnahmen wie auch die neu eingeführte Maßnahme der statischen Information letztlich lineare Fortentwicklungen der bestehenden VSBM darstellen, haben die Maßnahmen "Verminderung der Risiken" und "Kommunikation" eine neue Qualität und weden daher gelegentlich als "dritte Generation" der VSBM (nach der ersten Generation der VBM von Helsinki und der zweiten Generation der Stockholmer VSBM) bezeichnet. Diese Maßnahmen entsprechen inhaltlich unmittelbar der grundlegenden Philosophie vertrauensbildender Maßnahmen, durch Information und Kommunikation zur Verminderung der Gefahr von bewaffneten Konflikten und von Mißverständnissen oder Fehleinschätzungen beizutragen, wie sie bereits in der Schlußakte von Helsinki formuliert worden war. Sie bedürfen aber zu ihrem Einsatz entsprechender institutioneller Vorkehrungen.[64]

(2) Die Krisenmechanismen der KSZE

Die Krisenmechanismen der KSZE beruhen im wesentlichen auf Treffen der Teilnehmerstaaten, die auf Antrag eines oder mehrerer Teilnehmerstaaten einzuberufen sind.[65] Die Krisenmechanismen wurden zunächst im Bereich der militärischen vertrauens- und sicherheitsbildenden Maßnahmen, dann aber auch im allgemeinpolitischen Bereich und schließlich spezifisch für die menschliche Dimension der

62 Im Gegensatz zur bereits früher eingeführten "dynamischen" Information über Vorgänge, wie etwa Manöverankündigungen; die Terminologie wurde in den Wiener Verhandlungen geprägt.

63 Vgl. zum Ergebnis der VVSBM insgesamt *Borawski*, Security for a New Europe, S. 115ff, sowie Karl *Liko*, Das Wiener Dokument 1990, in: ÖMZ, (1991) 2, S. 108-112.

64 Gelegentlich wird die Ansicht vertreten, die "dritte Generation" der VSBM bestehe in der Schaffung der Institutionen selbst, was aber eine verkürzte Sicht ist. Ohne die konkreten Maßnahmen würden die Institutionen allein kaum der VSBM-Philosophie entsprechen. Dagegen stellen die konkreten Maßnahmen, wie ausgeführt, bereits für sich Vertrauensbildende Maßnahmen dar, die allerdings konkrete Einrichtungen erfordern, um funktionieren zu können. Die Institutionalisierung ist damit akzessorisch, nicht aber konstitutiv für die "dritte Generation" dieser Maßnahmen.

65 Es ist fraglich, ob auch die im Stockholmer und Wiener Dokument vorgesehenen Maßnahmen der Verifikation im militärischen Bereich (Inspektionen) als "Krisenmechanismen der KSZE" anzusehen sind. Sie finden sich zwar in einem KSZE-Dokument und sind für Situationen vorgesehen, in denen Unsicherheit besteht, werden aber ausschließlich im bilateralen Verhältnis zwischen den Teilnehmerstaaten angewendet. Demgegenüber sehen die angeführten Krisenmechanismen als letzte Stufe die Einberufung eines KSZE-Gremiums vor und entsprechen damit im eigentlichen Sinn der Bezeichnung "KSZE-Krisenmechanismus", da sie auf die Zusammenkunft (= Konferenz) aller Teilnehmerstaaten abstellen.

KSZE entwickelt. Die Mechanismen wurden im Zuge dieser Entwicklung immer differenzierter ausgestaltet.

Krisenmechanismen im Bereich der militärischen Vertrauens- und Sicherheitsbildung

Die ersten KSZE-Krisenmechanismen wurden im Rahmen der VVSBM vereinbart und im Wiener Dokument 1990 festgelegt. Die Schaffung von Krisenmechanismen und Institutionen verlief dabei auf mehreren Schienen. Bereits der erste westliche Vorschlag in den VVSBM enthielt die "Entwicklung von Kommunikationsmitteln"[66] zusätzlich zu den bisher üblichen diplomatischen Kanälen von Mitteilungen über vereinbarte Maßnahmen.[67] Nach einer späteren detaillierten Variante dieses Vorschlags[68] sollte jeder Staat eine Kontaktstelle nennen, die geeignet sei, solche Informationen – vorzugsweise rund um die Uhr – entgegenzunehmen. Der gleichzeitig eingebrachte Vorschlag von Staaten der damaligen Warschauer Vertragsorganisation (WVO) – Bulgarien, DDR, CSSR und Ungarn[69] – sah parallel dazu den "Aufbau eines eigenen Kommunikationsnetzes zur gegenseitigen Klärung von Situationen [vor], die bei irgendeiner Seite Zweifel oder Befürchtungen aufkommen lassen" (Pkt. V/8). Weiters enthielt der Vorschlag die "Abhaltung bilateraler und multilateraler Konsultationen auf regelmäßiger Basis (oder auf Ersuchen eines Teilnehmerstaates) zu Fragen, die im Zusammenhang mit den Zielen und Aufgaben der Verhandlungen über vertrauens- und sicherheitsbildende Maßnahmen besprochen werden" (Pkt. V/5), sowie ausdrücklich die "Schaffung eines Zentrums zur Verringerung der Kriegsgefahr und Verhinderung eines Überraschungsangriffs in Europa, das eine Informations- und Beratungsfunktion ausüben könnte" (Pkt. V/7).

Die Entwicklung eines Kommunikationssystems wurde auch im Vorschlag Rumäniens[70] "für Konsultationen zwischen den Staats- und Regierungschefs und für die Einberufung von Treffen auf hoher Ebene in Krisensituationen" (Pkt. 5) unterstützt, ebenso im Vorschlag der Gruppe der Neutralen und Nichtblockgebundenen

---

66 CSCE/WV/1 vom 9. März 1989, Pkt. 11.

67 Dieses Konzept läßt sich letztlich auf die Errichtung des "heißen Drahtes" zwischen den USA und der UdSSR im Gefolge der Kuba-Krise von 1962 zurückführen; vgl. Memorandum of Understanding between the United States of America and the Union of Socialist Soviet Republics Regarding the Establishment of a Direct Communications Link, Genf 1963, sowie Agreement between the United States of America and the Union of Socialist Soviet Republics on Measures to Improve the USA-USSR Direct Communciations Link, Washington 1971. Die in Wien vorgeschlagene und dann auch vereinbarte Maßnahme stellt damit die multilaterale Anwendung eines bilateral bereits akzeptierten Verfahrens dar.

68 CSCE/WV/1 amplified vom 9. Juni 1989.

69 CSCE/WV/2 vom 9. März 1989; der Vorschlag datierte aus der Zeit vor der demokratischen Revolution und reflektierte damit in anderen Elementen noch das "alte Denken" der Sicherheitspolitik der WVO.

70 CSCE/WV/3 vom 22. März 1989.

(N+N-) Staaten.[71] Die bestehende Praxis sollte gemäß diesem Vorschlag "durch ein System rascher Kommunikation verbessert werden, um die Verläßlichkeit und Rechtzeitigkeit der Übermittlung sicherzustellen; moderne Kommunikationsmittel sollten genutzt werden, um ... auch graphische Daten übermitteln zu können; schließlich könnte die Durchführung der Vertrauens- und Sicherheitsbildenden Maßnahmen zu einem erhöhten Bedarf an Klarstellungen und Konsultationen führen. Diesbezüglich wären geeignete Wege und Mittel zu prüfen".

Damit hatten alle an den VVSBM teilnehmenden Staaten und Staatengruppierungen zunächst die grundlegende Idee verbesserter Kommunikation in ihre Vorschläge aufgenommen. Es lagen aber auch schon die Ideen zur Schaffung geeigneter Konsultationsmechanismen, wie auch schließlich zur Schaffung permanenter Institutionen in Form des "Zentrums zur Verringerung der Kriegsgefahr" auf dem Verhandlungstisch. In der Folge wurden die Vorstellungen über die Ausgestaltung des Kommunikationsnetzes wie auch der Konsultationsmechanismen deutlicher. Nachdem die westliche Staatengruppe bereits in ihrem Vorschlag vom 23. Februar 1990[72] ein jährliches Treffen zur Beurteilung der Anwendung der VSBM vorgeschlagen hatte (Maßnahme 14), schlug sie am 18. Mai 1990[73] unter anderem hinsichtlich der Entwicklung von Kommunikationsmitteln die Optionen

- Telegrammnetz;
- Direktverbindung zwischen Datenverarbeitungsendgeräten;
- Verwendung der vorhandenen kommerziellen Netze, ausschließlich oder teilweise über das internationale Telefonnetz,

vor (Maßnahme 11), weiters einen bereits detailliert ausgearbeiteten "Mechanismus zur Erörterung ungewöhnlicher Aktivitäten militärischer Art" (Maßnahme 15) und Maßnahmen zur Verminderung des Risikos gefährlicher Zwischenfälle und Berichterstattung über solche Zwischenfälle (Maßnahme 16). Maßnahme 15 sah vor, daß ein Teilnehmerstaat, der Bedenken bezüglich einer ungewöhnlichen, militärisch bedeutsamen Aktivität hat, an der konventionelle Streitkräfte auf dem Territorium eines anderen Teilnehmerstaates im Rahmen nicht geplanter Aktivitäten außerhalb ihres Standortes beteiligt sind, binnen 48 Stunden Aufklärung darüber verlangen könne. Der Staat könnte aber auch um ein bilaterales Treffen mit dem anderen Staat ersuchen, das binnen 48 Stunden abgehalten werden müßte. Schließlich könnte der Teilnehmerstaat auch um ein Treffen aller 35 Teilnehmerstaaten ersuchen; hier wären aber die organisatorischen Modalitäten noch auszuarbeiten. Maßnahme 16 sah den Austausch von Einzelheiten über Kontaktstellen vor, die imstande sind, sich mit gefährlichen Zwischenfällen im Falle ihres Eintretens zu befassen.

---

71 CSCE/WV/5 vom 12. Juli 1989.

72 CSCE/WV/7.

73 CSCE/WV/8.

Diese Konzepte wurden dann in dem umfangreichen Vorschlag Frankreichs vom 8. Juni 1990 zum Entwurf eines Schlußdokuments[74] im wesentlichen übernommen. Er enthält die Anregung, "als Ergänzung zu den bisher benutzten diplomatischen Wegen und zur Übermittlung von Informationen in bezug auf vereinbarte Maßnahmen andere Mittel zur raschen und direkten Kommunikation zwischen Hauptstädten, am besten über festgelegte Kontaktstellen, [zu] untersuchen und entwickeln" (Pkt. 103). Hinsichtlich der Konsultation enthält der Vorschlag sowohl den bereits im vorherigen westlichen Vorschlag vorgesehenen "Stufenbau" für den Mechanismus[75] als auch die Kontaktstellen für gefährliche Zwischenfälle (Pkt. 99), überläßt aber ebenfalls die Ausarbeitung der näheren Modalitäten den weiteren Verhandlungen.

Das Wiener Dokument folgt im wesentlichen diesen Konzepten. Maßnahme IX (Kommunikation) sollte die erforderliche Infrastruktur schaffen. Sie sieht die Einrichtung eines direkten Kommunikationsnetzes zur Übermittlung von Mitteilungen zwischen den Hauptstädten der Teilnehmerstaaten (Pkt. 143) vor sowie in jedem Teilnehmerstaat die Einrichtung einer Kontaktstelle, "die in der Lage ist, solche Mitteilungen rund um die Uhr zu übermitteln und von anderen Teilnehmerstaaten zu empfangen" (Pkt. 144). Die technischen Einzelheiten des Netzes werden im Anhang II zum Wiener Dokument spezifiziert.

Maßnahme II (Verminderung der Risiken) enthält die Vorkehrung, daß "die Teilnehmerstaaten ... bezüglich jeglicher ungewöhnlicher und unvorhergesehener Aktivitäten ihrer Streitkräfte, die außerhalb ihrer normalen Friedensstandorte ... stattfinden, militärisch bedeutsam sind und bezüglich derer ein Teilnehmerstaat Besorgnis hinsichtlich seiner Sicherheit äußert, in Übereinstimmung mit den folgenden Bestimmungen einander konsultieren und zusammenarbeiten" (Pkt. 17). Der operative Teil sieht folgenden Vorgang vor: Der "Teilnehmerstaat, der bezüglich einer solchen Aktivität besorgt ist, kann ... ein Ersuchen um eine Erklärung übermitteln, das auch Angaben über ... die Gründe für die Besorgnis und, soweit möglich, über Art und Ort oder Gebiet der Aktivität enthalten" sollte (Pkt. 17.1 und 17.1.1). Die Antwort darauf ist binnen 48 Stunden zu übermitteln (Pkt. 17.1.2) und hat *die* gestellten "Fragen [zu] beantworten und jede andere zweckdienliche Information [zu] geben, die zur Klarstellung der ... Aktivität beitragen könnte" (Pkt. 17.1.3). Nach Prüfung der Antwort kann der ersuchende Staat ein Treffen zur Erörterung der Angelegenheit verlangen (Pkt. 17.2), das mit dem antwortenden Staat (Pkt. 17.2.1) oder aber mit allen Teilnehmerstaaten (Pkt. 17.2.2) stattfinden und jeweils binnen 48 Stunden beginnen wird.[76] Ersuchen um Erklärung, Antwort

---

74 CSCE/WV/12.

75 Erklärung; bilaterales bzw. multilaterales Treffen; jeweils 48 Stunden Frist; Pkt. 98.

76 Soweit die deutsche Textfassung. Demgegenüber spricht die englische Fassung von "within not more than 48 hours" und deutet damit die Möglichkeit einer kürzerfristigen Einberufung einer

und Ersuchen um ein Konsultationstreffen werden jeweils den anderen Teilnehmerstaaten unverzüglich übermittelt (Pkt. 17.1.4 sowie 17.2.1.2).

Ein Staat kann sich auch zu einem multilateralen Treffen entschließen, wenn er beim bilateralen Treffen erfolglos war. Letzteres "wird an einem ... einvernehmlich zu vereinbarenden Ort ... [oder,] falls kein Einvernehmen erzielt wird, ... im Konfliktverhütungszentrum abgehalten" (Pkt. 17.2.1.4). Ein Treffen aller Teilnehmerstaaten wird am Konfliktverhütungszentrum abgehalten (Pkt. 17.2.2.2).

Der Mechanismus wurde während der Jugoslawienkrise dreimal in Gang gesetzt. Zunächst richteten Österreich und Italien nach Ausbruch der Kämpfe in Slowenien im Juni 1991 eine schriftliche Anfrage an Jugoslawien. Nach einer schwerwiegenden Verletzung des österreichischen Luftraumes beantragte Österreich ein multilaterales Treffen, das am 1. Juli 1991 stattfand.[77]

Am 1. September 1991 kam es auf Antrag Ungarns zu einem bilateralen Treffen mit Jugoslawien. Auch dieses Treffen bezog sich auf Verletzungen des Luftraumes durch jugoslawische Militärflugzeuge. Die Konsultationen zielten also nicht primär auf die Verringerung der Gewalt im damaligen Jugoslawien, sondern auf die Vermeidung der Eskalation zu einem möglichen zwischenstaatlichen Grenzkonflikt, und erfüllten damit ihren Zweck. Am 8. April 1992 forderte Jugoslawien von einem Nachbarstaat Aufklärung über militärische Aktivitäten an der gemeinsamen Grenze. Hier erschöpfte sich der Mechanismus in der schriftlichen Beantwortung der Anfrage und führte zu keinen weiteren Konsultationen.

Punkt 18 regelt die Zusammenarbeit bei gefährlichen militärischen Zwischenfällen. Die Teilnehmer verpflichten sich zur Zusammenarbeit beim Melden und Klarstellen von gefährlichen Zwischenfällen sowie zur Bezeichnung einer Kontaktstelle für solche Meldungen (Pkt. 18 und 18.1). Mitteilungen werden "vorzugsweise über das VSBM-Kommunikationsnetz übermittelt" (Pkt. 18.3). Das KVZ hat die Aufgabe, die Liste der Kontaktstellen zu führen (Pkt. 18.1) und dient als Forum zur allfälligen Erörterung solcher Zwischenfälle (Pkt. 18.4), entweder bei den jährlichen oder bei zusätzlich anberaumten Treffen. Dieser Mechanismus wurde bisher nicht aktiviert.

Die Krisenmechanismen im Bereich der militärischen Vertrauens- und Sicherheitsbildung resultieren aus verschiedenen Inputs im Zuge der Verhandlungen. Das Konzept eines Kommunikationssystems zwischen den Teilnehmerstaaten wurde sowohl von der westlichen wie auch der östlichen und der N+N-Staatengruppe frühzeitig in die Vorschläge aufgenommen. Die weiteren Verhandlungen dienten seiner Ausgestaltung, die immer anspruchsvoller wurde und schließlich im

---

Konsultation an. Der spanische, französische, italienische und russische Text sprechen hingegen bloß von "nicht mehr als 48 Stunden" und lassen diese Frage offen.

77 Vgl. zum folgenden Heinz *Vetschera*, Die KSZE-Krisenmechanismen und ihr Einsatz in der Jugoslawienkrise, in: ÖMZ, 29 (1991) 5, S. 405-411.

Beschluß der Einrichtung eines eigenständigen Netzes für den Datenverbund mündete. Der Konsultationsmechanismus beruhte dagegen zunächst auf einem Vorschlag der östlichen Staatengruppe, der aber in seiner äußeren Form sehr vage blieb. Seine Inhalte wurden von der westlichen Staatengruppe in die konkrete Form des "Stufenbaus" gebracht, die dann auch Eingang in das Wiener Dokument fand. Als einziger wesentlicher Zusatz ist die Bestimmung zu sehen, die das KVZ als Forum für die Konsultationstreffen für ungewöhnliche militärische Aktivitäten (subsidiär bei bilateralen Treffen, unmittelbar bei multilateralen Treffen) wie auch bei gefährlichen Zwischenfällen vorsieht. Dieses Element greift wiederum auf die Idee eines "Zentrums zur Verringerung der Kriegsgefahr" zurück, die im ersten Vorschlag der östlichen Staatengruppe enthalten war.[78]

Der nichtmilitärische Krisenmechanismus

Die Charta von Paris wie auch das dazugehörige Zusatzdokument sahen bereits die Möglichkeit vor, den AHB zu Dringlichkeitssitzungen einzuberufen, und ließen diese Möglichkeit prüfen. Als Ergebnis dieser Prüfung beschloß der Rat der Außenminister auf seinem ersten Treffen in Berlin vom 19./20. Juni 1991 die Annahme eines "Mechanismus für Konsultation und Zusammenarbeit in dringlichen Situationen".[79] Gemäß diesem Mechanismus werden die Teilnehmer "einander in schwerwiegenden dringlichen Situationen, die auf Grund der Verletzung eines Prinzips der Schlußakte oder größerer, den Frieden, die Sicherheit oder die Stabilität gefährdender Zwischenfälle entstehen können, ... konsultieren und zusammenarbeiten".[80] Wenn ein Teilnehmerstaat der Ansicht ist, daß eine solche dringliche Situation entstanden ist, kann er von dem betroffenen Staat oder den betroffenen Staaten Klarstellung verlangen (Pkt. 1). Der ersuchte Staat bzw. die ersuchten Staaten stellen innerhalb von 48 Stunden alle zweckdienlichen Informationen zur Verfügung, um die Situation zu klären (Pkt. 1.1). Bleibt die Situation weiterhin ungelöst, kann jeder der betroffenen Staaten an den amtierenden Vorsitzenden des AHB[81] ein Ersuchen um Einberufung einer Dringlichkeitssitzung des Aus-

78 Die Idee der Schaffung ständiger Institutionen im Rahmen der KSZE gehörte zu den ursprünglichen Forderungen der östlichen Seite seit Beginn der KSZE. Da sie zu diesem Zeitpunkt stets auch mit der impliziten Forderung nach Mitsprache in der westlichen Sicherheitspolitik verbunden war, wurde sie von der westlichen Seite konsequent abgelehnt. Erst unter den geänderten Verhältnissen nach der Wende 1989 konnte erwartet werden, daß solche Einrichtungen nicht der Konfrontation, sondern der Kooperation in Europa dienen würden. Daher ergriff nun der Westen die Initiative zur Schaffung konkreter Institutionen und machte in der Londoner Erklärung des NATO-Gipfels von 1990 die entsprechenden Vorschläge; vgl. *Borawski*, Security for a New Europe, S. 93ff.

79 Berliner Treffen, Zusammenfassung der Schlußfolgerungen, Kap. II, Pkt. 6.

80 Ebd., Anhang 2.

81 Der Vorsitz rotiert in alphabetischer Reihenfolge unter den Teilnehmerstaaten.

schusses richten (Pkt. 2). Der Vorsitzende benachrichtigt unverzüglich alle Teilnehmerstaaten sowie das KSZE-Sekretariat von dem Ersuchen (Pkt. 2.4) und nimmt innerhalb 24 Stunden mit den betroffenen Staaten Kontakt auf (Pkt. 2.5). Sobald zwölf oder mehr Teilnehmerstaaten das Ersuchen innerhalb von höchstens 48 Stunden durch eine entsprechende Mitteilung an den Vorsitzenden unterstützt haben, beruft dieser das Treffen aller Teilnehmerstaaten ein, das frühestens 48 Stunden und spätestens drei Tage nach dieser Mitteilung abzuhalten ist (Pkt. 2.6).

Das Treffen "findet am Sitz des Sekretariats statt und dauert höchstens zwei Tage, sofern nichts anderes vereinbart wurde" (Pkt. 2.8), seine Tagesordnung besteht aus einem einzigen Punkt, der in demselben Wortlaut zu formulieren ist wie in der Mitteilung (Pkt. 2.9). Das Treffen kann je nach Situation Empfehlungen oder Schlußfolgerungen zur Herbeiführung einer Lösung vereinbaren oder beschließen, ein Treffen auf Ministerebene einzuberufen (Pkt. 2.13). Das Ersuchen sowie die Antwort werden allen KSZE-Teilnehmerstaaten mitgeteilt. Die Mitteilungen im Rahmen des Dringlichkeitsverfahrens werden vorzugsweise durch das VSBM-Kommunikationsnetz übermittelt (Pkt. 4).[82] Weiters legen die einschlägigen Bestimmungen ausdrücklich fest, daß diese Verfahren nicht anstelle des Mechanismus für ungewöhnliche militärische Aktivitäten angewendet werden (Pkt. 3).

Der Mechanismus wurde ebenfalls erstmals mit Beginn der Jugoslawienkrise im Juli 1991 aktiviert. Er führte unter anderem zur Unterstützung der EG-Beobachtermission in Jugoslawien, die durch die Beteiligung anderer KSZE-Teilnehmerstaaten erweitert wurde.[83] In der Folge fanden auf der Grundlage dieser ersten Krisensitzung weitere Krisensitzungen des AHB statt, wann immer es die Lage erforderte. Sie trugen zur Herausbildung einer konkordierten Sicht der Lage im früheren Jugoslawien zwischen den übrigen KSZE-Teilnehmerstaaten bei. Eine ausdrückliche zweite Krisensitzung wurde während des Helsinki-Folgetreffens der KSZE am 6. Mai 1992 zur Situation in Bosnien-Herzegowina einberufen. Schließlich wurde der Mechanismus im April 1993 im Zuge der Eskalation der Krise um Nagorny-Karabach durch Aserbaidschan aktiviert und führte zu einer Krisensitzung des AHB vom 27. bis 29. April.

Der humanitäre Krisenmechanismus

Der humanitäre Krisenmechanismus leitet sich von den Bestimmungen des Schlußdokuments des Wiener Folgetreffens 1986-1989 über die menschliche Dimension der KSZE ab. Die Teilnehmerstaaten beschlossen, "Informationen auszu-

82 Damit besteht eine institutionelle Brücke zwischen dem "zivilen" Krisenmechanismus des AHB und dem Bereich der VSBM.

83 Vgl. Neue Zürcher Zeitung, 2.7.1991 und 8.7.1991; Frankfurter Allgemeine Zeitung, 2.7.1991, sowie Le Monde, 5.7.1991.

tauschen sowie Informationsersuchen und Vorstellungen, die von anderen Teilnehmerstaaten zu Fragen der menschlichen Dimension der KSZE an sie herangetragen werden, zu beantworten" (Abs. 1) und bilaterale "Treffen mit anderen Teilnehmerstaaten, die darum ersuchen, abzuhalten, um Fragen betreffend die menschliche Dimension der KSZE, einschließlich Situationen und konkreter Fälle, mit dem Ziel ihrer Lösung zu prüfen" (Abs. 2). Die Teilnehmer beschlossen ferner, eine Konferenz über die menschliche Dimension der KSZE einzuberufen, um weitere Fortschritte bei der Achtung aller Menschenrechte und Grundfreiheiten, bei den menschlichen Kontakten und anderen Fragen von gleichfalls humanitärer Art zu erzielen. Es kam zu einem ersten Treffen (30.5.-23.6.1989) in Paris, einem zweiten (5.-29.6.1990) in Kopenhagen und einem dritten (10.9.-4.10.1991) in Moskau.

Das Kopenhagener Treffen wandelte die genannten Bestimmungen in einen obligatorischen Mechanismus mit festgelegtem Prozedere um. Die Staaten sind nunmehr verpflichtet, Informationsansuchen und schriftlich eingebrachte Vorstellungen, die von anderen Teilnehmerstaaten gemäß Absatz 1 des Wiener Schlußdokuments an sie herangetragen werden, so rasch wie möglich, jedoch spätestens binnen vier Wochen schriftlich zu beantworten;[84] bilaterale Treffen gemäß Absatz 2 des Wiener Schlußdokuments sind so schnell wie möglich, in der Regel innerhalb von drei Wochen ab dem Tag des Ersuchens durchzuführen (Abs. 42.2). Diese Bestimmungen wurden auf dem Moskauer Treffen dahingehend abgeändert, daß die Staaten "auf Informationsansuchen und Vorstellungen, die von anderen Teilnehmerstaaten ... in schriftlicher Form an sie herangetragen wurden, eine schriftliche Antwort in kürzestmöglicher Zeit, jedoch spätestens nach zehn Tagen, erteilen werden". Bilaterale Treffen werden so rasch wie möglich, üblicherweise aber innerhalb einer Woche nach dem Ersuchen abgehalten.[85] Weiters sieht das Mokauer Dokument die Erstellung einer Liste von Experten vor, von denen eine unparteiische Wahrnehmung ihrer Aufgaben erwartet werden kann (Abs. I/[3]).

Jeder Teilnehmerstaat kann um Beistand einer aus höchstens drei Experten bestehenden KSZE-Mission ersuchen, "die sich mit Fragen der Menschlichen Dimension der KSZE auf seinem Staatsgebiet befassen und zu deren Lösung beitragen soll" (Abs. I/[4]). Zweck einer solchen Mission ist es, "die Lösung einer bestimmten Frage oder eines Problems der menschlichen Dimension der KSZE zu erleichtern". Sie "kann die für die Durchführung ihrer Aufgaben erforderlichen Informationen einholen und, wenn angebracht, ihre guten Dienste und Vermittlerdienste dazu nutzen, Dialog und Zusammenarbeit zwischen interessierten Parteien zu fördern" (Abs. I/[5]). Schließlich können "ein Teilnehmerstaat oder mehrere,

---

84 Dokument des Kopenhagener Treffens der Konferenz über die Menschliche Dimension der KSZE, Abs. 42.1.

85 Dokument des Moskauer Treffens der Konferenz über die menschliche Dimension der KSZE, Abs. I/(2).

die die Punkte 1 oder 2 des Mechanismus der Menschlichen Dimension zur Anwendung gebracht haben, ersuchen, daß die KSZE-Institution[86] bei einem anderen Teilnehmerstaat anfragt, ob er mit der Einladung einer Expertenmission zur Behandlung einer spezifischen, klar umrissenen Frage der Menschlichen Dimension der KSZE auf seinem Staatsgebiet einverstanden ist" (Abs. I/[8]).

Falls jedoch ein Teilnehmerstaat entweder eine solche Anfrage an einen anderen Teilnehmerstaat gerichtet hat oder befindet, daß die Expertenmission keine Lösung der betreffenden Frage erbracht hat, kann er – mit Unterstützung von mindestens fünf weiteren Teilnehmerstaaten – die Einberufung einer Mission von bis zu drei KSZE-Berichterstattern einleiten (Abs. I/[9]). Die Berichterstatter "werden die Tatsachen feststellen und darüber berichten und ... können Empfehlungen für mögliche Lösungen der aufgeworfenen Frage abgeben. ... Der ersuchte Staat wird – falls nicht anders vereinbart – spätestens drei Wochen nach Vorlage des Berichts der KSZE-Institution alle Bemerkungen zum Bericht zuleiten". Der Bericht kann auf die Tagesordnung des nächsten ordentlichen Treffens des AHB gesetzt werden, der über mögliche weitere Schritte entscheiden kann (Abs. I/[11]). In ähnlicher Weise kann ein Teilnehmerstaat, falls er "der Meinung ist, daß in einem anderen Teilnehmerstaat eine besonders schwerwiegende Gefahr für die Verwirklichung der Bestimmungen der Menschlichen Dimension der KSZE aufgetreten ist, ... mit Unterstützung von mindestens neun weiteren Teilnehmerstaaten ... das Verfahren in Gang setzen" (Abs. I/[12]).

Weiters kann der AHB auf Antrag eines Teilnehmerstaates beschließen, eine Mission von Experten bzw. KSZE-Berichterstattern einzusetzen (Abs. I/[13]). Die Beschlüsse des zweiten Ratstreffens in Prag[87] benannten das Büro für Demokratische Einrichtungen und Menschenrechte[88] in Warschau als die KSZE-Einrichtung, die mit Aufgaben im Zusammenhang mit Experten- und Berichterstattermissionen gemäß Moskauer Dokument betraut wurde.[89]

Der Mechanismus wurde bisher einmal im Zusammenhang mit der Jugoslawienkrise aktiviert. Am 5. August 1992 wurde das BDIMR von Großbritannien informiert, daß es mit Unterstützung Italiens, Portugals, Dänemarks, der USA, Griechenlands, Spaniens, der Niederlande, Irlands und Deutschlands den humanitären Mechanismus aufgrund der Lage in Bosnien-Herzegowina und Kroatien in Gang gesetzt habe. In der Folge schlossen sich auch Frankreich und Belgien an. Die Gruppe der Berichterstatter war mit dem 4. September 1992 etabliert. Das Man-

86 Aller Wahrscheinlichkeit nach das BDIMR in Warschau.

87 Prager Treffen des Rates der KSZE, 30.-31. Januar 1992; Prager Dokument über die weitere Entwicklung der KSZE-Institutionen und -Strukturen.

88 Diese Bezeichnung wurde auf dem Prager Ratstreffen eingeführt.

89 Prager Dokument über die weitere Entwicklung der KSZE-Institutionen und -Strukturen, Kap. III, Pkt. 14.

dat der Berichterstattermission bezog sich zunächst auf Übergriffe gegen unbewaffnete Zivilpersonen in Bosnien-Herzegowina und Kroatien, wurde dann aber um die Untersuchung von Gebieten, die von "ethnischen Säuberungen" bedroht sind, sowie um die Prüfung der Anschuldigungen über willkürliche Verhaftungen von Serben in Kroatien erweitert. Die Berichterstatter bereisten Kroatien vom 30. September bis zum 5. Oktober und legten anschließend ihren Bericht vor, in dem sie unter anderem die Einrichtung eines Gerichtshofes zur Aburteilung von Straftätern vorschlagen.

Zusammenfassung und Vergleich der Mechanismen

Die Entwicklung der Krisenmechanismen und der Institutionen im Rahmen des KSZE-Prozesses ist eng miteinander verflochten, geht aber auf mehrere unterschiedliche Wurzeln zurück. Ihr liegen die insbesondere von der östlichen Seite langjährig geforderte Institutionalisierung der KSZE ebenso zugrunde wie die vom Westen seit langem erhobenen Forderungen, durch vermehrten Informationsaustausch auf militärischem Gebiet zur Verbesserung der sicherheitspolitischen Situation beizutragen, und die westlichen Forderungen nach verbessertem Schutz der Menschenrechte.

Die Entwicklung der beiden ersten Krisenmechanismen verlief zunächst einigermaßen parallel,[90] aber nicht völlig synchron. So entwickelte sich der Mechanismus für ungewöhnliche militärische Aktivitäten zunächst ohne Bezug zu einer konkreten Institution, die dann erst im Wiener Dokument damit verbunden erscheint. Es wurde also mit dem KVZ gewissermaßen um den vorgesehenen Mechanismus herum eine Institution geschaffen, die vor allem der Durchführung dieser konkreten Aufgabe dienen sollte. Demgegenüber wurde der AHB wie auch das KSZE-Sekretariat zunächst ohne definierte Aufgabe im Krisenmanagement geschaffen. Sie war zwar schon in der Charta von Paris und im dazugehörigen Schlußdokument angekündigt, wurde aber erst auf dem Berliner Ratstreffen definiert.[91] Die Entwicklung des humanitären Mechanismus folgte schließlich erst mit relativ großem zeitlichen Abstand auf die Schaffung einer entsprechenden KSZE-Institution, die außerdem erst eine Erweiterung des ursprünglich auf freie Wahlen beschränkten Mandats auf allgemeine Menschenrechtsfragen erfahren mußte. Der humanitäre Mechanismus weist einerseits eine Parallele zum militärischen Krisenmechanismus auf, da er ebenfalls im Rahmen einer Sonderkonferenz der KSZE geschaf-

---

90 Nämlich durch die zeitliche Parallele der Endphase der VVSBM bis zur Annahme des Wiener Dokuments 1990 mit der Arbeit des Vorbereitungsausschusses für den Pariser KSZE-Gipfel.

91 Diese unterschiedliche Setzung der Prioritäten läßt sich auch in den jeweiligen Bestimmungen der Charta von Paris erkennen. Bei den Bestimmungen über den Konsultativausschuß wird die Aufgabe des Krisenmechanismus an erster Stelle angeführt; demgegenüber führen die Bestimmungen über den AHB die mögliche Funktion als Krisenorgan erst an letzter Stelle an.

fen wurde. Andererseits verweist er die Beschlußfassung an den AHB und steht so dem allgemein-politischen Mechanismus nahe.

Die genannten Mechanismen haben nur bedingt klar definierte und voneinander abgrenzbare Aufgabenbereiche. Der VSBM-Mechanismus des KVZ nimmt ausdrücklich auf "militärische Aktivitäten" Bezug und schließt damit andere Anwendungsfälle grundsätzlich aus. Ähnlich spezifiziert ist der Anwendungsbereich des humanitären Mechanismus. Der allgemein-politische Mechanismus des AHB bezieht sich dagegen auf den breiten Bereich der zehn Prinzipien und erweitert ihn noch um größere, den Frieden, die Sicherheit oder die Stabilität gefährdende Zwischenfälle.[92] Er würde damit die beiden anderen Bereiche prinzipiell mit abdekken. Andererseits legen die entsprechenden Bestimmungen der Berliner Beschlüsse ausdrücklich fest, daß der Mechanismus des AHB nicht anstelle des Mechanismus betreffend ungewöhnliche militärische Aktivitäten anzuwenden ist. Die Abgrenzung ist somit formal vorgeschrieben. Allerdings hat die bisherige Praxis gezeigt, daß Anlaßfälle zur Aktivierung des militärischen Krisenmechanismus sich kaum von denen zur Aktivierung des allgemein-politischen AHB-Krisenmechanismus trennen lassen. Hinsichtlich des humanitären Mechanismus besteht mit dem allgemein-politischen Mechanismus die Überschneidung in der Beschlußfassung durch den AHB.

Die Abläufe der Krisenmechanismen weisen teilweise eine hohe Ähnlichkeit auf, insbesondere in der Stufung des Verfahrens (Ersuchen um Erklärung, Antwort und erst dann Einberufung eines Treffens). Dies resultiert zweifellos aus der inkrementalen Entwicklung der Mechanismen aus dem ursprünglichen militärischen Mechanismus nach dem Wiener Dokument. Eine weitere Parallele besteht zwischen dem militärischen und dem allgemein-politischen Mechanismus in der Fristsetzung von jeweils 48 Stunden für die einzelnen Schritte sowie in der Informationspflicht gegenüber den anderen Teilnehmerstaaten. Andererseits weichen beide Mechanismen insofern voneinander ab, als der militärische Mechanismus die Option bilateraler oder multilateraler Treffen aufweist, der AHB-Mechanismus jedoch nur multilaterale Treffen. Der AHB-Mechanismus sieht eine ausdrückliche zeitliche Begrenzung der Dauer des Treffens vor und enthält Bestimmungen über die möglichen Ergebnisse der Treffen (Empfehlungen, Schlußfolgerungen, Beschluß beim Treffen auf Ministerebene); gleichartige Aussagen fehlen beim VSBM-Mechanismus. Im humanitären Mechanismus werden Beschlüsse über die Konsequenzen aus den Expertenberichten dem AHB zur Beschlußfassung

92 Vereinfacht könnte man den militärischen Mechanismus auf den ersten Korb und den humanitären Mechanismus auf den dritten Korb beziehen. Dies trifft aber nur bedingt und nur so lange zu, bis man den Geltungsbereich des allgemein-politischen Mechanismus einbezieht, der *alle* KSZE-Prinzipien betrifft. Da einerseits auch die "Achtung der Menschenrechte" als Prinzip der Schlußakte angeführt wird, sich der Prinzipienkatalog andererseits ebenfalls im ersten Korb befindet, ist damit eine solche lineare Zuordnung ausgeschlossen.

zugewiesen. Schließlich enthalten die Bestimmungen über den AHB-Mechanismus die erstmalige, wenngleich verklausuliert formulierte Durchbrechung des in der KSZE dominierenden Konsensprinzips,[93] die beim humanitären Mechanismus explizit erfolgt. Gleichartige Bestimmungen fehlen im VSBM-Mechanismus.

(3) Friedliche Streitbeilegung

Neben den eigentlichen Krisenmechanismen wurde im Rahmen der KSZE schon früh die Frage der friedlichen Streitbeilegung angesprochen,[94] die im weitesten Sinne ebenfalls als "krisenhemmend" angesehen werden kann.[95] Dies führte schließlich zur Schaffung eines Mechanismus der friedlichen Streitbeilegung, der auf einem Expertentreffen in Valletta (Malta) erarbeitet[96] und vom Berliner Ratstreffen angenommen wurde.[97] Er sieht Dritt-Parteien-Funktionen vor, die von qualifizierten Kandidaten[98] in der Vermittlung unterschiedlicher Standpunkte wahrzunehmen sind, um damit die Eskalation von Streitfällen zu eigentlichen Konflikten zu unterbinden. Der Mechanismus wurde auf dem KSZE-Treffen über die friedliche Streitbeilegung in Genf vom 12. bis 23. Oktober 1992 hinsichtlich des Verfahrens zur Auswahl der Personen aus der Liste abgeändert.[99] Auf diesem Treffen wurde auch die Errichtung eines Schlichtungs- und Schiedsgerichtshofes beschlossen[100] sowie in Ergänzung des KSZE-Verfahrens zur friedlichen Beilegung von Streitfällen ein Verfahren durch eine Schlichtungskommission eingerichtet.[101] Diese Ergebnisse wurden auf dem Stockholmer Ratstreffen angenommen.[102] Der Rat beschloß ferner, daß "der Rat oder der Ausschuß Hoher Beamter der KSZE

93 Anhang 2, Pkt. 2.7 der Berliner Beschlüsse bestimmt, daß "weder eine Beurteilung der Fakten noch eine mögliche Meinungsverschiedenheit über die Stichhaltigkeit der für die Einberufung einer Dringlichkeitssitzung geltend gemachten Gründe Anlaß zur Verschiebung oder Verhinderung einer Dringlichkeitssitzung geben" kann. Dies schließt die Behinderung der Einberufung einer solchen Sitzung durch Konsensverweigerung aus und weicht damit vom bisher gültigen Erfordernis des Konsenses für alle Entscheidungen – einschließlich der Verfahrensschritte – ab.

94 Vgl. die entsprechenden Richtlinien in Punkt V der Prinzipienerklärung in der Schlußakte von Helsinki.

95 Da die friedliche Streitbeilegung eben nur im weiteren Sinn als "Krisenmechanismus" bezeichnet werden kann, wird sie an dieser Stelle nicht eingehender behandelt.

96 Bericht über das KSZE-Expertentreffen über die friedliche Regelung von Streitfällen, Valletta, 8. Februar 1991.

97 Berliner Treffen, Zusammenfassung der Schlußfolgerungen, Anhang 3: Friedliche Beilegung von Streitigkeiten.

98 Bericht über das KSZE-Expertentreffen über die friedliche Regelung von Streitfällen, Bestimmungen für ein KSZE-Verfahren zur friedlichen Beilegung von Streitigkeiten, Abschn. V, Pkt. 1.

99 Ergebnisse des Genfer KSZE-Treffens über die friedliche Beilegung von Streitfällen, 23. Oktober 1992, Anhang 1.

100 Ebd., Anhang 2.

101 Ebd., Anhang 3.

102 Beschlüsse des Stockholmer Ratstreffens, Pkt. 4, lit. (a) bis (c).

zwei beliebige Teilnehmerstaaten anweisen kann, sich einem Vergleichsverfahren zu unterziehen, um sie bei der Lösung einer Streitigkeit zu unterstützen, die sie nicht innerhalb eines angemessenen Zeitraums beizulegen vermochten".[103] Dieser Mechanismus wurde bisher nicht aktiviert.

(4) Friedenserhaltende Operationen

Die Einrichtung friedenserhaltender Operationen im Rahmen der KSZE wurde auf Empfehlung des Prager Ratstreffens auf dem Helsinki-Folgetreffen beschlossen. Solche Operationen "können in Konfliktfällen, die es innerhalb oder zwischen Teilnehmerstaaten gibt, durchgeführt werden, um dazu beizutragen, Frieden und Stabilität zur Unterstützung einer laufenden Bemühung um eine politische Lösung aufrechtzuerhalten".[104] Sie können unter anderem dazu genutzt werden, "Feuereinstellungen zu überwachen und zu deren Aufrechterhaltung beizutragen, Truppenrückzüge zu überwachen, die Aufrechterhaltung von Recht und Ordnung zu unterstützen, humanitäre ... Hilfe zu leisten und Flüchtlinge zu unterstützen";[105] Operationen können ziviles und/oder militärisches Personal umfassen, einen unterschiedlichen Umfang haben und eine Vielfalt von Formen annehmen, einschließlich Beobachter- und Überwachungsmissionen sowie größere Einsätze von Streitkräften.[106] Friedenserhaltende Operationen der KSZE werden unter Berücksichtigung der Verantwortlichkeit der Vereinten Nationen in diesem Bereich und in Übereinstimmung mit den Zielen und Prinzipien der VN-Charta durchgeführt. KSZE-Friedenserhaltung wird insbesondere im Rahmen von Kapitel VIII der Charta der Vereinten Nationen stattfinden.[107] Gemäß den Helsinki-Beschlüssen sind bei friedenserhaltenden Operationen verschiedene Prinzipien zu befolgen. Sie werden keine Zwangsmaßnahmen umfassen; sie erfordern die Zustimmung der direkt betroffenen Parteien; sie werden unparteiisch durchgeführt; sie können nicht als Ersatz für eine Verhandlungslösung betrachtet und müssen daher als zeitlich begrenzt verstanden werden.[108] Ihre Voraussetzungen sind

- eine wirksame und dauerhafte Feuereinstellung;
- die Vereinbarung der notwendigen Memoranda of Understanding[109] mit den betroffenen Parteien und

---

103 Ebd., Pkt. 4, lit. (d).

104 Beschlüsse von Helsinki, Kap. III, Pkt. 17.

105 Ebd., Kap. III, Pkt. 18.

106 Ebd.

107 Ebd., Pkt. 19.

108 Ebd., Pkt. 22-25.

109 Das heißt die Abkommen, die die Rechtsstellung als Grundlage der Tätigkeiten sowie die sonstigen Beziehungen der Missionen zum Aufenthaltsstaat regeln.

– Garantien für die jederzeitige Sicherheit des eingesetzten Personals.[110]

Das Recht, solche Operationen zu beschließen, liegt beim Rat oder beim AHB, der gemäß den Helsinki-Beschlüssen auch die gesamte "politische Kontrolle und Führung" ausübt.[111] Die operative Gesamtleitung hat der Ratsvorsitzende, der von einer beim KVZ eingerichteten Ad-hoc-Gruppe[112] unterstützt wird.[113] Diese Gruppe wird sich in der Regel aus Vertretern des Vorgängers und des Nachfolgers des amtierenden Vorsitzenden, der kontingentstellenden Staaten und solcher Staaten, die andere wesentliche praktische Beiträge zu der Operation leisten, zusammensetzen und die operative Unterstützung der Mission gewährleisten und sie überwachen.[114] Die Ad-hoc-Gruppe wird rund um die Uhr als Kontaktstelle für den Leiter der Mission dienen und ihn, soweit erforderlich, unterstützen.[115]

Die Führung im Einsatzraum (operative Kommandogewalt) obliegt dem Leiter der Mission, der vom Ratsvorsitzenden benannt wird und durch den AHB zu bestätigen ist. Er ist dem Ratsvorsitzenden verantwortlich, konsultiert mit der und wird geführt durch die Ad-hoc-Gruppe.[116] Die Verbindung zwischen der Operation und den übrigen Teilnehmerstaaten der KSZE läuft über den Konsultativausschuß des KVZ. Das KVZ ist auch für die Durchführung all jener Aufgaben in bezug auf friedenserhaltende Operationen zuständig, die ihm vom AHB zugewiesen werden.[117]

Die Vorbereitung einer friedenserhaltenden Operation im Nagorny-Karabach-Konflikt

Bereits im Februar 1992 wurde auf Veranlassung des damaligen amtierenden Ratsvorsitzenden, des tschechoslowakischen Außenministers Jirí Dienstbier, eine Berichterstattermission nach Nagorny-Karabach entsandt. Diese Mission berichtete an die 7. Sitzung des AHB, der am 28. Februar 1992 unter anderem die Teilnehmerstaaten der KSZE aufforderte, ein Embargo über alle Waffen- und Munitionslieferungen an die beteiligten Streitkräfte zu verhängen und darüber dem Konfliktverhütungszentrum zu berichten.[118] Das 8. Treffen des AHB beschloß am 13. März 1992 die Abhaltung eines zusätzlichen Treffens des Rates für den 24. März und empfahl dem Rat, den amtierenden Vorsitzenden der KSZE zu ersuchen, sobald

110 Beschlüsse von Helsinki, Kap. III, Pkt. 30.

111 Ebd., Pkt. 28.

112 Eine solche Gruppe ist bisher nicht etabliert worden.

113 Beschlüsse von Helsinki, Pkt. 39.

114 Ebd., Pkt. 40 und 41.

115 Ebd.

116 Ebd., Pkt. 43-45.

117 Ebd., Pkt. 41 und 42; vgl. auch die zwischenzeitlich erfolgte Einrichtung einer "mission support group" im Rahmen des KVZ.

118 7. Treffen des AHB, Journal No. 2, Anhang 1, Pkt. 4; diese Aufforderung wurde von den Teilnehmerstaaten zumindest hinsichtlich der Meldung unterschiedlich befolgt.

wie möglich eine Konferenz über Nagorny-Karabach unter Schirmherrschaft der KSZE abzuhalten.[119] Die zusätzliche Ratstagung beschloß daraufhin die Abhaltung einer solchen Konferenz, die unter Teilnahme von Armenien, Aserbaidschan, Belarus', der CSFR, Frankreichs, Deutschlands, Italiens, der Russischen Föderation, Schwedens, der Türkei und der USA in Minsk stattfinden sollte; der amtierende Vorsitzende sollte den Vorsitzenden der Konferenz ernennen.[120]

In der Folge wurden Vorbereitungen für eine KSZE-Beobachtermission in Nagorny-Karabach getroffen,[121] der diesbezügliche Beschluß des AHB wurde gefaßt.[122] Die Unvereinbarkeit der Standpunkte der beiden Seiten sowie die Fortsetzung der Kampfhandlungen verhinderte aber bis auf weiteres die Entscheidung über eine Entsendung der geplanten Beobachtermission.[123] Das 17. Treffen des AHB beschloß die Einsetzung einer Ad-hoc-Gruppe zur Vorbereitung der Entsendung einer Voraus-Beobachtergruppe nach Nagorny-Karabach,[124] die schließlich nach Entscheidung der Wiener AHB-Gruppe vom 11. März im Auftrag des amtierenden Vorsitzenden in der Zeit vom 6. bis 24. April 1993 den Einsatzraum bereiste und ihren Bericht dem AHB auf seinem 21. Treffen am 26./27. April 1993 vorlegte. In der Folge wurde beim KVZ ein Planungsstab eingerichtet, um die praktische Durchführung einer möglichen Überwachungsmission in Nagorny-Karabach vorzubereiten, und ein Stufenplan für den Einsatz entwickelt, der vom Abschluß eines Waffenstillstandes an mit der Entsendung einer Vorausgruppe beginnen sollte und in der letzten Stufe eine Überwachungsgruppe von etwa vierhundert Beobachtern und anderem Personal vorsah.

(5) KSZE-Missionen der präventiven Diplomatie

Die Praxis seit dem Helsinki-Folgetreffen und seinen Beschlüssen sowie die nachfolgenden Beschlüsse des Stockholmer Ratstreffens zeigen allerdings, daß sich das Schwergewicht in der Konfliktverhütung von friedenserhaltenden Operationen tra-

---

119 8. Treffen des AHB, Journal, Annex 2, Pkt. 3 und 4.

120 Erstes Zusätzliches Treffen des KSZE-Rates, Zusammenfassung der Schlußfolgerungen, Helsinki, 24. März 1992, Pkt. 9 und 10. Am 7. April 1992 ernannte der amtierende Vorsitzende Prof. M. Rafaelli aus Italien zum Vorsitzenden der geplanten Konferenz.

121 Draft Modalities for CSCE Monitor Mission in connection with the situation in and around Nagorno Karabakh, Prag, 17. April 1992.

122 Das 10. Treffen des AHB beschloß am 29. April 1992 die Bildung einer Mission zur Überwachung der Feuereinstellung unter der Voraussetzung des Zustandekommens einer wirksamen und dauerhaften Feuereinstellung, der Zustimmung und Zusammenarbeit aller betroffenen Parteien und des Abschlusses der erforderlichen Memoranda of Understanding (Stationierungsabkommen), Journal, Anhang 6.

123 Vgl. die Erklärung des Vorsitzenden des AHB, 12. Sitzung des AHB (Journal No. 3, 10.6.1992), die Erklärung der italienischen Delegation als Vorsitzender der geplanten Konferenz über Nagorny-Karabach auf dem 14. Treffen des AHB (Journal No. 9, Juli 1992) und die Erklärung des AHB auf dem 16. Treffen (Journal No. 3, 18.9.1992).

124 Journal No. 2, 6.11.1992.

ditionellen Zuschnitts zunehmend auf solche der "präventiven Diplomatie" verlagert, die allerdings im weiteren Sinne ebenfalls der Friedenserhaltung zuzurechnen sind. Sie entsprechen jedenfalls den Zielsetzungen der Friedenserhaltung, wie sie sowohl semantisch als auch nach den Helsinki-Beschlüssen zu verstehen ist.[125]

Die KSZE-Missionen im früheren Jugoslawien

Die KSZE war bereits beim Aufflammen der Kämpfe in Slowenien und Kroatien durch die Aktivierung der Krisenmechanismen mit der Jugoslawienkrise befaßt worden. Die Ausdehnung der kriegerischen Handlungen auf Bosnien sowie die Gefahr weiterer Eskalation in den potentiellen Krisenregionen Makedonien, Kosovo, Sandschak und Vojvodina führte zur Schaffung von Missionen, in denen sich der Übergang von traditionellen friedenserhaltenden Operationen zu einer KSZE-spezifischen Form der präventiven Diplomatie manifestierte.

Die Plenarsitzung der Helsinki KSZE-Nachfolgekonferenz verabschiedete am 15. April 1992 eine Erklärung, die die Anwendung bewaffneter Gewalt und die Verletzung der territorialen Integrität Bosnien-Herzegowinas verurteilte und die beteiligten Parteien, insbesondere die Führung Serbiens und der Jugoslawischen Volksarmee (JVA) aufrief, die Feindseligkeiten einzustellen. Der AHB stellte zunächst das Bestehen einer Aggression von seiten der JVA und von ihr unterstützter Freischärler fest und erklärte seine Unterstützung für die Friedensbemühungen der EG und der VN in Lissabon.[126] In der Folge beauftragte er den Konsultativausschuß des Konfliktverhütungszentrums mit der Entsendung einer Ermittlungsmission zur Erkundung der militärischen Lage im Kosovo,[127] die vom 27. Mai bis zum 2. Juni 1992 durchgeführt wurde und über den Konsultativausschuß des KVZ an den AHB berichtete. Wenngleich die Mission keine unmittelbare Gefahr einer steigenden militärischen Spannung erkennen konnte, wies sie doch auf die Gefahr eines Konflikts hin, der mit Geduld und gutem Willen zu begegnen sei.

Der AHB setzte nun eine Einsatzgruppe ein, bestehend aus Österreich, Kanada, der CSFR, Deutschland, Griechenland, Portugal (für die EG), der Russischen Föderation, Schweden, der Schweiz, der Türkei und den USA, die unter anderem "Empfehlungen für die Rolle erarbeiten sollte, die künftige kürzer oder länger dauernde KSZE-Missionen bei der Förderung von Frieden, der Abwendung von Gewalt und der Wiederherstellung der Wahrung der Menschenrechte und Grundfreiheiten in Kosovo, Vojvodina und Sandschak sowie bei der Unterstützung der

---

125 In gewisser Hinsicht könnte man die präventive Diplomatie sogar als eher dem Ziel der Friedenserhaltung entsprechend definieren, da sie bereits *vor* einem Friedensbruch zum Einsatz kommt. Traditionelles Peacekeeping würde dagegen zumeist erst *nach* einer bewaffneten Auseinandersetzung zur Stabilisierung von Waffenstillständen durchgeführt.

126 10. Treffen des AHB, Journal, 29.4.1992, Anhang 4.

127 11. Treffen des AHB, Journal No. 3, 20.5.1992, Anhang 2.

Friedenskonferenz der Europäischen Gemeinschaft spielen könnten".[128] Diese Gruppe wurde in der Folge in eine Lenkungsgruppe umgewandelt[129] und die Entsendung der auf dem 12. Treffen vereinbarten Erkundungsmission beschlossen.[130]

Auf Empfehlung dieser Erkundungsmission[131] beschloß der AHB einerseits, in Zusammenarbeit mit den einschlägigen Behörden eine ständige Präsenz in Kosovo, Sandschak und Vojvodina in Form von Langzeitmissionen einzurichten, die folgende Aufgaben haben sollte:

- "Den Dialog zwischen den in Frage kommenden Behörden und den Vertretern der Bevölkerungen und Gemeinschaften[132] in den drei Regionen fördern";
- "Informationen über alle Aspekte sammeln, die Aufschluß über Verletzungen der Menschenrechte und Grundfreiheiten geben, und sich für die Lösung solcher Probleme einsetzen";
- "Kontaktstellen zur Lösung von Problemen, die gegebenenfalls identifiziert werden, einrichten";
- "Bei der Bereitstellung von Informationen über einschlägige Rechtsvorschriften zum Thema Menschenrechte, Minderheitenschutz, freie Medien und demokratische Wahlen Hilfestellung leisten".[133]

Auf demselben Treffen beschloß der AHB andererseits die Ausdehnung der Überwachungsmissionen der Europäischen Gemeinschaften auf die Nachbarländer Serbiens und Montenegros zu unterstützen, das heißt die Ausweitung des Mandats der EG-Beobachtermissionen (European Community Monitoring Missions, ECMM). In diesem Zusammenhang beschloß der AHB weiters, mit den Behörden in Skopje[134] die Möglichkeit der Entsendung ähnlicher Missionen unter der Schirmherrschaft der KSZE zu erkunden.

Darüber hinaus ersuchte der AHB den amtierenden Vorsitzenden, Gespräche aufzunehmen, um Möglichkeiten der Unterstützung entsprechender, an Serbien und Montenegro grenzender Staaten in der Stärkung der durch die Vereinten Nationen verhängten Sanktionen zu prüfen.[135] Schließlich beschloß der AHB, eine

128 12. Treffen des AHB, Journal No. 3, 10.6.1992, Anhang.

129 13. Treffen des AHB, Journal No. 7, 7.7.1992, Anhang. Dabei wurde Portugal als Folge des Wechsels im EG-Vorsitz durch Großbritannien ersetzt.

130 13. Treffen des AHB, Journal No. 7, 7.7.1992, Anhang, Pkt. 7.

131 Report of the CSCE Exploratory Mission to Kosovo, Vojvodina and Sandzak, 2.-8. August 1992, Wien, 9. August 1992.

132 Diese Formulierung reflektiert offensichtlich die im früheren jugoslawischen Verfassungsrecht bestehende Unterscheidung in für Jugoslawien konstitutive "Staatsvölker" ("narodi" wie etwa Serben, Kroaten, Slowenen, Moslems, Makedonier und Montenegriner) und "Volksgruppen" (narodnosti), die nicht originär "jugoslawisch" sind (wie etwa Albaner, Ungarn, Rumänen, Bulgaren, Slowaken usw.).

133 15. Treffen des AHB, Journal No. 2, 14.8.1992, Anhang 1.

134 Das heißt der bis dahin nicht anerkannten und zur KSZE nicht als Teilnehmer zugelassenen Republik Makedonien.

135 15. Treffen des AHB, Journal No. 2, 14.8.1992, Anhang 1.

Beobachtermission zur Untersuchung behaupteter Menschenrechtsverletzungen im früheren Jugoslawien einzurichten; ihre Aufgabe sollte in erster Linie darin bestehen, in enger Zusammenarbeit mit dem Internationalen Komitee vom Roten Kreuz und der Menschenrechtskommission der Vereinten Nationen zu gewährleisten, daß alle angeblichen Internierungsstandorte innerhalb kürzester Zeit inspiziert werden.[136]

In der Folge wurden die Leiter der Missionen ernannt, die zur Vorbereitung der Einrichtung in die Einsatzräume reisten[137] und dem 16. Treffen des AHB vom 16. bis 18. September 1992 berichteten. Auf der Grundlage dieser Berichte beschloß der AHB,

- "sich in geeigneter Weise mittels Langzeitmissionen nach Kosovo, Sandschak und Vojvodina und Erkundungsaktionen der präventiven Diplomatie zu bedienen";
- "eine KSZE-Mission nach Skopje zu entsenden, um ein Übergreifen des Konflikts zu verhindern";
- "sofern es die Umstände rechtfertigen, weitere Berichterstattermissionen zu humanitären Aspekten der Krise zu entsenden, insbesondere im Hinblick auf die dringend notwendige Schließung der Internierungslager, und in Abstimmung mit den Aktivitäten der Vereinten Nationen, des Europarats, des UNHCR und des IKRK."[138]

Hinsichtlich der Langzeitmissionen beauftragte der AHB den Leiter der drei Missionen, "unverzüglich mit der Schaffung der Voraussetzungen für eine ständige Präsenz in den drei Regionen zu beginnen, unverzüglich in Abstimmung mit dem amtierenden Vorsitzenden, auf Empfehlung der Lenkungsgruppe, eine erste Abteilung von Personal zusammenzustellen und sie in die drei Regionen zu entsenden, die Organisation der Missionen, einschließlich der personellen Anforderungen, zu übernehmen, und in Zusammenarbeit mit dem Leiter der (vorherigen) Erkundungsmission in Abstimmung mit den Vertretern der jeweiligen Bevölkerungsgruppen und Gemeinschaften sowie der Minderheiten in den drei Regionen und den Belgrader Behörden einen Entwurf von Modalitäten vorrangig zu erarbeiten". Die Modalitäten sollten Bestimmungen enthalten über:

- Sicherheit und Bewegungsfreiheit der Mitglieder der Missionen;

---

136 Ebd. Diese Mission ist nicht identisch mit der Beobachtermission im Rahmen des humanitären Krisenmechanismus.

137 Der Verfasser nahm an der Fahrt zur Vorbereitung der "Missionen langer Dauer" nach Serbien teil und unterstützte den Leiter der Mission in administrativen/logistischen Fragen. In der Folge entwickelte sich aus den Kontakten zwischen den Missionen und dem KVZ de facto die Unterstützung von KSZE-Missionen (mission support) durch das KVZ, die dann durch die Entscheidungen des Stockholmer Ratstreffens im Dezember 1992 formalisiert wurde.

138 16. Treffen des AHB, Journal No. 3, 18.9.1992, Anhang 1.

- Zugang zu den ortsansässigen Bevölkerungsgruppen, Gemeinschaften, Minderheiten und Behörden;
- Vorrechte und Immunitäten;
- Stationierungsorte;
- Dauer.

Der AHB begrüßte die Fortschritte, die bei der Bildung der Überwachungsmission in Skopje erzielt wurden, erklärte seine Unterstützung für die Bemühungen, Operationen der Mission in nächster Zukunft in Gang zu setzen, und nahm den Bericht der Mission zur Kenntnis. Die Ausarbeitung der Modalitäten wurde der Lenkungsgruppe übertragen. Weiters wurde beschlossen, daß die operative Kontrolle der Mission durch den amtierenden Vorsitzenden unter Mithilfe anderer Mitglieder der KSZE-Troika und mit der praktischen Unterstützung der entsprechenden KSZE-Institutionen aufrechterhalten werden sollte. Zudem beschloß der AHB, die Errichtung von Missionen zur Unterstützung der durch Resolution 757 des Sicherheitsrates verhängten Sanktionen gegen Restjugoslawien zunächst in Bulgarien, Ungarn und Rumänien zu unterstützen. Dazu wurde eine Verbindungsgruppe in Wien eingerichtet. Die Teilnahme an allen Missionen wurde allen KSZE-Teilnehmerstaaten freigestellt, die hiefür Personal nominieren können.

Die Missionen begannen nunmehr mit ihrem Aufbau und parallel dazu bereits mit ihren Operationen. Die Langzeitmissionen rekrutierten ihr Personal vorwiegend aus dem diplomatischen Bereich, wobei Personen bevorzugt wurden, die eine frühere Verwendung im damaligen Jugoslawien gehabt hatten sowie die erforderlichen Kenntnisse der Landessprache und der lokalen Gegebenheiten mitbrachten. Diese Art von Missionen unterscheidet sich damit maßgeblich von traditionellen friedenserhaltenden Operationen, die in erster Linie ein militärisches "Beobachten und Melden" etwa entlang von Waffenstillstandslinien vorsehen, aber praktisch keine Vermittlungstätigkeit auf lokaler Ebene, so daß sie auf Kenntnisse der Landessprache weitgehend verzichten können. Während traditionelle Operationen daher zumeist personalintensiv sind, wurde bei den Langzeitmissionen eher Wert auf die Qualifikation des Personals als auf die Zahl gelegt. Dennoch ist ein bestimmtes Kontingent von Personen erforderlich, um innerhalb der Einsatzräume mit der erforderlichen Frequenz präsent zu sein. Die ersten Planungen sahen zunächst einen Umfang von insgesamt 12 Teilnehmern für diese Missionen vor. Die Stockholmer Ratstagung beschloß dann aber eine substantielle Aufstockung, mit besonderem Schwergewicht auf dem Kosovo.[139]

Die Mission in Skopje begann ebenfalls im September 1992 den Aufbau. Da ihre Aufgabe eher den traditionellen friedenserhaltenden Operationen gleicht, ist

139 Neben den bereits anfänglich errichteten und ständig besetzten Büros in Priština (Kosovo), Novi Pazar (Sandschak) und Subotica (Vojvodina) konnten in Ausführung dieses Beschlusses Anfang Februar 1993 im Kosovo weitere Büros in Prizren und Pec errichtet und besetzt werden.

sie auch ähnlich strukturiert und weist einen höheren Anteil an militärischem Personal auf, wobei aber auch hier Wert auf die erforderlichen Sprachkenntnisse gelegt wird. Dies wurde durch den geringen Umfang der Mission (mit anfänglich bis zu acht Personen) um so nötiger. In der Praxis hat allerdings auch diese Mission eine Vermittlungstätigkeit übernommen, insbesondere hinsichtlich der Stellung der albanischen Volksgruppe.

Während die ersten Teilnehmer an beiden Missionen in den ersten Wochen nach den Beschlüssen des AHB in den Einsatzräumen eintrafen, mußten sie ihre Tätigkeit zunächst praktisch ohne Rechtsgrundlage ausüben, da die Memoranda of Understanding mit den jeweiligen Regierungen der Gaststaaten erst Ende Oktober/Anfang November 1992 unterzeichnet werden konnten.[140] Ferner fehlte es zunächst an ausreichenden Geldmitteln, da die Teilnehmerstaaten in den jährlichen Budgets der KSZE-Institutionen hierfür keine Ansätze vorgesehen hatten. Anfänglich stand daher lediglich ein geringer Betrag zur Einrichtung der Missionen zur Verfügung (start-up fund), mit dem weder die erforderlichen Fahrzeuge noch Fernmeldemittel beschafft werden konnten. Zusätzliche Budgets bedurften erst eines Beschlusses der Teilnehmerstaaten.[141] Trotz dieser erschwerten Bedingungen etablierten sich die Missionen aber in den Einsatzräumen und sandten ihre Berichte, wobei seit Anfang November eine regelmäßige Übermittlung erfolgt. Weiters vermittelten sie wie vorgesehen in Streitfällen.

In der Praxis zeichnet sich als besonders relevanter Aufgabenbereich ab, das Auswachsen an sich geringfügiger Zwischenfälle oder individueller Gewaltanwendung von zumeist unpolitischer Natur zwischen Angehörigen verschiedener Volksgruppen zu Konfrontationen zwischen den Volksgruppen zu verhindern. Hier waren sowohl die Missionen von langer Dauer als auch die Mission in Skopje bisher erfolgreicher, als in der Öffentlichkeit bekannt werden konnte. Eine größere Anzahl lokaler Zwischenfälle konnte durch die Arbeit der Angehörigen dieser Missionen emotionslos auf ihren zumeist unpolitischen Charakter reduziert werden, ohne daß dies groß publik gemacht worden wäre, was wahrscheinlich zur weiteren Eskalation beigetragen hätte.

Die Langzeitmissionen gerieten allerdings zunehmend einerseits in das Spannungsfeld einer Radikalisierung der serbischen Innenpolitik und wurden anderer-

---

140 Beim Abschluß der Memoranda wurde allerdings klargestellt, daß seine Unterzeichnung kein Präjudiz für die Anerkennung der Bundesrepublik Jugoslawien und ihrer Stellung in der KSZE bedeutet.

141 Der entsprechende – zunächst noch provisorische – Beschluß wurde am 14. Oktober gefaßt. Dabei wurde die Fälligkeit der ersten Tranche erst mit dem 1. Dezember 1992 festgelegt, so daß bis zu diesem Zeitpunkt an eine geregelte Finanzierung der Operation nicht zu denken war. Dennoch mußten bereits die laufenden Kosten der Operation im Einsatzraum gedeckt wie auch die notwendigen ersten Einkäufe von Sachgütern (insbesondere Fahrzeugen) bezahlt werden. Dies erforderte entsprechende Improvisationen der durchführenden Stelle, das heißt des KVZ.

seits zum Faustpfand für die Forderung Restjugoslawiens nach Zulassung zur KSZE. Nach Ablauf des ersten Memorandum of Understanding am 28. April 1993 stimmte die Regierung in Belgrad noch einer Verlängerung um zwei Monate zu. Eine weitere Verlängerung wurde aber Ende Juni 1993 verweigert und zwang zum Rückzug der Langzeitmissionen im Juli 1993.

Die Mission in Georgien

Der AHB ersuchte auf seinem 16. Treffen den amtierenden Vorsitzenden um die Ernennung eines persönlichen Vertreters, der aus Anlaß des Südossetienkonflikts eine Erkundungsmission nach Georgien unternehmen und Empfehlungen für eine Mission militärischer Experten zur Überwachung des im Abkommen von Sotschi geschlossenen Waffenstillstandes geben sollte.[142] Auf der Grundlage dieser Empfehlungen beauftragte der AHB auf seinem 17. Treffen den persönlichen Vertreter des amtierenden Vorsitzenden mit der Mission, "unterstützt von zwei diplomatischen Beratern und einer Gruppe von vier Offizieren unter Leitung eines hochrangigen Offiziers, und ersuchte die Mission",

- "unverzüglich Gespräche mit allen am georgisch-ossetischen Konflikt beteiligten Parteien aufzunehmen, um die Ursachen der Spannungen festzustellen und nach Möglichkeit auszuschalten, damit die zivile Ordnung und politische Versöhnung über die unmittelbare Feuereinstellungszone hinaus auf die umliegenden Städte und Dörfer ausgedehnt werden kann";
- "einen Anfang für eine sichtbare Präsenz der KSZE in der Region zu setzen und Kontakte mit den örtlichen Stellen und Vertretern der Bevölkerung aufzunehmen";
- "zur Unterstützung der bestehenden Feuereinstellung Verbindung mit den örtlichen Militärkommandeuren der durch das Abkommen von Sotschi gebildeten dreiseitigen Friedensstreitkräfte aufzunehmen sowie enge Kontakte im angemessenen Ausmaß zu ihnen im Rahmen der Gesamtbemühungen der KSZE herzustellen, regelmäßige Kontakte mit den örtlichen Militärkommandeuren zu unterhalten, Informationen über die militärische Lage zu sammeln, gewaltsame Zwischenfälle zu untersuchen und die örtlichen Kommandeure auf mögliche politische Folgen bestimmter militärischer Aktionen aufmerksam zu machen; sowie die Erweiterung des politischen Rahmens zu ermöglichen, in dem eine dauerhafte politische Versöhnung auf der Grundlage der KSZE-Prinzipien und -Verpflichtungen erzielt werden kann".[143]

Er ersuchte ihn ferner, "zur Schaffung eines Verhandlungsrahmens für die Konfliktparteien in Abchasien beizutragen, um eine dauerhafte Feuereinstellung zu er-

142 16. Treffen des AHB, Journal No. 3, 18.9.1992, Anhang 2.

143 17. Treffen des AHB, Journal No. 2, 6.11.1992, Anhang 2, Pkt. 1.

reichen und eine stabile politische Lösung des Konflikts zu finden".[144] In der Folge beschloß der AHB auf seinem 19. Treffen die Aufstockung der Teilnehmerzahl und verlängerte das Mandat um weitere sechs Monate.[145]

Die Mission in der Republik Moldau

Der amtierende Vorsitzende ernannte im Vorfeld des 15. Treffens des AHB einen persönlichen Verteter mit der Aufgabe, "den Appell an die KSZE, einen Beitrag zur Regelung des Konflikts in den Gebieten am linken Dnjestr-Ufer in der Republik Moldau zu leisten, zu prüfen und dem amtierenden Vorsitzenden nach Konsultationen mit den betroffenen Parteien, insbesondere in der Republik Moldau, geeignete Vorschläge darüber zu unterbreiten, wie die KSZE in geeignetster Weise Hilfestellung leisten kann".[146] Der persönliche Verteter des amtierenden Vorsitzenden berichtete in der Folge an den AHB, der auf seinem 19. Treffen die Einsetzung einer KSZE-Mission beschloß. Ihre Aufgabe ist es, die Herbeiführung einer dauerhaften, umfassenden politischen Lösung des Konflikts zu fördern. Ihre Ziele sind: "die Konsolidierung der Unabhängigkeit und Souveränität der Republik Moldau in ihren gegenwärtigen Grenzen und die Verstärkung ihrer territorialen Integrität sowie eine Übereinkunft über einen Sonderstatus der Trans-Dnjestr-Region; eine Vereinbarung über den Rückzug ausländischer Truppen; die wirksame Einhaltung internationaler Verpflichtungen bezüglich der Menschen- und Minderheitenrechte; und die Unterstützung bei der Überwachung der Verwirklichung von Vereinbarungen für eine dauerhafte politische Lösung".[147] Am 20. April 1993 ernannte der amtierende Vorsitzende den Leiter der Mission, die zunächst acht Personen umfassen sollte, und entsandte ihn in den Einsatzraum.

Die Mission in Estland

Der AHB befaßte sich auf seinem 17. Treffen mit der Situation in Estland und ersuchte den amtierenden Vorsitzenden um die Ernennung eines persönlichen Vertreters, um die Möglichkeiten einer KSZE-Mission in Estland zu erkunden.[148] Er beschloß dann auf seinem 18. Treffen die Einsetzung einer Mission in Estland, "um die Integration und ein besseres Verständnis unter den Gemeinschaften in Estland weiter zu fördern",[149] und legte auf dem 19. Treffen die Rahmenbedingungen fest. Die Mission soll "Stabilität, Dialog und Verständigung zwischen den

144 Ebd., Pkt. 2.

145 19. Treffen des AHB, Journal No. 3, 4.2.1993, Anhang 4.

146 15. Treffen des AHB, Journal No. 2, 14.8.1992.

147 19. Treffen des AHB, Journal No. 3, 4.2.1993, Anhang 3.

148 17. Treffen des AHB, Journal No. 2, 6.11.1992.

149 18. Treffen des AHB, Journal No. 3, 13.12.1992, Anhang 2.

Volksgruppen fördern und zu diesem Zweck unter anderem Kontakte mit den zuständigen Behörden und mit einschlägigen nichtstaatlichen Institutionen und Organisationen, darunter mit politischen Parteien, Gewerkschaften und Massenmedien, sowohl auf landesweiter als auch auf örtlicher Ebene herstellen und aufrechterhalten, Informationen zusammentragen und als Kontaktstelle für Informationen, technische Unterstützung und Beratung über Angelegenheiten dienen, die den Status der Volksgruppen in Estland sowie die Rechte und Pflichten ihrer Angehörigen betreffen". Die Mission wird anfänglich sechs Personen umfassen und mit dem BDIMR kooperieren. Sie arbeitet auf dem gesamten Staatsgebiet, der Schwerpunkt ihrer Tätigkeit wird jedoch in den nördlichen und nordöstlichen Landesteilen liegen.[150]

Die Entsendung eines persönlichen Vertreters nach Tadschikistan

Der AHB ersuchte auf seinem 19. Treffen den amtierenden Vorsitzenden zur "Entsendung eines persönlichen Vertreters, in Begleitung eines Angehörigen des BDIMR, nach Tadschikistan, um die Situation im Land zu untersuchen. Dieser Besuch sollte in Abstimmung mit den zuständigen Vertretern der Vereinten Nationen erfolgen und die laufenden Bemühungen der Vereinten Nationen in Tadschikistan berücksichtigen". Der persönliche Vertreter sollte der Wiener AHB-Gruppe Bericht über seine Erkenntnisse erstatten.[151]

Die Unterstützung der von den Vereinten Nationen verhängten Sanktionen

Die Missionen zur Unterstützung der von den Vereinten Nationen gegen Restjugoslawien verhängten Sanktionen unterscheiden sich in mehrfacher Hinsicht von den übrigen Operationen im Rahmen der KSZE. Einerseits erstrecken sie sich über mehrere Staaten, andererseits ist ihre Aufgabe nicht mehr der "kooperativen Sicherheit" zuzuordnen, sondern enthält eine ausdrücklich konfrontative Zielsetzung, da die Wirtschaftssanktionen in Ausübung der Zwangsgewalt des Sicherheitsrates im Rahmen der kollektiven Sicherheit der Vereinten Nationen verhängt worden sind. Ziel der Missionen ist es, die Nachbarstaaten Serbiens und Montenegros bei der Durchsetzung der Wirtschaftssanktionen zu unterstützen. Die eigentlichen Missionen bestehen aus Zollexperten verschiedener KSZE-Staaten. Sie unterstützen einerseits die Arbeit der lokalen Grenz- und Zollbehörden, bei denen sie zumeist auch stationiert sind. Andererseits wurden die Teilnehmerstaaten ersucht, Kontaktpunkte in ihren jeweiligen zentralen Zoll- und/oder Finanzstrafbehörden einzurichten, die von den Missionen im Verdachtsfall angerufen werden

150 19. Treffen des AHB, Journal No. 2, 3.2.1993, Anhang 1.
151 19. Treffen des AHB, Journal No. 3, 4.2.1993.

und zur Klärung von Zweifelsfällen beitragen können. Die Liste dieser Kontaktpunkte wird vom Konfliktverhütungszentrum evident gehalten. Zur verbesserten Koordination der Überwachung wurde vom AHB auf Vorschlag der Europäischen Gemeinschaften die Errichtung eines Sanktionskoordinators beschlossen, der seinen Sitz in Brüssel hat und im Zusammenwirken mit den Europäischen Gemeinschaften die Überwachung der Missionen steuert und ihr Zusammenspiel vor Ort mit der Kommunikationszentrale bei der EG-Kommission[152] koordiniert sowie Verbindung mit und zwischen den Staaten in der Region über die Durchführung der Sanktionen hält.[153]

III. Das Verhältnis der KSZE zu anderen sicherheitspolitischen Institutionen und Organisationen in Europa

1. Die Rolle der KSZE als regionale Abmachung gemäß Kapitel VIII der Charta der Vereinten Nationen

Das Verhältnis der KSZE zu den Vereinten Nationen wurde durch die Erklärung als "regionale Abmachung" gemäß Kapitel VIII der Charta der Vereinten Nationen in den Beschlüssen von Helsinki auf die Grundlage der Charta gestellt.

a. Charakteristik regionaler Abmachungen

Regionale Abmachungen stehen in einem gewissen Widerspruch zum grundsätzlich universalistischen Prinzip der Charta der Vereinten Nationen. Ihre Schaffung geht insbesondere auf Bestrebungen der lateinamerikanischen Staaten bei der Gründungskonferenz der Vereinten Nationen in San Francisco 1945 zurück, ihr bereits entwickeltes regionales Sicherheitssystem zu erhalten.[154] Der Kompromiß zwischen Universalismus und Regionalismus bestand schließlich darin, daß die VN-Charta im Gegensatz zu ihrer sonst universellen Konzeption in Kapitel VIII die Konzepte der Dezentralisation und des Regionalismus anerkannte, "aber nur auf den Gebieten der Friedenserhaltung und der friedlichen Streitbeilegung".[155] Gemäß Artikel 52 Absatz 1 der Charta der Vereinten Nationen schließt sie

> "das Bestehen regionaler Abmachungen oder Einrichtungen zur Behandlung derjenigen die Wahrung des Weltfriedens und der internationalen Sicherheit betreffenden Angelegenheiten nicht aus, bei denen Maßnahmen regionaler Art angebracht sind; Voraussetzung hierfür ist, daß diese Abmachungen oder Einrichtungen und ihr Wirken mit den Zielen und Grundsätzen der Vereinten Nationen vereinbar sind."

---

152 Sanctions Assistance Mission Communications, SAMCOMM.

153 19. Treffen des AHB, Journal No. 3, Anhang 1.

154 Waldemar *Hummer*/Michael *Schweitzer*, Kommentar zu Artikel 52 der VN-Charta, in: *Simma u.a.*, Charta, S. 636-676 (641).

155 Ebd.

Gemäß Absatz 2 desselben Artikels werden die

> "Mitglieder der Vereinten Nationen, die solche Abmachungen treffen oder solche Einrichtungen schaffen, ... sich nach besten Kräften bemühen, durch Inanspruchnahme dieser Abmachungen oder Einrichtungen örtlich begrenzte Streitigkeiten friedlich beizulegen, bevor sie den Sicherheitsrat damit befassen."

"Regional" bezieht sich dabei nicht auf eine geographische Abgrenzung oder Nachbarschaft,[156] sondern vorrangig auf die Teilnahme oder Mitgliedschaft in einer solchen Abmachung oder Einrichtung sowie vor allem auf ihren Zweck.[157] Der Zweck regionaler Abmachungen gemäß Kapitel VIII besteht darin, lokal und unter Ausnutzung größerer Sachnähe, Legitimität und Solidarität eine Ausweitung eines Konflikts – infolge der Intervention von an sich unbeteiligten Dritten – nach Möglichkeit zu vermeiden. Dies setzt zwar eine gewisse territoriale Verbundenheit der Mitglieder voraus, kann aber nicht im Sinne einer verpflichtenden Vizinität verstanden werden. "Regional" darf auch nicht so gedeutet werden, daß die Abmachung oder Einrichtung generell befugt wäre, in der "Region" für Friedenserhaltung zu sorgen, sondern limitiert diese Funktion auf die Beziehung *zwischen ihren Teilnehmern oder Mitgliedern*. Dritte können davon nicht erfaßt werden. Maßnahmen gegen sie können nur aufgrund anderer Bestimmungen der Charta oder als Ausfluß des Rechts auf Selbstverteidigung getroffen werden. Gelegentliche Versuche regionaler Organisationen, Zwangsmaßnahmen gegenüber dritten Staaten zu ergreifen,[158] beruhten auf einer unrichtigen Auslegung des Begriffs der "Regionalität", da es für die Zulässigkeit solcher Maßnahmen nicht darauf ankommt, ob sich ein Staat in einer "Region" befindet, sondern ob er Teilnehmer oder Mitglied dieser Abmachung oder Einrichtung ist.

Regionale sicherheitspolitische Abmachungen/Einrichtungen nach Kapitel VIII sind von regionalen kollektiven Selbstverteidigungsbündnissen abzugrenzen.[159] Formal haben letztere in Kapitel VII (Artikel 51) ihre Rechtsgrundlage.[160] Funktional dienen sie der kollektiven Verteidigung *nach außen*, gegen einen oder meh-

---

156 "Vizinität", vgl. *Hummer/Schweitzer*, Artikel 52, S. 643f.

157 Vgl. hierzu und zum folgenden ebd., S. 648f.

158 Wie etwa durch die Arabische Liga gegen Israel im Palästinakonflikt 1948, durch die OAS gegenüber Kuba im Jahre 1962 oder durch die OAU im Shaba-Konflikt 1977/78; alle Beispiele nach ebd., S. 648.

159 Vgl. ebd., S. 650; hier werden beispielhaft NATO, Warschauer Pakt, WEU und SEATO als Selbstverteidigungsbündnisse angeführt (unter Zitierung früherer Arbeiten von *Krezdorn*, Les Nations Unies et les Accords Régionaux, 1954, und *Pernice*, Die Sicherung des Weltfriedens durch regionale Organisationen und die Vereinten Nationen. Eine Untersuchung über die Kompetenzverteilung nach Kap. VIII der VN-Charta, 1972). Obgleich die WEU teilweise in der Literatur als "regionale Abmachung" im Sinne des Kap. VIII bezeichnet wird (vgl. *Pernice*, zitiert bei *Hummer/Schweitzer*, Artikel 52), hat sie bisher weder Verbindung mit den Vereinten Nationen aufgenommen noch über ihre Aktivitäten an den Sicherheitsrat berichtet.

160 Vgl. den Kommentar von Albrecht *Randelzhofer* zu Artikel 51, in: *Simma u.a.*, Charta, S. 617-635 (632).

rere dritte Angreifer, die nicht zum System gehören. Demgegenüber dienen regionale Abmachungen/Einrichtungen im Sinne des Kapitels VIII der (gegenseitigen) kollektiven Sicherheit *nach innen.*[161]

Allerdings wird diese Bezugnahme auf die regionale "kollektive Sicherheit" durch die Bestimmung des Artikels 52 Absatz 2 eingeschränkt, daß örtlich begrenzte Streitigkeiten mit "friedlichen Mitteln" beizulegen sind. Darunter sind, wie sich im Rekurs auf Kapitel VI[162] in Artikel 52 Absatz 4 ergibt, insbesondere folgende Techniken der friedlichen Streitbeilegung zu verstehen: Verhandlungen, Untersuchungen, Vermittlung, Vergleich, Schiedsspruch, gerichtliche Entscheidung usw.[163] Diese Aufzählung ist aber nicht erschöpfend und schließt andere Mittel gewaltloser Lösungen nicht aus.[164]

Zu Zwangsmaßnahmen kollektiver Sicherheit ermächtigt die Charta nur in einem äußerst eingeschränkten Umfang. Artikel 53 Absatz 1 gibt einerseits dem Sicherheitsrat die Ermächtigung, regionale Abmachungen oder Einrichtungen zur Durchführung von Zwangsmaßnahmen unter seiner Autorität in Anspruch zu nehmen. Er bestimmt andererseits ausdrücklich: "Ohne Ermächtigung des Sicherheitsrats dürfen Zwangsmaßnahmen aufgrund regionaler Abmachungen oder seitens regionaler Einrichtungen nicht ergriffen werden".[165]

Damit fehlt regionalen Abmachungen/Einrichtungen die Kompetenz, von sich aus Zwangsmaßnahmen etwa im Rahmen kollektiver Sicherheit zu ergreifen. Die Charta schließt zwar nicht aus, daß sie berechtigt seien oder sich in ihrer Charta das Ziel setzen können, Zwangsmaßnahmen anzuwenden.[166] Sie bindet solche Maßnahmen aber ausdrücklich an eine Ermächtigung des Sicherheitsrates. Damit ist ausschließlich der Sicherheitsrat zu ihrer Durchführung befugt. Er – und nur er – darf Staaten (d.h. auch regionale Organisationen) ermächtigen, derartige Zwangsmaßnahmen zu ergreifen.[167]

---

161 So *Hummer/Schweitzer*, Artikel 52, S. 650. Allerdings wird auch festgestellt, daß es in der Praxis zur Vermischung kommt und daß regionale Einrichtungen wie die OAS, die OAU oder die Arabische Liga auch die Funktion eines Systems kollektiver Selbstverteidigung gemäß Artikel 51 wahrnehmen.

162 So ebd., S. 652.

163 Vgl. Artikel 33 Absatz 1 der Charta der Vereinten Nationen.

164 Vgl. *Neuhold*, Internationale Konflikte, S. 357ff.

165 Die einzige Ausnahme, die Artikel 53 Absatz 1 vorsieht, richtet sich gegen einen Feindstaat (d.h. im Sinne des Artikels 53 Absatz 2 der VN-Charta gegen jeden Staat, der während des Zweiten Weltkriegs Feind eines Unterzeichners dieser Charta war), soweit sie in Artikel 107 oder in regionalen, gegen die Wiederaufnahme der Angriffspolitik eines solchen Staates gerichteten Abmachungen vorgesehen ist. Diese Bestimmung wird heute als obsolet angesehen.

166 Die Ergreifung von Zwangsmaßnahmen stellt damit zwar eine Möglichkeit dar, *die aber nicht in der Satzung einer regionalen Einrichtung vorgesehen sein muß*. Sie ist auch nicht konstitutiv für eine solche regionale Abmachung/Einrichtung.

167 Georg *Ress*, Kommentar zu Artikel 53 der VN-Charta, in: *Simma u.a.*, Charta, S. 681.

Auch hierin liegt ein wesentlicher Unterschied zu regionalen Verteidigungsbündnissen, die zur Ausübung ihrer Funktion keinerlei weitere Sanktionierung durch den Sicherheitsrat benötigen. Die Ausübung der Selbstverteidigung wird durch Artikel 51 als "Naturrecht" anerkannt; sie kann lediglich durch einen Beschluß der Sicherheitsrates beschränkt werden.

Somit liegt die wesentliche Aufgabe regionaler Abmachungen/Einrichtungen in der *kooperativen Sicherheit.* Sie betonen die friedliche Streitbeilegung und die Maßnahmen der Friedenserhaltung, und damit auch der präventiven Sicherheitspolitik. Dagegen liegt die Zuständigkeit für kollektive Sicherheit im eigentlichen Sinne beim Sicherheitsrat, der allein über Zwangsmaßnahmen entscheidet. Soweit regionale Abmachungen/Einrichtungen Elemente der kollektiven Sicherheit enthalten, sind auch diese dem Sicherheitsrat untergeordnet und können jedenfalls nicht ohne seine Zustimmung angewendet werden.

b. Bewertung der KSZE als regionale Abmachung

Die Entwicklung der Institutionen wie auch die bisher erkennbare Praxis der KSZE entsprechen zunehmend den Kriterien einer regionalen Abmachung im Sinne des Kapitels VIII der VN-Charta. Zum einen umfaßt sie tatsächlich alle Staaten einer Region, aber auch Staaten, die für die Sicherheit in dieser Region von Relevanz sind. Dies betrifft zunächst die bereits erwähnte Teilnahme von USA und Kanada seit Beginn der KSZE, aber auch die Teilnahme der nichteuropäischen Staaten auf dem Gebiet der ehemaligen Sowjetunion. Einerseits gehörten diese Gebiete durch ihre damalige Zugehörigkeit zur Sowjetunion von Anfang an zum Anwendungsbereich der Schlußakte von Helsinki (mit Ausnahme der militärischen Bestimmungen). Es wurde also die KSZE durch die Teilnahme dieser Staaten nicht "erweitert"; sie wäre vielmehr im Gegenteil durch die Nichtteilnahme dieser Staaten verkleinert worden, und es wäre sinnwidrig gewesen, sie aus Anlaß der Unbhängigkeit aus ihren Verpflichtungen, etwa im humanitären Bereich, zu entlassen. Andererseits besteht in einigen dieser Gebiete ein Konfliktpotential, das auf Europa überschlagen kann. Es erschiene daher verfehlt, dieses Potential auszugrenzen und zu ignorieren, anstatt es in den Anwendungsbereich der Mechanismen zur Konfliktverhütung und Friedenserhaltung einzubeziehen.[168]

---

168 Zwar erscheint die Kritik berechtigt, daß die Teilnahme einiger dieser Staaten ein Problem für die "europäische Sicherheitskultur" bedeutet und daß sich durch ihre Teilnahme der Grad der insgesamt vorhandenen Werteübereinstimmung und Werteverwirklichung in der KSZE verringert hat; vgl. Michael *Staack*, Eine europäische Sicherheitskultur: Aussichten für eine regionalspezifische Normen- und Regimebildung, S. 187-208 in diesem Band. Dieses Argument hätte aber auch gegenüber der Teilnahme der Sowjetunion und ihrer Verbündeten in der Frühphase der KSZE ins Treffen geführt werden können, die damals ebenfalls nicht die westliche Wertgrundlage teilten. Weiters zeigt die Inanspruchnahme des AHB-Krisenmechanismus durch Aserbaidschan und die darauf in Gang gesetzte Vorbereitung einer friedenserhaltenden Opera-

Zum anderen entsteht in der KSZE durch die Entwicklung der Krisenmechanismen wie auch der Vorkehrungen zur friedlichen Streitbeilegung, zur Durchführung friedenserhaltender Operationen und der präventiven Diplomatie zunehmend ein Instrumentarium, das dem Grundauftrag regionaler Abmachungen zur Friedenserhaltung und friedlichen Streitbeilegung voll entspricht. Hinzu tritt in letzter Zeit überdies zumindest in Teilbereichen auch die Mitwirkung an der Durchsetzung von Zwangsmaßnahmen des Sicherheitsrates gegenüber Restjugoslawien,[169] was ebenfalls der Rolle einer regionalen Abmachung entspricht.[170] Diese Einschätzung wird auch nicht dadurch in Frage gestellt, daß im Rahmen der KSZE selbst keine eigentlichen Maßnahmen kollektiver Sicherheit und Zwangsdurchsetzung vorgesehen sind. Wie ausgeführt, ist dieses Element für eine regionale Abmachung zwar möglich, aber nicht konstitutiv zwingend.

Auch die bisherige Praxis bestätigt die Rolle der KSZE als regionale Abmachung. Sie hat dort Erfolge zu verzeichnen, wo ihre Instrumente – entsprechend dem Aufgabengebiet einer regionalen Abmachung – rechtzeitig eingesetzt wurden, um einen potentiellen Konflikt an der untersten Eskalationsstufe zu verhüten. Insbesondere die Missionen der präventiven Diplomatie dürften in der Verhinderung einer möglichen Eskalation des Kosovo-Konflikts nach Aussage interessierter Parteien bisher durchaus erfolgreich agiert haben.[171]

Institutionen und Mechanismen wie auch die bisherige Praxis im Rahmen der KSZE entsprechen damit dem Bild einer grundsätzlich kooperativen und präventiven regionalen Abmachung im Sinne des Kapitels VIII geradezu archetypisch.[172] Maßnahmen im Rahmen der KSZE waren dann einigermaßen erfolgreich, wenn sie sich an diesem Leitbild orientierten. Sie mußten freilich fast zwangsweise

tion in Nagorny-Karabach, daß die Teilnahme dieser Staaten in der KSZE durchaus die Möglichkeit eröffnet, potentielle Krisenherde mit den Instrumenten der KSZE zu entschärfen.

169 Eine solche konfrontative Rolle ist auf die Dauer nur bedingt mit der Funktion einer "kooperativen" Sicherheitsstruktur vereinbar und müßte früher oder später zu Problemen führen. In diesem Sinne wurde etwa die Verweigerung der weiteren Zusammenarbeit bei den Langzeitmissionen von der Seite Restjugoslawiens mit der konfrontativen Haltung der KSZE begründet, Jugoslawien die Teilnahme an der KSZE bis auf weiteres nicht zu ermöglichen.

170 Hier war die KSZE allerdings die erste europäische Institution, die an der Durchsetzung der Maßnahmen mitwirkte. Ihre Missionen waren bereits im Einsatz, als sich die Seeblockade Jugoslawiens durch Kriegsschiffe der NATO und der WEU noch auf ein passives "Beobachten und Melden" beschränken mußte, ehe sie der Sicherheitsrat durch Resolution 787 am 16. November 1992 ermächtigte, auch Zwangsmaßnahmen gegen Blockadebrecher zu ergreifen.

171 Es ist naturgemäß schwierig, den Nichteintritt eines Ereignisses, etwa einer Eskalation in einem Konflikt, auf bestimmte Aktionen zurückzuführen. Es scheint aber, daß die Präsenz der KSZE-Missionen an bestimmten Orten im Kosovo etwa anläßlich der Auseinandersetzungen um den albanischen Schulunterricht im Herbst 1992 den Kontrahenten Zurückhaltung auferlegt hat. Wie ein Beobachter anführte, "ist dort, wo die KSZE-Vertreter waren, nicht geschossen worden, und dort, wo sie nicht waren, wurde geschossen".

172 Dies betrifft letztlich bereits die allerersten sicherheitspolitischen Schritte im Rahmen der KSZE bei der Schaffung vertrauensbildender Maßnahmen, die ebenfalls dem Ziel der Konfliktverhütung durch Kooperation dienen sollten.

erfolglos bleiben, wenn sie in einer Situation angewendet wurden, die über die Möglichkeit der Konfliktverhütung bereits hinauseskaliert war, wie etwa der Krieg in Bosnien-Herzegowina.

c. Beobachterstatus für die KSZE und Institutionalisierung der Zusammenarbeit mit den Vereinten Nationen

In seinem Bericht "Agenda for Peace" wies der Generalsekretär der Vereinten Nationen auf die wichtige Rolle regionaler Abmachungen und Organisationen im Bereich der Frühwarnung hin und lud solche Organisationen ein, die noch nicht um einen Beobachterstatus bei den Vereinten Nationen nachgesucht hatten, dies zu tun und durch entsprechende Vereinbarungen mit den Sicherheitsmechanismen der VN verbunden zu werden.[173] Daraufhin ersuchten die Minister auf dem Ratstreffen in Stockholm den AHB, die praktischen Auswirkungen der in Helsinki erfolgten Erklärung der KSZE als regionale Abmachung im Sinne von Kapitel VIII der Charta der Vereinten Nationen zu untersuchen, die Einladung des VN-Generalsekretärs zu prüfen und den Beobachterstatus zu beantragen.[174] Die Minister betonten, daß der amtierende Vorsitzende enge Kontakte mit den Vereinten Nationen halten sollte, um den regelmäßigen Informationsaustausch, die Zusammenarbeit und die Koordinierung zu fördern sowie Doppelarbeit zu vermeiden, und wiesen die amtierende Vorsitzende des AHB an, unverzüglich regelmäßige Kontakte mit dem VN-Generalsekretär aufzunehmen, um zu gewährleisten, daß sowohl die Vereinten Nationen als auch die KSZE-Teilnehmerstaaten über die jeweiligen Aktivitäten auf dem laufenden gehalten werden, insbesondere im Bereich der Frühwarnung, der Konfliktverhütung, der Bewältigung und Lösung von Konflikten sowie der Förderung demokratischer Werte und Menschenrechte.

Unter Bezug auf eine entsprechende Resolution der Generalversammlung der Vereinten Nationen[175] wurde schließlich am 26. Mai 1993 in einem Briefwechsel zwischen dem Generalsekretär der Vereinten Nationen und der amtierenden Vorsitzenden der KSZE der Rahmen für die Zusammenarbeit und Koordination zwischen den Vereinten Nationen und der KSZE abgesteckt. Demzufolge werden der Generalsekretär der Vereinten Nationen und der amtierende Vorsitzende und ihre jeweiligen Vertreter regelmäßig Konsultationen abhalten, insbesondere über die Zusammenarbeit und Koordination von Tätigkeiten von gemeinsamem Interesse. Die ständige Vertretung bei den Vereinten Nationen jenes KSZE-Teilnehmerstaates, der den amtierenden Vorsitzenden stellt, wird als Kontaktpunkt und als Repräsentant des amtierenden Vorsitzenden in New York und in Genf agieren.

---

173 Boutros *Boutros-Ghali*, An Agenda for Peace, New York 1992, Pkt. 27.

174 Beschlüsse des Stockholmer Ratstreffens, Pkt. 8.

175 Resolution No. XXXXVII/10, 2.12.1992.

Die KSZE-Delegation jenes KSZE-Teilnehmerstaates, der den amtierenden Vorsitzenden stellt, sowie der KSZE-Generalsekretär und andere KSZE-Institutionen in Wien werden als Kontaktpunkte in Wien dienen.

> "Kontakte werden stattfinden in Form von Konsultation über die Vorbereitung, Einleitung und Durchführung von Erkundungs- und anderen Missionen, des Austausches von Informationen zwischen den Vertretern der Vereinten Nationen und der KSZE im Einsatzraum über die Lage in ihren Verantwortungsbereichen und von anderen bedeutsamen Informationen, einschließlich der Bewegungen und anderen Tätigkeiten der Missionen; weitere Zusammenarbeit kann den Austausch von Informationen bei der Erstellung von Berichten der Missionen, die Untersuchung der Möglichkeit gemeinsamer Berichte und der Möglichkeit verschiedener Art der wechselseitigen Unterstützung im Einsatzraum und die Untersuchung der Möglichkeit gemeinsamer Missionen abdecken".[176]

Im Briefwechsel wird ausdrücklich festgestellt, daß die beschriebenen Formen der Zusammenarbeit auch auf friedenserhaltende Operationen anwendbar seien und daß die KSZE bei der Planung und Durchführung friedenserhaltender Operationen, soweit angemessen, auf die technische Hilfe und Beratung der VN zurückgreifen könne.

Mit der Erklärung der KSZE zur regionalen Abmachung im Sinne des Kapitels VIII der Charta der Vereinten Nationen durch die Helsinki-Beschlüsse war somit ein Rahmen geschaffen worden, der den Status der KSZE definierte, aber auch bereits einzelne Aufgaben vorgab.[177] Die Vereinbarungen vom 26. Mai eröffnen darüber hinaus auch die Möglichkeit der Zusammenarbeit in konkreten Bereichen, insbesondere bei der Friedenserhaltung. Ihre Inhalte entsprechen im wesentlichen den Vorstellungen über die Rolle regionaler Abmachungen und Organisationen, wie sie in den Punkten 64 und 65 der "Agenda for Peace" dargelegt sind.

2. Das Verhältnis der KSZE zu den europäischen Allianzen (NATO und WEU)

Das Verhältnis der KSZE zu den bestehenden Allianzen in Europa (NATO und WEU) beruht demgegenüber nicht auf einer ähnlich etablierten Grundlage. Sowohl hinsichtlich der Rechtsgrundlage als auch hinsichtlich der Aufgaben besteht ein wesentlicher Unterschied zwischen regionalen Abkommen im Sinne des Kapitels VIII einerseits und (regionalen wie auch anderen) Allianzen andererseits, die vorwiegend der kollektiven Selbstverteidigung dienen. NATO wie auch WEU fallen unzweifelhaft in die zweite Kategorie. Sowohl Artikel 5 des Nordatlantikvertrages vom 4. April 1949 als auch Artikel V des Brüsseler Vertrages vom 17. März

---

176 Übersetzung durch den Verfasser.

177 Wie etwa die Berichtspflicht an den Sicherheitsrat gemäß Artikel 54 der VN-Charta.

1948 beziehen sich ausdrücklich auf das Recht zur Selbstverteidigung gemäß Artikel 51 der Charta der Vereinten Nationen.

Die unterschiedliche Grundlage schließt aber eine mögliche Zusammenarbeit und sogar die Bildung von Grauzonen der Überlappung und der Doppelgleisigkeit zwischen der KSZE und den genannten Allianzen nicht zwangsweise aus.

a. NATO und WEU als mögliche "Teilmengen" der KSZE?

Eine Überschneidung könnte sich daraus ergeben, daß beide Verträge durchaus Elemente der "kooperativen Sicherheit" enthalten. So verpflichtet etwa Artikel 1 des Nordatlantikvertrages die Mitglieder zur friedlichen Streitbeilegung und zur Enthaltung der Androhung oder Anwendung von Gewalt. Artikel 2 verpflichtet sie zur Entwicklung friedlicher und freundschaftlicher Beziehungen, einschließlich der Beseitigung von Konflikten in ihren internationalen Wirtschaftsbeziehungen. In ähnlicher Weise verpflichten sich die Mitglieder der WEU in Artikel X des Brüsseler Vertrages, Streitigkeiten friedlich beizulegen und sie dem Internationalen Gerichtshof (IGH) zu unterbreiten, sofern sie unter Artikel 36 Absatz 2 des Statuts des IGH fallen.

Diese kooperativen Elemente betreffen aber nur die Beziehungen der Mitglieder dieser Organisationen untereinander[178] und schließen damit eine gesamteuropäische Funktion dieser Allianzen aus, solange ihre Mitgliedschaft eng gefaßt bleibt. Da aber alle Mitglieder dieser Allianzen auch Teilnehmer der KSZE sind, könnte man die Allianzen hinsichtlich ihrer "kooperativen" Elemente immerhin als Teilmengen der kooperativen Sicherheit im Rahmen der KSZE sehen. Selbst diese Sicht erscheint aber problematisch. Die Allianzen weisen nämlich keinerlei Beziehungen zu den Vereinten Nationen im Sinne des Kapitels VIII auf,[179] so daß sie ihre "kooperative" Funktion gegenüber den Vereinten Nationen allenfalls durch die KSZE mediatisiert wahrnehmen könnten. Mangels eines entsprechenden Abkommens mit der KSZE fehlt aber derzeit die Grundlage für solch eine Rolle.

Trotz der bestehenden "kooperativen" Elemente und der Überschneidung im Kreis der Mitglieder/Teilnehmer können die beiden Allianzen daher derzeit weder für sich als "regionale Organisationen" noch auch als Teilmengen einer regio-

178 Auch diese Eigenschaft ist nur beschränkt gegeben. So erklärte etwa der damalige amerikanische Außenminister John Foster *Dulles* im Jahre 1956, daß die NATO keine Zuständigkeit zur Streitbeilegung unter den Mitgliedern habe und daher keine regionale Organisation im Sinne der Charta der Vereinten Nationen sei; Department of State Bulletin, (1956) 884, S. 925, zitiert nach *Hummer/Schweitzer*, Artikel 52, S. 650 (Anm. 112).

179 Allerdings können die Allianzen auf der Grundlage des Artikels 48 der Charta der VN Aufgaben bei der Durchsetzung von Zwangsmaßnahmen übernehmen, die vom Sicherheitsrat verhängt worden sind. Gemäß dieser Bestimmung werden Beschlüsse des Sicherheitsrates zur Wahrung des Weltfriedens "von den Mitgliedern der Vereinten Nationen unmittelbar sowie durch Maßnahmen in den geeigneten internationalen Einrichtungen durchgeführt, deren Mitglieder sie sind" (Abs. 2); die letztere Aussage bezieht sich auch auf militärische Allianzen.

nalen Abmachung verstanden werden. Ihre primäre Funktion ist nach wie vor die kollektive Selbstverteidigung im Sinne des Artikels 51[180] der Charta der Vereinten Nationen, was wiederum eine Funktion als Subsystem der KSZE funktional ausschließen müßte.

b. Friedenserhaltende Operationen

Derzeit wird vorwiegend über die Mitwirkung der Allianzen an friedenserhaltenden Operationen im Rahmen der KSZE debattiert. So erklärte der Nordatlantikrat auf seiner Ministertagung am 4. Juni 1992, das Bündnis besitze

> "die Fähigkeit, zu wirksamen Aktionen der KSZE entsprechend ihrer neuen und größeren Verantwortung für Krisenmanagement und die friedliche Beilegung von Streitigkeiten beizutragen. In diesem Zusammenhang sind wir bereit, von Fall zu Fall, in Übereinstimmung mit unseren eigenen Verfahren, friedenserhaltende Aktivitäten unter der Verantwortung der KSZE einschließlich der Bereitstellung von Ressourcen und Fachwissen des Bündnisses zu unterstützen".[181]

Ähnlich erklärte der Ministerrat der WEU bei seinem Treffen am 19. Juni 1992 in Petersberg (Bonn) die Bereitschaft,

> "auf einer Fall-zu-Fall-Grundlage und in Übereinstimmung mit unseren Verfahren die wirksame Erfüllung von Maßnahmen der Konfliktverhütung und der Krisenbewältigung, einschließlich friedenserhaltender Aktivitäten der KSZE oder der Vereinten Nationen oder des VN-Sicherheitsrates [zu unterstützen]. Dies wird ohne Präjudiz für die möglichen Beiträge anderer KSZE-Staaten und anderer Organisationen zu diesen Aktivitäten geschehen".[182]

Eine korrespondierende Formulierung enthalten schließlich die Helsinki-Beschlüsse:

> "Die KSZE kann Ressourcen und mögliche Erfahrung sowie Sachkenntnis bestehender Organisationen, wie der EG, der NATO und der WEU nutzen und könnte sie deshalb ersuchen, ihre Ressourcen zur Verfügung zu stellen, um sie bei der Durchführung friedenserhaltender Aktivitäten zu unterstützen. Andere Institutionen und Mechanismen, ein-

---

180 Vgl. hierzu die Aussage von Wim *van Eekelen*: "CSCE will never be able to provide the same kind of collective security, which at present NATO and WEU offer their members and thus cannot replace collective defence organizations" (Wim F. *van Eekelen*, The Future of Multinational Security Institutions, S. 29-47 in diesem Band. Diese Aussage trifft einerseits zu, da die KSZE tatsächlich in nächster Zukunft kaum die Rolle von Bündnissen zur kollektiven Verteidigung übernehmen wird, was aber auch nicht ihr Zweck sein kann. Andererseits vermengt diese Aussage die Begriffe "collective security" und "collective defence" und erscheint insofern mißverständlich.

181 Kommuniqué der Ministertagung des Nordatlantikrates, Oslo, 4. Juni 1992, Pkt. 10, Abs. 2 und 3; Bulletin des Presse- und Informationsamts der Bundesregierung (Bonn), (12.6.1992) 64, S. 614f.

182 WEU Ministerial Council, 19. Juni 1992; Petersberg Declaration, Pt. No. 2, in: Europe Documents (Brüssel), No. 1787, 23. Juni 1992 (Übersetzung durch den Verfasser).

> schließlich des Mechanismus zur Friedenserhaltung der Gemeinschaft Unabhängiger Staaten (GUS), können ebenfalls von der KSZE ersucht werden, Friedenserhaltung im KSZE-Gebiet zu unterstützen."[183]

Diese Erklärungen könnten die Grundlage einer Kooperation zwischen den verschiedenen Einrichtungen im Bereich der Friedenserhaltung bilden, so daß die gegebenen Möglichkeiten optimal nutzbar wären. Allerdings wird ihr Inhalt oftmals verflacht und ins Gegenteil verkehrt. So wird gelegentlich die Meinung vertreten, die KSZE verfüge weder über Erfahrungen bei friedenserhaltenden Operationen noch über eigene Truppen,[184] weshalb NATO und WEU zu solchen Operationen herangezogen werden müßten.

Einer solchen Sicht ist freilich entgegenzuhalten, daß die Erfahrung der genannten Organisationen im Bereich friedenserhaltender Aktivitäten ebenso groß oder gering ist wie die der KSZE. Sowohl NATO wie WEU sind – wie ausgeführt – ihrer Grundkonzeption nach Verteidigungsallianzen und haben daher bislang keinerlei friedenserhaltende Aktivitäten im genannten Sinne geplant, vorbereitet oder ausgeführt. Zwar existieren insofern entsprechende Erfahrungen im Rahmen der genannten Organisationen, als einige ihrer Teilnehmer- oder Mitgliedstaaten darüber verfügen. Sie sind aber wiederum kein exklusives Merkmal der Allianzmitglieder.[185] Insofern sie jedoch allesamt Teilnehmer der KSZE sind, können diese Staaten ihre Erfahrungen auch direkt in Operationen der KSZE einbringen.

Ähnliches gilt auch für die Stellung von Truppenkontingenten. Die Allianzen verfügen ebensowenig wie die KSZE über eigene Truppen, sondern sind auf Kontingente ihrer Mitgliedstaaten angewiesen. Insofern diese Staaten selbst Teilnehmer der KSZE sind, können sie ihre Kontingente durchaus direkt der KSZE zur Verfügung stellen, ohne die entsprechenden Allianzen zwischenzuschalten.[186]

Der originäre Beitrag der Allianzen ist also nicht dort zu suchen, wo er in der plakativen Darstellung ihrer Vorzüge gerne gesehen wird, nämlich im angeblich angesammelten Fachwissen im eigentlichen Bereich der Friedenserhaltung und in der Stellung von Truppen. Er wäre vielmehr dort zu suchen, wo die Allianzen tat-

---

183 Beschlüsse von Helsinki, Kap. III, Pkt. 52.

184 So etwa die Ausführungen bei *Staack*, Eine europäische Sicherheitskultur. Danach habe die KSZE vorerst darauf verzichtet, eigene Friedenstruppen aufzustellen. Aufstellung eigener, multi- oder gar supranationaler Verbände im Bereich der Friedenserhaltung stehe im Gegensatz zur bisherigen jahrzehntelangen Praxis im Rahmen der Vereinten Nationen und sei daher ein ausgesprochenes Novum.

185 Neben den NATO-Mitgliedern Belgien, Dänemark, Frankreich, Großbritannien, Italien, Niederlande und Norwegen weisen insbesondere Finnland, Irland, Österreich und Schweden langjährige Erfahrung im Bereich friedenserhaltender Operationen auf und haben teilweise über mehr als drei Jahrzehnte Truppen, Beobachter und Kommandanten gestellt. Vgl. *Arbeitsgemeinschaft "Truppendienst"* (Hrsg.), Handbuch für Soldaten im Dienst der Vereinten Nationen, Wien 1985 (Truppendienst-Taschenbuch No. 29).

186 Dies entspräche auch der bisherigen Praxis im Rahmen der Vereinten Nationen, wo Truppen ebenfalls von den Mitgliedstaaten direkt gestellt wurden, ohne Mediatisierung durch Allianzen.

sächlich originäre Kapazitäten aufweisen, die die Fähigkeit der einzelnen Mitgliedstaaten der Allianzen übersteigen und im Rahmen der KSZE nicht erbracht werden können. Dies werden vor allem die Planungs-, Führungs-, Transport- und Versorgungskapazitäten sein, wie sie insbesondere in der nordatlantischen Allianz bereits existieren und auch im Rahmen der WEU im Entstehen begriffen sind. Hier wären tatsächlich "Ressourcen und Fachwissen" spezifischer Art durch die Allianzen in die friedenserhaltenden Operationen im Rahmen der KSZE einzubringen, um bestehende Defizite abzudecken.[187]

Aus diesen Ausführungen ließe sich nunmehr der Schluß ziehen, die genannten Allianzen stünden auf derselben Stufe wie die KSZE und könnten von sich aus friedenserhaltende Operationen gesamteuropäischen Ausmaßes durchführen; denn sie haben ebenso wie die KSZE den Zugriff auf Truppenkontingente von Staaten, die vielfach ebenfalls Erfahrungen mit solchen Operationen haben, und sie verfügen überdies (zumindest teilweise) über die erforderlichen Planungs-, Führungs-, Transport- und Versorgungskapazitäten, die sie unmittelbar einsetzen könnten. Dem ist aber entgegenzuhalten, daß sie einerseits nicht den Status einer regionalen Abmachung oder Organisation aufweisen und daß andererseits friedenserhaltende Operationen einen breiten politischen Rahmen erfordern, der nicht nur die kontingentstellenden Staaten erfassen muß, sondern auch (und vor allem) alle betroffenen Staaten. Dies trifft aber in den meisten angesprochenen Szenarien für friedenserhaltende Operationen der Allianzen in Europa nicht zu. Jedes Einschreiten einer Staatengruppe oder Allianz in einen Konflikt zwischen Nichtmitgliedern erschiene jedoch problematisch. Es wäre schlechthin unmöglich, wäre eine der Konfliktparteien Allianzmitglied, da eine Intervention dann mit Sicherheit als Parteinahme verstanden würde.

Insgesamt ergänzen sich also die Funktionen der Allianzen und der KSZE bei friedenserhaltenden Operationen. Die KSZE kann den breiten politischen Rahmen bieten, der für solche Operationen geboten erscheint, während die Allianzen – richtig verstanden – "Ressourcen und Fachwissen", insbesondere in den Bereichen Planung, Führung, Transport und Versorgung beisteuern können. Die eigentliche Leistung wäre freilich von den kontingentstellenden Staaten zu erbringen.

c. Mögliche Grauzonen und Doppelgleisigkeiten

Angesichts der unterschiedlichen primären Ziele (kollektive Selbstverteidigung bei den Allianzen einerseits und kooperative Sicherheitspolitik im Rahmen der KSZE andererseits) ist es zunächst schwer vorstellbar, daß jenseits einer möglichen Zusammenarbeit in allfälligen friedenserhaltenden Operationen Grauzonen überlappender Tätigkeiten oder Doppelgleisigkeiten zwischen den Allianzen und der

---

187 Kritisch zu den Kapazitäten der Allianzen selbst in diesen Bereichen *van Ekelen*, The Future.

KSZE entstehen können. Solche Grauzonen scheinen sich aber in der letzten Zeit insofern zu entwickeln, als sich die Allianzen für "kooperative" Aufgaben über den Bereich ihrer Mitglieder hinaus öffnen, insbesondere in der Rüstungskontrolle. So hat die NATO mit dem Nordatlantischen Kooperationsrat (NACC) ein Gremium geschaffen, in dem sie mit den Mitgliedstaaten der ehemals gegnerischen Allianz "kooperative" Sicherheitspolitik betreibt.[188] Der Teilnehmerkreis ist damit zwar zunächst enger als in der KSZE, so daß sich noch keine wirkliche Grauzone bilden konnte. Allerdings erscheint eine solche Orientierung an der früheren Mitgliedschaft in der gegnerischen Allianz zunehmend als Anachronismus. Sollte demzufolge der Kooperationsrat durch die Einbeziehung anderer interessierter Staaten schließlich auf den gesamten Bereich der KSZE-Teilnehmerstaaten ausgeweitet werden, müßte in der Tat eine Überlappung mit bestehenden KSZE-Einrichtungen, wie etwa dem Sicherheitsforum, erwartet werden, die einer Klärung bedürfte.

d. Die mögliche Weiterentwicklung des Verhältnisses zu anderen europäischen Organisationen

Die zunehmende Institutionalisierung der KSZE einerseits und die genannte Ausweitung der Tätigkeiten bestehender europäischer Organisationen andererseits wirft die Frage auf, in welchem Verhältnis zu den anderen sicherheitspolitischen Institutionen und Organisationen in Europa sich die KSZE weiterentwickeln kann. Derzeit präsentiert sich die KSZE als der einzig umfassende europäische Rahmen. Demgegenüber weisen die genannten wie auch die anderen Organisationen der europäischen Integration einen höheren Organisationsgrad auf. Auf dieser Grundlage scheinen konzeptuell folgende Möglichkeiten denkbar:

(1) Die KSZE wird eine umfassende gesamteuropäische internationale Organisation

Diese Option würde die bisherige Entwicklung der KSZE mit zunehmender Organisationsdichte und Institutionalisierung hin zu einer umfassenden internationalen Organisation extrapolieren. Eine solche Organisation würde aller Voraussicht nach die Gesamtheit der bisherigen Teilnehmerstaaten auf der einen Seite und den Gesamtbereich der bisherigen Aufgaben (Körbe) auf der anderen Seite umfassen. Damit würde sie allerdings die in den jeweiligen Aufgabenbereichen bereits tätigen europäischen Einrichtungen duplizieren. So würde die humanitäre Dimension weitestgehend jenen Bereich erfassen, der bereits von der Europäischen Menschenrechtskonvention und den auf ihrer Grundlage geschaffenen Einrichtungen abgedeckt wäre. Der zweite Korb würde in gewisser Hinsicht jene Bereiche

---

188 Hierzu detailliert John *Barrett*/Hans Jochen *Peters*, NACC and the CSCE: A Contribution in the Context of the Concept of Interlocking Institutions, S. 249-263 in diesem Band.

duplizieren, die von den (west)europäischen Gemeinschaften und gesamteuropäisch von der ECE erfaßt sind. Die sicherheitspolitische Dimension würde weitestgehend die Funktionen des Nordatlantischen Kooperationsrates duplizieren, insbesondere hinsichtlich der rüstungskontrollpolitischen Aufgaben. In einer weiteren Entwicklungsstufe wäre schließlich der Aufbau einer gemeinsamen gesamteuropäischen Verteidigung denkbar, was auch die verteidigungspolitische Komponente der atlantischen Allianz duplizieren müßte.

Sollte die KSZE tatsächlich eine solche Entwicklung nehmen, würde sie zwangsläufig die bestehenden Institutionen und Organisationen überrunden und schließlich hinfällig machen, da sie aufgrund ihres Teilnehmer-(oder dann Mitglieder-)kreises umfassender wäre als die genannten Organisationen oder Institutionen.[189] Langfristig müßten somit die bestehenden Organisationen, die sowohl hinsichtlich der Mitglieder als auch des Aufgabenbereiches nur Teilmengen des umfassenderen KSZE-Rahmens darstellten, in diesem größeren Rahmen vollständig aufgehen.

Diese Entwicklung erscheint freilich wenig realistisch, da derzeit wenig Bereitschaft zu erkennen ist, die Rolle bestehender Institutionen und Organisationen zugunsten einer umfassenderen, wenn nicht ausschließlichen Rolle der KSZE aufzugeben.

(2) Die KSZE ist eine Übergangslösung für den Einstieg in existierende Organisationen und Strukturen

Die bestehende und teilweise noch zunehmende parallele Ausrichtung bereits existierender europäischer Institutionen und Organisationen einerseits und der KSZE andererseits könnte freilich auch zur gegenteiligen Entwicklung führen. In dieser Sicht wäre es dann die Hauptaufgabe der KSZE, die bisher außerhalb des (praktisch ausschließlich westeuropäischen) Integrationsrahmens befindlichen Staaten schließlich in ihn hineinzuleiten. Sobald sie diese Aufgabe erfüllt hätte, wäre sie letztlich überflüssig. Im Bereich der humanitären Dimension wäre es etwa die Aufgabe der KSZE, alle Staaten zur Ratifikation der Europäischen Menschenrechtskonvention und zur Anwendung der entsprechenden Mechanismen zu bewegen. Sobald diese Mechanismen überall in Europa anwendbar wären, würde sich die humanitäre Dimension der KSZE weitgehend erübrigen. In ähnlicher Weise würde eine allumfassende Mitgliedschaft der derzeitigen KSZE-Teilnehmerstaaten in den Europäischen Gemeinschaften den zweiten Korb obsolet machen. Die Staaten würden durch solch eine Mitgliedschaft voraussichtlich größere Wirkung erzielen als durch die bloße Berufung auf die entsprechenden KSZE-Bestimmun-

189 Sie müßte dann voraussichtlich auch ihre Verfahrensvorschriften ändern und spezialisierte Entscheidungsorgane etwa in der Form des VN-Sicherheitsrates entwickeln, wobei sie zunächst auf Verfahrensregeln bestehender Organisationen zurückgreifen könnte.

gen. Schließlich würde in sicherheitspolitischer Hinsicht die Teilnahme aller Staaten am Nordatlantischen Kooperationsrat oder in der Nordatlantischen Allianz selbst den ersten Korb weitgehend obsolet machen.[190] Zusammenfassend wäre damit die Existenz der KSZE als bloße "Wartehalle" für die schließliche Mitgliedschaft aller Staaten in den bereits existierenden europäischen Organisationen und Institutionen gerechtfertigt.

Auch diese Ansicht erweist sich aber als unrealistisch. Zwar erschiene es zunächst konzeptuell logischer, bestehende Institutionen oder Organisationen auszubauen als neue zu schaffen, doch ist bei diesen derzeit nur wenig Bereitschaft festzustellen, ihren Mitgliederkreis in der angesprochenen Art zu erweitern. Am geringsten scheinen die Widerstände im Bereich der humanitären Dimension, insbesondere gegen die Idee, möglichst alle Staaten der Europäischen Menschenrechtskonvention zu unterwerfen. Es sollte jedoch nicht übersehen werden, daß die Ratifikation dieser Konvention durch die nichteuropäischen Staaten (einschließlich USA und Kanada) durchaus nicht als selbstverständlich angenommen werden dürfte, womit selbst in diesem wenig kontroversen Bereich die Mitgliedschaft vermutlich nicht so umfassend wäre wie die Teilnahme an der KSZE.

Die Realisierung der Option erscheint in den beiden anderen Körben noch weniger wahrscheinlich. Die EG hat bisher gezögert, ihren Mitgliederkreis um die bereits marktwirtschaftlich orientierten Demokratien zu erweitern, und zunächst der Vertiefung vor der Erweiterung Vorrang gegeben. Hier hat sich erst in der letzten Zeit vorsichtig eine entgegenkommendere Haltung entwickelt. Es scheint jedoch unwahrscheinlich, daß die Gemeinschaften in naher Zukunft bereit wären, sich auch nur den neuen Demokratien in Mittel- und Osteuropa zu öffnen, die eben erst den Übergang zur Marktwirtschaft vollziehen. Ähnlich zögernd haben die bestehenden westlichen Allianzen auf die Entwicklungen in Europa reagiert. Der oftmals geäußerte Wunsch mancher neuen Demokratie nach Mitgliedschaft in der NATO wurde bisher nur abschlägig beschieden. Als Minimallösung wurde der Nordatlantische Kooperationsrat geschaffen, der aber nur den "kooperativen" Teil der militärischen Sicherheitspolitik abdeckt. Allerdings steht er derzeit nur den früheren Mitgliedern der ehemals gegnerischen Allianz offen, nicht aber den langjährig befreundeten neutralen Demokratien in Europa, so daß er nicht einmal im Ansatz gesamteuropäisch ist. Ähnliches gilt für die WEU, bei der die Bestimmungen über die Mitgliedschaft noch restriktiver gefaßt sind und demzufolge noch weniger Optionen für Nichtmitglieder der EG oder der NATO bestehen. Auch diese Option muß daher als unrealistisch angesehen werden.

---

190 Vgl. zu diesem Szenario der "Aufteilung" der KSZE entlang der Inhalte der verschiedenen Körbe *Barrett/Peters*, NACC and the CSCE.

(3) Fortdauer der bisherigen Situation

Die beiden genannten extremen Optionen erschienen zwar konzeptuell jeweils als logische Entwicklungen aus der derzeitigen Situation, sie sind aber unrealistisch, da sie keine Zustimmung bei den bisherigen Mitgliedern von bestehenden Institutionen und Organisationen finden. Hier ist vielmehr eine eigenartige Diskrepanz in der Haltung dieser Organisationen festzustellen, die einerseits keinerlei oder nur eine restriktive Neigung zeigen, sich der Neuaufnahme von Mitgliedern zu öffnen, andererseits aber geradezu eifersüchtig darüber wachen, daß die KSZE nicht zu viele Funktionen erhält. Solange die Tendenz besteht, sich weder dem umfassenderen Rahmen der KSZE unterzuordnen noch auch im Mitgliederkreis so umfassend wie die KSZE werden zu wollen, muß daher für die Zukunft davon ausgegangen werden, daß die vorhandenen Organisationen sowie die KSZE weiterhin nebeneinander bestehen werden, ohne daß sie ineinander aufgehen.

In dieser Entwicklungsperspektive wird die KSZE daher auch in absehbarer Zukunft mit ihren bestehenden Gremien und Institutionen den einzigen tatsächlich umfassenden Rahmen der gesamteuropäischen Sicherheitspolitik bilden, in dem alle europäischen (sowie für die europäische Sicherheitspolitik relevanten nichteuropäischen) Staaten vertreten sind und agieren können. Dies schmälert die Rolle anderer sicherheitspolitischer Einrichtungen nicht. Es muß aber bewußt gemacht werden, daß ihnen aufgrund ihrer begrenzten Mitgliederzahl eben nur beschränkte Funktionen zukommen können, die nicht genuin "gesamteuropäisch" sind, sondern zunächst nur ihren Mitgliederkreis betreffen. Eine gesamteuropäische Rolle können sie nur in einem größeren gesamteuropäischen Rahmen übernehmen, den derzeit nur die KSZE bietet.

IV. Die sicherheitspolitische Rolle der KSZE: Geltende Stereotype, Verbesserungsvorschläge und realistische Zukunftserwartungen

Es kann nicht bestritten werden, daß die KSZE viele Erwartungen nicht erfüllt hat, die in sie gesetzt worden sind. Oftmals entstanden Erwartungen aus mangelhafter Kenntnis der bisherigen Entwicklung und der daraus resultierenden Eigenschaften der KSZE, aus unzutreffenden Analogien mit anderen Einrichtungen oder durch eine irreleitende Terminologie.[191]

1. Stereotype

Inzwischen sind über die KSZE mehrere Stereotype gebildet worden, die eine realistische Einschätzung ihrer sicherheitspolitischen Grenzen und Möglichkeiten er-

191 So hat der Begriff "Konfliktverhütungszentrum" gelegentlich die Erwartung geweckt, diese Einrichtung könnte von sich aus aktiv werden, um das Entstehen von Konflikten zu verhüten.

schweren, wenn nicht verhindern, ebenso aber auch die Beurteilung ihres Stellenwertes im Rahmen der "interlocking" oder "mutually reinforcing institutions".

a. Die KSZE hat sich als zu schwach erwiesen, da sie den Jugoslawienkonflikt nicht verhindert/gelöst hat

Als häufigstes Stereotyp ist der Vorwurf zu hören, die KSZE habe in der Jugoslawienkrise versagt. Dabei haben auch die Bemühungen von als effizienter dargestellten sicherheitspolitischen Institutionen auf europäischer (EG, WEU, NATO) wie auf globaler Ebene (VN) den Krieg im früheren Jugoslawien bisher nicht beenden können.

Der Vorwurf ignoriert die grundlegende Tatsache, daß internationale sicherheitspolitische Einrichtungen nicht unabhängig von ihren Mitgliedern oder Teilnehmerstaaten funktionieren.[192] Sie erfordern vielmehr deren koordinierte Zusammenarbeit, sei es im Plenum oder in einem kleineren Entscheidungsgremium. Bestehen zwischen maßgeblichen Staaten Meinungsverschiedenheiten darüber, wie einer Krise beizukommen und welches Ergebnis wünschenswert sei, läßt sich die Krise auch im Rahmen von Organisationen oder Institutionen nicht lösen. Solche Uneinigkeiten waren hinsichtlich der Entwicklungen im früheren Jugoslawien sowohl im Vorfeld als auch beim Ausbruch der Gewaltanwendung manifest.[193] Maßgebliche westliche und andere Staaten schienen lange Zeit geneigt, die Zuspitzung der Lage zu ignorieren[194] und dann eher die Gewaltanwendung als den Zerfall Jugoslawiens zu tolerieren.[195] Damit war aber die KSZE ebenso wie jedes andere internationale Gremium in ihrer Handlungsfähigkeit behindert.[196]

---

192 Vgl. hierzu explizit Ingo *Peters*, Normen- und Institutionenbildung der KSZE im Widerstreit politischer Interessen: Die Durchsetzung des Gewaltverzichts als Prüfstein für die KSZE, S. 155-185 in diesem Band.

193 Vgl. ebd. sowie James B. *Steinberg*, The Response of International Institutions to the Yugoslavia Conflict: Implications and Lessons, in: F. Stephen *Larrabee* (Hrsg.), Europe's Volatile Powderkeg: Balkan Security after the Cold War, Washington, D.C.: American University Press (im Erscheinen).

194 Versuche der österreichischen Außenpolitik, auf die aufwachsende Krise hinzuweisen, wurden vielfach als "Sarajevo-Komplex" belächelt. Zu den "Signalen", die bereits lange vor Ausbruch der Krise erkennbar waren, vgl. ausführlich Heinz *Vetschera*/Andrea *Smutek-Riemer*, Signale zur Früherkennung von krisenhaften Entwicklungen am Beispiel der Entwicklung zur Jugoslawienkrise, in: Wolfgang *Heydrich*/Joachim *Krause*/Uwe *Nerlich*/Jürgen *Nötzold*/Reinhardt *Rummel* (Hrsg.), Sicherheitspolitik Deutschlands: Neue Konstellationen, Risiken, Instrumente, Baden-Baden: Nomos Verlag 1992, S. 287-330.

195 Zu den wahrscheinlichen Gründen vgl. *Steinberg*, The Response, sowie *Vetschera/Smutek-Riemer*, Signale, S. 323-327. Unter ausdrücklicher Nennung Großbritanniens, Frankreichs und Rußlands, die jegliche serbische Aktionen abdeckten, vgl. Andreas *Unterberger*, in: Die Presse, 21.7.1993.

196 Die genannten Staaten Großbritannien, Frankreich und Rußland sind gleichzeitig ständige Mitglieder des VN-Sicherheitsrats.

Umgekehrt läßt sich gerade anhand der Jugoslawienkrise belegen, daß viele Stereotype, die über die KSZE existieren und oftmals mit vorwurfsvollem Unterton vorgetragen werden, nicht zutreffen. Ebenso läßt sich belegen, daß viele der oftmals gut gemeinten Verbesserungsvorschläge für die KSZE insofern verfehlt sind, als sie von unzutreffenden Prämissen ausgehen oder die konstatierten Probleme in Wahrheit nicht lösen.

b. Die KSZE ist entscheidungsschwach

Der Vorwurf der Entscheidungsschwäche ist einerseits der weitestgehende und dient andererseits auch als Angelpunkt für andere Stereotype, die als Begründungen für diese Schwäche genannt werden, nämlich

- der Umfang der Teilnehmerzahl, insbesondere ihr Anwachsen durch die Aufnahme der Nachfolgestaaten der früheren Sowjetunion, sowie
- das Konsensprinzip, das angesichts der großen Teilnehmerzahl rasche, entschlossene Entscheidungen verhindert habe.

Diesem Vorwurf liegt eine fehlerhafte Analogie zum System der Vereinten Nationen zugrunde, das im Rahmen der kollektiven Sicherheit tatsächlich in konfrontativer Art, nämlich *gegen* den festgestellten Aggressor Entscheidungen zu treffen hat. Demgegenüber ist die primäre Aufgabe der KSZE als Einrichtung der kooperativen Sicherheitspolitik, mögliche Konfliktpotentiale durch Frühwarnung, vorbeugende Diplomatie, Vermittlung und ähnliche kooperative Maßnahmen an ihrem Aufwachsén zu hindern, ohne den Anspruch auf zwangsweise Durchsetzung. Da mithin das System der KSZE primär nicht streitige, sondern kooperative Entscheidungen bedingt, erscheinen die zur Begründung der angeblichen Entscheidungsschwäche angeführten Stereotype unzutreffend.

(1) Der Teilnehmerkreis ist zu groß geworden

Insbesondere die Aufnahme der neuen Staaten aus dem Gebiet der ehemaligen Sowjetunion wird oftmals kritisiert. Wie bereits angeführt, wäre aber einerseits eine Verweigerung der Teilnahme dieser Staaten insofern problematisch gewesen, als ihr Territorium bereits seit 1975 zum Geltungsbereich der KSZE-Bestimmungen (mit Ausnahme der Anwendung der V[S]BM) gehört.[197] Andererseits läßt sich die Ansicht auch empirisch nicht belegen, daß durch die Aufnahme besonders dieser Staaten die KSZE "zu unbeweglich" geworden sei. Diese Staaten sind nicht immer bei Sitzungen vertreten, und wenn sie vertreten sind, haben sie sich bisher in keiner Weise blockierend verhalten. Beschlüsse wurden viel häufiger durch etablierte Staaten blockiert, die bereits von Anfang an in der KSZE vertreten

---

197 Die einzige tatsächliche Erweiterung des KSZE-Raumes erfolgte mit der Aufnahme Albaniens.

waren.[198] Bemerkenswert erscheint hier insbesondere der Zeitbedarf der Gruppe der EG-Staaten, um vor Sitzungen intern eine einheitliche Linie festzulegen, was oftmals zu verspäteten Sitzungsbeginnen führt.[199]

Der erweiterte Teilnehmerkreis kann auch nicht als Begründung für das angebliche Versagen der KSZE in der Jugoslawienkrise angeführt werden. Die entscheidende Phase im Vorlauf und bei unmittelbarem Ausbruch der Krise,[200] als noch eine Möglichkeit zum Handeln im Rahmen der KSZE bestanden hätte, lag nämlich *vor* dem Zerfall der Sowjetunion, als die damaligen Sowjetrepubliken noch durch die zentrale Regierung in Moskau vertreten waren. Ebensowenig hat die Teilnahme der neuen Staaten die Maßnahmen zur Jugoslawienkrise im Rahmen der KSZE behindert.

(2) Das Konsensprinzip verhindert Entscheidungen

Dieses Stereotyp wird zwar vielfach im Zusammenhang mit der gewachsenen Teilnehmerzahl angesprochen, war aber schon zu hören, als die KSZE lediglich 35 Teilnehmerstaaten umfaßte. Als Verbesserung werden einerseits ein weitgehendes Abgehen vom Konsensprinzip (jenseits der bereits bestehenden "Konsens minus eins"-Regel) und andererseits die Konzentration der Entscheidungsfindung durch Schaffung kleinerer Entscheidungsgremien, etwa in Form des VN-Sicherheitsrates, vorgeschlagen.

Unter der Prämisse einer vorrangig kooperativ-präventiven Funktion geht allerdings die Kritik am Konsensprinzip fehl. Es ermöglicht immerhin Ergebnisse, denen alle Beteiligten zugestimmt haben, so daß sie sich in der Folge auch schwer davon distanzieren können.[201] Die Einführung des Majoritätsprinzips erschiene erst dann erforderlich, wenn die KSZE in Zukunft auch eine konfrontativ-repressive Funktion übernehmen sollte.

---

198 So werden gelegentlich Arbeitssitzungen durch Fragen verzögert, die aus dem ungelösten Zypernproblem zwischen den ursprünglichen Teilnehmerstaaten Zypern, Griechenland und Türkei entstehen. Diese Kontroverse hat die Konferenzarbeit seit 1974 beeinträchtigt, nachdem die türkische Invasion auf Zypern erfolgt war.

199 Da die bezahlte Zeit der Konferenzdolmetscher vom vorgesehenen Sitzungsbeginn ab gerechnet wird, ist dies auch eine Kostenfrage.

200 Nämlich der Krieg der Jugoslawischen Volksarmee gegen Slowenien und anschließend gegen Kroatien Ende Juni sowie Juli 1991.

201 So erfordert etwa die Entsendung von Beobachtermissionen oder die Stationierung von Friedenstruppen auf jeden Fall den Konsens aller Beteiligten und sonstigen relevanten Akteure (einschließlich möglicher "troublemakers") und bedarf damit einer Konsensentscheidung. Dies wurde am Beispiel der Langzeitmissionen nach Jugoslawien besonders deutlich. Wenngleich Jugoslawien an der Entscheidung über die Missionen nicht beteiligt war, hing deren Durchführung letztlich von seiner Kooperationsbereitschaft und Zustimmung ab.

2. Verbesserungsvorschläge

Auf der Grundlage dieser Kritik wurden vor allem von akademischer Seite mehrfach Vorschläge zur Verbesserung der Arbeit der KSZE gemacht, die die vermeintlichen Schwächen überwinden sollen.

a. Die KSZE braucht einen Sicherheitsrat

Diese Forderung wird zumeist im Zusammenhang mit der Kritik am großen Teilnehmerkreis sowie am Konsensprinzip vorgebracht, wobei teils der Sicherheitsrat der Vereinten Nationen zum Vorbild genommen wird, teils aber auch durchaus eigenständige Modelle vorgestellt werden.[202] Wie die Praxis der Vereinten Nationen gezeigt hat, garantiert aber auch eine solche Konstruktion nicht zwangsläufig eine erhöhte Effizienz; der Entscheidungsprozeß wird lahmgelegt, sobald divergierende Auffassungen aufeinandertreffen, die erst wieder die Suche nach einem Konsens innerhalb des Gremiums erfordern.

Damit ist auch die Ansicht widerlegt, daß im Rahmen der KSZE ein verkleinertes Entscheidungsorgan in der Art des VN-Sicherheitsrates eher in der Lage gewesen wäre, wirksame Entscheidungen oder Lösungen in der Jugoslawienkrise zu finden. In einem solchen Gremium wären nämlich in der einen oder anderen Weise jene widersprüchlichen Positionen vertreten worden, die auch das Plenum blokkierten. Die Unfähigkeit, Entscheidungen zu treffen, wäre damit nur in ein anderes Gremium verlagert, nicht aber aufgehoben worden.

b. Straffung der Organisation und/oder Stärkung bestehender Organe

Diese Vorschläge betreffen einerseits die Verdichtung der KSZE-Strukturen zu einem "Hauptquartier"[203] und andererseits die Umfunktionierung des Konfliktverhütungszentrums zu einer selbständig handlungsfähigen Einrichtung[204] bzw. die Stärkung der Position des amtierenden Vorsitzenden oder des Generalsekretärs.[205] Berücksichtigt man allerdings die unterschiedlichen Positionen der Teilnehmerstaaten hinsichtlich der Schaffung und Kompetenzverteilung der bisher bestehenden KSZE-Institutionen, erscheinen solche Vorschläge wenig realistisch.

---

202 So schlägt Peters einen "Europäischen Sicherheitsrat" vor, der sich aus der KSZE-Troika und fünf bis zehn weiteren, in Regionalzonen gewählten Vertretern zusammensetzen sollte. Um die negativen Erfahrungen der Vereinten Nationen zu berücksichtigen, sollte es dabei weder eine ständige Mitgliedschaft noch ein Vetorecht geben; vgl. Ingo *Peters*, Normen- und Institutionenbildung.

203 *Dixon/Hirschfeld*, Adapting the CSCE. Kritik am "Wanderzirkus" der verschiedenen Tagungsorte übt auch Ingo *Peters*, Normen- und Institutionenbildung.

204 *Dixon/Hirschfeld*, Adapting the CSCE; *Steinberg*, The Response.

205 *Steinberg*, The Response, schlägt eine solche Stärkung sowie eine verbesserte Koordination des Generalsekretärs mit dem KVZ vor.

c. Bessere Nutzung bestehender Instrumente

Die Fehleinschätzung der Lage und die Uneinigkeit der Akteure angesichts der Jugoslawienkrise verhinderte aber auch, daß von den in der KSZE vorhandenen Instrumenten zur Konfliktverhütung Gebrauch gemacht wurde, als noch Gelegenheit dafür gewesen wäre. Erst nach Zustandekommen einer mehr oder weniger koordinierten Ansicht zwischen den Teilnehmerstaaten der KSZE beginnt man sich in der letzten Zeit selbstkritisch zu fragen, ob (und allenfalls warum) nicht im Vorfeld der Jugoslawienkrise besserer Gebrauch von den existierenden Krisenmechanismen, aber etwa auch vom Instrumentarium militärischer Inspektionen hätte gemacht werden können. Dies wäre der sicherheitspolitischen Funktion und dem Instrumentarium der KSZE adäquater gewesen – das zunächst geschaffen, dann aber von den Teilnehmerstaaten nicht genutzt worden war[206] – als die Erwartung, im Rahmen der KSZE schließlich eine Lösung für einen bereits ausgebrochenen Konflikt zu finden.

3. Schlußfolgerungen für die künftige sicherheitspolitische Rolle der KSZE im Bereich der "mutually re-inforcing institutions"

a. Hauptfunktionen der KSZE

Für die KSZE lassen sich aus der bisherigen Entwicklung und der derzeitigen Struktur zwei Hauptfunktionen im Rahmen der gesamteuropäischen Sicherheitspolitik ableiten.

Einerseits wird die KSZE in ihren Folgetreffen, aber auch im Rahmen der Ratstreffen weiterhin die "legislative Funktion" der gesamteuropäischen Konferenz ausüben, auf welcher die Teilnehmerstaaten sich die Regeln für das künftige Zusammenleben in Europa geben. Hier stellt die oftmals kritisierte Anzahl der Teilnehmer einen positiven Faktor dar, da kein potentieller Adressat der gesamteuropäischen sicherheitspolitischen Verhaltensregeln ausgegrenzt wird. Die sicherheitspolitische Bedeutung dieser legislativen Funktion liegt darin, durch Verhaltensregeln für Stabilität und Vorhersehbarkeit zu sorgen. Die Bewältigung dieser Aufgabe erscheint heute weniger kompliziert als zur Zeit der Ost-West-Konfrontation, da die ideologische Unvereinbarkeit der Standpunkte nunmehr weggefallen ist und sich alle Teilnehmerstaaten zumindest formal zu einem einheitlichen Wertesystem bekennen.[207]

---

206 Immerhin gab es selbst bei der Aktivierung des militärischen Krisenmechanismus durch Österreich am 1. Juli 1991 noch seitens einiger Teilnehmerstaaten Kritik am österreichischen Vorgehen.

207 Die KSZE nahm in ihrem Ansatz die Überwindung des Ost-West-Konfliktes gewissermaßen vorweg. Zwar fehlte zunächst die gemeinsame Wertgrundlage für eine stabile europäische Normenordnung, doch konnten erste Fundamente bereits während der Konfrontation gelegt wer-

Andererseits wird es die Aufgabe der KSZE sein, Instrumente der kooperativen, präventiven Sicherheitspolitik zu schaffen und weiterzuentwickeln. Diese Instrumente stehen dann den Teilnehmerstaaten für Friedenserhaltung und Konfliktverhütung zur Verfügung. Die Entscheidung über ihren Einsatz liegt freilich nicht bei der KSZE. Es liegt im Ermessen der Teilnehmerstaaten selbst, sie gegebenenfalls auch tatsächlich zu benützen.

b. Grenzen und Möglichkeiten der KSZE

Die Grenzen und Möglichkeiten der KSZE liegen in der kooperativen und präventiven Sicherheitspolitik. Sie wird keine maßgeblichen Funktionen übernehmen können, die der "konfrontativen" Sicherheitspolitik zuzurechnen sind.[208] Aufgaben der kollektiven Verteidigung werden jedenfalls weiterhin in die Kompetenz der existierenden Verteidigungsbündnisse wie NATO oder WEU fallen.[209] Die KSZE kann jedoch nach den bisherigen Erfahrungen Instrumente und Mechanismen kooperativer Sicherheit anbieten, die durchaus geeignet erscheinen, auf der untersten Stufe einer Eskalation das Aufwachsen von Konflikten zu verhüten.

Will man daher die gegenwärtige und die wahrscheinliche sicherheitspolitische Rolle der KSZE bewerten, müssen Maßstäbe angelegt werden, die ihren Eigenschaften angemessenen sind. Es wäre verfehlt, von ihr Ergebnisse zu erwarten, die sie als grundsätzlich kooperative, auf Prävention ausgerichtete regionale Sicherheitsabmachung nicht erbringen kann. Solche Erwartungshaltungen erscheinen um so überzogener, wenn man bedenkt, daß selbst die ihrer Satzung nach zur Durchsetzung geschaffenen internationalen Institutionen und Organisationen keinerlei Erfolge verzeichnen können. Andererseits hat die Praxis gezeigt, daß der rechtzeitige Einsatz der Mittel, die in der KSZE geschaffen worden sind, durchaus zur Erhaltung der Stabilität und zur Verhinderung weiteren Eskalierens beitragen kann.

---

den. Es ist daher sinnwidrig, die KSZE als "Produkt des Kalten Krieges zu bezeichnen, das heute keinen Stellenwert mehr hat". Zu beachten sind allerdings die Vorbehalte bei Staack, daß die Teilnahme der nichteuropäischen Staaten auf dem Gebiet der ehemaligen Sowjetunion ein Problem für die europäische "Sicherheitskultur" bedeute; vgl. *Staack*, Eine europäische Sicherheitskultur.

208 Abgesehen von Maßnahmen wie der Beteiligung an nichtmilitärischen Sanktionen, etwa der Unterstützung des Wirtschaftsembargos gegen Restjugoslawien. Diese Einschränkung beruht allerdings auf dem in diesem Aufsatz vertretenen Verständnis friedenserhaltender Maßnahmen als "kooperativ", da sie zumindest die Duldung, wenn nicht sogar das Einverständnis aller Beteiligten voraussetzen. Dagegen rechnet Peters friedenserhaltende Maßnahmen zum "konfrontativen Konfliktmanagement"; vgl. Ingo *Peters*, Normen- und Institutionenbildung.

209 Wobei sie allerdings auf deren Mitglieder beschränkt sind; diese Organisationen sind eben noch lange nicht "gesamteuropäisch" und zeigen auch keine Tendenz, sich so umfassend zu entwickeln.

V. Anhang

Sitzungen der KSZE-Gremien seit der Charta von Paris 1990

(A) Helsinki-Nachfolgetreffen

24.3.-10.7.1992

(B) Ratstreffen

1. Ratstreffen, Berlin, 19.-20.6.1991
2. Ratstreffen, Prag, 30.-31.1.1992
3. Ratstreffen, Stockholm, 14.-15.12.1992

(C) Treffen des AHB

1. Treffen, Wien, 28.-29.1.1991
2. Treffen, Prag, 23.-24.5.1991
3. Treffen, Berlin, 17.-18.6.1991
4. Treffen, Prag, 22.-24.10.1991
5. Treffen, Prag, 8.-10.1.1992
6. Treffen, Prag, 27.-29.1.1992
7. Treffen, Prag, 27.-28.2.1992
8. Treffen, Helsinki, 13.3.1992
9. Treffen, Helsinki, 19.3.1992
10. Treffen, Helsinki, 29.4.1992
11. Treffen, Helsinki, 18.-21.5.1992
12. Treffen, Helsinki, 8.-10.6.1992
13. Treffen, Helsinki, 29.6.-7.7.1992
14. Treffen, Helsinki, 9.7.1992
15. Treffen, Prag, 13.-14.8.1992
16. Treffen, Prag, 16.-18.9.1992
17. Treffen, Prag, 5.-6.11.1992
18. Treffen, Prag, 11.-13.11.1992
19. Treffen, Prag, 2.-4.2.1993
20. Treffen Prag, 16.-18.3.1993 (als Wirtschaftsforum)
21. Treffen, Prag, 26.-27.4.1993
22. Treffen, Prag, 29.-30.6.1993

(C.1) Dringlichkeitstreffen des AHB

1\. Treffen, 3.-4.7.1991

1\. Zusätzliches Treffen, 8.8.1991

2\. Treffen, 6.5.1992

2\. Zusätzliches Treffen, 3.9.1991

3\. Treffen, 26.-29.4.1993

3\. Zusätzliches Treffen, 10.10.1991

4\. Zusätzliches Treffen, 9.11.1991

(D) TREFFEN DES KONSULTATIVAUSSCHUSSES

1. Treffen, 3.12.1990
2. Treffen, 25.2.1991
3. Treffen, 16.4.1991
4. Treffen, 13.5.1991
5. Treffen, 14.6.1991
6. Treffen, 1.-2.7.1991
   (gem. Art.17.2.2 des Wiener Dokuments 1990)
7. Treffen, 12.7.1991
8. Treffen, 16.9.1991
9. Treffen, 7.10.1991
   Jährl. Treffen zur Beurteilung der Durchführung 1991, 11.-13.11.1991
10. Treffen, 18.11.1991
11. Treffen, 2.12.1991
12. Treffen, 16.12.1991
13. Treffen, 14.1.1992
14. Treffen, 17.1.1992
15. Treffen, 20.1.1992
16. Treffen, 22.1.1992
17. Treffen, 23.-24.1.1992
18. Treffen, 17.2.1992
19. Treffen, 16.3.1992
20. Treffen, 28.4.1992
21. Treffen, 15.5.1992
22. Treffen, 23.5.1992
23. Treffen, 5.6.1992
24. Treffen, 19.6.1992
25. Treffen, 14.6.1992
26. Treffen, 21.9.1992
27. Treffen, 19.10.1992
28. Treffen, 28.10.1992
29. Treffen, 2.11.1992
30. Treffen, 23.11.1992
31. Treffen, 7.12.1992
32. Treffen, 9.12.1992
33. Treffen, 18.1.1993
34. Treffen, 8.2.1993
35. Treffen, 15.3.1993
36. Treffen, 20.4.1993
   Jährl. Treffen zur Beurteilung der Durchführung 1993, 4.-5.5.1993
37. Treffen, 10.5.1993
38. Treffen, 14.6.1993
39. Treffen, 12.7.1993

6. Normen- und Institutionenbildung der KSZE im Widerstreit politischer Interessen: Die Durchsetzung des Gewaltverzichts als Prüfstein für die KSZE

Ingo Peters

I. Die Durchsetzung des Gewaltverzichts als Prüfstein für die KSZE

Nach dem Ende des Ost-West-Gegensatzes sind die politisch verbindlichen KSZE-Prinzipien, Normen und Regeln für die Politik der Staaten und Regierungen im Grundsatz unumstritten.[1] Die Bestimmungen der Helsinki-Schlußakte von 1975, die in der *Charta von Paris für ein neues Europa* von 1990 bestätigt und erweitert worden sind, werden formal von allen 53 KSZE-Staaten anerkannt.[2] Trotz wünschenswerter Konkretisierung in Einzelfragen ist die Setzung gemeinsamer Normen im Rahmen der KSZE damit weitgehend abgeschlossen. Angesichts des gemeinsamen Bekenntnisses zu Demokratie, Marktwirtschaft und Menschenrechten entwickelt sich Europa offenbar zu einer politisch-ideologisch weitgehend homogenen Region.

Partikularinteressen, die von den gemeinsam formulierten politischen Zielen und Interessen abweichen, bestehen jedoch fort. Sie werden von einzelnen Staaten bzw. deren Regierungen vertreten, aber zunehmend auch von nichtstaatlichen politischen Akteuren wie ethnischen oder religiösen Volksgruppen oder deren Führern. Einzelinteressen sind mit den KSZE-Prinzipien und Zielen spätestens dann unvereinbar, wenn die Bereitschaft besteht, zu ihrer Verwirklichung gewaltsame Mittel einzusetzen. Die gewaltsamen Konflikte im ehemaligen Jugoslawien sowie in und zwischen den Nachfolgestaaten der Sowjetunion sind die augenfälligsten Beispiele für die eklatanteste Form der Verletzung von KSZE-Normen und -Regeln. Als Kehrseite des Wegfalls des Ost-West-Systemgegensatzes sind neue sicherheitspolitische Herausforderungen unübersehbar, durch welche die Sicherheit und Zusammenarbeit in Europa in Frage gestellt wird: althergebrachte nationale, ethnische oder religiöse Gegensätze brechen wieder hervor oder es sind neue entstanden; Minderheitenprobleme und wirtschaftliche Mißstände führen ebenso wie

---

1 An verschiedenen Stellen dieses Aufsatzes gehen Informationen des Verfassers aus Hintergrundgesprächen im Auswärtigen Amt und dem Verteidigungsministerium in Bonn, mit Mitgliedern verschiedener Delegationen auf dem KSZE-Folgetreffen in Helsinki, den VSBM-Verhandlungen in Wien und bei der NATO in Brüssel ein. Diese Informationen sind aus Gründen des Vertrauensschutzes nicht einzeln ausgewiesen. Der Verfasser dankt jedoch allen Gesprächspartnern herzlich für ihre hilfreiche Offenheit. Anja *Jetschke*, Friedrich *Erbacher* und besonders Henning *Riecke* danke ich für ihre unermüdliche Zuarbeit und einige wichtige Hinweise.

2 Vgl. die Texte der Dokumente in: *Auswärtiges Amt* (Hrsg.), Sicherheit und Zusammenarbeit in Europa. Dokumentation zum KSZE-Prozeß, Bonn 1990; *dass.* (Hrsg.), Sicherheit und Zusammenarbeit in Europa. Dokumentation zum KSZE-Prozeß 1990/91, Bonn 1991.

Vormacht- oder Territorialansprüche zu Sezessionsbestrebungen, innerstaatlichen und zwischenstaatlichen Konflikten.[3] Der Beitritt neuer Mitglieder zur KSZE setzt die formale Anerkennung bisheriger KSZE-Dokumente voraus und suggeriert eine neuartige politisch-kulturelle Homogenität in Europa. Spätestens durch die Erweiterung der KSZE um die asiatischen Republiken der ehemaligen Sowjetunion wird diese Homogenität jedoch erneut in Frage gestellt: Die "politische Kultur" der Mitglieder wird derart vielschichtig, daß die Umsetzung der Normen und der erforderliche Konsens für weiterführende Beschlüsse erneut zweifelhaft werden.[4]

Der Prüfstein für die Funktionalität und die politische Glaubwürdigkeit der KSZE ist die Durchsetzung des Gewaltverzichtsgebots. Bei den meisten in den verschiedenen KSZE-Dokumenten festgeschriebenen Normen handelt es sich um Verhaltensgebote, die mehr oder weniger eingehalten werden können, also um Ziele, die in einem stetigen Prozeß schrittweise verbesserter Umsetzung in der politischen Praxis erreicht werden sollen. Bestimmungen wie die des Gewaltverzichts hingegen sind nicht schrittweise umzusetzen, sondern es sind Regeln, die entweder eingehalten oder gebrochen werden.[5] Die zentrale Frage lautet daher, welchen Beitrag die KSZE zur Konfliktverhütung und gegebenenfalls Konfliktbewältigung in Europa leistet, um das Gewaltverzichtsgebot durchzusetzen?

Normensetzung ist an sich bereits eine Form der Konfliktverhütung, weil durch sie die politischen Kosten für eine Gewaltanwendung erhöht werden.[6] Darüber hinaus erfordert das Gewaltverzichtsgebot alternative Handlungsoptionen zur Durchsetzung bzw. zum Ausgleich gegensätzlicher Ziele und Interessen. Zu diesem Zweck haben sich die KSZE-Staaten im November 1990 auf dem Gipfeltreffen in Paris Institutionen geschaffen, die seither schrittweise ausgebaut worden sind. In der Praxis sind diese Institutionen indes offensichtlich unzulänglich: Die Organe und Instrumente sowie die Prozeduren der Entscheidungsfindung in der KSZE haben angesichts der Verletzungen von KSZE-Normen im ehemaligen Jugoslawien und der ehemaligen Sowjetunion bisher die Konflikte nicht bewältigen,

3 Vgl. Stephen *Van Evera*, Primed for Peace: Europe after the Cold War, in: International Security, 15 (Winter 1990/91) 3, S. 7-57 (48f); Kalevi J. *Holsti*, A "Zone of Civility" in European Diplomatic Relations? The CSCE and Conflict Resolution. Vorlage auf dem Jahrestreffen der International Studies Association, Atlanta, GA, 31.3.-4.4.1992.

4 Vgl. Bernard *von Plate*, Die Neuordnung in der ehemaligen Sowjetunion: Eine Herausforderung für die KSZE, in: Europa-Archiv, (1992) 10, S. 288-294; Ingo *Peters*, Sicherheit in Europa nach dem Ost-West-Konflikt. Der KSZE-Prozeß als regionale Sicherheitsinstitution, in: Christopher *Daase u.a.* (Hrsg.), Regionalisierung der Sicherheitspolitik, Baden-Baden: Nomos 1993, S. 89-108.

5 Vgl. hierzu die Unterscheidung zwischen *Normen* und *Regeln* in der Regimetheorie bei Norbert *Ropers*/Peter *Schlotter*, Regimeanalyse und KSZE-Prozeß, in: Beate *Kohler-Koch*, Regime in den internationalen Beziehungen. Baden-Baden: Nomos 1989, S. 315ff (328).

6 Vgl. *Holsti*, A "Zone of Civility"?, S. 12.

geschweige denn verhüten können: Versagt die KSZE angesichts der neuen sicherheitspolitischen Herausforderungen trotz der neuen Institutionen?

Das zentrale politische Problem besteht heute offensichtlich nicht in der Normensetzung, sondern vor allem in der Um- bzw. Durchsetzung gemeinsam deklarierter Ziele und Werte.[7] Eine effektive Normendurchsetzung setzt funktionale und politische Faktoren voraus, die hier lediglich skizziert werden können: Auf funktionaler Ebene sind Instrumente und Handlungsoptionen notwendig, die zeitlich und inhaltlich eine effektive Problemlösung ermöglichen. Selbst bei Einvernehmen der Konfliktparteien über die Einhaltung des Gewaltverbotes ist eine funktionale Problemlösung als Vorstufe zur Konfliktlösung zwar geboten, aber nicht in jedem Falle möglich. Meist werden daher Kompromisse unabwendbar sein, um einen Interessenausgleich unter Wahrung des Gewaltverzichts herbeizuführen. Voraussetzung hierfür ist indes, daß die Konfliktparteien überzeugt sind bzw. werden, daß der Versuch, ihre Interessen gewaltsam durchzusetzen, mehr kostet als ein Kompromiß.[8] Bei bereits erfolgter Gewaltanwendung stellt sich die Aufgabe, den Konflikt einzudämmen, das heißt seine horizontale und vertikale Eskalation möglichst zu verhindern sowie den Konflikt auf friedliche Formen des Konfliktmanagements zurückzuführen. Ob die Konfliktparteien dazu politisch bereit sind, hängt zentral von dem Gegenstand des Konflikts ab und den relativen Interessen, die die Parteien damit verbinden.

Im positiven Falle können diplomatische Mittel (gute Dienste, Streitschlichtung, Vermittlung etc.) erfolgreich angeboten und eingesetzt werden. Ist hingegen ein derartiges kooperatives Konfliktmanagement unter konstruktiver Beteiligung der Konfliktparteien nicht mehr erreichbar, dann stellt sich vor allem im Falle gewaltsamer Konfliktaustragung die Aufgabe des konfrontativen Konfliktmanagements, das heißt, KSZE-Normen müßten gegen eine oder mehrere Konfliktparteien durchgesetzt werden. Hierzu sind abgestufte politische oder wirtschaftliche Sanktionsmaßnahmen bis hin zu Militäreinsätzen als Instrumente denkbar. Ob sie allerdings im Sinne der Durchsetzung des Gewaltverzichts effektiv sein würden, ist fraglich und vor allem vom jeweils interessengebundenen Einlenken der Konfliktparteien abhängig. Im früheren Jugoslawien etwa könnten durch den Einsatz kollektiver Militäraktionen die Konflikte vielleicht eingedämmt und dadurch Schlimmeres verhindert werden. Selbst dann würden die der Gewalt zugrunde liegenden

7 *Umsetzungsprobleme* bestehen dann, wenn trotz glaubhafter Bemühungen die Verwirklichung der KSZE-Normen nicht ad hoc möglich ist. Unterbleibt die Normenerfüllung hingegen vorsätzlich und wider bessere Möglichkeiten, so stellt sich das Problem der *Durchsetzung* der KSZE-Normen.

8 Vgl. I. William *Zartman*, The Strategy of Preventive Diplomacy in Third World Conflicts, in: Alexander *George* (Hrsg.), Managing US-Soviet Rivalry: Problems of Crisis Prevention, Boulder, CO: Westview Press, 1983, S. 341-364 (352).

politischen Konflikte jedoch keinesfalls gelöst sein, wenn nicht darüber hinaus ein politischer Interessenausgleich stattfindet.

Normendurchsetzung ist nicht allein eine Frage geeigneter Instrumente zur funktionalen Problemlösung bzw. zur Konfliktbewältigung. Eine zweite unverzichtbare politische Voraussetzung ist eine zeitlich und inhaltlich effektive Handlungsfähigkeit der Staatengemeinschaft gegenüber den Regelverletzern. Dies wiederum setzt eine schnelle und gezielte, politisch legitimierte Entscheidungsfindung der KSZE, also aller übrigen KSZE-Staaten, über den Einsatz geeigneter Mittel voraus, unter Umständen auch unter Einschränkung der Souveränität des jeweils betroffenen Staates oder der Staaten. Erschwerend für eine internationale Handhabe kommt hinzu, daß die Regelverletzer nicht oder nicht ausschließlich Staaten sind, sondern auch politische Gruppen (z.B. ethnische oder religiöse Volksgruppen), die weder die internationalen Vereinbarungen unterzeichnet haben, noch sich an diese gebunden fühlen. Innerstaatliche Konflikte bzw. die Verletzung von KSZE-Normen und -Regeln sind für internationale Instrumente nur dann zugänglich, wenn die Staaten auch für derartige Fälle zumindest teilweise auf ihre Souveränität verzichten und das Nichteinmischungsgebot relativiert oder zu einem bedingten Einmischungsgebot umformuliert wird.[9]

Angesichts der hier kurz diskutierten funktionalen und politischen Voraussetzungen für eine effektive Normendurchsetzung sollen die bisher im Rahmen der KSZE eingerichteten Organe und Instrumente zur Konfliktverhütung und zur Konfliktbewältigung anhand der in der Übersicht zusammengestellten Kriterien hinsichtlich folgender Fragen analysiert werden:

- Welche Merkmale kennzeichnen nach dem Helsinki-Folgetreffen die Organe, Instrumente und Mechanismen zur Umsetzung der KSZE-Normen?
- Welche institutionellen Defizite sind zu konstatieren und welche politischen Positionsunterschiede der KSZE-Staaten liegen der institutionellen Entwicklung zugrunde?
- Welche Folgerungen ergeben sich aus den bisherigen Erfahrungen und welche Handlungsempfehlungen lassen sich ableiten, um dem deklarierten Ziel der Konfliktverhütung und des möglichst frühzeitigen Konfliktmanagements im Rahmen der KSZE näher zu kommen?

---

9 Vgl. *Holsti*, A "Zone of Civility"?, S. 9 und S. 19; *ders*., Peace and War: Armed Conflict and International Order 1648-1989, Cambridge: Cambridge University Press, 1992, Kap. 12; Jost *Delbrück*, Die internationale Gemeinschaft vor neuen Herausforderungen: Zur Neubestimmung der Reichweite des Interventionsverbotes der Charta der Vereinten Nationen, in: Wolfgang *Heydrich u.a.* (Hrsg.), Sicherheitspolitik Deutschlands: Neue Konstellationen, Risiken, Instrumente, Baden-Baden: Nomos 1992, S. 547-556.

KRITERIEN FÜR DIE BEURTEILUNG DER KSZE-INSTITUTIONEN
ZUR KONFLIKTVERHÜTUNG UND KRISENBEWÄLTIGUNG

Kriterium A: Bandbreite von Instrumenten für verschiedene Konflikttypen/-stadien

a. zur Früherkennung von Konflikten mit Eskalationspotential

Indikatoren:
- Instrumente zur kollektiven Gewinnung von Informationen
- Instrumente für bi- und multilaterale Konsultationen und Verhandlungen

b. zum kooperativen Konfliktmanagement

Indikatoren:
- Instrumente für den Einsatz "guter Dienste"
- Instrumente für Konsultationen unter Vermittlung Dritter
- Instrumente zur freiwilligen Streitschlichtung
- Instrumente zur obligatorischen Streitschlichtung, Schiedsgerichtsbarkeit

c. zum konfrontativen Konfliktmanagement

Indikatoren:
- Instrumente zur Verhängung von politischen und wirtschaftlichen Sanktionen
- Instrumente zum Einsatz friedenserhaltender Maßnahmen (peacekeeping)
- Instrumente zum Einsatz militärischer Zwangsmaßnahmen (peacemaking)

Kriterium B: Anpassungsfähigkeit der Instrumente an spezifische Konfliktkonstellationen;

Indikatoren:
- Einsatzmöglichkeit in verschiedenen Politikfeldern (Menschenrechte, Minderheitenkonflikte, Wirtschaftskonflikte, militärische Sicherheit)
- zeitlich abstufbare Routine- oder Krisenkonsultationen
- Abstufbarkeit nach Teilnehmerkreis, bi- oder multilateral
- nach Art und Intensität abstufbare Sanktionen (politische, wirtschaftliche, militärische)

Kriterium C: Handlungsfähigkeit durch effektive Entscheidungsprozeduren

Indikatoren:
- klare Entscheidungsstruktur, eindeutige Zuständigkeit und Arbeitsteilung zwischen den Organen
- Initiierungsmodus für die Instrumente (Fristen?, Quoren?)
- Entscheidungsmodus (Mehrheit oder Konsens?)
- partieller Souveränitätsverzicht (vorweggenommener Konsens)
- Rückkopplungsprozesse zur Erfolgskontrolle bzw. Nachbesserung
- Verfügbarkeit erforderlicher Finanz- und Sachmittel (Logistik, Gerät, Waffen etc.)

I. Institutionenbildung in der KSZE als politischer Prozeß

1. Bestandsaufnahme: KSZE-Institutionen als intergouvernementale Struktur

Auf dem Helsinki-Folgetreffen ist die KSZE von den Teilnehmerstaaten zu einer *regionalen Abmachung* im Sinne von Kapitel VIII der Charta der Vereinten Nationen (VN) erklärt worden. Dadurch ist sie für die regionale Konfliktverhütung und

Krisenbewältigung zuständig.[10] Die KSZE als Kollektiv bzw. die einzelnen KSZE-Staaten haben in bezug auf diese beiden neuen Aufgaben das Recht, sich auch mit den inneren Angelegenheiten der Staaten zu befassen, insoweit sie KSZE-Regelungen berühren. Dies gilt für die *Menschliche Dimension* und für die Friedenserhaltung sowohl zwischen als auch innerhalb der Teilnehmerstaaten.[11]

Seit 1989 sind institutionelle Strukturen der KSZE aufgebaut und entwickelt worden, die als operatives Unterfutter erforderlich sind, damit die KSZE ihre neuen Aufgaben erfüllen kann: Die Verdichtung des politischen Konsultationsnetzes (regelmäßige Gipfel- und Folgetreffen, halbjährliche Treffen der Außenminister etc.), die Einrichtung permanenter Organe und deren Ausstattung mit spezifischen Mechanismen bilden die operativen Instrumente zur Bewältigung der neuen sicherheitspolitischen Herausforderungen und zur kooperativen Gestaltung der zwischenstaatlichen Beziehungen. Der *Rat* der Außenminister – bzw. stellvertretend der *Ausschuß Hoher Beamter* (AHB) – ist das zentrale politische Konsultations- und Entscheidungsgremium für alle Problemfelder.[12] Dem Rat der Außenminister oder dem AHB, unterstützt durch das Sekretariat in Prag als administratives Organ, obliegen Übersicht, Leitung und Koordinierung der KSZE-Aktivitäten zur Konfliktverhütung und Krisenbewältigung. Darüber hinaus tritt der AHB einmal im Jahr als *Wirtschaftsforum* zusammen, da für Fragen der wirtschaftlichen Zusammenarbeit kein eigenes Organ eingerichtet worden ist.[13]

---

10 Vgl. Helsinki-Dokument 1992, Gipfelerklärung vom 10.7.1992, Ziff. 25, in: Bulletin des Presse- und Informationsamts der Bundesregierung, Bonn (kurz: Bulletin), (23.7.1992) 82, S. 777ff (780).

11 Ebd., Ziff. 8 und Ziff. 20, S. 777 bzw. 779.

12 Vgl. zur Kompetenz des Rates: Charta von Paris für ein neues Europa vom 21.11.1990 (kurz: Charta von Paris), Zusatzdokument über die Durchführung einiger Maßnahmen, Abschn. I/A (Aufgaben), in: Bulletin, (24.11.1990) 137, S. 1416; Prager Dokument über die weitere Entwicklung der KSZE-Institutionen und Strukturen vom 31.1.1992 (kurz: Prager Dokument), ebd., (4.2.1992) 12, S. 84f, Ziff. 16 (Maßnahmen gegen TNS) und 41; Helsinki-Dokument 1992, Beschlüsse, S. 781ff, Abschn. I, Ziff. 6-7 (Aufgaben), Ziff. 12-14 (Amtierender Vorsitzender), Ziff. 15 (Troika), Ziff. 17 (Ad-Hoc-Lenkungsgruppen), Ziff. 22 (Persönlicher Vertreter), Abschn. II/Ziff. 9 (Ernennung des Hochkommissars), Abschn. III (Frühwarnung, Konfliktverhütung, Krisenmanagement).
Vgl. zur Kompetenz des AHB: Charta von Paris, Zusatzdokument, Abschn. I/B (Aufgaben), S. 1416; Zusammenfassung der Schlußfolgerungen des Treffens des KSZE-Außenministerrates in Berlin, 19.-20.6.1991 (kurz: Berliner Dokumente), Anhang 2 (Mechanismus für dringliche Situationen), in: Bulletin, (22.6.1991) 72, S. 582f; Dokument des Moskauer Treffens über die Menschliche Dimension der KSZE vom 3.10.1991 (kurz: Moskauer Dokument), Ziff. 13, in: Bulletin, (18.10.1991) 115, S. 912; Prager Dokument, Ziff. 2-4 (Aufgabendelegierung), 7-12 (Menschliche Dimension), 16 (Maßnahmen gegen TNS), 19 (Wirtschaftsforum), S. 83f; Helsinki-Dokument 1992, Beschlüsse, Abschn. I, Ziff. 9-11 (Aufgaben), Abschn. III (Rat), Abschn. VII, Ziff. 21-32 (Wirtschaftsforum), S. 781f, bzw. S. 785ff und 799f.

13 Vgl. zum Wirtschaftsforum, das erstmals vom 16. bis zum 18.3.1993 in Prag stattfand, Helsinki-Dokument 1992, Beschlüsse, S. 799f, Abschn. VII.

Dem Rat/AHB sind funktional differenzierte permanente Organe nachgeordnet: Für militärische Sicherheit und friedliche Streitschlichtung ist das *Konfliktverhütungszentrum* (KVZ) in Wien zuständig, für die Menschliche Dimension das *Büro für Demokratische Institutionen und Menschenrechte* (BDIMR) in Warschau. Diese Organe besitzen für die Durchführung ihrer spezifischen Aufgaben in bezug auf vorbeugende Maßnahmen zur Konfliktverhütung zwar eine eigenständige Kompetenz. Letztlich sind sie jedoch von den Vorgaben und Entscheidungen des Rates oder AHB abhängig, vor allem wenn es um die politische Krisenbewältigung geht, die allein dem Rat oder AHB vorbehalten ist. Das KVZ und das BDIMR hingegen dienen bei der Krisenbewältigung als Exekutivorgane, die aufgrund von Vorgaben des AHB gezielte Maßnahmen durchführen können.[14]

Zusätzlich sind der Rat bzw. AHB sowie das KVZ und das Büro mit spezifischen Instrumenten ausgerüstet worden, um die ihnen übertragenen Aufgaben verwirklichen zu können: Für den Rat und den AHB sind dies vor allem der Mechanismus für dringliche Situationen und friedenserhaltende Maßnahmen, für das BDIMR der Mechanismus über die Menschliche Dimension und der *Hohe Kommissar für nationale Minderheiten*, für das KVZ die Vertrauens- und Sicherheitsbildenden Maßnahmen (VSBM), besonders der Mechanismus für Konsultationen und Zusammenarbeit in bezug auf ungewöhnliche militärische Aktivitäten und der Mechanismus für friedliche Streitbeilegung.[15] Letzterer ist auf dem Stockholmer Ratstreffen durch die Schaffung einer Streitschlichtungskommission ergänzt worden. Für die Signatarstaaten (derzeit 30 der 53 KSZE-Staaten) besteht weiterhin die Möglichkeit zur Schlichtung auf Anweisung des Rates/AHB sowie der Anrufung des KSZE-Streitschlichtungs- und Schiedsgerichts in Genf.[16]

---

14 Vgl. zu den Aufgaben und Zuständigkeiten des KVZ: Charta von Paris, Zusatzdokument, S. 1417, Abschn. I/F, Ziff. 2 und 4 (VSBM); Wiener Dokument 1990 der Verhandlungen über Vertrauens- und Sicherheitsbildende Maßnahmen vom 19.11.1991, in: Bulletin, (6.12.1990) 142, S. 1493ff, und Wiener Dokument 1992 vom 4.3.1992, ebd., (21.3.1992) 3, S. 31ff; Berliner Dokumente, Zusammenfassung, S. 583, Anhang 3, Ziff. 1 (friedliche Beilegung von Streitigkeiten); Prager Dokument, S. 85, Ziff. 26-40 (Sicherheitsforum); Helsinki-Dokument 1992, Beschlüsse, S. 785ff, Abschn. III (Rat).
Vgl. zum BDIMR: Charta von Paris, Zusatzdokument, S. 1417, Abschn. I/G., Ziff. 1-4 (noch Büro für freie Wahlen, Aufgaben); Moskauer Dokument, S. 909ff; Prager Dokument, S. 85, Ziff. 9-15 (Menschliche Dimension, bezogen auf Moskauer Dokument); Helsinki-Dokument 1992, S. 783 bzw. S. 785ff, Beschlüsse, Abschn. II, Ziff. 10 (Hochkommissar), Abschn. III (Rat).

15 Vgl. die Einzelbestimmungen zu den Mechanismen: Berliner Dokumente, Zusammenfassung, S. 582, Anhang 2 (Mechanismus für Konsultation und Zusammenarbeit in dringlichen Situationen); Dokument des Moskauer Treffens, S. 910ff, Abschn. I, sowie Helsinki-Dokument 1992, Beschlüsse, S. 794f, Abschn. VI, Ziff. 7 (Mechanismus über die Menschliche Dimension); Wiener Dokument 1990, S. 1494f, Ziff. 17; ebenso Wiener Dokument 1992, S. 296f, Ziff. 17; sowie Prager Dokument, S. 85, Ziff. 29 (Mechanismus für Konsultation und Zusammenarbeit in bezug auf ungewöhnliche militärische Aktivitäten); Berliner Dokumente, Zusammenfassung, S. 583, Anhang 3 (Mechanismus für friedliche Beilegung von Streitfällen).

16 Vgl. Dokumente des dritten KSZE-Außenministertreffens in Stockholm, 14.-15.12.1992, in: Bulletin, (18.12.1992) 138, S. 1257ff, Zusammenfassung der Schlußfolgerungen, Beschlüsse (kurz:

Welchen Aufgaben können die einzelnen Instrumente dienen? Für die Früherkennung von gewaltträchtigen Konflikten in bzw. zwischen den KSZE-Staaten stehen zunächst eine Reihe von Instrumenten zur Verfügung, mit denen Informationen zur kollektiven Lagebeurteilung und Entscheidungsfindung gewonnen werden können. Für das Problemfeld militärische Sicherheit sind dies vor allem einige der VSBM, das heißt Informations- und Überprüfungsmaßnahmen sowie Verhaltensregeln, durch die Routineaktivitäten von außergewöhnlichen und besorgniserregenden militärischen Aktivitäten unterschieden werden können.[17] Hinzu kommt der Dialog über politisch-militärische Sicherheitsfragen im Konsultativausschuß des KVZ, im KSZE-Forum für Sicherheitskooperation zudem der "ergebnisorientierte Sicherheitsdialog".[18]

Die Frühwarnung in bezug auf die *Menschliche Dimension* obliegt dem *Hohen Kommissar für nationale Minderheiten* (HCM), der als Sensor für problematische Entwicklungen dient und für entsprechende Informationsdienste gegenüber dem Rat/AHB in diesem Problemfeld zuständig ist.[19] Darüber hinaus kann das BDIMR als Ort für Konsultationen auf verschiedenen Ebenen genutzt werden. Routinemäßig dienen die jährlichen Implementationstreffen im BDIMR wie auch im KVZ zur Diskussion problematischer Entwicklungen im jeweiligen Politikfeld, die dann zur weiteren Beschlußfassung an den Rat/AHB weitergeleitet werden können. Dort kann dann über möglicherweise als erforderlich erachtete Nachbesserungen von Maßnahmen in beiden Bereichen entschieden werden.

Zusätzlich besteht die Möglichkeit, *Erkundungs- und Berichterstattermissionen* einzusetzen. Sie können vom AHB für alle Politikfelder sowie vom KVZ oder BDIMR entsprechend ihrer funktionalen Zuständigkeit entsandt werden. Im Gegensatz zu den Mechanismen oder Inspektionen bei den VSBM sind die Missionen ein kollektives Instrument, das zwar von einem einzelnen Teilnehmer angeregt werden kann, der sich betroffen fühlt. Die Durchführung von Missionen setzt jedoch einen Konsensbeschluß und ein eindeutiges Mandat voraus, in dem Ziele, Dauer und andere Modalitäten festgelegt sind. Missionen sind als Maßnahme zur Informationsgewinnung nicht allein ein Instrument zur Frühwarnung, sondern insbesondere auch zur Krisenbewältigung zweckmäßig und haben daher bereits zahlreiche Anwendung gefunden.

Stockholmer Dokument). Beschluß über friedliche Beilegung von Streitigkeiten des 3. Treffens des KSZE-Rates in Stockholm, in: Bulletin, (8.1.1993) 2, S. 5ff.

17 Vgl. Ingo *Peters*, Sicherheitspolitische Vertrauensbildung im neuen Europa. Herausforderungen und Entwicklungen in der VSBM-Politik, in: Erhard *Forndran*/Hartmut *Pohlman* (Hrsg.), Europäische Sicherheit nach dem Ende des Warschauer Paktes, Baden-Baden: Nomos 1993, S. 363-389.

18 Vgl. Helsinki-Dokument 1992, S. 790ff, Beschlüsse, Abschn. V.

19 Nach langdauernden Kontroversen auf den zahlreichen Folge- und Expertentreffen werden Minderheitenrechte heute wie die Menschenrechte als Individualrechte, nicht als Kollektivrechte behandelt.

Für akute Konflikte, denen einerseits greifbare Besorgnisse bzw. Bedrohungsperzeptionen oder Interessengegensätze zugrunde liegen, bei denen andererseits aber keine oder noch keine Gewalt angewendet wird, besteht Bedarf an Instrumenten zum kooperativen Konfliktmanagement. Diese Instrumente dienen dazu, einen Interessenausgleich zwischen den Konfliktparteien herbeizuführen und Kompromisse zu ermöglichen. Je rechtzeitiger ein Konflikt bearbeitet wird, desto größer ist die Chance, ein gewaltsames Ausufern zu verhindern.[20] Für diesen Zweck stehen im Bereich militärischer Sicherheit bestimmte VSBM zur Verfügung, vor allem die Vor-Ort-Inspektionen auf Verlangen oder Einladung sowie Evaluierungsbesuche zur Überprüfung bestimmter Aktivitäten oder Potentiale. Dadurch können gegebenenfalls Befürchtungen als grundlos ausgeräumt und kann "Vertrauen", im Sinne einer begründeten Erwartung, in die defensiven Absichten einer Regierung oder die Routine bestimmter Aktivitäten gestärkt werden.

Hinzu kommt sowohl für die militärische Sicherheit als auch für die *Menschliche Dimension* die Möglichkeit, die jeweils eingerichteten Mechanismen zur Aufklärung spezifischer Zweifelsfälle einzusetzen. Die Mechanismen sind vorstrukturierte Dialogprozesse, die zur Rückversicherung dienen und dadurch zur Deeskalation von Konfliktsituationen durch den Abbau akuter Bedrohungsperzeption beitragen können. Sie sind in ihren Anwendungsmodalitäten, hinsichtlich der Teilnehmer als auch der Zeit, durchaus flexibel. Dem bloßen Ersuchen um Klarstellung einer bestimmten Situation können – je nach Einschätzung der Dringlichkeit oder Zweckmäßigkeit – bilaterale oder multilaterale Konsultationen sogleich oder nacheinander folgen. Im Falle des Mechanismus für die *Menschliche Dimension* sind die anfänglich festgelegten dysfunktional langen Fristen inzwischen schrittweise verkürzt und die Konsultationsbestimmungen dadurch wesentlich verbessert worden. Die Frist für die Beantwortung eines Informationsersuchens des bereits auf dem Wiener Folgetreffen (1989) eingerichteten Mechanismus wurde auf dem 2. Treffen über die Menschliche Dimension in Kopenhagen (Juni 1990) auf vier Wochen, auf dem 3. Treffen über die Menschliche Dimension in Moskau (Oktober 1991) auf 10 Tage verkürzt; gleichzeitig wurde in Kopenhagen für die Einberufung bilateraler Treffen ein Zeitraum von drei Wochen eingeführt, der nach den Beschlüssen von Moskau lediglich noch eine Woche beträgt.[21]

---

20 Vgl. zum Problem des "richtigen Zeitpunkts": *Zartman*, The Strategy of Preventive Diplomacy, S. 352ff, sowie Jacob *Bercovitch u.a.*, Some Conceptual Issues and Empirical Trends in the Study of Successful Mediation in International Relations, in: Journal of Peace Research, 28 (Februar 1991) 1, S. 7-17.

21 Vgl. Abschließendes Dokument des Wiener Folgetreffens der KSZE vom 15.1.1989, Die Menschliche Dimension, Abs. 1, in: Bulletin, (31.1.1989) 10, S. 94; Dokument des Kopenhagener Treffens über die Menschliche Dimension vom 29.6.1990, Ziff. 42.1, in: Bulletin, (4.7.1990) 88, S. 767; Moskauer Dokument, S. 910, Ziff. 2; bzw. Dokument des Wiener Folgetreffen, Menschliche Dimension, Abs. 2, S. 94; Dokument des Kopenhagener Treffens, S. 767, Ziff. 42.3.

Zur kooperativen Konfliktbewältigung in Minderheitenfragen können nach entsprechender Ermächtigung durch den AHB außerdem "gute Dienste" und Vermittlung im Rahmen der "Frühmaßnahmen" des Hohen Kommissars genutzt werden.[22] Für längerfristige Vermittlungsaktionen steht auch der *La-Valletta-Mechanismus* für friedliche Streitbeilegung bereit.[23] Beide Vermittlungsoptionen setzen indes die Zustimmung und aktive Mitarbeit der Konfliktparteien voraus, sind also auf freiwillige Schlichtungsmaßnahmen beschränkt.

Eine obligatorische Streitschlichtung ist für die gesamte KSZE bisher nicht vereinbart worden. Allerdings enthalten die im Stockholmer Dokument vereinbarten Prozeduren zur Schlichtung auf Anordnung sowie die KSZE-Schiedsgerichtsbarkeit zwingende Elemente, weil nach freiwilliger Unterstellung eines Falles bzw. für die Unterzeichner des Gerichtsstatus Entscheidungen mit Mehrheitsbeschluß getroffen werden und bindend sind.[24]

Wenn "Prinzipien der Schlußakte verletzt werden oder ein Zwischenfall vorliegt, der Frieden, Sicherheit oder Stabilität gefährdet", oder wenn bereits Gewalt angewendet worden ist, dann handelt es sich um besonders *dringliche Situationen*.[25] Die Anforderungen an die Problemlösungskapazität der KSZE gehen dann auf die Ebene der konfrontativen Konfliktbewältigung über. Die Schwelle vom kooperativen zum konfrontativen Konfliktmanagement stellt der Mechanismus für *dringliche Situationen* dar. Er sieht bilaterale Klarstellungsgesuche, aber auch Dringlichkeitssitzungen des AHB als dem für die politische Krisenbewältigung zuständigen Organ vor. Der AHB kann Empfehlungen bzw. Schlußfolgerungen formulieren, um die Kompromißfindung zu erleichtern, oder auch ein Treffen des Ministerrats einberufen, um einer akuten Krise Herr zu werden.

Als "Ergänzung zum politischen Prozeß der Lösung von Streitfällen" kann die KSZE nach den Beschlüssen von Helsinki als *regionale Abmachung* im Sinne von Kapitel VIII der VN-Charta auch friedenserhaltende Maßnahmen anwenden, also KSZE-Blauhelme nach dem Vorbild der Vereinten Nationen einsetzen. Sie können zum Beispiel dazu dienen, Konfliktparteien geographisch zu trennen und Waffenstillstandsvereinbarungen zu überwachen. Allerdings verfügt die KSZE weder über einen eigenen Militärapparat noch über eigene Truppen. Vielmehr ist sie in dieser Frage von entsprechenden Beschlüssen im Rahmen der NATO, der WEU oder auch der GUS, letztlich indes weiterhin von der Bereitschaft der einzelnen Regierungen abhängig, der KSZE Peacekeeping-Truppen zur Verfügung zu stel-

---

22 Vgl. Helsinki-Dokument 1992, Beschlüsse, S. 784, Abschn. II, Ziff. 17.

23 Vgl. Bericht des Expertentreffens über friedliche Regelung von Streitfällen in La Valletta vom 8.2.1991, in: *Auswärtiges Amt*, Sicherheit und Zusammenarbeit... 1990/91, S. 181ff.

24 Vgl. Helsinki-Dokument 1992, Beschlüsse, S. 788, Abschn. III, Ziff. 58-62; Stockholmer Dokumente, Beschluß über friedliche Beilegung von Streitigkeiten, Art. 26, S. 10ff.

25 Vgl. zu diesem Mechanismus die Definition einer "dringlichen Situation" und die einzelnen Modalitäten, Berliner Dokumente, Zusammenfassung, S. 582, Anhang 2, Präambel.

len. Diese Peacekeeping-Aktionen schließen indes in Übereinstimmung mit Artikel 53 der VN-Charta militärische Zwangsmaßnahmen aus, die ausdrücklich den Vereinten Nationen überlassen bleiben. Außerdem ist wie im Falle der VN die Zustimmung der betroffenen Parteien und der Konsens aller KSZE-Staaten über den Einsatz friedenserhaltender Maßnahmen erforderlich.[26]

Die Handlungsfähigkeit der KSZE als kollektive Institution ist vor allem vom Entscheidungsmodus abhängig, der dem Einsatz der verschiedenen Werkzeuge zur Konfliktverhütung und Krisenbewältigung vorausgeht. Der allgemeine Informationsaustausch ist eine grundsätzliche vereinbarte Routinesache, zum Beispiel der Datenaustausch im Rahmen der VSBM. Gute Dienste, Vermittlung bzw. Streitschlichtung finden auf Wunsch und ausschließlich unter Zustimmung der beteiligten Konfliktparteien statt.

Die Mechanismen bedürfen, um in Gang gesetzt zu werden, zunächst eines Ersuchens durch einen Teilnehmer, dann der Unterstützung durch eine unterschiedliche Anzahl von anderen Teilnehmerstaaten, denn die Quoren sind je nach Mechanismus verschieden festgelegt.[27] Beschlüsse über weiterführende Schritte zur Bewältigung einer Konfliktgefahr oder einer akuten Krise können hingegen grundsätzlich nur durch eine Konsensentscheidung aller Teilnehmerstaaten gefaßt werden. Dies gilt bis hin zum möglichen Einsatz friedenserhaltender Maßnahmen.

Eine wichtige Ausnahme bestätigt indes diese Regel: In besonderen Fällen, das heißt bei "eindeutigen, groben und nicht behobenen Verletzungen einschlägiger KSZE-Verpflichtungen zu Menschenrechten, Demokratie und Rechtsstaatlichkeit" können bestimmte Maßnahmen auch gegen den Willen des betroffenen Teilnehmerstaates, also auch ohne dessen Zustimmung vom Rat/AHB eingeleitet werden. Diese Regelung basiert auf einem "vorweggenommenen Konsens", das heißt die KSZE-Staaten haben diesem Verfahren für bestimmte Situationen vorweg zugestimmt (Konsens-minus-eins-Regelung). Allerdings kommen als Maßnahmen lediglich "politische Erklärungen oder andere politische Schritte, die außerhalb des Territoriums des betroffenen Staates anwendbar sind", in Betracht.[28] Das liest sich zwar relativ unverbindlich, schließt aber genauer betrachtet immerhin die Verhängung von politischen oder wirtschaftlichen Sanktionen ein. Dazu gehört zum Beispiel auch die Unterstützung der KSZE-Staaten für das von den VN beschlossene Waffenembargo gegen "Jugoslawien".[29]

---

26 Helsinki-Dokument 1992, Gipfelerklärung, S. 780 und S. 786f, Ziff. 25, und Beschlüsse, Abschn. III, vor allem Ziff. 19, 22, 23 und 29.

27 Vgl. Anm. 15.

28 Vgl. Prager Dokument, S. 84, Ziff. 16.

29 Vgl. Resolution 713 (1991) des Sicherheitsrates der Vereinen Nationen über ein bindendes Waffenembargo gegen Jugoslawien, verabschiedet in New York am 25.9.1991, in: Europa-Archiv, (1991) 21, S. D550-D552. Am 30.5.1992 wurden durch die VN-Resolution 757 umfassende Sanktionen gegen Serbien-Montenegro verhängt, vgl. Europa-Archiv, (1992) 12, S. Z156.

Die Handlungsfähigkeit der KSZE-Institutionen könnte durch eine Überlastung in Frage gestellt werden, zum Beispiel wenn – wie es gegenwärtig tatsächlich der Fall ist – mehrere Krisenherde gleichzeitig der Aufmerksamkeit und Entscheidung sowie der Durchführung von Maßnahmen durch die KSZE bedürfen. Gegen eine drohende Überlastung des jeweiligen Vorsitzenden im Rat/AHB sind in Helsinki verschiedene Maßnahmen verabschiedet worden. So hat der Vorsitzende die Möglichkeit, Krisenherde durch externe Experten begutachten zu lassen und dadurch die Expertise für die Entscheidungsfindung im KSZE-Rahmen zu verbessern. Weiterhin wird der amtierende Vorsitzende durch seinen Vorgänger und seinen Nachfolger unterstützt, mit denen er die KSZE-*Troika* bildet. Außerdem kann er Aufgaben an *Ad-hoc-Lenkungsgruppen* delegieren und *persönliche Vertreter* für spezifische Krisensituationen bzw. Konfliktfälle ernennen, die ihn in seinen exekutiven Funktionen unterstützen, ihn allerdings nicht von seiner Verantwortlichkeit gegenüber der Gesamtkonferenz entbinden. Die erforderliche Formulierung eindeutiger Mandate für die Aktionen und Maßnahmen sowie die vereinbarten Berichtspflichten der im Auftrag der KSZE tätigen Akteure ermöglichen darüber hinaus Feedback-Prozesse, so daß Nachregelungsversuche möglich sind, um eine spezifische Entwicklung angemessen begleiten zu können. *Persönliche Vertreter* sind bereits bei verschiedenen Missionen, etwa in die "Dnjestr-Republik"/Moldawien oder in Nagornyj-Karabach zum Einsatz gekommen.[30]

Im Lichte der eingangs aufgestellten Kriterien für effektive KSZE-Institutionen läßt sich somit zusammenfassen:

- Nach den Beschlüssen von Helsinki verfügt die KSZE über einen breiten Fächer von Instrumenten, die bei verschiedenen Konflikttypen (z.B. bei zwischen- und innerstaatlichen) bzw. in unterschiedlichen Stadien von Konflikten sinnvoll eingesetzt werden können.
- Für spezifische Krisen oder Bedrohungen stehen zahlreiche Mechanismen und Instrumente zur Verfügung, die auf die verschiedenen Problemfelder anwendbar sind. Diese Werkzeuge können flexibel gehandhabt und spezifischen Anforderungen angepaßt werden.
- Die KSZE besitzt somit ein erhebliches funktionales Potential für die Früherkennung von Konflikten, für das kooperative und das notfalls erforderliche konfrontative Konfliktmanagement.
- Die politischen Entscheidungsstrukturen und die Durchführungsmöglichkeiten sind in Helsinki nachhaltig ausgebaut worden, so daß die institutionellen Vor-

30 Vgl. Helsinki-Dokument 1992, S. 782, Abschn. I, Ziff. 15 (Troika), Ziff. 16-21 (Ad-hoc-Lenkungsgruppen) und Ziff. 22 (Persönlicher Vertreter); zu Berichtspflichten beispielsweise für den Hohen Kommissar für nationale Minderheiten ebd., S. 784, Abschn. II, Ziff. 17-22; für den Vorsitzenden des Konsultativausschusses vgl. Prager Dokument, S. 85, Ziff. 37.

aussetzungen für eine erfolgreiche Konfliktverhütung und Krisenbewältigung insgesamt verbessert worden sind.

- Nach dem Helsinki-Folgetreffen ist die Hierarchisierung der KSZE-Institutionen abgeschlossen. Im Gegensatz zu den Anfängen in der Pariser Charta besteht heute eine klare Über- und Unterordnung: Der Rat/AHB ist das politische Entscheidungsgremium, BDIMR und KVZ sind exekutive Organe.
- Trotz dieser Klärung bleibt die Institutionenstruktur mit einem dysfunktionalen Manko behaftet: Die KSZE bleibt ein "Wanderzirkus". Die Verteilung der drei Organe auf drei Hauptstädte (Prag, Wien, Warschau) macht es zunehmend notwendig, daß die nationalen Vertreter von Sitzung zu Sitzung zwischen den Organen pendeln, weil sie häufig zugleich Repräsentanten im Konsultativausschuß des KVZ und im KSZE-Forum für Sicherheitskooperation in Wien wie auch im AHB in Prag sind, was sachlich im Interesse kontinuierlicher Arbeit durchaus sinnvoll ist.
- Notwendig sind vor allem zahlreiche Detailverbesserungen (Quoren, Fristen, Durchführungsformen etc.), die sich möglicherweise aus der weiteren Anwendungspraxis ergeben. Außerdem ist die Ausstattung (Personal und Mittel) der Organe für ihre umfangreichen und anspruchsvoll formulierten Aufgaben unzureichend.
- Insgesamt bilden die KSZE-Institutionen eine intergouvernementale Struktur ohne jegliche Abtretung staatlicher Souveränität an den KSZE-Rat oder AHB. Es gibt also auch keine unabhängige politische Kompetenz für eines der Organe, und trotz der verschiedenen Aufweichungen des Konsensprinzips ist die notwendige Einstimmigkeit weiterhin das zentrale Merkmal der KSZE-Entscheidungsfindung, auch im Rat und im AHB.

2. Politische Kontroversen: KSZE-Institutionen zwischen Allmacht und Ohnmacht

Die Bewegung und Bewegungsrichtung des KSZE-Prozesses ist seit 1989 nicht mehr durch das Spannungsverhältnis zwischen Ost und West bestimmt. Heute vollzieht sich der Verhandlungsprozeß über die KSZE-Institutionalisierung – vereinfacht gesagt – zwischen zwei Positionen, die von in Einzelfragen durchaus unterschiedlich zusammengesetzten Staatengruppierungen vertreten werden. Die Grundpositionen unterscheiden sich vor allem im Stellenwert, der in ihrem jeweiligen Zielkatalog der Erhaltung staatlicher Souveränität im Verhältnis zur Herstellung der Handlungsfähigkeit internationaler Organisationen beigemessen wird.

Die eine Position steht für eine "starke" KSZE, das heißt für den Aufbau handlungsfähiger Institutionen, denen auch politische Kompetenzen übertragen werden. Den Regierungen wird daher letztlich – im Interesse der effektiven Konfliktverhütung und Krisenbewältigung – zumindest ein partieller Souveränitätsverzicht abverlangt, also eine faktische Einschränkung ihres nationalen Handlungsspielraumes. Die andere Position indes ist eher darauf bedacht, die staatliche Souveränität und Handlungsfreiheit nicht oder möglichst wenig anzutasten, die Entscheidungen und Aktionen im Rahmen der KSZE möglichst uneingeschränkt auf einen Konsens zu gründen und so die KSZE am kurzen Zügel national definierter politischer Ziele und Interessen zu führen. Die bisherigen Entwicklungsschritte beruhen auf weitreichenden Vorstellungen und greifbaren Vorschlägen der ersten Gruppe. Deren Vorschläge werden dann im internationalen Abstimmungsprozeß wegen der im Einzelfall unterschiedlich motivierten Widerstände (auf die unten im einzelnen eingegangen wird) der zweiten Gruppe auf den jeweils kleinsten gemeinsamen Nenner zurechtgeschnitten und als Verhandlungsergebnis verabschiedet. Diese Kompromisse machen die KSZE und ihre Institutionen weder allmächtig noch ohnmächtig, sondern definieren ihren Einfluß und Handlungsspielraum je nach Politikfeld und Konfliktlage unterschiedlich und lassen sie daher weitgehend abhängig vom jeweils bestehenden Interessenkalkül und den Machtverhältnissen.

Der Grundkonflikt zwischen diesen Positionen zeigte sich seit Beginn der neuen Institutionalisierungsdebatte, die zunächst zwischen den Hauptstädten, ab dem 21. Juli 1990 dann im Vorbereitungskomitee für den KSZE-Gipfel im November 1990 in Paris und seither auf den halbjährlichen Treffen des KSZE-Außenministerrates bzw. praktisch permanent im AHB, aber auch auf den Expertentreffen und schließlich auf dem Folgetreffen in Helsinki geführt worden ist. Wie sollten die Entscheidungs- und Exekutivstrukturen der KSZE gestaltet werden?

Die Grobstruktur, die in Paris verabschiedet wurde, mit dem Außenministerrat als oberstem politischem Entscheidungsgremium, geht auf Vorstellungen der EG-Staaten zurück, deren eigene Struktur offensichtlich dabei Pate gestanden hat.[31] Die jeweilige Zuständigkeit und die Arbeitsteilung zwischen dem AHB und dem KVZ bzw. dessen *Konsultativausschuß* war damals indes unbestimmt geblieben.[32] Ursache hierfür waren die divergierenden Ziele und Interessen der KSZE-Staaten: Einige Staaten, unter anderem Deutschland, Rußland oder Kanada, setzten sich dafür ein, das KVZ mit weitreichenden politischen Kompetenzen auszustatten. Das Wiener Zentrum sollte nicht auf militärische Fragen und die Durchführung der VSBM beschränkt bleiben, sondern auch für einen politischen Sicherheitsdialog zuständig sein. Es bestand die Absicht, das KVZ als zentrales Organ der KSZE in der einen oder anderen Form allmählich zu einem Europäischen Sicherheitsrat auszubauen. Staaten wie die USA, Frankreich oder Großbritannien

31 Vgl. Heinrich *Schneider*, Vom KSZE-Prozeß zum gesamteuropäischen Kooperationssystem: Die europäische Sicherheit und ihr Architekturdilemma, in: Integration, (Oktober 1990), S. 150-164.

32 Vgl. Charta von Paris, Zusatzdokument, S. 1416-1422 (1416f).

waren hingegen bestrebt, der KSZE und insbesondere einzelnen Organen keine politischen Kompetenzen zu geben. Die Aufgaben des KVZ waren daher auf militärische Fragen, konkret auf die Koordinierung der VSBM-Implementierung zu beschränken. Politische Entscheidungen und die Aufsicht über die anderen Organe sollten beim Rat und dem AHB liegen und dadurch eng an die Hauptstädte gebunden werden.

Vordergründig wurde diese Haltung häufig mit dem Ziel begründet, einen bürokratischen Wasserkopf zu verhindern. Entscheidendes Motiv war indes die Wahrung der nationalen Entscheidungskompetenz. Ein bezeichnendes Schlaglicht warf in diesem Sinne die Diskussion über die Einrichtung eines Mechanismus zur friedlichen Streitbeilegung in La Valletta, Malta, im Februar 1991. Dort wurden unter anderem Vorschläge der Bundesrepublik Deutschland und Kanadas diskutiert, dem KVZ ein autonomes Initiativrecht für das Vermittlungsverfahren zu übertragen. Weil weiterreichende politische Kompetenzen für ein KSZE-Organ für einige Regierungen nicht akzeptabel waren, allen voran für die der USA und Frankreichs, wurden entsprechende Beschlüsse jedoch blockiert. Es blieb daher bei der unbefriedigenden Regelung, daß dieser Mechanismus lediglich von den Konfliktparteien eingeleitet werden kann.[33]

Ein anderes Beispiel für das Bestreben, das Konsensprinzip und die nationale Prärogative möglichst uneingeschränkt zu erhalten, war der Widerstand gegen die Aufwertung und Ausweitung des AHB bzw. genauer, der Position und Rolle des jeweiligen Vorsitzenden. Bereits anläßlich des Prager Ratstreffens hatte Außenminister Genscher den Vorschlag unterbreitet, zukünftig einen Lenkungsausschuß oder nach EG-Modell eine *Troika* für die operativen Aufgaben des Rates bzw. AHB einzusetzen. Restjugoslawien (Serbien/Montenegro) sprach sich damals (es wurde erst im Sommer 1992 suspendiert!) ebenso wie Großbritannien gegen derartige Pläne aus – London insbesondere, weil es nicht die VN-Strukturen in Form eines KSZE-Sicherheitsrates dupliziert sehen wollte, in dem die Rolle Großbritanniens im Unterschied zu seiner herausgehobenen Stellung als ständigem Mitglied im VN-Sicherheitsrat erst noch zu bestimmen war. Belgien hingegen widersprach diesen Plänen, weil es darin vor allem ein Instrument der großen Staaten in der KSZE sah, das zu Lasten der vielen kleinen gehen könnte.[34]

Durch die inzwischen erfolgte klare institutionelle Hierarchisierung ist die Kontroverse dadurch zugunsten einer intergouvernementalen Struktur ohne jegliche Abtretung staatlicher Souveränität an KSZE-Rat oder AHB, geschweige denn an

---

33 Vgl. im einzelnen die folgenden "non-papers", die im Vorbereitungskomitee für den Pariser Gipfel in Wien beraten wurden: Schweizer Vorschlag vom 26.4.1990; Benelux-Vorschlag vom Juli 1990; westdeutscher Vorschlag 26.7.1990; kanadischer Vorschlag vom 26.7. und 20.9.1990. Auf den Valletta-Mechanismus wird unten vertiefend eingegangen.

34 Vgl. Aufnahme aller GUS-Mitglieder in die KSZE, in: Neue Zürcher Zeitung (NZZ), 1.2.1992, Belgien kritisiert KSZE-Initiative Bonns, in: Süddeutsche Zeitung (SZ), 18.2.1992.

einzelne Organe, entschieden worden. Trotz dieser Klärung der Institutionenstruktur bleibt die KSZE – wie bereits angesprochen – ein "Wanderzirkus". Die Verteilung der drei Organe auf drei Hauptstädte ist ausschließlich politisch begründet. Diese Entscheidung im Vorfeld zum Pariser Gipfeltreffen im November 1990 war eine politische Geste gegenüber den neuen Demokratien in Osteuropa. Das BDIMR, damals noch Büro für freie Wahlen, verdankt seine Existenz vor allem dem von den USA propagierten Ziel, die *Menschliche Dimension* der militärischen Dimension mit dem KVZ gleichzustellen. Die Verteilung der Organe war ursprünglich auch Ausdruck des kleinsten gemeinsamen Nenners zwischen allen KSZE-Staaten, demzufolge keine komplexen KSZE-Strukturen geschaffen werden sollten. Keinesfalls sollte ein starkes KSZE-Zentrum oder eine KSZE-Hauptstadt entstehen. Im Sinne der *normativen Kraft des Faktischen* und der daran gebundenen politischen Interessen ist eine schnelle Beseitigung dieses institutionalisierten Mangels der KSZE-Institutionenbildung hingegen kaum vorstellbar. Immerhin ist auf dem Stockholmer Ratstreffen im Dezember 1992 der Posten eines *KSZE-Generalsekretärs* geschaffen worden, der schneller als erwartet bereits im April 1993 besetzt worden ist. Der Generalsekretär wird die Arbeit der verschiedenen Sekretariate zu bündeln haben und vor allem Vorschläge für eine grundsätzliche Strukturreform der KSZE-Institutionen erarbeiten.[35]

Befürchtungen hinsichtlich möglicher Einmischung in die inneren Angelegenheiten oder der Einschränkung des nationalen Handlungsspielraums bestimmten auch die Diskussion über die Einrichtung und Entwicklung der Mechanismen. Problematisch war dabei, daß die Wirksamkeit der jeweiligen Instrumente davon abhängt, inwieweit die KSZE zur Frühwarnung fähig oder in konkreten Krisensituationen befugt ist, in die Konfliktentwicklung einzugreifen und insbesondere, ob dies gegebenenfalls auch gegen den Willen der betroffenen Staaten bzw. Regierungen geschehen kann. Die Einschränkungen des Konsensprinzips wurden im Falle aller Mechanismen nur schrittweise möglich, indem bestehende Widerstände nach und nach aufgegeben wurden. Erleichtert wurde diese Nachgiebigkeit durch entsprechend vorsichtig formulierte Bestimmungen, durch die letztlich die nationale Prärogative sichergestellt blieb.

Der Mechanismus für Konsultationen und Zusammenarbeit in bezug auf ungewöhnliche militärische Aktivitäten laut Wiener VSBM-Dokument von 1990 kann bei Bedenken wegen ungewöhnlicher oder unvorhergesehener militärischer Aktivitäten außerhalb der normalen Friedensstandorte der jeweiligen Truppen von einzelnen Regierungen durch ein entsprechendes Ersuchen um Aufklärung in Gang gesetzt werden. Für weiterführende Beschlüsse und Maßnahmen bedarf es jedoch des Konsenses der KSZE-Staaten. Die erste Anwendung des Mechanismus durch

35 Vgl. Stockholmer Dokumente, Beschlüsse, Abschn. VII, S. 1262f.

Österreich anläßlich der Entwicklung in Jugoslawien im Sommer 1990 führte zwar zu Appellen, die von allen Teilnehmerstaaten unterstützt wurden. KSZE-Beobachter konnten aufgrund des mangelnden Konsenses jedoch nicht in die Kampfgebiete entsandt werden.[36] Erst auf dem Prager Ratstreffen im Januar 1992 wurde dieser Mechanismus um die Möglichkeit des KVZ-Konsultativausschusses erweitert, Erkundungs- und Überwachungsmissionen im Zusammenhang mit dem Mechanismus zu veranlassen und (unabhängig vom AHB) durchzuführen.[37]

Zum Mechanismus für die *Menschliche Dimension* wurde auf dem Moskauer Treffen (10.9.-4.10.1991) beschlossen, daß Berichterstattermissionen zur Kontrolle der Minderheitenpolitik einzelner Staaten auch ohne vorgeschaltete Konsultationen gegen deren Willen möglich sein sollten, wenn mindestens zehn Teilnehmerstaaten einen entsprechenden Antrag unterstützen. Dem waren eine Reihe von Zwischenschritten vorausgegangen. In Kopenhagen, auf der 2. Konferenz über die Menschliche Dimension der KSZE, waren hierzu vor allem Vorschläge Dänemarks und Kanadas diskutiert worden. Im dänischen Vorschlag wurde dem betroffenen Staat noch ein Ablehnungsrecht eingeräumt, während im kanadischen eher das Einmischungsrecht betont wurde.[38] Die Schweiz und Österreich brachten dann in Genf, beim Expertentreffen über nationale Minderheiten, relativ weitgehende Vorschläge ein, die jedoch erneut nicht verabschiedet wurden. Auf dem 3. Treffen über die Menschliche Dimension in Moskau schließlich erfuhr der Vorschlag massive Unterstützung, vor allem durch Deutschland, die skandinavischen Staaten, viele N+N- und die MOE-Staaten. Die USA hingegen setzten sich lediglich für einen Vorschlag ein, die Möglichkeiten für Vermittlungen auf freiwilliger Basis zu erweitern. Paris und London unterstützten den Ansatz Washingtons und verhinderten dadurch eine gemeinsame Position der EG in dieser Frage. Gründe hierfür waren zum einen Befürchtungen der Regierungen, die Mechanismen könnten wegen brisanter Minoritätenfragen im eigenen Lande angewendet werden; dies galt für die Sowjetunion und Jugoslawien ebenso wie für Frankreich oder Großbritannien.[39] In Frankreich kam eine spezifische politische Tradition hinzu: Nach jakobi-

---

36 Vgl. Die KSZE-Mechanismen im Falle Jugoslawiens, in: NZZ, 3.7.1991; siehe die Dokumentation der Protokolle der AHB-Sitzungen in: Europa-Archiv, (1991) 21, S. D534ff; Heinz *Vetschera*, Die KSZE-Krisenmechanismen und ihr Einsatz in der Jugoslawien-Krise, in: Österreichische Militärische Zeitschrift, (1992) 5, S. 405-411.

37 Vgl. Prager Dokument, S. 83ff, Ziff. 29.

38 Vgl. Sylvia *Rohde-Liebenau*, Menschenrechte und internationale Sicherheit, in: Michael *Staack* (Hrsg.), Aufbruch nach Gesamteuropa. Die KSZE nach der Wende im Osten, Münster: Lit-Verlag 1992, S. 247-278 (270).

39 Vgl. Murren über den Bremser EG, in: Frankfurter Rundschau (FR), 23.9.1991; Udo *Berdoll*, Alle gegen einen in Europa, in: SZ, 4.10.1991. In Frankreich bestehen beispielsweise Minderheitenprobleme mit den Korsen, Bretonen und Basken, in Großbritannien mit den Wallisern und Schotten.

nischem Selbstverständnis gibt es nur eine Nation und eine Nationalität, also keine Minderheiten.[40]

Bei der Diskussion in Helsinki über die Befugnisse und Handlungsrichtlinien für den *Hohen Kommissar für nationale Minderheiten* äußerten einige Staaten Vorbehalte wegen der Verbindung zwischen Minderheitenfragen und Terrorismus. Die Türkei und Großbritannien waren aufgrund ihrer spezifischen Problemlagen (radikale Kurden/PKK bzw. Nordirland/IRA) besonders daran interessiert, diese Verbindung aus der Zuständigkeit des HCM auszugrenzen. Im Ergebnis wurde dem Hohen Kommissar laut Helsinki-Dokument verboten, mit Personen/Organen, die Terror oder Gewalt ausüben, Kontakt aufzunehmen.[41] Problematisch bleibt die Frage, wer die Grenzfälle entscheidet. Denn häufig kommt es in der Frühphase eines Minderheitenkonflikts bereits zur Gewaltanwendung auf seiten der Minderheit. Dadurch könnte der HCM jederzeit in seinen Handlungsmöglichkeiten blockiert werden und nationale Minderheitenpolitik freie Hand gewinnen.

Gleichermaßen schrittweise wurde der Dringlichkeitsmechanismus etabliert und verbessert. Beim Pariser Gipfel war ein solcher Mechanismus bereits diskutiert worden, jedoch wegen des vorhandenen Widerstandes einiger Teilnehmer lediglich als zukünftige Option in das Dokument eingeflossen. Anläßlich des Berliner Ratstreffens konnte zuletzt der Widerstand Rußlands, der Türkei und Jugoslawiens überwunden und der Mechanismus eingerichtet werden. Bezeichnenderweise war die Voraussetzung dafür jedoch, daß das Prinzip der Nichteinmischung in die inneren Angelegenheiten ausdrücklich hervorgehoben wurde. Der Mechanismus fand dann umgehend wegen der Zuspitzung der Situation in Jugoslawien praktische Anwendung.[42] Die Konsens-minus-eins-Regel, derzufolge die KSZE-Staaten in Fällen von "eindeutigen, groben und nicht behobenen Verletzungen einschlägiger KSZE-Verpflichtungen" politische Erklärungen und Maßnahmen gegen einen Teilnehmerstaat ohne dessen Zustimmung ergreifen können, wurde jedoch erst anläßlich des Prager Ratstreffens im Januar 1992 verabschiedet. Auch hier waren Einwände aus Washington, London und Paris, aber auch aus Bukarest zu überwinden. Die grundsätzlichen Bedenken richteten sich unter anderem dagegen, daß diese Konsens-minus-betroffener-Staat-Regel im konkreten Fall jeweils eine Einmischung in die inneren Angelegenheiten bedeuten könnte.[43]

Auch das Fehlen einer obligatorischen Streitschlichtung im Rahmen der KSZE ist vor allem durch politische Konflikte bzw. das ausgeprägte Interesse einiger Re-

---

40 Vgl. Konrad *Mrusek*, Im Schatten der Balkan-Krise. Nur geringe Fortschritte bei der Genfer KSZE-Konferenz über Minderheiten, in: Frankfurter Allgemeine Zeitung (FAZ), 22.7.1991.

41 Vgl. Helsinki-Dokument 1992, Beschlüsse, S. 784, Abschn. II, Ziff. 25.

42 Die erste Dringlichkeitssitzung fand am 3./4. Juli 1991 in Prag statt; siehe auch Anm. 36.

43 Vgl. Prager Dokument, Ziff. 16, S. 84; vgl. auch Genscher und Havel fordern KSZE-Friedenstruppen, in: SZ, 31.1.1992.

gierungen erklärbar, ihre Souveränität nicht durch internationale Vereinbarungen oder Institutionen einschränken zu lassen. Der *Valletta-Mechanismus für friedliche Streitbeilegung* mittels einer freiwilligen Einschaltung von Vermittlern entsprach bei weitem nicht den Ansprüchen der Vorschläge zu diesem Thema.[44] Im Wiener Mandat war die Aufgabe für das Treffen in La Valletta noch anspruchsvoll formuliert worden: Es sollte eine Liste mit Kategorien von Streitfällen erstellt werden, die obligatorisch zur Vermittlung durch Dritte führen sollten; ebenso sollte die Möglichkeit der Verbindlichkeit getroffener Regelungen geprüft und möglichst festgelegt werden. In Valletta waren die Widerstände gegen derart weitreichende Regelungen indes so stark, daß zum Beispiel keine Definition der Streitkategorien akzeptiert wurde, welche die wahrscheinlichsten Konfliktursachen im neuen Europa, innerstaatliche oder "ethnonationalistische" Konflikte,[45] erfaßt hätte. Immerhin war eine einseitige Einleitung des Verfahrens vorgesehen. Aber sie sollte auch einseitig durch die Regierungen blockierbar bleiben, wenn "der Streitfall Fragen ihrer territorialen Integrität oder ihrer Landesverteidigung, ihrer Hoheitsansprüche auf Landgebiete oder konkurrierende Ansprüche hinsichtlich der Hoheitsgewalt über andere Gebiete berührt".[46] Auf dieser Regelung bestanden vor allem die Türkei und Griechenland wegen ihrer territorialen Ansprüche gegeneinander sowie Großbritannien angesichts seines Konflikts mit Spanien über Gibraltar.[47]

Im Vorfeld zum Helsinki-Folgetreffen setzte Paris – erstaunlich angesichts der in La Valletta eingenommenen eher restriktiven Position, weniger allerdings angesichts der traditionell verbreiteten legalistischen Politik- bzw. Staatsauffassung in Frankreich – mit einem umfassenden Vorschlag für einen "Sicherheitspakt" neue Akzente in dieser Frage. Frankreich propagierte darin die Weiterentwicklung der KSZE zu einer internationalen Organisation und die Umwandlung der bisherigen KSZE-Schlußakte und der weiterführenden Dokumente in einen völkerrechtlichen Vertrag. Auf dem Prager Ratstreffen unterbreiteten Paris und Bonn die Idee, ein Expertengremium zu beauftragen, einen "Entwurf eines Statuts für ein KSZE-Gremium für Vergleichs- und Schiedsspruchverfahren" auszuarbeiten. Dieser Vor-

44 Vgl. hierzu Oliver *Mietzsch*, Die KSZE als regionale Institution zur Konfliktverhütung und Streitbeilegung, in: *Staack*, Aufbruch nach Gesamteuropa, S. 91-117 (96ff).

45 Vgl. Peter *Schlotter*, Es gibt in diesem Konflikt nicht nur Gut und Böse: Im jugoslawischen Bürgerkrieg kann nur noch die KSZE vermitteln, in: FR, 29.8.1991; *Holsti*, A "Zone of Civility"?, S. 6 und S. 16-19.

46 Vgl. Abschnitt XII des Berichts von La Valletta vom 8.2.1991, S. 189. In der Praxis wird indes nicht überprüft, ob ein Staat zu Recht behauptet, daß einer der Ausschlußgründe laut Abschnitt XII anzuwenden sei. Siehe hierzu Stefan *Lehne*, The CSCE in the 1990s. Common European House or Potemkin Village?, Wien: Braunmühl 1991, S. 31ff.

47 Vgl. Berthold *Meyer*/Peter *Schlotter*, Auf dem Weg zu einer europäischen Friedensordnung, in: Johannes *Schwerdtfeger*/Egon *Bahr*/Gert *Krell* (Hrsg.), Friedensgutachten 1991, Münster: Lit-Verlag 1991, S. 111f; siehe auch Dieter *Senghaas*, Friedliche Streitbeilegung und kollektive Sicherheit im neuen Europa, in: Europa-Archiv, (1991) 10, S. 311-317.

schlag fand die Zustimmung des Ratstreffens.[48] Angesichts des grundsätzlichen Widerstandes Washingtons und Londons nahm die französische Regierung aber Abstand von den Plänen für einen umfassenden Sicherheitsvertrag und unterbreitete in Helsinki statt dessen lediglich Teile seines umfangreichen Ausgangsvorschlags: den Vorschlag zur Einrichtung eines Schlichtungs- und Schiedsgerichtshofes im Rahmen der KSZE und für einen erweiterten Verhaltenskodex (Code of Conduct) im Bereich militärischer Sicherheitsfragen.[49] Unterstützt wurden diese Vorschläge zunächst vor allem von Deutschland, später auch von anderen Teilnehmerstaaten.[50]

Der Widerstand Washingtons und Londons richtet sich nicht in erster Linie gegen diese Vorschläge für eine Verbesserung der Schlichtungsvorkehrungen. Dies zeigt der Vorschlag, den die USA als Antwort auf die französischen Vorstellungen einbrachte. Washington propagierte darin eine erweiterte politische Schlichtung durch den Rat bzw. den AHB.[51] Die amerikanischen Vorbehalte bezogen sich vor allem auf die vorgesehene Form, also dagegen, daß der Gerichtshof bzw. der Verhaltenskodex ausdrücklich als eine Vorstufe zu einem umfassenden KSZE-Sicherheitsvertrag bezeichnet wurde. Die rechtliche Formalisierung der KSZE, das heißt deren Umwandlung in eine internationale Organisation im Sinne des Völkerrechts, war und ist für die amerikanische Regierung unannehmbar. Washington sieht darin weiterhin – im Zusammenhang mit der Debatte um die westeuropäische Gemeinsame Außen- und Sicherheitspolitik (GASP) und das deutsch-französische Korps – den Versuch, die NATO zu schwächen. Dadurch würde der Einfluß der USA auf die europäische Sicherheitspolitik weiter zurückgedrängt, was Washington nicht hinzunehmen bereit ist.[52] Paris zielt auf die Stärkung einer (west-)europäischen Sicherheitsidentität, auch im Rahmen der KSZE. Washington hingegen sieht in der NATO *die* zentrale sicherheitspolitische Institution, deren Stellenwert durch die Entwicklung der KSZE auf gesamteuropäischer Ebene nicht beeinträchtigt werden darf.

48 Vgl. Prager Dokument, Zusammenfassung der Schlußfolgerungen, Ziff. 21, S. 88.

49 Vgl. Helsinki-Dokument 1992, zum Schiedsgerichtshof S. 788, Abschn. III, Ziff. 58, zum Verhaltenskodex S. 793, Ziff. 12.

50 Der Vorschlag für einen Verhaltenskodex wurde von Frankreich beim Helsinki-Folgetreffen zusammen mit Belgien, Bulgarien, Estland, Deutschland, Griechenland, Irland, Malta, Polen, Rumänien, Rußland und Spanien eingebracht.

51 Vgl. den Vorschlag der USA auf dem Helsinki-Folgetreffen vom 15.6.1992 (CSCE/WG1/11).

52 Vgl. als Hintergrund z.B. Wer sorgt für Frieden und Sicherheit in Europa (Leitartikel, gezeichnet H. K.), in: NZZ, 31.5./1.6.1992; Erich *Hauser*, Washington hat die Verbündeten ausgetrickst, in: Bonner Generalanzeiger, 3.6.1991; Karl-Heinz *Kamp*, Ein Spaltpilz für das Atlantische Bündnis? Das deutsch-französische "Eurokorps", in: Europa-Archiv, (1992) 15-16, S. 445-452; Eurokorps in die NATO eingebunden, in: SZ, 22.1.1993.

Dieses politische Spannungsverhältnis zwischen den westlichen Bündnispartnern Paris und Washington[53] hat seit dem Ende des Ost-West-Konflikts die KSZE-Verhandlungen bis in die Diskussion über Einzelheiten verschiedener Vorschläge geprägt. Ein wichtiger Streitpunkt war die Frage der Verbindung zwischen der KSZE und anderen internationalen Organisationen, namentlich der NATO. Obgleich nach einigen Mühen darüber grundsätzliches Einvernehmen erreicht schien, tauchte die Frage erneut auf, als es um die Festlegung der Einzelheiten bei den friedenserhaltenden Missionen im KSZE-Rahmen ging. Angesichts der fehlenden Infrastruktur und Truppen der KSZE wurde dabei konkret über die Frage gestritten, ob und wie die NATO oder die WEU (oder auch die GUS) in die Durchführung entsprechender Maßnahmen einbezogen werden könne. Während Paris die Rolle und den Beitrag der einzelnen Staaten herausstellen, die Organisation als solche hingegen kleinschreiben wollte, war Washington (unterstützt von anderen Bündnisstaaten, besonders Großbritannien und den Niederlanden) bemüht, als Ansprechpartner die NATO als Organisation herauszustellen.

Ergebnisse dieser Kontroversen waren pragmatische Regelungen, die den Interessenkonflikt sicher nicht endgültig gelöst haben: Zur obligatorischen Streitbeilegung findet sich im Helsinki-Dokument 1992 die Perspektive, daß die KSZE-Staaten die Vorschläge auf einem speziellen Treffen weiterverwenden werden und eine obligatorische Streitbeilegung unter Einbeziehung von Zwangselementen auf dem Ratstreffen in Stockholm im Dezember 1992 wenn möglich verabschieden wollten.[54] Dies geschah dann auch, allerdings ohne die USA und einige andere Staaten, die dem dort vereinbarten KSZE-Schiedsgerichtshof nicht beigetreten sind. Darüber hinaus bleibt es trotz der neuen Prozeduren und Mechanismen (Schlichtungskommission und Schlichtung auf Anordnung) bei der Veto-Option für den Fall, daß die betroffenen Staaten ihre "territoriale Integrität, oder ihre Landesverteidigung, ihre Hoheitsansprüche auf Landgebiete oder konkurrierende Ansprüche der Hoheitsgewalt über andere Gebiete" berührt sehen. Im Falle friedenserhaltender Maßnahmen wurde schließlich festgelegt, daß die KSZE andere Organisationen um Unterstützung ersuchen kann, daß dieses Ersuchen indes von Fall zu Fall beschlossen wird.[55]

Diese Ergebnisse wurden nach oftmals langwieriger und intensiver Überzeugungsarbeit trotz der vielschichtigen grundsätzlichen Widerstände zentraler Akteure erreicht. Zwei Faktoren begünstigten dies: Zum einen sahen sich die KSZE-Staaten sehr bald nach der Überwindung des Ost-West-Konflikts durch neue, akute Krisen herausgefordert. Da andere Institutionen aufgrund ihrer funktional oder

---

53 Flora *Lewis*, Tedious: French and Americans, in: International Harald Tribune, 24.7.1992.

54 Vgl. Helsinki-Dokument 1992, Beschlüsse, Abschn. III, Ziff. 57-62, S. 788.

55 Vgl. Helsinki-Dokument 1992, Beschlüsse, Abschn. III, Ziff. 52ff, S. 788. Bericht des KSZE-Treffens über Friedliche Streitbeilegung in La Valletta vom 8.2.1991, Art. XII, Ziff. 2.

geographisch beschränkten Zuständigkeit nicht geeignet waren bzw. zumindest zunächst nicht entsprechend umorganisiert werden sollten, bot sich allein der Ausbau der KSZE als gesamteuropäische Antwort an. Zum zweiten kam die Forderung aus den Staaten Osteuropas, nach der Auflösung der ehemals von der Sowjetunion dominierten internationalen Organisationen (WVO, RGW) in die westlichen Institutionen aufgenommen zu werden, vor allem in die EG und die NATO. Dazu gehörten auch weitreichende Vorstellungen über den Ausbau der KSZE, der trotz verschiedener Widerstände in einigen westlichen Staaten zumindest teilweise zugestanden wurde. Östliche Regierungen konnten dies zu Recht als ein Trostpflaster dafür verstehen, daß die westlichen Staaten nicht bereit waren, ihnen kurzfristig und umfassend die Vollmitgliedschaft in der EG oder der NATO anzubieten.

III. Normendurchsetzung und Institutionenbildung in der KSZE: Zusammenfassung

1. Bewertung der KSZE-Institutionalisierung

Warum steht die auf den ersten Blick positiv anmutende Bilanz der KSZE-Institutionalisierung in so krassem Widerspruch zu den bisher erbrachten Leistungen bei der Konfliktverhütung und Konfliktbewältigung? Warum ist der Ausbau der KSZE so weit fortgeschritten und bleibt dennoch der Vorwurf an die KSZE, ein "zahnloser Papiertiger" zu sein?

Durch das Ende des Ost-West-Konflikts sind weder das Sicherheitsdilemma noch die Möglichkeit des Versuchs einseitiger Interessendurchsetzung mit militärischen Mitteln als Unsicherheitsfaktoren in der internationalen Politik beseitigt worden. Unübersehbar stellen sich angesichts der fortbestehenden anarchischen Struktur der internationalen Gemeinschaft souveräner Staaten daher im Rahmen der KSZE erneut die alten Probleme bei dem Versuch, ein System "kollektiver Sicherheit" zu schaffen:[56] Wie kann im Konfliktfall die Staatengemeinschaft funktional effektiv und politisch legitimiert eingreifen? Mindestvoraussetzungen hierfür sind eine konsensuale Beurteilung der jeweiligen Lage und darüber hinaus des akuten Handlungsbedarfs, also Einvernehmen zwischen den normen- und regeltreuen Staaten über die politisch und funktional angemessenen Aktionen zur Durchsetzung der KSZE-Normen gegen "Gewalttäter". Unter welchen Bedingungen kommt es zur internationalen Intervention in zwischen- oder innerstaatlichen Konflikten? Wird auf Hilferufe im Falle von Verletzungen international verein-

56 Josef *Joffe*, Collective Security and the Future of Europe, in: Survival, 34 (Frühling 1992) 1, S. 36-50; Clifford *Kupchan*/Charles A. *Kupchan*, A Tune for Europe from a Concert of Old, in: International Security, 16 (Sommer 1991) 1, S. 114ff; Reinhard *Wolf*, Kollektive Sicherheit und das neue Europa, in: Europa-Archiv, (1992) 13, S. 365-374.

barter Normen kollektiv reagiert, auch wenn "nationale" Sicherheitsinteressen nicht unmittelbar bedroht sind?

Auf den ersten Blick ergeben sich Möglichkeiten und Grenzen für den Erfolg des Versuchs, die internationale Anarchie durch internationale Institutionen abzuschwächen, vor allem aus dem Grad an Unabhängigkeit von staatlicher Kontrolle, also von der Fähigkeit der Institution, als "objektiver", unabhängiger Akteur in das zwischenstaatliche Geschehen einzugreifen, um international ausgehandelte Ziele und Normen durchzusetzen. Die bisherige Institutionalisierung der KSZE hat indes lediglich zu internationalen Einrichtungen geführt. Das heißt, sie verfügt über keine supranationalen Elemente, so daß jeder Staat ein Vetorecht bei Beschlüssen und Aktionen im Namen der KSZE hat. Das Konsensprinzip ist also – trotz einiger Ausnahmen – nach wie vor die Grundlage für alle weiterführenden Beschlüsse und Aktionen der KSZE.

Die bisherigen Ergebnisse der Verhandlungen zwischen den zwei grundsätzlich unterschiedlichen Positionen der Regierungen zur Institutionalisierung haben die staatliche Kontrolle des KSZE-Prozesses letztlich unangetastet gelassen. Was die Institution KSZE als kollektiver Akteur darf und kann, hängt daher im Einzelfall vom Konsens der Teilnehmerstaaten bzw. von der Qualität der Organe, Mechanismen und Prozeduren ab, die für bestimmte Zwecke eingerichtet worden sind. Im Falle der Konsens-minus-eins-Regelung ist die Leistungsfähigkeit der KSZE davon abhängig, inwieweit die Staaten dazu bereit gewesen sind, vorab die kollektive Entscheidung zu delegieren und die Mittel für geeignete Maßnahmen vorab zur Verfügung zu stellen, sowie vom notwendigen Konsens zwischen den übrigen, den normen- und regeltreuen Staaten. Vorwürfe, die KSZE sei in konkreten Konfliktsituationen machtlos, fallen daher auf jene Regierungen zurück, die sich gegen weitergehende Kompetenzen der KSZE ausgesprochen haben. In dieser Grundstruktur unterscheidet sich die KSZE im übrigen kaum von anderen Institutionen, etwa den VN, der NATO, der WEU oder der EG.[57]

Die Notwendigkeit von Konsensentscheidungen kann in akuten Konfliktsituationen ein Hindernis für Eingriffe der KSZE (oder anderer internationaler Organisationen) bedeuten. Beispiele liefert der Konflikt zwischen Armenien und Aserbaidschan um und in Nagornyj-Karabach: Die Konfliktparteien waren nicht gewillt, Waffenstillstandsvereinbarungen zu treffen, die die unverzichtbare Voraussetzung für die beschlossenen friedenserhaltenden Maßnahmen der KSZE wären.[58] Gleichfalls hat der Konflikt in Jugoslawien wiederholt gezeigt, wie zweifelhaft in derartigen Situationen die Zustimmung der Konfliktparteien zu kollektiven Maßnahmen der Friedenserhaltung sein kann, weil sie meist taktisch bedingt

57 Vgl. z.B. zur Leistungsfähigkeit der VN *Holsti*, Peace and War, Kap. 12.

58 Militärbeobachter der KSZE nach Nagornyj-Karabach, in: FAZ, 10.7.1992; Konferenz in Rom boykottiert, in: SZ, 6.8.1992.

ist. Darüber hinaus haben sich die wirtschaftlichen Sanktionsmaßnahmen einmal mehr als stumpfe Waffen erwiesen.[59]

Selbst wenn es um Maßnahmen im Rahmen der *Konsens-minus-eins-Regelung* geht, also dem Regelverletzer keine Vetomöglichkeit eingeräumt ist, ist es offensichtlich bereits bei wirtschaftlichen Sanktionen problematisch, einen "Mehrheitskonsens" herzustellen, denn es ist keinesfalls garantiert, daß die normen- und regeltreuen Staaten einig sind in der Beurteilung der Lage und die gleichen Maßnahmen für erforderlich halten, geschweige denn, daß sie bei deren Umsetzung konzertiert handeln. Jüngste Beispiele lieferte die langwierige Diskussion auf dem Helsinki-Folgetreffen über den (zeitweiligen) Ausschluß Restjugoslawiens. Ganz abgesehen vom Widerstand Rußlands konnten selbst die EG-Staaten aufgrund der abweichenden Position Frankreichs nur mit erheblichen Problemen zu einer gemeinsamen Position finden. Allerdings scheint heute, nachdem trotz aller Schwierigkeiten ein gemeinsamer Beschluß vorliegt, das Problem der weiteren Aktivitäten im Rahmen des Rates/AHB nicht länger beim politischen Konsens, sondern bei der Suche nach funktional geeigneten Maßnahmen zu liegen.

Seit der Grundlegung in der Pariser Charta ist die Institutionenbildung im Rahmen der KSZE beachtlich vorangeschritten. Der Versuch, wirksame Organe, Instrumente und Entscheidungsprozeduren zur Durchsetzung der KSZE-Normen zu schaffen, hat jedoch das Spannungsverhältnis zwischen nationalstaatlicher Souveränität und handlungsfähigen KSZE-Institutionen bisher nicht überwunden, sondern reproduziert. Das Instrumentarium zur Konfliktverhütung und Krisenbewältigung weist daher vor allem dort Lücken auf, wo die Abtretung von Souveränität an internationale Institutionen am stärksten gefordert wäre: bei der obligatorischen Streitbeilegung und bei den friedenschaffenden Maßnahmen, also der Möglichkeit, militärische Zwangsmaßnahmen gegen Regelverletzer anzuwenden.

Das Spannungsverhältnis besteht weniger offensichtlich ebenfalls unter der Oberfläche bereits getroffener Vereinbarungen. Denn hinter zahlreichen Einzelbestimmungen der eindrucksvollen Institutionen-Kulisse der KSZE verbergen sich Formelkompromisse, die trotz verbleibender inhaltlicher Differenzen die Zustimmung aller ermöglichen. Die Tragfähigkeit dieser Kompromisse, also die Einhaltung der vereinbarten Normen oder die Akzeptanz und die jeweilige Anwendung der KSZE-Institutionen, bleiben letztlich fraglich und vor allem abhängig von der jeweiligen politischen Opportunität. Kritische Sollbruchstellen sind in dieser Hinsicht vor allem diejenigen Beschlüsse, die auf Vorschläge zurückgehen, die von einigen Regierungen nicht zuletzt wegen der mit diesen Maßnahmen einhergehenden Souveränitätsverzichte bzw. Einschränkungen des nationalen Handlungsspielraums als "illusionär" abgestempelt wurden und politisch grundsätzlich umstritten

59 Embargo wird umgangen, in: SZ, 21.7.1992; Sanktionen zeigen nur wenig Wirkung, in: SZ, 6.8.1992.

waren. Dies betraf vor allem die angesprochenen Fragen der Kompetenzausstattung der Organe und das Recht der KSZE, in die einzelstaatliche Politik auch gegen den Willen des betroffenen Staates durch internationale Instrumente, besonders die verschiedenen Mechanismen, einzugreifen.

Die einhegende Wirkung internationaler Institutionen auf die anarchische Struktur der Staatenwelt geht indes über die von den einzelnen Staaten und Regierungen kontrollierte und absichtlich durchgeführte Normensetzung und Schaffung von Instrumenten hinaus. Als unabsichtliche Konsequenzen sind auch zukünftig Einschränkungen der staatlichen Autonomie durch die systemische Wirkung der Institutionen nicht auszuschließen. Diese könnten die Konsensfindung im politischen Prozeß erleichtern und die Bedeutung erzielter Vereinbarungen verstärken. So wie sich in der Vergangenheit die Einflüsse des KSZE-Prozesses auf den Ost-West-Konflikt nur langfristig analysieren ließen,[60] ist eine mögliche systemische Wirkung auch künftig vermutlich nur langfristig feststellbar.

Die bisher letztlich unbefriedigende Wirksamkeit der KSZE bei der akuten Konfliktverhütung und der Konfliktbewältigung ist durch den grundsätzlich politischen Charakter der Konflikte bedingt. Für politische Konflikte gibt es keine "technischen Lösungen". Auch der umfassendste Katalog von Instrumenten und Mechanismen wäre keine Garantie für eine erfolgreiche Konfliktbewältigung oder wenigstens eine gewaltfreie Konfliktaustragung. Selbst wenn alle denkbaren oder wünschenswerten Instrumente und Mechanismen vorhanden wären, eröffnete dies noch nicht in jedem Fall die Möglichkeit, Regelverletzungen zu verhindern oder gegen Regelverletzer wirksam vorzugehen.

Die derzeitigen Erfahrungen der KSZE in den akuten Krisensituationen zeigen, daß trotz aller wertvollen Versuche, die Machtpolitik einzuhegen, nicht in erster Linie international vereinbarte Normen und Institutionen, sondern machtpolitisches Kalkül und "nationale" Sicherheitsinteressen die Handlungen der politischen Akteure – ob Staaten, Regionen oder Gruppen, ob auf seiten der Regelverletzer oder der herausgeforderten internationalen Gemeinschaft – bestimmen. Das Problem der Durchsetzung des Gewaltverzichts besteht nicht allein, weil Mißverständnisse und Fehlperzeptionen zwischen den Akteuren herrschen, sondern auch wegen gegensätzlicher Interessen bzw. der Bereitschaft bestimmter Akteure, für ihre Ziele und Interessen gewaltsame Mittel einzusetzen. Die KSZE-Institutionen, insbesondere die Mechanismen und die militärischen VSBM sind wegen ihres großenteils kooperativen Charakters vor allem wirksam gegenüber Unsicherheit, die aus dem Sicherheitsdilemma erwächst, aber wenig oder gar nicht, wenn es um einen offensiv agierenden, entschlossenen Aggressor geht.[61]

---

60 Vgl. *Peters*, Sicherheit in Europa nach dem Ost-West-Konflikt.

61 Vgl. *Wolf*, Kollektive Sicherheit und das neue Europa, S. 372f; *Holsti*, A "Zone of Civility"?, sowie Ingo *Peters*, Die Möglichkeiten der Politik militärischer Vertrauens- und Sicherheitsbil-

Im Falle der Konflikte in Jugoslawien waren die übrigen Staaten (abgesehen von divergierenden Interessenkalkülen) unter anderem deswegen unfähig, einen Konsens zu erreichen und damit zu wirksamen konzertierten Aktionen zu gelangen, weil Gewichtung und Legitimität des Territorialprinzips und des Prinzips der nationalen Selbstbestimmung strittig waren und noch sind. Während die USA, Großbritannien und Frankreich das Prinzip territorialer Integrität und Staatsbürgerschaft (citizenship) favorisierten, taten Deutschland, Österreich und Italien gleiches mit dem Selbstbestimmungsrecht und mit nationaler Identität.[62]

Die Funktionsbedingungen für ein System kollektiver Sicherheit gelten offensichtlich gleichermaßen für wirtschaftliche wie militärische Sanktionen und sind schwierig zu verwirklichen. Ein Manko liegt vor allem in der Konsensfindung und in der mangelhaften Umsetzung internationaler Beschlüsse aufgrund unterschiedlicher Interessenkalküle der Staaten und Regierungen. Die historischen und die aktuellen Probleme und Mißerfolge kollektiver Aktionen sind, wie Wolf schreibt, eben nicht zufällig, sondern in der Logik des Konzepts angelegt.[63] Daran würde sich auch nichts ändern, wenn es gelingen sollte, der KSZE und den KSZE-Vereinbarungen statt der politischen Verbindlichkeit einen völkerrechtlichen Status zu verleihen. Völkerrecht bleibt schwaches Recht in einem anarchischen internationalen System souveräner Staaten, in dem es per Definition kein Sanktionsmonopol gibt, durch das Übeltäter abgeschreckt oder bestraft werden könnten.[64]

Das letzte Kriterium aus der im Eingangsabschnitt vorgestellten Übersicht, also die Verfügbarkeit erforderlicher Finanz- und Sachmittel, ist bisher noch nicht offen angesprochen worden, verbirgt sich aber als zusätzliches Problem hinter einigen der bereits diskutierten Konfliktlinien über die institutionelle Ausgestaltung der KSZE. Die Friedensdividende aus der Abrüstung der zu Zeiten des Ost-West-Konflikts angehäuften Rüstungspotentiale ist bereits mehrfach ausgegeben, bevor diese Mittel für die aufwendigen internationalen Institutionen zur Konfliktverhütung und -bewältigung bereitgestellt werden konnten. Konferenzen, Konsultationen, Missionen und andere kooperative Instrumente bis hin zu friedenserhaltenden Maßnahmen sind jedoch kostenintensiv. Die Knappheit finanzieller Ressourcen setzt bereits heute der Kooperation enge Grenzen, zum Beispiel im Falle der Teilnahme der GUS-Staaten am *Nordatlantischen Kooperationsrat*, die teilweise

---

dender Maßnahmen sind größer als erwartet, in: Beiträge zur Konfliktforschung, (1988) 4, S. 91-116 (94-96 und 110ff).

62 Vgl. *Holsti*, A "Zone of Civility"?, S. 23; James *Mayall*, Nationalism and International Security after the Cold War, in: Survival, 34 (Frühling 1992) 1, S. 19-35 (32ff).

63 Vgl. *Wolf*, Kollektive Sicherheit und das neue Europa, S. 371.

64 Vgl. Wolfgang *Wagner*, Acht Lehren aus dem Fall Jugoslawien, in: Europa-Archiv, (1992) 2, S. 31-41. Wagner weist in seiner These 6 richtigerweise darauf hin, daß Regeln und Appelle gegen entschlossene Rechtsbrecher auch im innerstaatlichen Bereich nicht helfen – trotz des dort in der Regel vorhandenen Gewalt- und Sanktionsmonopols.

von der NATO finanziert wird. Der finanzielle Faktor beeinflußt auch die Fähigkeit und Bereitschaft der Regierungen, einer Weiterentwicklung internationaler Institutionen zuzustimmen. Funktional gilt es also, das allseits propagierte Ziel zu verwirklichen, die verschiedenen europäischen Sicherheitsinstitutionen komplementär zu entwickeln. Politisch stehen dem jedoch wiederum zumindest teilweise konfligierende Interessen und Ziele der Akteure gegenüber, die mit den einzelnen Institutionen verbunden sind.[65]

IV. Schlußfolgerungen und Handlungsempfehlungen

Welche Handlungsmöglichkeiten bieten sich im Lichte dieser Problemanalyse zur bisherigen Institutionalisierung der KSZE an, um die Institutionenbildung voranzutreiben und dadurch die Chancen für die Durchsetzung der KSZE-Normen, insbesondere des Gewaltverzichts, zu verbessern? Entlang der vorne entwickelten Kriterien sollen abschließend einige Folgerungen aus den bisherigen Erfahrungen der Institutionalisierung zu Handlungsempfehlungen zugespitzt werden, die normativ am Ziel orientiert sind, den friedlichen Wandel international zu befördern.

Kriterium A: Instrumente zur Früherkennung von Konflikten, zum kooperativen und konfrontativen Konfliktmanagement

- Die bisherigen Erfahrungen in der KSZE haben gezeigt, daß auch zunächst als illusionär bezeichnete Vorstellungen und Vorschläge trotz einiger Abstriche schließlich als neue Instrumente oder Maßnahmen der KSZE angenommen wurden. Weitreichende Vorschläge dienten dem Verhandlungsprozeß mehrfach als wichtige Orientierungsmarke und ermöglichten häufig Fortschritte, ohne sogleich greifbare Ergebnisse zu produzieren. Es gibt daher keinen Grund, sich von zeitweiligen Rückschlägen irritieren zu lassen. Weitreichende Vorschläge machen durchaus Sinn, wenn die Erwartungen nicht von vornherein unrealistisch überhöht sind.
- Die Möglichkeiten zur Früherkennung und Frühwarnung von Konfliktpotentialen müssen ausgebaut werden. Das Augenmerk ist auf die Erfahrungen zu richten, die mit dem HCM gesammelt werden. Sollten sich hier tatsächlich Barrieren zeigen, die sich aus nationalen Einspruchsmöglichkeiten gegen dessen Aktivitäten ergeben, dann sind Veränderungen der Bestimmungen anzustreben, die Auftrag und Handlungsspielraum des HCM neu definieren.
- Frühwarnung setzt voraus, daß nicht erst im Konfliktfall Ad-hoc-Arbeitsgruppen mit einzelnen Konfliktherden befaßt werden. Vielmehr sollten für ein-

65 Vgl. u.a. Anand *Menon*/Anthony *Forster*/William *Wallace*, A Common European Defence?, in: Survival, 34 (Herbst 1992) 3, S. 98-118; Edward *Mortimer*, European Security after the Cold War, London 1992 (IISS, Adelphi Paper 271).

schlägige "trouble spots" permanente Beobachtungsgruppen eingerichtet werden, die im Zuge eines Berichtssystems die Entwicklungen überwachen und dem Rat/AHB Empfehlungen geben könnten. Um die Kosten hierfür gering zu halten, sollten die nationalen diplomatischen Vertretungen in den entsprechenden Gebieten in das Berichtssystem einbezogen werden.

- Eine internationale Schiedsgerichtsbarkeit im Rahmen der KSZE, die für alle gleichermaßen verbindlich ist, bleibt ein sinnvolles politisches Ziel. Trotz der strukturell begrenzten Reichweite könnte diese Institution auch ohne Sanktionsmöglichkeiten helfen, die KSZE-Normen in der Politik der Teilnehmerstaaten fester zu verankern.
- Die gleiche Wirkung wäre vermutlich mit dem Schritt verbunden, die KSZE zu einer völkerrechtlichen Organisation "aufzuwerten". Allerdings müssen dabei kurzfristige Erfolge gegen die langfristigen Wirkungen abgewogen werden. Niemandem wäre damit gedient, wenn die KSZE zu einer Bürokratie verkrustete, die vom politischen Prozeß abgekoppelt wäre.
- Dem (Pseudo-)Hegemonialkonflikt zwischen den USA und Frankreich im Zuge ihrer KSZE-Politik und im Zusammenhang mit einer Verknüpfung europäischer und atlantischer Institutionen muß auf bi- und multilateraler Ebene weiterhin behutsam gegengesteuert werden. Denn es ist kontraproduktiv, die Bemühungen um die Zivilisierung und Einigung Europas auf Kosten transatlantischer Konflikte und einer Entfremdung der Amerikaner zu betreiben. In Frankreich besteht immerhin die Chance einer entspannteren Haltung gegenüber den USA nach dem nächsten Regierungs- bzw. Präsidentenwechsel. Die USA und Kanada haben eigene politische Interessen in Europa und können in Europa auch künftig positive Wirkungen entfalten, auch wenn die militärische Präsenz an direkter Bedeutung verliert.

Kriterium B: Anpassungsfähigkeit der Instrumente

- Das Instrument der Wirtschaftssanktionen gegen Regelverletzer muß entwickelt werden. Die Erfahrungen im Jugoslawienkonflikt sind mit dem Ziel auszuwerten, Maßnahmen zur Überwachung und Durchsetzung von Sanktionen zu vereinbaren, um diese soweit wie möglich zu standardisieren und im Bedarfsfall zügig umsetzen zu können.
- Militärische Interventionen müssen prinzipiell zwar ein letztes Mittel bleiben, dürfen aber nicht von vornherein ausgeschlossen sein, um ihre abschreckende Wirkung auf Regelverletzer glaubwürdig zu erhalten. Kraftmeierei mit Militäraktionen ohne greifbare Zielvorgabe ist indes inakzeptabel. Militärische Inter-

ventionen sind kaum gerechtfertigt, solange die Regierungen nicht in der Lage sind, Wirtschaftssanktionen effektiv einzusetzen.[66]

Kriterium C: Handlungsfähigkeit durch effektive Entscheidungsprozesse

- Der "Quantensprung" von der internationalen zur supranationalen Gesellschaft ist nicht in Sicht. Mitsprache und ein kontinuierlich entwickelter Konsens sind weiterhin Voraussetzungen dafür, daß die Institutionen und Strukturen der KSZE als im Interesse eines jeden Teilnehmerstaates liegend angesehen und als legitim anerkannt werden.
- Das Konsensprinzip sollte daher weiterhin die Regel für die Beschlußfassung sein und die Möglichkeit von Maßnahmen gegen einzelne Staaten die Ausnahme für die wichtigsten Regelverletzungen bleiben.
- Der Souveränitätsverzicht wird vor allem von jenen Staaten propagiert, deren Handlungsspielraum ohnehin eingeschränkt ist und die deshalb relativ wenig zu verlieren haben. Problematisch bleiben die Mächte, die tatsächlich über den relativ größten Handlungsspielraum verfügen, und jene, bei denen die Souveränität einen im Verhältnis zur Realität überhöhten Symbolwert besitzt.
- Daher ist es ratsam, die Bemühungen um teilweise Einschränkungen des nationalen Handlungsspielraums kontinuierlich zu konzertieren, ohne den Eindruck zu erwecken, dies geschehe lediglich aus Machtinteresse, gewissermaßen als Ersatzbefriedigung der Schwachen.
- Die aktuellen Konfliktherde in der ehemaligen Sowjetunion und im ehemaligen Jugoslawien sind Beispiele für Verletzungen internationaler Normen auf innerstaatlicher und internationaler Ebene, die sich großenteils aus der Auflösung des staatlichen Gewaltmonopols ergeben. Denn dort handelt es sich nicht allein um staatliche Gewaltanwendung durch Militär, sondern auch um die Normenverletzung etwa durch Milizen oder Freischärler (Tschetniks etc.).
- Einschränkungen des Konsensprinzips sind nur in dem Maße sinnvoll, in dem die Souveränität der Staaten tatsächlich das zentrale oder alleinige Hindernis für die Durchsetzung der KSZE-Normen ist. Sie helfen hingegen nicht direkt gegen Regelverletzungen durch nichtstaatliche Akteure.
- Die ersten greifbaren Erfahrungen mit der *Konsens-minus-eins-Regelung* und der international im Rahmen der KSZE legitimierten Intervention in inner- bzw. zwischenstaatliche Konflikte verdeutlichen, daß sehr bald eine Grundsatzdebatte über das Spannungsverhältnis zwischen dem Territorialprinzip und dem Prinzip der nationalen Selbstbestimmung notwendig ist.

---

66 Vgl. Hanns *Maull*, Zivilmacht Bundesrepublik Deutschland. Vierzehn Thesen für eine neue deutsche Außenpolitik, in: Europa-Archiv, (1992) 10, S. 269-278 (274).

- Diese Debatte ist mit dem Ziel zu initiieren, den relativen Stellenwert der beiden Prinzipien und die jeweiligen Konsequenzen unter verschiedenen Konfliktbedingungen festzulegen.

  Soweit möglich sollten für zukünftige Konflikte in realistischen Szenarien Handlungsoptionen im Sinne von *Standing Operational Procedures* als vorweggenommener Konsens für verschiedene Interventionsoptionen erarbeitet und soweit möglich festgelegt werden. Allerdings sollte die Bewältigung lokaler Bedrohungen flexibel bleiben und Rücksicht auf den Grad an Betroffenheit der einzelnen KSZE-Mitglieder nehmen. Angesichts der oben weiterhin als problematisch gewerteten Konzeption der kollektiven Sicherheit sollten einerseits nichtbetroffene KSZE-Mitglieder nicht über Gebühr beansprucht und in ihren jeweiligen Reaktionen festgelegt werden.[67] Andererseits muß ebenfalls gesichert sein, daß subregionale Akteure mit direkten Interessen und direkter Betroffenheit ihren Partikularinteressen nicht uneingeschränkt nachgehen. International kontrollierte und gleichzeitig zeitlich und funktional effektive Intervention bleibt eine Gratwanderung und ein politisch heikles Thema.

Forum für Sicherheitskooperation

- Die derzeitigen Konfliktherde im KSZE-Europa sind besonders dadurch gekennzeichnet und daher schwierig zu bearbeiten, weil sie zumindest teilweise mit der Auflösung des staatlichen Gewaltmonopols einhergehen.
- Dies führt zu der ebenso einsichtigen wie schwierig zu verwirklichenden Forderung, in den zukünftigen Rüstungskontrollverhandlungen im Rahmen des *KSZE-Forums für Sicherheitskooperation* sehr bald über die Kontrolle der leichten Infanterie- und Artilleriewaffen zu verhandeln, die von den bisherigen Reduzierungen und Beschränkungen im Rahmen der KSE-Vereinbarungen nicht erfaßt worden sind. Ziel dabei ist, diese Waffengattungen möglichst strengen und effektiven Restriktionen zu unterwerfen und den Freischärlern dadurch ihre Hauptkampfmittel zu entziehen.[68]
- Darüber hinaus gilt es, den internationalen Waffenhandel mit konventionellen Waffen allgemein zunächst innerhalb des zielorientierten Sicherheitsdialogs ins Visier zu nehmen, besonders weil der Markt durch die von der "Abrüstung" in Europa freigesetzten Rüstungsgüter zusätzlich angereichert wird!

---

67 Vgl. die Parallelargumentation in bezug auf die NATO bei Reinhard *Wolf*, Opfer des eigenen Erfolgs? Perspektiven der NATO nach dem Kalten Krieg, in: Aus Politik und Zeitgeschichte. Beilage zur Wochenzeitung Das Parlament, (1992) 13, S. 3-16 (15).

68 Vgl. Heinrich *Vogel*, Integration und Desintegration: Das europäische Dilemma, in: Europa-Archiv, (1992) 15-16, S. 433-438 (436).

Innenpolitische Rückkopplung

- Institutionen sind nur so mächtig, wie es die "souveränen" Staaten ihnen gemeinsam einräumen. Daher sollten die Anforderungen und Erwartungen an diese internationalen Institutionen nicht überstrapaziert werden. Insbesondere sollte *innenpolitisch* deren Leistungsfähigkeit nicht übersteigert dargestellt werden. Andernfalls könnte es leicht aus innenpolitischen, populistischen Gründen dazu kommen, daß Konflikte mit Mitteln bekämpft werden, die der "objektiven" Lage nicht angemessen sind, so daß die gesetzten Ziele unter Umständen geradezu konterkariert werden.

Politik, Konflikte und staatliche Souveränität können nicht per Deklamation abgeschafft werden. Dennoch ist Resignation angesichts der Wiederkehr immer gleicher, letztlich offenbar unlösbarer Problemstrukturen in der internationalen Politik keine verantwortbare Alternative. Zweifellos sind die Voraussetzungen für ein funktionierendes System kollektiver Sicherheit im Rahmen der KSZE derzeit jedoch nicht oder nur partiell gegeben. Dennoch gibt es hoffnungsvolle Ansätze, die bei gleichzeitig wirklichkeitsnaher Einschätzung der Möglichkeiten und Grenzen erweitert und vertieft werden sollten. Daher bleibt nur, den politischen Problemen weiterhin mit politischen Mitteln zu begegnen, auch wenn dadurch allenfalls zweitbeste Maßnahmen zur Konfliktverhütung und -bewältigung vereinbart werden. Politik ist und bleibt unvermeidlich das "Bohren harter Bretter" (Max Weber)!

7. Eine europäische Sicherheitskultur: Aussichten für eine regionalspezifische Normen- und Regimebildung

Michael Staack

I. Problemaufriß

Der die Nachkriegszeit prägende System- und Werteantagonismus zwischen freiheitlich-demokratischem Westen und kommunistischem Osten gehört seit den Herbstrevolutionen des Jahres 1989, spätestens aber seit dem mißlungenen Putsch in der Sowjetunion (August 1991), der Vergangenheit an. Mit der "Charta von Paris", am 21. November 1990 von den Staats- bzw. Regierungschefs der KSZE-Staaten feierlich unterzeichnet, wurden Demokratie, Rechtsstaatlichkeit, Marktwirtschaft und Gewaltverzicht als gemeinsames Wertefundament für ein "Neues Europa" festgelegt. Als hochrangiger internationaler politischer Verhaltensstandard hat sich die Charta seitdem mehrfach bewährt, vor allem während des versuchten Umsturzes in Moskau. Dennoch sind noch längst nicht alle ihre programmatischen Postulate schon gesamteuropäische Wirklichkeit. Die kriegerischen Auseinandersetzungen auf dem Gebiet des auseinandergefallenen Jugoslawien sind kein singuläres Phänomen, sondern stehen stellvertretend für das explosive Potential, das sich auch in anderen Teilen Europas aus Nationalismus, Wohlstandsgefälle, willkürlichen Grenzziehungen, Mangel an gefestigter Demokratie und anderen Lasten der Vergangenheit gebildet hat. Im bisherigen Verlauf des Jugoslawienkonfliktes wurde außerdem deutlich, daß die internationale (VN) bzw. die KSZE-Gemeinschaft auf derartige Konflikte zunächst kaum vorbereitet war und sich auch nachfolgend als nicht hinreichend fähig zur Konfliktbeendigung erwies.

Vor diesem Hintergrund stellt sich die Frage nach der Möglichkeit, nach der Wünschbarkeit und nach den Erfolgsbedingungen für eine regionalspezifische Sicherheitskultur im KSZE-Europa, in der Kooperation und gewaltfreie Konfliktregelung gefördert werden. Wird die Herausbildung einer solchen Sicherheitskultur durch besondere historische, ökonomische oder politisch-kulturelle Faktoren begünstigt? Welche Bedingungen müssen gegeben sein, um eine solche Sicherheitskultur aufzubauen? Was wurde im Rahmen der KSZE bereits erreicht? Können bestimmte Konstanten der Entwicklung Westeuropas nach 1945 – Souveränitätsverzicht und Integrationsbereitschaft – modellhaft für den Osten sein und gesamteuropäische Zusammenarbeit generieren? Sollte der KSZE-Raum geographisch neu bestimmt werden oder bietet die derzeitige KSZE-Welt den erfolgversprechenden Rahmen für eine regionalspezifische Sicherheitskultur?

Daß eine regionalspezifische Sicherheitskultur eine wünschbare Zielvorstellung darstellt, wird im folgenden aus zwei Gründen vorausgesetzt. Erstens hat der bisherige Verlauf des KSZE-Prozesses bereits zu einer erheblichen, von den Teilnehmerstaaten positiv bewerteten Normen- und Regimebildung geführt. Und zweitens erhöht eine regionale Beschränkung die Wahrscheinlichkeit, daß sich dieser Prozeß erfolgversprechender fortsetzt, als dies im globalen Rahmen etwa einer weitaus unspezifischeren "Neuen Weltordnung" möglich wäre.

Wenn im folgenden von "Sicherheit" die Rede ist, so wird im Sinne eines erweiterten Sicherheitsbegriffes argumentiert, der über die militärische Dimension von Sicherheit hinaus auch innenpolitische, ökonomische oder ökologische Faktoren einbezieht. Sicherheit bzw. Stabilität in Gesamteuropa bleiben auch unter den Bedingungen komplexer Interdependenz[1] von militärischen Regelungen mit abhängig, lassen sich aber keinesfalls auf diesen Sachbereich begrenzen.

In dieser Studie wird die These vertreten, daß sich die Sicherheitskultur des gesamteuropäischen Raums im Vergleich zu anderen Weltregionen vor allem durch zwei Spezifika auszeichnet. Erstens: Eine Wertegemeinschaft, beruhend auf der Akzeptanz von Demokratie, Rechtsstaat und Marktwirtschaft, ist prinzipiell vorhanden. Zweitens: Gesamteuropa ist geprägt durch einen hohen Grad der Verregelung durch Regime bzw. Institutionen. Hinzu kommt, daß nahezu alle politischen Führungen an dauerhafter gesamteuropäischer Kooperation interessiert sind und eine Mehrzahl der europäischen Staaten, insbesondere die größeren, politisch führenden bzw. wirtschaftlich wichtigen, die Aufrechterhaltung der gegenwärtigen europäischen Ordnung als ein erstrebenswertes Ziel ansehen.

Die nachfolgenden Überlegungen können im Rahmen dieser Studie nicht vollständig ausgearbeitet werden. Ziel ist es, einen umfassenden Themenaufriß mit ersten Handlungsorientierungen vorzulegen.

II. Demokratie als notwendige Bedingung des Friedens

Aus einer Analyse der Gründe, die zum Ende des Ost-West-Konflikts führten, ergeben sich wesentliche Schlußfolgerungen für die Gestaltung einer gesamteuropäischen Sicherheitskultur. Die Beendigung dieses Konflikts wurde durch verschiedenartige Strukturveränderungen beeinflußt, unter anderem durch den Bedeutungsgewinn des Sachbereichs Wirtschaft/Wohlfahrt gegenüber dem Sachbereich militärische Sicherheit und durch die Attraktivität der prosperitätsfördernden Integration Westeuropas. Der Konflikt löste sich aber erst auf mit dem Zusammenbruch des kommunistischen Herrschafts- und Wirtschaftssystems. Aus Gorbatschows Versuch der radikalen Systemreform wurde eine Systemüberwindung.

In den späten 40er und frühen 50er Jahren als Macht- und Systemkonkurrenz angelegt, war aus dem Ost-West-Konflikt spätestens mit den Volksaufständen 1953

---

1 Siehe Robert *Keohane*/Joseph *Nye*, Power and Interdependence: World Politics in Transition, 2. Aufl., Boston 1989.

(DDR) und 1956 (Ungarn) in erster Linie eine Machtkonkurrenz geworden. Bedingt durch den Expansionsanspruch der kommunistischen Diktaturen und deren systemnotwendige Abschottung aus Gründen der Selbsterhaltung wurde der Systemunterschied konfliktpolitisch aufgeladen. Die Interessen der regierenden Minderheit entwickelten sich immer weniger kongruent zu denen einer gesellschaftlichen Mehrheit, für die die Staats-, Gesellschafts- und Wirtschaftsordnung der demokratischen Industriestaaten längst zum Modell geworden war. Als sich die östlichen Gesellschaften ihrer kaum noch handlungsfähigen Herrschaftssysteme entledigten, ging daher auch die Nachkriegsordnung antagonistischer Blöcke zu Ende. Daraus ergibt sich "die wichtigste Lehre des Ost-West-Konflikts ...: Demokratisierung ist die einzig wirksame Strategie zur Eliminierung der Gewalt und zur Institutionalisierung gewaltfreier Konfliktbearbeitungsmodi."[2]

Seit Kants Schrift "Zum Ewigen Frieden" (1795) ist die These schlüssig begründet, daß Demokratien untereinander keine Kriege führen. Diese Aussage wird von der quantitativen Kriegsursachenforschung nahezu einhellig unterstützt.[3] Für die These von der Friedfertigkeit von Demokratien untereinander sprechen vor allem die folgenden sechs Argumente: (1) Demokratisch gewählte Eliten müssen nicht auf äußere Expansion zurückgreifen, um ihre Herrschaft zu sichern. (2) Die Gruppe der Wahlbevölkerung als Hauptleidtragende eines Krieges kann den politischen Prozeß mit Aussicht auf Erfolg nutzen, um Eliten an der Kriegführung zu hindern. (3) Im demokratischen Willensbildungsprozeß hat eine kriegerische Politik nur geringe Chancen, akzeptiert zu werden. (4) Demokratische Wahlen produzieren in der Regel risikoabgeneigte, zentristisch orientierte Eliten. (5) Demokratische Staaten respektieren eher die politischen Strukturen einer anderen Demokratie und verhalten sich deshalb ablehnend gegenüber dem Rückgriff auf Gewaltanwendung im Verhältnis zu einer solchen Demokratie. Schließlich fördert (6) die Existenz von zivilen Gesellschaften und Rechtsstaatlichkeit im Innern die Akzeptanz entsprechender Verhaltensstandards (z.B. Völkerrecht, friedliche Konfliktbeilegung) auch nach außen.[4]

---

2 Ernst-Otto *Czempiel*, Weltpolitik im Umbruch. Das internationale System nach dem Ende des Ost-West-Konflikts, München 1991, S. 28.

3 Vgl. dazu mit weiteren Nachweisen "Democracy and Foreign Policy: Community and Constraint", Sondernummer der Zeitschrift Journal of Conflict Resolution, 35 (Juni 1991) 2; Klaus Jürgen *Gantzel*/Jens *Siegelberg*, Krieg und Entwicklung. Überlegungen zur Theoretisierung von Kriegsursachen unter besonderer Berücksichtigung der Zeit seit 1945, in: Politische Vierteljahresschrift, 31 (1990) Sonderheft 21 (Theorien der Internationalen Beziehungen. Bestandsaufnahme und Forschungsperspektiven), S. 219-239; Zeev *Maoz*/Nasrin *Abdolali*, Regime Types and International Conflicts, 1816-1976, in: Journal of Conflict Resolution, 33 (März 1989) 1, S. 3-35; Randall *Schweller*, Domestic Structure and Preventive War: Are Democracies More Pacific?, in: World Politics, 44 (Januar 1992) 2, S. 235-269.

4 Charles A. *Kupchan*/Clifford A. *Kupchan*, Concerts, Collective Security, and the Future of Europe, in: International Security, 16 (Sommer 1991) 1, S. 149; vgl. außerdem Michael *Doyle*, Liberalism and World Politics, in: American Political Science Review, 80 (Dezember 1986) 4,

Auch unter Demokratien bestehen selbstverständlich unterschiedliche bzw. gegensätzliche Interessen fort. Ihre Gesellschaften lassen deren gewaltsame Austragung aber nicht zu. Sie bevorzugen auch für die Konfliktbearbeitung im demokratischen Binnenverhältnis gewaltfreie Lösungsstrategien, wie sie ihrer innerstaatlichen Politik eigen sind, so "daß sich in der internationalen Politik eine Insel des Friedens in einem Meer von Konflikten herausgebildet hat" und "seit (mindestens) 1816 ... Demokratien (fast) keine Kriege mehr gegeneinander geführt"[5] haben. Die empirische Evidenz zugunsten der Friedfertigkeit von Demokratien untereinander kann aber nicht zu der generellen Annahme führen, daß Demokratien per se friedlich seien. Gegenüber nicht-demokratischen Staaten besteht ihre Gewaltbereitschaft fort und äußert sich in einer entsprechender Konflikthäufigkeit.[6] Wie läßt sich diese Differenz erklären?

Die Antwort ist in der Perzeption von Demokratien untereinander zu suchen. Innerstaatliche demokratische Verfaßtheit wirkt auf andere Demokratien offensichtlich als "vertrauensbildende Maßnahme", während ein nicht-demokratisches Herrschaftssystem als potentielle Bedrohung wahrgenommen wird. Demokratische Verhältnisse tragen wiederum dazu bei, daß diese Perzeption wesentlich schwieriger manipuliert werden kann als es in autokratischen oder teildemokratischen Systemen der Fall ist. Demokratische Staaten neigen also dazu, von der Gewalthaltigkeit der Herrschaftsstruktur auf die Außenpolitik von Staaten zu schließen und sich dementsprechend zu verhalten.[7] Diese Verhaltensnorm wird abgestützt durch die Offenheit von bzw. Öffentlichkeit in demokratischen Entscheidungsprozessen. Schließlich tragen auch die transnationalen, zwischengesellschaftlichen Beziehungen über Staatsgrenzen hinweg zur Vertrauensbildung bei. Sie fördern sowohl die zwischenstaatliche Friedfertigkeit als auch, darüber hinaus, die Fähigkeit und Bereitschaft zur Kooperation.

Die Demokratisierung der Staatenwelt stellt folglich die wirksamste und dauerhafteste Friedensstrategie dar. Der Demokratisierungsprozeß in Osteuropa ordnet sich ein in einen globalen, seit den 70er Jahren anhaltenden Trend hin zur Demokratisierung und damit zur Ausweitung der liberalen Friedenszone im internatio-

---

S. 1151-1169; *ders.*, Kant, Liberal Legacies, and Foreign Affairs, in: Philosophy and Public Affairs, Part I, 12 (Sommer 1983) 3, S. 205-235; Part II, ebd., 12 (Herbst 1983) 4, S. 323-353; T. Clifton *Morgan*/Sally Howard *Campbell*, Domestic Structure, Decisional Constraints, and War: So Why Kant Democracies Fight?, in: Journal of Conflict Resolution, 35 (Juni 1991) 2, S. 187ff.

5 Thomas *Risse-Kappen*, Unfriedliche Demokratien? Demokratischer Frieden? Überlegungen zu einem theoretischen Puzzle. Arbeitspapier für die HSFK-Konferenz "Frieden und Konflikt in den internationalen Beziehungen" zu Ehren von Ernst-Otto Czempiels 65. Geburtstag, Frankfurt a.M., 29.-31.5.1992, S. 7.

6 Vgl. hierzu die in Anm. 3 genannte Literatur.

7 *Risse-Kappen*, Unfriedliche Demokratien?, S. 32ff.

nalen System.[8] Das Ende des Ost-West-Konflikts hat insofern außerordentlich gute Bedingungen geschaffen, um den politischen Großraum Europa zu einer Zone des "demokratischen Friedens" (so US-Außenminister James Baker) werden zu lassen. Außer dem amerikanischen Kontinent gibt es keine Region mit einem vergleichbar hohen Demokratisierungsgrad.

Um eine Sicherheitskultur auf dieser Grundlage auszugestalten, sind jedoch noch erhebliche politische Anstrengungen notwendig: (1) Die Demokratie als staatliche Verfassungsform in den ehemals kommunistischen Staaten muß sich stabilisieren können. (2) Die zunächst vielfach nur "aufgesetzte" demokratische Verfassung muß abgestützt werden durch eine demokratische politische Kultur; durch die Entwicklung "ziviler Gesellschaften". (3) Beide Zielsetzungen können nur erreicht werden, wenn nach dem Zusammenbruch des planwirtschaftlichen Systems eine positive Wirtschaftsentwicklung sichtbar wird.

Die relative Stabilität der westlichen Demokratien resultiert wesentlich daraus, daß sie aufgrund ihrer ökonomischen Leistungsfähigkeit die materiellen Bedürfnisse einer großen Mehrheit ihrer Bürger befriedigen können. Die politische Kompromißfähigkeit und damit die Fähigkeit zu friedlicher Konfliktregulierung in demokratischen Gesellschaften hängt maßgeblich von den vorhandenen materiellen Verteilungsspielräumen ab. Wenn die Grenzen dieses Spielraums erreicht werden und sich das ökonomische und soziale Gefälle vergrößert, spitzen sich Konflikte zu. Wo der Staat immer weniger in der Lage ist, in den Konflikten zu vermitteln und einen gesellschaftlichen Konsens herzustellen, verliert er zunehmend an Legitimität. Autoritäre Strömungen gewinnen in derartigen Situationen an Bedeutung und die demokratische Konfliktlösungskultur wird in Frage gestellt.

Daraus ergeben sich auch Konsequenzen für die Außenpolitik: "Historische und aktuelle Erfahrungen sowie systematische friedenstheoretische Überlegungen belegen, daß eine der wesentlichen Ursachen für politisch virulente Konflike in der ökonomischen Zerklüftung von Gesellschaften und im ökonomischen Gefälle zwischen Gesellschaften besteht."[9] Kurzfristig erforderlich ist daher, mindestens, die Bekämpfung von Massenarmut und sozialer Entwurzelung.

Letztlich entscheiden die genannten innenpolitischen Bedingungsfaktoren über die Stabilität der betreffenden Staaten und damit auch über die Stabilität des europäischen Systems. Stabile politische Systeme sind generell weniger konfliktgeneigt als instabile. Stabile Strukturen lassen sich aber nur erreichen, wenn verläßliche Zukunftserwartungen über das wechselseitige Verhalten vorhanden sind. Für

8 Vgl. dazu *Czempiel*, Weltpolitik im Umbruch, S. 88-98, sowie – mit kritischen Einschränkungen – Wolf-Dieter *Eberwein*, Demokratisierung und Krieg. Zurück in die Zukunft oder Ewiger Frieden? Manuskript zur Veröffentlichung des Arbeitskreises für Sicherheitspolitik, Februar 1992, insbesondere S. 11-21.

9 Dieter *Senghaas*, Friedensprojekt Europa, Franfurt a.M. 1992, S. 57.

die ehemals kommunistischen Staaten hängt die Bildung gefestigter demokratischer Staatswesen maßgeblich von ihrer ökonomischen Entwicklungsperspektive ab.[10] Gelingt eine sichtbare ökonomische Annäherung Osteuropas an Westeuropa nicht, drohen nicht nur weitere Migrationsbewegungen von Ost nach West. Eine zunehmende Instabilität der neuen politischen Systeme müßte auch deren Berechenbarkeit in den internationalen Beziehungen beeinträchtigen; ohne diese Berechenbarkeit entfällt aber eine kardinale Bedingung für Vertrauensbildung und Sicherheit. Deshalb stellt die ökonomische Entwicklung des postkommunistischen Ostens eine dringliche gesamteuropäische Aufgabe dar.

Stabile Demokratisierung allein reicht, wie am Beispiel der ökonomischen Dimension gezeigt, für eine neue Sicherheitskultur noch nicht aus. Diese ist auch davon abhängig, inwieweit es gelingt, die latente Anarchie des internationalen Systems – hier des europäischen Subsystems – einzuhegen.[11] Internationale Organisationen und Foren[12] liefern den Rahmen für den Prozeß der Normen- und Regimebildung. Welche Leistungen hat die gesamteuropäische KSZE auf diesem Gebiet aufzuweisen und welche Entwicklungsperspektiven im Sinne einer regionalspezifischen Sicherheitskultur sind darin beinhaltet?

III. Die Normen- und Regimebildung in der KSZE als Beitrag zu einer regionalspezifischen Sicherheitskultur

Unter dem Vorzeichen des Ost-West-Konflikts diente der KSZE-Prozeß vorrangig als Forum für den Dialog zwischen beiden Konfliktparteien, in den auch die neutralen und nichtgebundenen Staaten einbezogen wurden, sowie als Rahmen zur schrittweisen Erarbeitung eines entspannungspolitischen Verhaltensstandards auf der Grundlage der Schlußakte von Helsinki. Hierbei erwies sich die KSZE als erstaunlich erfolgreich, obwohl sie keine internationale Organisation wurde, sondern eine Konferenzabfolge blieb, und obwohl ihre Normenbildung keine völkerrechtliche, sondern lediglich politische Verbindlichkeit für sich beanspruchen konnte.[13]

---

10 *Senghaas* (ebd., S. 58) weist zu Recht darauf hin, daß die ökonomisch ungleichgewichtige Entwicklung des West- und des Ostteils von Europa durch das zentralbürokratische Wirtschaftssystem zwar verschärft wurde, aber bereits im späten Mittelalter bzw. in der frühen Neuzeit begonnen hatte. Daraus ergibt sich unter anderem die Konsequenz, daß eine Neuauflage des "Marshallplanes" für Osteuropa nur bedingt wirksam sein würde, da wesentliche Voraussetzungen für eine marktwirtschaftliche Entwicklung überhaupt erst geschaffen werden müssen.

11 Auf ein weiteres Erfordernis, nämlich die strategische Kompetenz der Akteure (Eliten) im Sinne zielgerichteten politischen Handelns, kann an dieser Stelle nur verwiesen werden. Vgl. dazu Ernst-Otto *Czempiel*, Die Organisation der Sicherheit in und für Europa, in: Beate *Kohler-Koch* (Hrsg.), Staat und Demokratie in Europa, 18. Wissenschaftlicher Kongreß der Deutschen Vereinigung für Politische Wissenschaft, Opladen 1992, S. 209f.

12 Vgl. zur Begrifflichkeit Clive *Archer*, International Organizations, New York/London 1992.

13 Vgl. dazu Wilfried *von Bredow*, Der KSZE-Prozeß. Von der Zähmung zur Auflösung des Ost-West-Konflikts, Darmstadt 1992.

Auch ohne Rechtsverbindlichkeit bzw. ohne eine sanktionsbewehrte zentrale Instanz wurden die im KSZE-Prozeß erarbeiteten Normen weitgehend respektiert und wirkten als ein bedeutsamer Maßstab für die Konfliktregulierung zwischen den Staatengruppen.[14] Der entsprechende Verhandlungs- bzw. Überprüfungsprozeß trug, ungeachtet teilweise erheblicher Auffassungsunterschiede zwischen Ost und West, zur Zivilisierung der Konfliktstruktur im KSZE-Raum bei. 1989, am Vorabend der Beendigung des Ost-West-Konflikts, wurde das europäische System – im offenkundigen Widerspruch zur Anarchie-These – bereits durch einen hohen Grad der Verregelung gekennzeichnet, an den bei der nachfolgenden Neuordnung Europas und beim Ausbau der KSZE zu einer Organisation angeknüpft werden konnte.[15]

Internationale Organisationen bilden das tauglichste Instrument zur Zivilisierung der prinzipiellen Anarchie des internationalen Systems.[16] Internationale Organisationen formieren und entwickeln sich aufgrund gemeinsamer Interessen ihrer Teilnehmer. Auf der Basis gemeinsamer Werte und Überzeugungen sowie durch deren Festigung können sie ein bestimmtes Maß an staatenübergreifendem politischen Konsens herbeiführen. Die eigene Bereitschaft zur Kooperation wird verstärkt durch die Kooperationsbereitschaft der anderen Staaten. Die Einhegung von Anarchie durch Zusammenarbeit wird gefördert, indem Information und Interaktionen intensiviert und formalisiert, das wechselseitige Verhalten also transparent, verläßlich bzw. berechenbar wird und somit Vertrauen gebildet und Sicherheit gewährleistet werden können.

1. Demokratie und Menschenrechte

Der in der Schlußakte von Helsinki enthaltene, auf den Folgekonferenzen von Belgrad, Madrid und Wien bekräftigte und ergänzte Normenkatalog beinhaltet zentrale Ordnungsprinzipien des internationalen Systems, die sich seit dem Westfälischen Frieden (1648) entwickelt haben: insbesondere die Grundsätze der souveränen Gleichheit der Staaten, des Verzichts auf die Androhung bzw. den Gebrauch von Gewalt sowie der friedlichen Regelung von Konflikten. Er konzentrierte sich also auf Verhaltensregeln für die Ordnung zwischen Staaten. Die zentralen Themen der innerstaatlichen Herrschaft – Demokratie, Menschenrechte,

---

14 Zur Bedeutung von Normen im internationalen System siehe Robert *Axelrod*, An Evolutionary Approach to Norms, in: American Political Science Review, 80 (1986) 4, S. 1095-1111.

15 Vgl. Manfred *Efinger*/Volker *Rittberger*/Michael *Zürn*, Internationale Regime in den Ost-West-Beziehungen. Ein Beitrag zur Erforschung der friedlichen Behandlung internationaler Konflikte, Frankfurt a.M. 1988.

16 Vgl. dazu Robert *Axelrod*, Die Evolution der Kooperation, München 1987; Robert O. *Keohane*, After Hegemony: Cooperation and Discord in the World Political Economy, Princeton, NJ 1984; Kenneth A. *Oye* (Hrsg.), Cooperation under Anarchy, Princeton, NJ 1986.

Rechtsstaatlichkeit – waren zwar ebenfalls Bestandteil der KSZE-Dokumente, blieben aber zwischen West und Ost heftig umstritten und mußten stets mit dem prinzipiellen Zusatz "gültig in den jeweiligen Systemgrenzen" gelesen werden.[17]

Die Bedeutung der Menschenrechtsdiskussion im KSZE-Prozeß bis 1989 lag dementsprechend nicht so sehr in detaillierter Normenbildung, als vielmehr in der kontroversen Auseinandersetzung über menschenrechtliche Grundprinzipien, wie in der Schlußakte verankert. Dadurch konnten die kommunistischen Staaten kontinuierlich zur Rechtfertigung ihrer Innenpolitik und, in der Folge, zu Korrekturen bzw. vielen "kleinen Schritten" der Veränderung veranlaßt werden. Bei allen systembedingten Grenzen hatte die fortgesetzte Implementierungsdebatte schließlich auch Konsequenzen für die Normenbildung. Im Jahr 1989, als Ergebnis der schon von einer Aufweichung der alten Konfliktstruktur gekennzeichneten KSZE-Folgekonferenz in Wien, kam es sogar zur Einberufung einer besonderen "Konferenz über die Menschliche Dimension der KSZE". Echte Fortschritte konnten aber nur bei Teilaspekten erzielt werden, bei der Ausgestaltung des Rechts auf Freizügigkeit.

Dieser Zustand änderte sich erst nach dem Umbruch im Osten. Nicht nur die innerstaatliche Verfassung der KSZE-Staaten, auch die Frage ihrer Wirtschaftsordnung, wurden nunmehr – im Gegensatz zur Schlußakte von Helsinki – einvernehmlich und bis ins Detail gehend normiert. Das alte Defensivargument der kommunistischen Staaten, bei Demokratie und Menschenrechten handele es sich um "innere Angelegenheiten", für die das Prinzip der Nichteinmischung gelte, wanderte vorerst in die diplomatische Asservatenkammer; die Einrichtung neuer Institutionen und Überprüfungsmechanismen wurde möglich. Mit der "Charta von Paris für ein Neues Europa" (21.11.1990),[18] den Schlußdokumenten der Menschenrechtskonferenzen von Kopenhagen (29.6.1990)[19] und Moskau (3.10.1991)[20] und dem "Helsinki-Dokument 1992" (10.7.1992)[21] entstand ein gesamteuropäisches Demokratie- und Menschenrechtsregime, das in seiner Präzision und Reichweite in keiner anderen Subregion der VN zu finden ist. Diese im KSZE-Raum besonders weit vorangeschrittene Entwicklung paßt sich ein in einen Veränderungsprozeß sowohl des klassischen Souveränitätsbegriffs als auch des Völkerrechts: Der Verkehr der staatlichen Akteure mit den Bürgern unterliegt mittlerweile Eingrif-

17 Siehe dazu Michael *Staack*, Menschenrechte und Sicherheit. Produktives Spannungsverhältnis oder Sollbruchstelle für den Dialog der Weltmächte?, Berlin 1989.

18 Die "Charta von Paris" ist dokumentiert in: *Auswärtiges Amt* (Hrsg.), Sicherheit und Zusammenarbeit in Europa. Dokumentation zum KSZE-Prozeß 1990/91, Bonn 1991, S. 147-179.

19 Für den Wortlaut siehe ebd., S. 35-57.

20 "Konferenz über die Menschliche Dimension der KSZE. Dokument des Moskauer Treffens vom 3.10.1991", in: Bulletin des Presse- und Informationsamts der Bundesregierung, (18.10.1991) 115, S. 909-919.

21 "Helsinki-Dokument 1992. Herausforderung des Wandels", ebd., (23.7.1992) 82, S. 777-804.

fen von außen, die mit der Verfügungsgewalt des "klassischen Souveräns" über seine "Untertanen" unvereinbar gewesen wären. Die Einhaltung eines menschenrechtlichen (Mindest-)Standards wird immer stärker zu einem Maßstab zwischenstaatlicher Beziehungen, der sich auch auf die Kooperationsbereitschaft in anderen Politikbereichen auswirkt.

Auf nahezu jeder KSZE-Tagung seit 1990 konnten Fortschritte bei der Normenbildung erzielt werden; außerdem wurden immer mehr osteuropäische Staaten als Vollmitglieder oder Beobachter in den Europarat aufgenommen. Besonders wichtig bleibt das KSZE-Dokument von Kopenhagen, das in der Qualität seiner Programmaussagen, zur Rechtsstaatlichkeit und zum Schutz von Minderheitenrechten einer europäischen Verfassungscharta gleichkommt. Wären diese Programmsätze seit längerem erprobte gesamteuropäische Verfassungswirklichkeit, so wäre auch die Zahl der Konfliktregionen in der KSZE-Welt weitaus geringer. Damit ist ein Dilemma angesprochen, das den KSZE-Prozeß immer stärker behindert: Im Widerspruch zu den eingegangenen Verpflichtungen werden die KSZE-Normen in den ehemals kommunistischen Staaten nur teilweise umgesetzt. Dafür ist sowohl die fehlende rechtliche Verbindlichkeit ursächlich als auch der Mangel an einer entsprechenden politischen Kultur. Außerdem fehlt es an Sanktionsinstrumenten oder diese werden nur zögerlich angewandt. Zwar ist das Nichteinmischungsprinzip inzwischen wenn nicht aufgehoben, so doch vielfach durchbrochen, aber die Ausgestaltung der entsprechenden KSZE-Mechanismen hat mit dem inhaltlichen Normenbildungsprozeß nicht Schritt gehalten. Das betrifft sowohl den spezifischen Mechanismus für die "Menschliche Dimension" als auch die umfassenden Regelungen für Konfliktvermeidung und Streitbeilegung.

Das Problem ist hierbei weniger ein Dissens über die funktionale Notwendigkeit als der entschlossene politische Wille, die Verwirklichung von Demokratie und Menschenrechten als Kernbestandteil europäischer Sicherheitskultur wieder zu einem zentralen Gegenstand der KSZE-Debatte werden zu lassen. Sollte sich dieser Prozeß fortsetzen, würde auch die politisch maßstabbildende Funktion der KSZE-Normenbildung immer mehr in Mitleidenschaft gezogen: Handlungsbedarf ist folglich offenkundig. Innerhalb der KSZE ist eine neue Menschenrechts- und Demokratiedebatte überfällig, um der Forderung nach Erfüllung der eingegangenen Verpflichtungen politischen Nachdruck zu verleihen. Für die KSZE geht es also um eine Bewährungsprobe auf altem Terrain unter neuen Bedingungen.[22] Dazu bedarf es keiner gänzlich neuen Instrumente, sondern einer Prioritätenveränderung vor allem in der Politik des Westens, der sich in der KSZE zuletzt zu stark auf die Sicherheitspolitik konzentriert hat. Auch und gerade nach dem Ende

22 Vgl. dazu Sylvia *Rohde-Liebenau*, Menschenrechte und internationale Sicherheit – das Beispiel Europa, in: Michael *Staack* (Hrsg.), Aufbruch nach Gesamteuropa. Die KSZE nach der Wende im Osten, Münster 1992, S. 247-278 (273-278).

des Ost-West-Konflikts bleiben Demokratisierungs- und Menschenrechtspolitik außerordentlich wichtig, denn von ihrer Respektierung hängt maßgeblich die Entwicklung der Sicherheitskultur ab.

2. Kooperative Sicherheit

Positiver fällt die Bilanz in der Sicherheitspolitik aus. Regellosigkeit wurde schrittweise durch Verhaltensdisziplinierung ersetzt. An die Stelle klassisch souveräner Machtpolitik trat die Ächtung des Krieges und ein faktisches "Eroberungsverbot". Die Forderung, daß nationalstaatliches Rüstungsverhalten grundsätzlich Verhandlungen zugänglich sein muß, wird akzeptiert; ebenso die Norm, das eigene Territorium internationaler Verifikation zu öffnen. Ein weiterer, regional realisierbarer Entwicklungsschritt könnte im Verbot von offensiven Militärstrategien bestehen.[23] Auch sicherheitspolitisch erfolgten die wesentlichen Verregelungsschritte für den KSZE-Raum nach 1989, aber auch hier konnte auf vorhandene Regime zurückgegriffen werden.[24] Mit dem KSE-Vertrag über die Reduzierung konventioneller Bewaffnung (19.11.1990)[25] und der ergänzenden "Abschließenden Akte" über die Begrenzung der Mannschaftsstärken (10.7.1992)[26] wurde zwischen den Mitgliedsstaaten der NATO und den ehemaligen Mitgliedsstaaten des Warschauer Paktes bzw. deren Nachfolgestaaten ein umfassender Abrüstungsprozeß eingeleitet, der die während des Ost-West-Konflikts entstandenen Disparitäten beseitigen wird. Durch die Einrichtung des "Forums für Sicherheitskooperation" als Ergebnis der Gipfelkonferenz von Helsinki ist nunmehr der institutionelle Rahmen geschaffen, um im Kreis aller KSZE-Teilnehmer sämtliche sicherheitspolitischen Fragen – auch Streitkräfteplanung, Nichtverbreitung und Rüstungskonversion – erörtern und weitere Vereinbarungen vorbereiten zu können.[27]

---

23 Vgl. Harald *Müller*, Institutionen und internationale Ordnung. Arbeitspapier für die HSFK-Konferenz "Frieden und Konflikt in den internationalen Beziehungen" zu Ehren von Ernst-Otto Czempiels 65. Geburtstag, Frankfurt a.M., 29.-31.5.1992, S. 28.

24 Vgl. Oliver *Meier*, Auf dem Weg zu einer Sicherheitsgemeinschaft? Die sicherheitspolitische Integration in der KSZE, in: *Staack*, Aufbruch nach Gesamteuropa, S. 54-90.

25 Für den Wortlaut des "Vertrags über Konventionelle Streitkräfte in Europa" siehe *Auswärtiges Amt*, Sicherheit und Zusammenarbeit in Europa, S. 119-146.

26 "Abschließende Akte der Verhandlungen über Personalstärken der Konventionellen Streitkräfte in Europa", in: Bulletin des Presse- und Informationsamts der Bundesregierung, (17.7.1992) 79, S. 753-759.

27 Um das "Forum für Sicherheitskooperation" leistungsfähig auszugestalten, bedarf es einer Klarstellung der Aufgabenzuweisung gegenüber dem Nordatlantischen Kooperationsrat (NAKR). Dieser wurde geschaffen, um die Kommunikation mit den ehemaligen Sicherheitsgegnern zu verbessern und weil eine Erweiterung der NATO nicht stattfinden sollte. Im Gegensatz zum NAKR verfügt das Forum über ein klares, umfassendes und gesamteuropäisches Mandat zur "Schaffung neuer Sicherheitsbeziehungen untereinander auf der Grundlage kooperativer und gemeinsamer Ansätze zur Sicherheit" (Helsinki-Dokument 1992). Außerdem bezieht es die früheren N+N-Staaten ein. Als Verhandlungsrahmen sollte dem Forum daher eindeutige Priorität

Von besonderer Bedeutung für die regionalspezifische europäische Sicherheitskultur sind jedoch die seit der Stockholmer "Konferenz über Vertrauensbildende Maßnahmen und Abrüstung in Europa" (KVAE) im KSZE-Rahmen erzielten Vereinbarungen über vertrauens- und sicherheitsbildende Maßnahmen. Ihre Implementierung – zusammen mit den Verifikationsregeln der KSE-Abkommen – hat zu einer historisch einzigartigen Transparenz militärischer Strukturen und Bewegungen geführt, die eine verdeckte Vorbereitung zwischenstaatlicher militärischer Konflikte verhindert.[28] Mit den Vereinbarungen der Jahre 1990/92 hat sich der Ansatz kooperativer Sicherheit für die Sicherheitsbeziehungen in Gesamteuropa durchgesetzt. Ursprünglich auf den Abbau des Ost-West-Gegensatzes bezogen, weisen sie über diesen hinaus. Das vorhandene Regelwerk stellt eine gute Ausgangsbasis dafür dar, nunmehr regionale Sicherheitsarrangements anzustreben und qualitative Rüstungskontrollprobleme zu bearbeiten.

Die Regime- bzw. Institutionenbildung im KSZE-Rahmen stellt nur einen Ausschnitt der gesamteuropäischen Verregelung dar. Auch teileuropäische Institutionen wie die EG (u.a. mit ihren Assoziierungs- bzw. Handelsabkommen) oder die NATO (mit ihrer Kooperationsbereitschaft gegenüber den früheren Gegnern) tragen zu einer hohen Regelungsdichte bei. Diese Regelungsdichte kann eine gesamteuropäische Sicherheitskultur stabilisieren und fördern, wenn sie auf Kooperation zwischen möglichen Konfliktpartnern angelegt ist, allen Interessenten grundsätzlich offensteht, faire Beteiligungschancen beinhaltet und Transferleistungen (sowohl im Politikfeld Sicherheit als auch im Politikfeld Wohlfahrt) zugunsten der schwächeren Systemmitglieder ermöglicht. Das Ende des Großkonflikts zwischen Ost und West hat wichtige Probleme gelöst, aber auch neue hervorgebracht. Die Rahmenbedingungen dafür, diese durch Regime und Institutionen zu regeln bzw. "kleinzuarbeiten", wurden gleichwohl erheblich verbessert.[29]

IV. Kann die europäische Sicherheitskultur eine Einbeziehung der "Gemeinschaft Unabhängiger Staaten" verkraften?

Das Auseinanderfallen der Sowjetunion in – bezieht man auch Estland, Lettland und Litauen ein – 15 Nachfolgerepubliken hat die Rahmenbedingungen für gesamteuropäische Zusammenarbeit grundlegend verändert. Solange die UdSSR unter der reformerischen Gorbatschow-Führung als einheitlicher Verhandlungs- und

zukommen, eine Doppelung von Funktionszuweisungen vermieden und der NAKR auf konsultative Prozesse im Verhandlungsvorfeld beschränkt werden.

28 Vgl. dazu Günter *Joetze*, Verhandlungen über Vertrauens- und Sicherheitsbildende Maßnahmen in Wien und das "Wiener Dokument 1990", in: Europa-Archiv, 46 (1991) 14, S. 422-428.

29 Vgl. zum Verhältnis von Konfliktqualität und Regelungsmöglichkeit Volker *Rittberger*/Michael *Zürn*, Transformation der Konflikte in den Ost-West-Beziehungen. Versuch einer institutionalistischen Bestandsaufnahme, in: Politische Vierteljahresschrift, 32 (1991) 3, S. 399-424.

Vertragspartner bestand, reichte es aus, mit diesem zu Vereinbarungen zu gelangen. Für die europäische Staatengemeinschaft war es vorrangig, daß sich der Gesamtstaat an diese Verpflichtungen hielt. Für die Sicherheitspolitik genügte dies im wesentlichen auch, nicht aber für die Demokratie- und Menschenrechtspolitik. Bei der Verwirklichung der entsprechenden KSZE-Verpflichtungen bildeten der politische Wille des Zentrums und die Situation in den Metropolen die entscheidenden Maßstäbe. Der Demokratisierungsprozeß im Baltikum – und die sich erhebenden starken Gegenkräfte – fanden noch hinreichende öffentliche Aufmerksamkeit, während die Situation in anderen Landesteilen als Gegenstand internationaler Konferenzdiplomatie weitgehend ausgeblendet wurde.

Ein solches Verhalten kann sich der Rest der KSZE-Welt nach der Aufnahme aller GUS-Mitglieder in die KSZE und den Nordatlantischen Kooperationsrat Anfang 1992 nicht mehr leisten.[30] Für die Einbeziehung aller GUS-Staaten wurden vor allem folgende Gründe angeführt: (1) der entsprechende Wille dieser Staaten, (2) die Unmöglichkeit einer nicht-diskriminierenden Ungleichbehandlung, (3) die Notwendigkeit, diese Staaten auf die KSZE-Rüstungskontrollabmachungen zu verpflichten sowie (4) die Absicht, laizistische und wenigstens potentiell demokratiefähige Regime in Zentralasien nicht dem Machtanspruch des islamischen Fundamentalismus zu überlassen. Vor allem die regional besonders interessierte Türkei, aber auch die Vereinigten Staaten drängten auf entsprechende Entscheidungen, die auch von Deutschland unterstützt wurden. Rückblickend kann festgestellt werden, daß eine sorgfältige Abwägung der Frage, welcher dieser Staaten in welche Organisation bzw. in welchen Kooperationszusammenhang aufgenommen werden sollte, nicht stattgefunden hat.

Die bisherigen Erfahrungen mit den GUS-Staaten im Nordatlantischen Kooperationsrat, vor allem aber in der KSZE, ergeben ein sehr zwiespältiges Bild. Während sich eine Staatengruppe, bestehend aus Belarus, Kasachstan, der Russischen Föderation, der Ukraine und Kirgistan, um eine kooperative Verhandlungspolitik und die Respektierung der eingegangenen Verpflichtungen bemüht,[31] zeigt eine andere Staatengruppe (Tadschikistan, Turkmenistan, Usbekistan) weder besonderes Interesse an den betreffenden Institutionen noch an der Normeneinhaltung. In eine dritte Staatengruppe gehören Armenien, Aserbaidschan, Georgien und Moldowa, die jeweils in Bürgerkriege bzw. bewaffnete Konflikte mit anderen KSZE-Teilnehmern verwickelt sind. Sie haben zwar ihr Mitwirkungsinteresse bekundet, KSZE-Konfliktbeobachter eingeladen bzw. akzeptiert, aber gleichwohl die KSZE-Normen wiederholt verletzt; und zwar sowohl für die zwischenstaatlichen Bezie-

---

30 Vgl. Bernard *von Plate*, Die Neuordnung in der ehemaligen Sowjetunion: Eine Herausforderung für die KSZE, in: Europa-Archiv, 47 (1992) 10, S. 288-294.

31 Das gilt sowohl für Sicherheits- bzw. Rüstungskontrollvereinbarungen als auch für die Verankerung von Minderheitenrechten der deutschen Minderheiten in diesen Staaten.

hungen als auch in ihrer innerstaatlichen Politik. Ähnlich wie in Mittelost- bzw. Südosteuropa verhalten sich generell jene GUS-Staaten am kooperativsten, die bzw. deren Eliten auf bestimmte demokratische Traditionen zurückblicken können. In anderen Staaten sind diese entweder gar nicht vorhanden oder nur außerordentlich schwach ausgeprägt.

Durch die Teilnahme sämtlicher GUS-Staaten hat sich der Grad der insgesamt vorhandenen Werteübereinstimmung und Werteverwirklichung in der KSZE verringert. Ihr programmatischer Demokratiestandard hat sich teilweise ebensoweit von den Realitäten entfernt wie zu Zeiten des Ost-West-Konflikts. Auch sicherheitspolitisch fällt die Bilanz ambivalent aus: Der Bindung an die KSE-Abkommen steht ein von diesen nicht oder nur unzureichend erfaßter Handel mit Rüstungsgütern unter Einschluß von Massenvernichtungswaffen gegenüber. Auch das Argument einer Absicherung gegen den islamischen Fundamentalismus kann nicht überzeugen, denn dieses Ziel kann in den betreffenden Staaten kaum durch internationale Organisationen gefördert werden. Eingetreten ist eher eine ganz andere Entwicklung: Die abnehmende Bereitschaft einer sich als regionale Vormacht definierenden, ein autoritäres Entwicklungsmodell anbietenden Türkei, sich dem gesamteuropäischen Demokratie- und Menschenrechtsregime zu unterwerfen.

Obwohl die Aufnahme aller GUS-Staaten im nachhinein als Fehlentscheidung bewertet werten muß, lassen sich nur schwer klare Schlußfolgerungen aus dieser Analyse ableiten. Ein Ausschluß bestimmter Staaten kommt nur dann in Frage, wenn diese dauerhaft und willentlich gegen die KSZE-Normen verstoßen. Die realpolitische Schwelle für einen derartigen Schritt liegt, wie sich am Beispiel Restjugoslawiens gezeigt hat, sehr hoch, ist als Sanktionsmaßnahme aber unverzichtbar. Aus guten Gründen hat sich der Europarat dafür entschieden, die asiatischen GUS-Republiken nicht in seine Arbeit einzubeziehen.[32] Demokratische Erfahrungen, auf die zurückgegriffen werden könnte, sind hier nicht vorhanden, und ganz andere politisch-kulturelle Traditionen bestimmend. Wenn diese Staaten mittel- und langfristig in die spezifische europäische Sicherheitskultur hineinwachsen sollen, hilft der gegenwärtig vielfach vorherrschende Ansatz eines "benign neglect" nicht weiter.[33] Solange sich die KSZE-Gemeinschaft nicht für das äußerste Mittel eines Ausschlusses entscheidet, bleibt als einzig wirksame Alternativstrategie der Versuch einer umfassenden Einbeziehung aller GUS-Staaten in die gesamteuropäische Zusammenarbeit mit dem Ziel einer Förderung bzw. Entwicklung ihres demokratischen Potentials. Dazu sollten auch gesellschaftliche Kontakte gezielt ermutigt und gefördert werden.

---

32 Vgl. Michael *Thumann*, Wer nach Westen will, muß warten, in: Die Zeit, 18.9.1992, S. 12.

33 Vgl. Peter *Glotz*, Die Einheit und die Spaltung Europas. Die Auswirkungen der mitteleuropäischen Revolution von 1989 auf Gesamteuropa, in: Aus Politik und Zeitgeschichte. Beilage zur Wochenzeitung Das Parlament, (31.1.1992) B6, S. 50-61.

V. Auf dem Weg zu einer europäischen Sicherheitskultur: Erfolgsbedingungen und Handlungsorientierungen

Obwohl von einer das Verhalten der Staaten und Gesellschaften im KSZE-Raum wirklich umfassend bestimmenden "europäischen Sicherheitskultur" noch nicht gesprochen werden kann, lassen sich unverzichtbare Bestandteile einer solchen, sich entwickelnden Regionalkultur bereits identifizieren. Gesamteuropa wird – trotz der im Osten aufbrechenden bzw. eskalierenden Konflikte – geprägt durch ein hohes Maß der Zivilisierung in den zwischen- und innerstaatlichen Beziehungen. Im Vergleich zu anderen Weltregionen konnte das Gewaltelement im Konfliktaustrag erheblich reduziert werden. Diese Entwicklung hat bemerkenswerterweise schon unter dem Vorzeichen des Ost-West-Gegensatzes begonnen und sich danach beschleunigt fortgesetzt. Sie hat zwei Hauptursachen: Demokratisierung mit der Folge eines hohen Maßes an Werteübereinstimmung im KSZE-Raum und Verregelung mit der Folge der Förderung weiterer Kooperationsbereitschaft unter der Voraussetzung wechselseitigen Gewinns. Weil nahezu alle KSZE-Staaten an der Aufrechterhaltung der bestehenden Ordnung interessiert sind, sind die Aussichten für die Entwicklung einer regionalspezifischen Sicherheitskultur durchaus positiv zu bewerten, wenngleich Ist-Zustand und Idealprogramm immer noch weit auseinanderklaffen. Dazu sind jedoch, klare Zielvorgaben vorausgesetzt, erhebliche politische Anstrengungen erforderlich, die nicht weniger Leistungen erfordern werden als die während des Ost-West-Konflikts erbrachten.

1. Demokratisierungspolitik

Weil demokratische Verhältnisse in Staaten die notwendige Bedingung für friedliche Konfliktregelung zwischen Staaten bilden, ist eine aktive Demokratisierungspolitik die entscheidende Erfolgsbedingung zur Förderung einer europäischen Sicherheitskultur. Sowohl die KSZE als auch der Europarat müssen als Foren bzw. Instrumente der Demokratisierungs- und Menschenrechtspolitik verstärkt genutzt werden, aber das reicht nicht aus: auch besondere Anstrengungen der nationalen Außenpolitik, vor allem aber aus dem gesellschaftlichen Bereich (z.B. durch Stiftungen, Parteien sowie thematisch interessierte Vereinigungen) und durch transnationale Beziehungen sind vonnöten. Nachdem die Jahre 1990/92 für die gesamteuropäische Normen- und Regimebildung auf dem Gebiet von Demokratie und Menschenrechten außerordentlich fruchtbar gewesen sind, kommt es nun darauf an, den programmatisch erreichten hohen Demokratiestandard schrittweise in der Praxis zu verwirklichen. In der gesamteuropäischen Konferenzdiplomatie muß die Verwirklichung von Demokratie und Menschenrechten wieder einen erheblich höheren Stellenwert erlangen. Dabei sollte stets berücksichtigt werden, daß Demokratie als innerstaatliche Verfassungsform der Abstützung durch eine günstige Wohlstandsentwicklung und durch eine zivile politische Kultur bedarf.

2. Kooperative Verknüpfungspolitik

Um diejenigen Staaten, deren Praxis durch erhebliche Demokratiedefizite gekennzeichnet wird, zur Respektierung des KSZE-Standards zu veranlassen, kann die Strategie einer kooperativen Verknüpfungspolitik eingeschlagen werden. Dabei sollten die seit 1975 im KSZE-Rahmen gesammelten Erfahrungen nutzbar gemacht werden. Es bietet sich insbesondere an, Menschenrechts- und Demokratiefragen mit Angeboten wirtschaftlicher, technologischer oder umweltpolitischer Zusammenarbeit zu verbinden; und zwar sowohl national als auch multilateral.[34] Das heißt unter anderem, daß die Teilnahme an Hilfsprogrammen bzw. Leistungen der EG an die Einhaltung von KSZE-Normen gebunden werden sollte. Auch eine solche kooperativ angelegte Politik kann paradoxerweise zu neuen Konflikten führen. Demokratisierungspolitik bedeutet einen expliziten und kontinuierlichen Eingriff in die innerstaatliche Entwicklung von nicht- oder teildemokratischen Staaten. Als mögliche Reaktion wären sowohl der erneute Rückgriff auf das Prinzip der Nichteinmischung in innerstaatliche Angelegenheiten zu erwarten als auch eine Abschottungspolitik unter Einschluß des Rückzuges aus internationalen Kooperationszusammenhängen. Gleichwohl ist diese Gefahr geringer, wenn die Einmischung durch internationale Organisationen – statt durch nationalstaatliche Politik – erfolgt.

3. Zwischengesellschaftliche Beziehungen

Wenn Demokratisierungsstrategien zur Drohpolitik werden, sind sie im Grunde schon gescheitert. Im Zweifelsfall setzt sich Abgrenzung aus Selbsterhaltungsinteresse immer gegen äußeren Veränderungsdruck durch. Deshalb kommt es darauf an, eine staatliche kooperative Verknüpfungspolitik durch einen Ausbau transnationaler Beziehungen zu ergänzen. Die Entspannungspolitik hat gelehrt, daß auf diesem Wege die jeweiligen innerstaatlichen Reformkräfte, auf deren Durchsetzungskraft es letztlich ankommt, am sichersten gestärkt werden können. Eine Ausweitung zwischengesellschaftlicher Beziehungen führt zur Zunahme von Kommunikation und Information und erhöht dadurch die Chancen für wechselseitige Empathie. Ein solcher Ansatz transnationaler Vertrauensbildung, der im Westteil Europas alte Gräben weitgehend eingeebnet hat, beeinflußt auch die Entscheidungsprozesse im politischen System im Sinne erhöhter Kooperations- und Inte-

---

34 Dieser Ansatz funktioniert wenigstens ansatzweise für die Rüstungspolitik: Die Bereitschaft zu Rüstungskonversion und Nichtverbreitung wird durch Finanzhilfen, Umschulungs- bzw. Beschäftigungsprogramme gestärkt.

grationsbereitschaft. Dazu kann auch eine wichtigere Rolle gesellschaftlicher Akteure in zwischenstaatlichen Verhandlungsprozessen beitragen.

4. Förderung regionaler Integration und Kooperation

Gefördert sowohl durch den Ost-West-Konflikt als auch durch die gemeinsame Anerkennung demokratischer Werte und Verhaltensmaßstäbe, entwickelte sich im Westen Europas ein vielfältiges Netz regionaler Integrations- und Kooperationsformen mit der Europäischen Gemeinschaft als dem wichtigstem Bestandteil. Weil sich die Staaten von dieser Zusammenarbeit wechselseitige Gewinne versprachen, schloß dies die Bereitschaft zum Souveränitätsverzicht ein. Das entstandene institutionelle Netzwerk erhöhte außerdem die Vorhersehbarkeit bzw. Berechenbarkeit politischen Verhaltens. Nach dem Zusammenbruch der hegemonial bestimmten kommunistischen Strukturen, die keine positiven Wirkungen hinterließen, fehlen derartige Kooperationsformen im Osten Europas weitgehend. Gesamteuropäische Zusammenarbeit und die Assoziierung an bisher rein westliche Organisationen können dieses Defizit nur partiell kompensieren.[35] Die Staaten des Ostens sollten deshalb zur Bildung regionaler Kooperationszusammenhänge – vor allem politisch und ökonomisch – ermutigt werden. Eine solche Entwicklung liegt auch im Interesse des Westens, denn sie erhöht die Stabilität in Gesamteuropa, wirkt der zunehmenden Fragmentierung entgegen und bewirkt damit günstigere Rahmenbedingungen für das Wachsen einer gesamteuropäischen Sicherheitskultur.

5. Gesamteuropäische Wirtschaftskooperation

In den Staaten des Westens ist trotz gegenteiliger Absichtserklärungen noch nicht in vollem Umfang erkannt worden, daß die schrittweise Verringerung des dramatischen ökonomischen Gefälles innerhalb Europas nicht nur eine Voraussetzung für einen gesamteuropäischen Wirtschaftsraum, sondern auch eine zentrale Bedingung kooperativer Sicherheit darstellt. Die Bereitschaft zu den notwendigen eigenen Belastungen, zu öffentlicher Sanierungshilfe und zu gezielter Förderung von Direktinvestionen in Osteuropa entspricht bei weitem nicht den Notwendigkeiten. Zwar wird die Herausbildung gesamteuropäischer Wirtschaftsbeziehungen von der KSZE nicht entscheidend geprägt sein, denn zentrale Aufgaben der weltwirtschaftlichen Integration Osteuropas werden vielmehr von der EG, von den internationalen Finanzinstitutionen (Weltbank, IWF, EBWE) sowie von der bilateralen Wirtschaftskooperation mit den OECD-Staaten wahrgenommen. Bis die sich mühsam entwickelnden Marktwirtschaften im Osten durch ein institutionalisiertes Netz in

---

35 Vgl. Heinrich *Vogel*, Integration und Desintegration. Das europäische Dilemma, in: Europa-Archiv, 47 (1992) 15/16, S. 433-444.

Form von Verträgen, Regelungs- und Abstimmungsmechanismen sowie durch die Zugehörigkeit zu internationalen Wirtschaftsorganisationen vollständig in einen gesamteuropäischen Wirtschaftsraum eingebunden sind, kann die KSZE aber als ein wichtiges Diskussionsforum dienen, in dem den Reformstaaten eine gleichberechtigte Mitsprache gewährleistet ist und "als politischer Stimulus für die Ausweitung der Formen und Gebiete der wirtschaftlichen Zusammenarbeit" (so der Präsident der EG-Kommission, Jacques Delors) dienen.

Die KSZE eignet sich als die Institution, in der die osteuropäischen Staaten eine entschiedene westliche Unterstützung im ökonomischen Transformationsprozeß anmahnen können. Hier können sie gemeinsame Ziele und Interessen auch gemeinschaftlich artikulieren, während sie bei Verhandlungen mit der EG als einzelstaatlicher Akteur auftreten. Mit der ordnungspolitischen Wende in Mittel- und Osteuropa, mit dem Übergang zu Demokratie und Marktwirtschaft, haben die Reformstaaten die grundlegende Voraussetzung für ein Zusammenwachsen Europas geschaffen. Eine auch ökologisch vertretbare Wirtschaftspolitik in Gesamteuropa verlangt Umdenken und Interessenausgleich sowohl im Osten als auch im Westen. Ob der Beschluß des Helsinki-Gipfels 1992, den Ausschuß Hoher Beamter regelmäßig auch als Wirtschaftsforum zusammentreten zu lassen, in diesem Sinne ausgestaltet wird, muß sich erst erweisen. Alternativ bzw. ergänzend denkbar und von höherem politischen Rang wäre auch eine gesamteuropäische Konferenz der Wirtschaftsminister unter dem Dach der KSZE.

6. Ausbau des Minderheitenschutzes

Nach dem Zusammenbruch des kommunistischen Systems befinden sich die Gesellschaften des Ostens auf der Suche nach identitätsstiftenden Mustern. Dazu gehört vorrangig der Bezug auf die eigene Nationalität, und zwar in ganz unterschiedlicher Intensität: von historischer Vergewisserung bis zu nationalistischem Absolutheitsanspruch. Diese Identitätsbestimmung kann ein Element der notwendigen nachholenden Modernisierung sein, sie kann aber auch, wie im ehemaligen Jugoslawien, zum Bürgerkrieg und zur Blockade gesamteuropäischer Zusammenarbeit führen.[36] Wenngleich die aktuelle politische Situation in den ethnonationalistischen Konflikten auf dem Gebiet der früheren UdSSR bzw. im Osten Europas dadurch gekennzeichnet ist, daß nahezu alle ethnischen Bewegungen separatistische Ziele vertreten und die Eskalation interethnischer Konflikte wenig Toleranz und Bereitschaft zu friedlichem Zusammenleben erkennen läßt, ändert dies nichts

---

36 Vgl. Dieter *Senghaas*, Vom Nutzen und Elend der Nationalismen im Leben von Völkern, in: Aus Politik und Zeitgeschichte. Beilage zur Wochenzeitung Das Parlament, (24.7.1992) B31/32, S. 23-32.

daran, daß nur wechselseitige Anerkennung und Respektierung längerfristig friedensichernd für die jeweilige Region wirken können.

Mit der autoritären Niederschlagung ethnisch motivierter Bestrebungen ist günstigenfalls eine zeitlich begrenzte Einhegung des Konflikts möglich, doch die Konfliktursachen werden nicht behoben. Ebensowenig realistisch erscheint eine friedensstabilisierende Wirkung der Neugründung von ökonomisch kaum überlebensfähigen Kleinstaaten: Es liegt nahe, daß sich die zuvor innergesellschaftlichen Konflikte dann auf die zwischenstaatliche Ebene verlagern, in Form von Grenzstreitigkeiten bzw. territorialen Ansprüchen. Weil die Konfliktparteien zur Konfliktregelung zumeist nicht selbst in der Lage sind, kommt dem vermittelnden, schlichtenden oder – auch durch Zwangsmittel – streitbeilegenden Eingreifen internationaler Organisationen wie der KSZE und der VN auf der Grundlage rechtlicher Vereinbarungen eine besondere Bedeutung zu (siehe unten "Konfliktschlichtung und Streitbeilegung"). Um eine präzise normative Grundlage für eine internationale Einmischung zu schaffen, sollte außerdem der Vorschlag, eine "Europäische Minderheitencharta" auszuarbeiten, vordringlich weiterverfolgt werden. Diese Charta sollte vorhandene KSZE-Regeln für den Schutz und die Förderung nationaler Minderheiten zusammenfassen und weiterentwickeln, insbesondere Normierungen für kulturelle Autonomie, für politische Repräsentanz und Partizipation sowie für den Gebrauch der Muttersprache in Erziehung und Ausbildung. Als institutioneller Rahmen bietet sich hierfür die gesamteuropäische KSZE an, während der Europarat mit seinen strikteren Aufnahme- und Verhaltensgeboten auf absehbare Zeit viele der in bezug auf den Minderheitenschutz "kritischen" Staaten nicht einschließen wird.

In diesen Kontext ist auch der Beschluß des Helsinki-Gipfels einzuordnen, einen "Hohen Kommissar der KSZE für nationale Minderheiten" einzusetzen, der eng mit dem Büro für Demokratische Institutionen und Menschenrechte zusammenwirken wird. Der Hohe Kommissar soll als "institutionalisiertes Frühwarnsystem" fungieren, kann dazu selbst die Initiative ergreifen, bleibt aber für ein mögliches Wirken in einem Land mit Konfliktpotentialen auf die Kooperation des jeweiligen Staates angewiesen. Obwohl seine Zuständigkeit zunächst mehr appellativ als operativ ausgestaltet ist, stellt die Einsetzung eines Hohen Kommissars einen qualitativen Fortschritt dar. Die Einmischung der KSZE-Gemeinschaft in die inneren Angelegenheiten der Teilnehmerländer wird für ein zentrales Politikfeld bekräftigt, eine herausgehobene Institution mit dieser Aufgabe betraut. Der KSZE-Hochkommissar kann die Vielzahl der Minderheitenprobleme nicht lösen, aber er kann sich zu einem wirksamen "gesamteuropäischen Gewissen" entwickeln: unabhängig von nationalstaatlichen Interessen und auf die frühzeitige Erkennung und Entschärfung sich abzeichnender Konflikte verpflichtet.

7. Konfliktschlichtung und Streitbeilegung

Der Rest der europäischen Staatenwelt, darüber besteht Konsens, kann nicht tatenlos zusehen, wenn Konflikte zwischen und innerhalb von KSZE-Staaten eskalieren. Während die Eingrenzung von Konflikten bisher immerhin weitgehend gelungen ist, reichen die Mechanismen zur Konfliktbeendigung nur aus, wenn ein entsprechender politischer Wille der Streitparteien vorausgesetzt werden kann. Die in den letzten zwei Jahren im Rahmen der KSZE entwickelten Mechanismen spezifischer Konfliktschlichtung und Streitbeilegung greifen nur, wenn ein Minimum an Kooperationsbereitschaft vorhanden ist. Die fehlende Verbindlichkeit der Mechanismen und die Ausklammerung wesentlicher – der innerstaatlichen Politik zugehörenden – Streitkategorien behindern ihre Wirksamkeit in Krisenfällen nach wie vor, woraus sich ein entsprechender Nachbesserungsbedarf ergibt, dem aber erhebliche politische Widerstände entgegenstehen.[37]

Die Geschichte des KSZE-Prozesses hat aber gerade in letzter Zeit gezeigt, daß sich, unter anderem unter dem Druck funktionaler Notwendigkeiten, zunächst nicht konsensfähige Zielvorstellungen dennoch durchsetzen ließen. Ein KSZE-Gerichtshof könnte, nachdem alle sonstigen Bemühungen um die friedliche Beilegung eines Streitfalles fehlgeschlagen sind und die Gefahr einer militärischen Eskalation droht, als letzte Streitbeilegungsinstanz tätig werden. Seine Entscheidungen wären für alle Beteiligten verbindlich, was die Schaffung entsprechender Instrumente erforderlich macht.

Ungeachtet der berechtigten Kritik sind schon die in letzter Zeit erreichten Normenbildungsschritte erstaunlich und haben zu einem gesamteuropäischen Regime der Konfliktregelung als Subsystem der VN geführt, dessen Potential noch keineswegs ausgeschöpft ist. Dabei ist es wahrscheinlich, daß eine Verregelung nichtmilitärischer Sanktionsmechanismen (z.B. Embargomaßnahmen) leichter erreicht werden kann als eine Einigung auf militärische Sanktionsinstrumente. Nach den Beschlüssen von Helsinki sollte nun mit der Ausarbeitung eines Kataloges von Wirtschaftssanktionen unter Einschluß der für Überwachung und Durchsetzung erforderlichen Instrumente begonnen werden, damit diese im Bedarfsfall ohne weitere Aushandlung angewendet werden können. Bevor ökonomische Sanktionen nicht ausgeschöpft worden sind, muß der Rückgriff auf militärische Optionen in der Regel unterbleiben. Entscheidend ist außerdem der Ausbau von Frühwarnsystemen (wie des Hochkommissariats für Minderheiten und der Erkundungs- bzw. Berichterstattungsmissionen), um national wie multilateral rechtzeitig politische Entscheidungs- bzw. Verständigungsprozesse zu ermöglichen.[38]

---

37 Vgl. Oliver *Mietzsch*, Die KSZE als regionale Institution zur Konfliktverhütung und Streitbeilegung, in: *Staack*, Aufbruch nach Gesamteuropa, S. 91-117.

38 Vgl. dazu die weiterführenden Überlegungen von *Senghaas*, Friedensprojekt Europa, S. 103-138.

8. Friedensichernde Missionen

Mit dem in Helsinki 1992 vollzogenen Schritt, sich zur regionalen Abmachung nach Kapitel VIII Artikel 52 der Charta der Vereinten Nationen zu erklären, hat sich die KSZE die rechtliche Grundlage zur bewaffneten Friedenssicherung verschafft. Sie kann nunmehr operative Maßnahmen durchführen, die bisher den VN vorbehalten waren, und in eigener Verantwortung und auf friedliche Weise die Lösung von Krisen und Konflikten zwischen Vancouver und Wladiwostok in Angriff nehmen. Das Helsinki-Dokument stellt dazu fest: "Je nach ihrem Mandat wird eine friedenserhaltende Operation der KSZE ziviles und/oder militärisches Personal umfassen, von kleinen bis zu großen Operationen reichen und eine Vielfalt von Formen annehmen können, einschließlich von Beobachter- und Überwachungsmissionen sowie größeren Einsätzen von Streitkräften. Friedenserhaltende Aktivitäten können unter anderem dazu dienen, Feuereinstellungen zu überwachen und zu deren Aufrechterhaltung beizutragen, Truppenrückzüge zu überwachen, die Aufrechterhaltung von Recht und Ordnung zu unterstützen, humanitäre und medizinische Hilfe zu leisten und Flüchtlinge zu unterstützen."[39] Friedenserhaltende Operationen der KSZE führen, so das Dokument weiter, nicht zu Zwangsmaßnahmen (Kampfeinsätzen), sie bedürfen eines genauen Mandats und der Zustimmung der direkt betroffenen Parteien.

Mit dieser neuen Regelung hat die KSZE einen wichtigen Beschluß gefaßt, um ihren diplomatischen Bemühungen Nachdruck zu verleihen. Mit entsprechenden Einsätzen hält sie sich noch zurück, denn nationalstaatliche Interessen und funktionale Notwendigkeit befinden sich gerade auf diesem Gebiet in heftigem Widerstreit.[40] Offensichtlich ist die Bereitschaft der KSZE-Staaten, auf nationale Souveränitätsrechte zu verzichten, nur schrittweise zu erlangen. Die KSZE hat vorerst darauf verzichtet, eigene Friedenstruppen aufzustellen oder entsprechende, permanente Kommando- bzw. Planungskapazitäten (Generalstabsausschuß) einzurichten. Bei ihren Friedensmissionen will sie sich auf vorhandene Potentiale (EG, NATO, WEU, GUS) stützen. Um als Regionalabmachung der Vereinten Nationen voll handlungsfähig zu werden, sollten auch die nächsten Schritte konsequent vollzogen werden, nämlich die Bereitschaft, notfalls auch Kampfeinsätze zu führen, sowie die Bildung einer KSZE-Friedenstruppe, die nicht auf die fallweise Kooperationsbereitschaft von Nationalstaaten oder anderen Organisationen angewiesen ist. Dadurch würden ihre Operationsfähigkeit gestärkt und ihre Legitimation erhöht, um veränderte Anforderungen bewältigen zu können.

---

39 Helsinki-Dokument 1992, S. 786f.

40 Vgl. die ausgezeichnete Diskussion bei Klaus *Hartung*, Wer will denn Bosnien retten?, in: Die Zeit, 21.8.1992, S. 4.

9. Stärkung der Handlungsfähigkeit

Der Ausbau handlungsfähiger Institutionen und Instrumente in der KSZE hat mit dem Normenbildungsprozeß nicht Schritt gehalten, obwohl in Helsinki das jeweils präsidierende KSZE-Teilnehmerland neue operative Kompetenzen erhielt, die KSZE-Troika (Präsidialstaat, Vorgänger und Nachfolger) rechtlich verankert, der Rat der Außenminister als wichtigstes Entscheidungsgremium gestärkt und der Ausschuß Hoher Beamter als zentrale Koordinierungsinstanz für die Tätigkeit der gesamten KSZE aufgewertet wurden. Nachdem die KSZE von 34 auf 53 Mitglieder angewachsen ist, muß der Erweiterung eine prozedurale Straffung folgen: (1) Erforderlich ist die Einrichtung eines "Europäischen Sicherheitsrates", der sich aus der Troika und 5 bis 10 weiteren, in Regionalzonen gewählten Vertretern zusammensetzen könnte. Eine ständige Mitgliedschaft in diesem Rat sollte es, negative Erfahrungen der VN berücksichtigend, ebensowenig geben wie ein Vetorecht. Eine begrenzte, genau festgelegte Delegierung von Entscheidungskompetenzen an den Sicherheitsrat würde die Reaktionsfähigkeit der KSZE in Krisensituationen wesentlich verbessern. (2) Das bereits mehrfach durchbrochene Konsensprinzip sollte prinzipiell beibehalten, aber sachbereichsspezifisch auch durch die Möglichkeit zu qualifizierten Mehrheitsentscheidungen ersetzt werden. Das betrifft insbesondere die Entscheidungsfindung in einem Sicherheitsrat. (3) Regionale Gesprächs- und Verhandlungsprozesse, die unter dem gemeinsamen Dach der KSZE stattfinden, aber nur einen Teil der Mitgliedsstaaten erfassen, können die zentralen Institutionen und Entscheidungsprozesse entlasten. Entsprechende positive Erfahrungen, bei den KSE-Verhandlungen, liegen bereits vor. Eine Regionalisierung erscheint sowohl im Bereich der Rüstungskontrolle als auch bei der Konfliktregelung wünschenswert.

VI. Schlußbemerkung

Mit der Ausdehnung auf alle GUS-Staaten hat das KSZE-System die Grenzen seiner Integrationsfähigkeit erreicht; und noch ist offen, ob diese nicht sogar schon überschritten wurden. Eine weitere Ausdehnung auf Staaten ohne demokratische politische Traditionen wird den erreichten Stand der Normen- und Regimebildung unweigerlich zurückwerfen müssen: sie darf nicht stattfinden. Normen können ihre Wirkung nur entfalten, wenn sie respektiert und verwirklicht werden. Nach der räumlichen Erweiterung muß nun die inhaltliche Vertiefung Priorität besitzen, wenn die Entwicklung einer regionalspezifischen Sicherheitskultur auf der Grundlage einer Wertegemeinschaft nicht zurückfallen soll auf den Status eines normativen Postulats. Dabei kann Europa durchaus auch eine Schrittmacherrolle für die Normenbildung im Rahmen der VN übernehmen, ohne aber der Gefahr zu erliegen, die Welt eurozentriert neu ordnen zu wollen.

Noch stärker als bisher wird sich gesamteuropäische Zusammenarbeit am Grundsatz der Subsidiarität ausrichten: nur dann, wenn andere, erprobte und funktional geeignete Institutionen nicht zur Verfügung stehen, sollte die KSZE neue Aufgaben übernehmen. Ohnehin sind die Grenzen der Problemlösungsfähigkeit in Gesamteuropa eng gesteckt. Viele der Problemlagen, die seit dem Ende des Ost-West-Konflikts die europäische Politik bestimmen und die Entwicklung einer Sicherheitskultur bedrohen – Nationalitätenkonflikte, Wohlstandsgefälle, die Notwendigkeit einer "nachholenden Modernisierung" im Osten –, sind nicht binnen kurzer Frist, sondern nur längerfristig bzw. sogar nur in geschichtlichen Zeiträumen zu lösen.

Das öffentliche Bewußtsein für die neuen Erfordernisse und die Grenzen der Problemlösungsfähigkeit ist aber noch weithin unterentwickelt. Gegenwärtig nehmen eher Tendenzen zu, die auf Abschottung, auf das Negieren von Problemen oder auf eine Überbewertung militärischer Konfliktlösung hinauslaufen und einer gemeinsamen Sicherheitskultur entgegenwirken. Auch Überforderung bedroht die Akzeptanz von internationalen Organisationen wie der KSZE. Deshalb sollte diese nur solche Aufgaben bearbeiten, zu deren Lösung sie derzeit auch wirklich beitragen kann. Ihre Leistungen können dabei nicht überzeugender ausfallen als die Bereitschaft ihrer Teilnehmer zu gesamteuropäischer Kooperation.

8. Die innerstaatliche Funktion der KSZE

Bernard von Plate

I. Grenzen der Machbarkeit, konzeptionelle Perspektiven

Den Kriegen, die dem Ende des Ost-West-Konflikts auf dem Fuße folgten, steht die KSZE weitgehend hilflos gegenüber. Die Gemeinschaft von 53 Staaten – nach dem Stand vom Frühjahr 1993 – hat im Zerfallsprozeß der Sowjetunion und der Jugoslawischen Föderation bislang keine auffallende und dauerhafte Rolle spielen können. Der gute Ruf, den sich die KSZE in den Jahren nach 1975 erworben hat, ist in Gefahr, verspielt zu werden. Ihr Renommee als Katalysator einer Entwicklung, die im Herbst 1989 schließlich in einen Wandel revolutionärer Größenordnung einmündete, ist kurz davor, zu einem nostalgischen Erinnerungsposten zu werden. Die Hoffnungen, von denen im November 1990 die "Charta von Paris für ein neues Europa" getragen war, haben einer harten Realität Platz machen müssen. Das neue "Zeitalter der Demokratie, des Friedens und der Einheit", das in Paris die damals noch 34 Teilnehmer der KSZE und der Präsident der Kommission der Europäischen Gemeinschaften voraussagten,[1] ist nicht näher gerückt.

Was rechtfertigt diese Beobachtungen? Bilden sie nur eine Momentaufnahme? Ist die KSZE lediglich von einer *konjunkturellen* Schwäche erfaßt, die demnächst von einem Aufschwung abgelöst werden wird, oder ist sie das Opfer *struktureller* Veränderungen, in denen sie ihren Platz nicht bzw. noch nicht gefunden hat? Die hier diskutierte Behauptung lautet, daß die Unzulänglichkeiten der KSZE nicht zuletzt ihre Überforderung ausdrücken, die wiederum *konzeptionelle* Gründe hat. Von der KSZE wird etwas verlangt, was sie nicht einlösen kann. Ihre komparativen Vorteile gegenüber anderen europäischen und atlantischen Institutionen finden hingegen ungenügende Beachtung und Förderung. Auf eine Kurzformel gebracht: Die Hypothek der KSZE sind die an sie gerichteten Erwartungen. Sie beziehen sich auf eine Leistungsbilanz, die sie bis 1989 erbringen konnte, die aber fälschlicherweise auch nach dem Ende der Ost-West-Konfrontation weiterhin als Bemessungsgrundlage dient. Daß "die KSZE ... bei [den] positiven Veränderungen eine Schlüsselrolle gespielt" hat, wie im Juli 1992 in der Schlußerklärung von Helsinki stolz vermerkt ist,[2] wird hier nachdrücklich unterstrichen. Bezweifelt wird jedoch, daß sich der Erfolg der KSZE in der Vergangenheit, den sie bei den Umwälzungen *in* den ehemals sozialistischen Staaten hatte, nach einigen chirurgischen

---

1 Charta von Paris für ein neues Europa, in: Bulletin der Bundesregierung (Bulletin), (24.11.1990) 137, S. 1409.

2 *Konferenz über Sicherheit und Zusammenarbeit in Europa*, Helsinki-Dokument 1992. Herausforderung des Wandels, in: Bulletin, (23.7.1992) 88, S. 777.

Eingriffen gewissermaßen in linearer Fortschreibung auch unter anderen Bedingungen auf der *zwischen*staatlichen Ebene wiederholen läßt.

Ernsthaft hat 1975, als schließlich die KSZE-Schlußakte von Helsinki unterzeichnet werden konnte, wohl kaum einer an die Gefahr eines militärischen Ost-West-Konflikts geglaubt. Wenn der Grundsatz der "Unverletzlichkeit der Grenzen" und die Verpflichtung der Staaten, auf die "Androhung oder Anwendung von Gewalt" zu verzichten, in der Schlußakte einen zentralen Platz einnehmen, dann hatte dies etwas mit der politischen Sanktionierung der Nachkriegsentwicklung zu tun, nicht jedoch mit der Gefahr eines drohenden Krieges. Die Wirkung der KSZE seit 1975 ist nicht vorrangig an der Frage zu bemessen, welchen Beitrag sie geleistet hat, um einen Ost-West-Konflikt oder generell einen Krieg zu verhindern. Ihr Erfolg ist allenfalls in zweiter Linie im Bereich der zwischenstaatlichen Beziehungen auszumachen. Ihr volles Gewicht hat die KSZE vielmehr als Bezugspunkt innerstaatlicher Systemveränderungen entfaltet. Diese zugespitzten Feststellungen leugnen natürlich nicht, daß es auch einen Anteil der KSZE im Prozeß des Systemwandels auf dem Feld der zwischenstaatlichen Politik gegeben hat. Die Nachfolgekonferenzen der KSZE seit 1975 haben hier eine durchaus wichtige Rolle gespielt. Dieser Sachverhalt relativiert die vorausgegangenen Aussagen, macht sie jedoch nicht ungültig.

Der innerstaatliche Maßstab ist nicht veraltet; er hat jedoch Konkurrenz bekommen. Auf der Latte, an der die KSZE gegenwärtig gemessen wird, steht nun auch, was sie dazu beitragen kann, Kriege zwischen ihren Teilnehmerstaaten zu verhindern oder sogar zu beenden, und wie groß ihre Fähigkeit sein wird, den Frieden zwischen den Staaten zu bewahren oder sogar wiederherzustellen. Diese Leistungsparameter sind für die KSZE weitgehend neu. Unter den Bedingungen des Ost-West-Antagonismus haben sie kaum eine Rolle gespielt. Die schlechten Noten, die die KSZE – aus politischer Rücksichtnahme oft allerdings nur hinter vorgehaltener Hand – einstecken muß, sind die Antwort darauf, daß sie den neuen Anforderungen bisher nicht gerecht werden konnte.

Kann die KSZE diesem Mangel abhelfen? Die laufende Diskussion erweckt den Eindruck, als sei es allein eine Frage des politischen Interesses, die KSZE in den Konflikten im postantagonistischen Zeitalter wirkungsvoller zur Geltung zu bringen. Gelingt es, so die Suggestion, sie mit den erforderlichen Instrumenten und Kompetenzen auszustatten, oder ihr da, wo die eigenen Möglichkeiten nicht ausreichen, den Zugriff auf andere europäische und atlantische Institutionen zu eröffnen, die über Ressourcen verfügen, die ihr unmittelbar nicht zu Gebote stehen, könnte sie zu einer zentralen Einrichtung in der Sicherheitsordnung Europas avancieren. Diese Vorstellung klingt verlockend. Sie ist auch nicht falsch; sie greift jedoch zu kurz, weil sie einer Vision der Machbarkeit erliegt. Die Hürden, vor der die KSZE-Teilnehmer stehen, sind eben nicht nur ihre divergierenden politischen Interessen. Sie könnten sich sogar, wenn auch der Verlauf der zweiten Helsinki-Konferenz wenig Anlaß zur Zuversicht bot, als nur zeitweilig herausstellen. Weitaus gravierender ist indessen die Natur der Probleme, sind die Ursachen, die den Konflikten zugrunde liegen. Sie sind einer politischen Willensentscheidung der KSZE-Teilnehmer nicht zugänglich. Womit die KSZE konfrontiert ist und was sie so hilflos erscheinen läßt, sind natürlich auch, aber nicht nur die Gewaltausbrüche, die den Ost-West-Konflikt in Europa abgelöst haben. Herausgefordert ist die KSZE bereits, bevor Gewalt angewendet wird. Dazu gehört, auf die Bedingungen einwirken zu können, die ein friedliches Zusammenleben erschweren oder gelegentlich unmöglich machen. Demokratie und Menschenrechte, so heißt es folgerichtig in der "Charta von Paris", bilden die Grundlage für den Frieden.

Diese Bemerkungen haben nicht den Zweck, die Aufbruchstimmung von Paris noch einmal in Erinnerung zu rufen. Die Absicht ist, auf die Verschiedenartigkeit der Probleme hinzuweisen, vor die die KSZE gestellt ist. Es verlangt andere Instrumente und Verfahrensgrundsätze, wenn es der KSZE darum geht, als Referenzgröße für den *Wandel* in den Staaten da zu sein, als sie dann gefragt sind, wenn die KSZE gebraucht wird, um Konflikte zu verhindern oder sogar zu beenden. Konkret: Die KSZE kann als ein völkerrechtlicher Vertrag auf die Ursachen vieler Probleme nicht besser einwirken als unter den Bedingungen eines offenen Dialogforums. Die rechtliche Selbständigkeit ihrer Institutionen wäre dagegen ein wichtiger Schritt in die Richtung einer größeren Handlungsfähigkeit, wenn die Aufgabe darin besteht, Konflikte zu vermeiden. Ähnliches gilt in Bezug auf die Konsensregel. Es ist keine Frage der Abstimmungsmodalitäten, wenn es um die Demokratiefähigkeit der Staaten geht. Es ist aber sehr wohl wichtig, welche Verfahrensgrundsätze gelten, um in der KSZE entscheidungsfähiger zu sein. Wenn über die Optionen der KSZE nachgedacht wird, sind diese beiden Wirkungsdimensionen auseinanderzuhalten. Hier geht es auf den nächsten Seiten nur um die Rolle der KSZE *in* ihren Teilnehmerstaaten.

II. Alte Stärken, neuer Bedarf

Angesichts der Enttäuschungen, die die KSZE bei vielen ausgelöst hat, ist zu fragen, ob die komparativen Vorteile, die den guten Ruf der KSZE unter den Bedingungen eines antagonistischen Europas begründet haben, aufgebraucht und hinfällig geworden sind. Geht es wirklich in jeder Hinsicht um eine umfassend erneuerte KSZE, in der die Funktionsprinzipien der Vergangenheit für die Zukunft nicht mehr taugen?

Nahezu 15 Jahre lang hat die KSZE mitgeholfen, die innerstaatlichen Voraussetzungen einer konfrontativen Ost-West-Struktur zu erodieren. Auf diesem Feld war sie weitgehend konkurrenzlos. Auch nach dem Ende der Ost-West-Teilung

Europas sind es die Verhältnisse *in* den Staaten und den sie tragenden Gesellschaften, die das Zusammenleben gefährden. *Zwischen*staatliche Auseinandersetzungen sind zwar im Vergleich zu den Jahren der ideologischen und machtpolitischen Zweiteilung Europas wahrscheinlicher geworden, doch ihre Ursachen liegen mehr denn je im Inneren der Länder. Es spricht kaum etwas für die Annahme, daß Konflikte mit einer Aggression beginnen. Als weitere Stufe in einem Konfliktverlauf sind sie eine reale Gefahr; es gehen ihnen jedoch Versäumnisse und Fehlentscheidungen in den Staaten voraus. Traditionelle Aggressionsgründe wie etwa die Absicht, das eigene Territorium zu erweitern, nehmen auf der Skala möglicher Kriegsgefahren in Europa allenfalls hintere Plätze ein. Die Konflike zu Beginn der 90er Jahre sind davon keine Ausnahme.

Eine Wurzel haben nahezu alle Spannungen gemeinsam. Sie wird hier stellvertretend für die Gefahrenquellen genannt, die in eine gründlichere Zusammenstellung gehören. Es ist die Art und Weise, in der Interessenunterschiede ausgetragen werden, nicht ihr Vorhandensein. Bedenklicher noch als das Fehlen institutioneller Konfliktregelungsmechanismen in nahezu allen krisenträchtigen Staaten ist der Mangel an einem Konfliktverständnis, das Kompromißfähigkeit ebenso einschließt wie die Fähigkeit zur Toleranz. Stattdessen wirken Verhaltensmuster, die sich an autoritären Traditionen, engstirnigen Identifikationsbedürfnissen und Überhöhungen historischer Erinnerungen orientieren. Schon diese wenigen Hinweise genügen, um feststellen zu können, daß es sich um emotionale Fluchtpunkte handelt, die nur in einer langfristigen Zeitperspektive entwertet werden können. Gefragt sind demnach Prozesse, die nicht "von oben" und mehrheitlich erzwungen werden können, sondern die "von unten" ausgehen müssen, um zu einem tragfähigen Wandel zu führen.

Ein besonderes Krisenpotential unterstreicht diese innerstaatliche Dimension zukünftiger Konfliktgefahren. Mit dem Zerfall der Sowjetunion hat ein völkerrechtlicher Grundsatz Aktualität erlangt, der in der Schlußakte von Helsinki mit der Verpflichtung, die "territoriale Integrität" der Staaten zu wahren, in einem Atemzug genannt wird: Das Recht auf eine friedliche Veränderung von Grenzen. 1975 hat insbesondere die Bundesrepublik Deutschland, unterstützt von ihren Verbündeten nachdrücklich das Interesse verfolgt, sich den Weg zu einer friedlichen Vereinigung mit der DDR nicht zu verstellen. Der deutschlandpolitische Bedarf ist mittlerweile gedeckt. Die Zahl weiterer Anwendungsfälle ist hingegen inflationär gestiegen. Die Befreiung der Staaten Ostmittel- und Südosteuropas vom machtpolitischen Zugriff der Sowjetunion war nur eine Hälfte des tiefgreifenden Umbruchs in Europa seit den augehenden 80er Jahren. Die andere betrifft die Sowjetunion selber. Der Zerfall gleicht einem Vorgang der Entkolonialisierung. In diesem geht es keineswegs nur darum, die – mitunter recht kurzlebige – Existenz vormalig unabhängiger Staaten wieder herzustellen. Die Zahl von Neugründungen ist nicht geringer. Ihr territorialer Zuschnitt beruht auf der ehemals gelegentlich willkürlichen Festlegung von Verwaltungsgrenzen. So ist die Annahme, daß aus 15 Sowjetrepubliken auch nur 15 Staaten entstehen, nicht gesichert. Ihre Gründung war ein erster Schritt, der weitere nicht ausschließt, die nicht nur bestehende Grenzen verändern, sondern zu völlig neuen Staaten führen werden. Angesichts dieser Erwartung erlangt der Grundsatz, daß Grenzveränderungen nur auf friedlichem Wege zulässig sind, eine Aktualität, die 1975 nicht in gleicher Dringlichkeit gegeben war. Festzuhalten ist, daß Sezessionen von Teilgebieten oder staatliche Neugründungen aus bestehenden Staaten heraus erwachsen und allenfalls erst im weiteren Verlauf von außen gewaltsam eingefordert werden. "Peaceful change" in der Bedeutung der 90er Jahre verlangt eine Konfliktkultur, die in großen Teilen Europas ohne Tradition ist.

Was bedeutet das Gesagte mit Blick auf die KSZE? Sie muß sich nicht um jeden Preis ein neues Wirkungsfeld suchen. Das Ende des systemischen und machtpolitischen Antagonismus in Europa heißt für die KSZE zunächst einmal, daß sich die Möglichkeiten, aber auch der Bedarf vergrößert haben, in die Staaten hineinzuwirken, wohingegen dies in der Vergangenheit allenfalls nur auf Umwegen geschehen konnte. Bedingung dafür ist jedoch, auch weiterhin dem Prozeßcharakter Rechnung zu tragen, in dem sich der Wandel in den KSZE-Teilnehmerstaaten nur vollziehen kann. Das heißt, sie muß sich den Grad an flexibler Offenheit bewahren, der gesellschaftliche Prozesse in den ganz unterschiedlichen Weltgegenden der KSZE-Teilnehmerstaaten auszeichnet. Mit der politischen Zeitenwende sind nicht notwendigerweise KSZE-Prinzipien hinfällig geworden, die für ihre Existenz unter Ost-West-Bedingungen konstitutiv waren. Wenn die KSZE, wie es im Helsinki-Dokument von 1992 heißt, "ein Forum für Dialog, Verhandlung und Zusammenarbeit, das der Gestaltung des neuen Europa Richtung und Impulse gibt"[3] bleibt, dann kann sie – Ausnahmen zunächst einmal außer Acht gelassen – nicht auf die völkerrechtliche Unverbindlichkeit ihrer Beschlüsse sowie den durch vage Formulierungen eingeschränkten Grundsatz der Einstimmigkeit verzichten. Die Durchsetzung von KSZE-Normen ist vor allem dann keine Angelegenheit von Mehrheitsentscheidungen, wenn in einer ganzen Reihe von Teilnehmerstaaten die Bedingungen für ihre Einhaltung nicht vorhanden und auch durch eine Kompetenzausweitung der KSZE nicht herstellbar sind. Die Fortgeltung beider Grundsätze drückt also keineswegs nur das Maß des Möglichen aus. Sie sind vielmehr durch ein Aufgabenfeld vorgegeben, das seit der Wende von 1989/90 nichts von seiner Bedeutung verloren hat.

Vor einem allzu vehementen Reformeifer warnt – nun allerdings nicht mehr aus der Binnensicht der KSZE-Teilnehmer argumentierend – auch der folgende

---

3 Bulletin, (23.7.1992) 88, S. 779.

Gesichtspunkt: Das Risikopotential in Europa ist keineswegs gleichmäßig verteilt. Der KSZE-Raum ist keine einheitliche "Konfliktlandschaft". Es bedarf keiner prognostischen Fähigkeiten, um vorauszusagen, was sich bereits deutlich abzeichnet: In Osteuropa ist die Dynamik der Veränderungen ungleich größer als im Westen des Kontinents. In Osteuropa ist deshalb auch der Normenkatalog der KSZE weitaus häufiger von Verletzungen bedroht, als dies in den Reihen der "alten" KSZE-Teilnehmer der Fall sein wird. Es gibt also schon jetzt ein West-Ost-Handlungsgefälle. Es wird in einer überschaubaren Zukunft nicht geringer werden und Europa dauerhaft prägen. Ebenso gehört nur wenig Phantasie dazu sich vorzustellen, welchen Zerreißproben die KSZE ausgesetzt sein würde, wenn an die Stelle kooperativer Strukturen mehrheitlich entschiedene Durchsetzungsmechanismen treten würden. Eine auf 53 Staaten angewachsene KSZE könnte dem nicht standhalten. Insofern hat die KSZE-Teilnahme aller ehemaligen Sowjetrepubliken ihren Preis. Er kann nicht zurückgefordert werden, zumal mit ihm dafür bezahlt wurde, die Tür zu neuen Staaten und Gesellschaften immerhin einen Spalt weit zu öffnen. Die KSZE würde auch dadurch nicht handlicher, indem sie etwas nachzuahmen versuchte, was mit Blick auf einzelne Bestimmungen im Vertrag von Maastricht erstmals festgeschrieben wurde: ein unterschiedliches Maß an Umsetzungsverpflichtung für einige Unterzeichnerstaaten. Sozial- und finanzpolitische Regelungsbereiche sind teilbar; menschen- und völkerrechtliche Mindeststandards sind dies nicht. Insofern ist Maastricht in dieser Hinsicht kein Modell für die KSZE.

III. Abwarten oder was dann?

Die Staatenwelt ist nicht dazu verdammt, defätistisch abzuwarten, bis überall das herangereift ist, was gemeinhin als eine konfliktfähige politische Kultur umschrieben wird. In der "Charta von Paris" haben sich die Teilnehmerstaaten der KSZE dazu verpflichtet, "die Demokratie als die einzige Regierungsform [ihrer] Nationen aufzubauen".[4] Die später hinzugekommenen KSZE-Teilnehmer haben sich dieser Verpflichtung angeschlossen. Im Helsinki-Dokument von 1992 bestätigen die Teilnehmerstaaten der KSZE die gemeinsamen Ziele wie "die Achtung der Menschenrechte und die Grundfreiheiten, einschließlich der Rechte Demokratie, Rechtsstaatlichkeit" usw. und fügen hinzu: "Die Einhaltung unserer Verpflichtungen bildet die Basis für Mitwirkung und Zusammenarbeit in der KSZE und einen Eckpfeiler für die weitere Entwicklung unserer Gesellschaften."[5]

Die Vorkehrungen, die die KSZE-Staaten seit dem Paris-Gipfel getroffen und die Hilfsmittel, die sie sich geschaffen haben, um den hehren Absichtserklärungen Nachdruck zu verleihen und sie umzusetzen, sind nach wie vor dürftig. So war und

4 Bulletin, (24.11.1990) 137, S. 1409.

5 Bulletin, (23.7.1992) 88, S. 777.

ist das in Warschau eingerichtete "Büro für freie Wahlen", später in "Büro Demokratischer Institutionen und Menschenrechte" (BDIMR) umbenannt, kaum mehr als eine Duftnote. Es hat weder die Ausstattung noch die Kompetenz, das zu sein, was es im Interesse der gemeinsamen Verpflichtungserklärungen sein sollte, ein "Dienstleistungsunternehmen" zugunsten der gesteckten Ziele. Dazu bedarf es – und das gilt für die anderen KSZE-Institutionen gleichermaßen – einer rechtlichen Aufwertung. Was für die KSZE insgesamt schädlich wäre, wollte man ihr den Charakter eines Prozesses nehmen und sie auf eine vertragliche Basis stellen, ist für ihre einzelnen institutionellen Einrichtungen ein herausragendes Ziel. Sie müssen vertraglich in die Lage versetzt werden, aus eigenem Recht heraus tätig werden zu können.

Es würde nicht nur einer rechtlichen Qualität des BDIMR bedürfen, sondern dieses zusätzlich aufwerten, wenn sich die Teilnehmerstaaten der KSZE dazu verpflichteten, ihre nationalstaatlichen Minderheitengesetze in Warschau zu registrieren und durch das Büro einer breiten Öffentlichkeit zugänglich zu machen. Es würde ihrer Einhaltung größeren Nachdruck verleihen, wobei die Regelung, völkerrechtliche Verträge bei den Vereinten Nationen zu hinterlegen, Pate stehen könnte. Eine entsprechende Vereinbarung wäre zugleich ein Schritt, mit dem die im Helsinki-Dokument vorgetragene Überzeugung, "daß die im Bereich der menschlichen Dimension der KSZE eingegangenen Verpflichtungen ein unmittelbares und berechtigtes Anliegen aller Teilnehmerstaaten und eine nicht ausschließlich innere Angelegenheit des betroffenen Staates darstellen",[6] Substanz erhielte. Beispielhaft und analog anwendbar ist in diesem Zusammenhang die Note, mit der die italienische Regierung im April 1992 Wien über den endgültigen Vollzug des Südtirolpakets in Kenntnis setzt. In ihr heißt es: "Die italienische Regierung sieht das Ergebnis, das bei der Verwirklichung der Autonomie der Provinz Bozen erzielt wurde, als einen wichtigen Bezugspunkt für den Minderheitenschutz an, wie er sich auch im KSZE-Rahmen herausbildet. *Auch dessen spezifische Überwachungsmechanismen können Anwendung finden, um sicher zu stellen, daß die Behandlung dieser Minderheit mit den Prinzipien übereinstimmt, welche man zum Zwecke eines friedlichen und harmonischen Zusammenlebens im Neuen Europa kodifizieren wird.*"

Den Wirkungsgrad der KSZE zu erhöhen und die Empfehlung, das Konsensprinzip nicht über die bereits vereinbarte Einschränkung hinaus zurückzunehmen, sind kein Widerspruch. Diese Feststellung geht allerdings davon aus, daß sich die KSZE, um noch einmal das Helsinki-Dokument von 1992 zu zitieren, mit den "Grundursachen der Probleme" auseinandersetzt.[7] Die Ausgangsbedingungen dafür sind mit dem Ende des Systemkonflikts ungleich günstiger, aber auch drin-

6 Ebd.

7 Ebd., S. 779.

gender geworden. Wozu die KSZE in der Vergangenheit nicht in der Lage war, jetzt kann sie es tun. Sie muß weitere Schritte unternehmen, die sie von ihrem Monopol entfernen, ein Forum der Staaten zu sein. Sie sollte mehr und mehr auch zu einer Bühne für Gesellschaft und gesellschaftliche Gruppen werden. Der Platz, der den nichtstaatlichen Organisationen bislang zugestanden wurde, darf nicht schon alles sein, was für sie erreichbar ist. Der Bedarf, daß sich demokratische, nichtstaatliche Kräfte in Teilnehmerstaaten der KSZE wie zu Zeiten der antagonistischen Systemauseinandersetzung auf die feierlichen Verabredungen und Verpflichtungserklärungen ihrer staatlichen Repräsentanten auf den KSZE-Konferenzen berufen, ist noch keineswegs erschöpft. Auffallend ist vielmehr, daß zwar immer wieder auf die Verletzung grundlegender Menschen- und Bürgerrechte als Quelle innerstaatlicher Krisen verwiesen wird – so auch in diesem Papier –, man aber kaum etwas davon hört, daß benachteiligte Einzelpersonen oder Gruppen die KSZE-Normen einfordern, auf die sich ihre Regierungen verpflichtet haben. Dieser Sachverhalt muß stutzig machen. Er verweist auf das doppelte Defizit, daß KSZE-Prinzipien als Berufungsgrundlage innergesellschaftlicher Konflikte nicht mehr den Stellenwert haben, der unter Ost-West-Bedingungen ihre Wirkung ausmachte, und daß es der KSZE nicht gelungen ist, diese Rolle – wenn auch unter veränderten äußeren Bedingungen – beizubehalten bzw. aufzunehmen.

IV. KSZE-Botschafter

Ein Ansatzpunkt, hier für Abhilfe zu sorgen, könnte in der praktischen Umsetzung der folgenden Überlegung enthalten sein. Wenn die KSZE als innerstaatliche Berufungsgrundlage an Bedeutung eingebüßt hat, muß sie den Staaten und Gesellschaften wieder näher gebracht werden. Da, wo früher die demokratischen Kräfte in den vormals sozialistischen Staaten in einem übertragenen Sinne zur KSZE gingen, muß heute die KSZE zu den Kräften gehen, die in den neuen Teilnehmerstaaten dafür eintreten, daß die Gelöbnisse von Paris keine Papierform bleiben. Die Idee ist die Einrichtung von "KSZE-Botschaftern". Nun ist es durchaus denkbar, das KSZE-Sekretariat – wie auch schon für das BDIMR empfohlen – in seinem Status so umzugestalten und aufzuwerten, daß es Repräsentanten aus den Teilnehmerstaaten bei sich akkreditieren könnte. Dem Zweck, die KSZE in den Demokratisierungsprozeß ihrer jungen Teilnehmerstaaten einzubringen, wäre damit jedoch nicht gedient. Ohnehin wären die Aussichten gering, daß sich die neuen Staaten im KSZE-Prozeß zusätzlich zu den bestehenden Anforderungen, die schon jetzt häufig ihre Möglichkeiten übersteigen, noch zu einer weiteren Belastung bereit finden. Nicht die Teilnehmerstaaten sind also bei der KSZE, sondern die KSZE ist bei den Teilnehmerstaaten anzusiedeln.

Hier geht es zunächst einmal um die Idee, nicht jedoch um ihre Ausgestaltung in allen Einzelheiten. Doch vorstellbar wäre es, die "KSZE-Botschaft" räumlich wie finanziell in der diplomatischen Vertretung eines KSZE-Staates unterzubringen, ohne sie damit jedoch von ihrer Gastbotschaft politisch abhängig zu machen. Der Zweck dieser Regelung wäre eine materielle Lastenverteilung. Das Ziel, Vertreter der KSZE zu akkreditieren, würde durch diese räumliche Zuordnung nicht beschnitten werden. Eine Etappe, die zweifellos noch weiter entfernt ist, könnte sein, daß es eines Tages die "KSZE-Botschafter" sind, die auf den "Überprüfungskonferenzen" die Berichte für die Implementierungsdebatte abgeben. Der erste Schritt, um diese Ideen zu realisieren, ist jedoch, daß die KSZE-Teilnehmer sich dazu entschließen, einer KSZE-Institution den "international anerkannten Status" zu verleihen, der sie dazu befugt, "KSZE-Botschafter" zu entsenden. Die im Helsinki-Dokument von 1992 verabredete Prüfung dieses Fragenkomplexes sollte die hier erwogenen Anregungen aufgreifen.[8]

8 Bulletin, (23.7.1992) 88, S. 782.

9. Adapting the CSCE to Modern Problems: Limits and Opportunities*

Anne M. Dixon/Thomas J. Hirschfeld

Abstract

The post-Cold War European security architecture consists of overlapping multilateral institutions all evolving to adapt to new circumstances. This article explores the recent developments in the Conference on Security and Cooperation in Europe (CSCE) with particular attention to how the CSCE can be enabled to promote peaceful resolution of disputes. The authors doubt that the CSCE potential should be judged by its halting responses to Nagorno-Karabakh and Bosnia – problems to which no institution, country or group of countries has effectively responded. Instead, we believe that the CSCE can be developed to fulfill certain defined and circumscribed roles. The article describes the measures that have strengthened and broadened the CSCE since the end of 1989, and the resulting mechanisms for action. It then briefly outlines the perspectives of selected members on the CSCE and its competencies and speculates about how diverse expectations may create limits for the development of CSCE structures. The second section examines the bases for legitimate collective action in conflict prevention, crisis management and conflict management against a background of CSCE norms and principles. Having concluded, albeit reluctantly, that structural adaptations alone are unlikely to make the CSCE much more effective, we suggest a modern adaptation of a 19th Century solution to earlier versions of many of the present problems – a new Congress of Berlin under CSCE member auspices.

I. Keeping in Step with the Times: New Members and New Missions

1. CSCE Expansion

Since its inception in Helsinki in 1975, CSCE membership has expanded from the original 34 signatories of the Helsinki Final Act to 52 members (excluding Serbia and Montenegro, currently suspended). Virtually all of Europe is included, as are the United States, Canada and all of the republics of the former Soviet Union; Japan and several non-member Mediterranean states have observer status. Much of this broadening followed the end of the Cold War division of Europe, in an attempt to involve former adversaries in a mutual security framework and to create a greater regional community. Under the Helsinki Final Act of 1975, CSCE

* The views expressed are those of the authors and are not necessarily shared by the Center for Naval Analyses (CNA) or its research sponsors.

understandings are divided among three "baskets" of issues, which were created to advance principles upon which the security of the community of members is believed to depend.

The first basket, General Principles and Security Issues, defines the ethos of the CSCE. Ten basic principles of international behavior are outlined, including respect for territorial integrity, peaceful settlement of disputes, human rights and equal rights, and self-determination. Confidence and Security Building Measures (CSBMs) now call for prior notification of military maneuvers and an exchange of observers, and members have assumed obligations regarding force reductions and verification in the Conventional Forces, Europe (CFE) Treaty process. The second basket covers Economics, Science and Technology and the Environment and involves measures to promote free market economies and economic cooperation as well as environmental protection measures. The third basket deals with Humanitarian Issues, including minority protection, dissemination of information and cultural cooperation.

2. Evolving CSCE Structures

a. The Paris Summit and the Charter for a New Europe

Since the fall of the Berlin Wall at the end of 1989, the CSCE has instituted several changes in order to become an effective institution with specified competencies rather than a loosely defined forum for dialogue. Several important structures were introduced at the Paris CSCE summit of November 1990, and by the resulting Charter of Paris for a New Europe. Following an October meeting of CSCE foreign ministers in New York, a Council of Ministers (COM) was established in Paris with a broad mandate. The COM is the main decision making body in the CSCE; all of its decisions are arrived at by full consensus. It is chaired by the state that hosts the most recent COM meeting (to take place at least annually). Following the meeting of CSCE foreign ministers in Prague in January 1992, Czechoslovakia assumed the chairmanship.

The Paris Charter also provided for the establishment of a Committee of Senior Officials (CSO), a subsidiary working group of the executive body, at the ambassadorial level. This group is charged with preparing meetings of the COM and implementing its decisions. The COM may delegate decision making authority to the CSO. The CSO reviews current issues and coordinates CSCE activities with other international organizations, including NATO, the WEU and the UN. CSO meetings are held at least quarterly, so CSO delegates may be more aware of current problems and more accustomed to working with each other. This in turn may make the CSO a potentially more effective forum than the COM.

A Council of Ministers of Foreign Affairs was established at the Paris summit. This group subsequently worked to establish the emergency mechanism that calls for the CSO to meet in emergency situations. The ministers also formed a CSCE parliamentary assembly on the model of the Parliamentary Assembly of the Council of Europe. Both of these structures strengthen the CSCE security dimension by creating a way to call attention to mounting tensions early on, and by providing for more regular dialogue thereafter.

The Paris Charter also established three offices that expand the CSCE security system. A Conflict Prevention Center (CPC) was established in Vienna in January of 1991 to monitor military data sharing and to host both annual implementation meetings and special meetings called under the unusual military activities mechanism.[1] The Paris Charter also provided for a CPC role in "reducing the risk of conflict" and in "broader tasks relating to dispute settlement;" these provisions have since been elaborated somewhat in the Helsinki II Document signed in the summer of 1992, and the CSCE Forum for Security Cooperation began meeting in Vienna on 22 September 1992, to continue work on CSCE conflict management tools. The Paris Charter also established a Conflict Prevention Center Consultative Committee (CPC/CC), a steering group at the ambassadorial level that was charged with oversight of CPC communications and the implementation of agreed Confidence and Security Building Measures (CSBMs).

A Secretariat opened in Prague in February 1991. It provides administrative support to the COM and CSO and houses an archive. It also provides information to the public, non-CSCE states and other international organizations. Finally, the Office for Free Elections (OFE) opened in April 1991 in Warsaw and was expanded in January 1992 into an Office for Democratic Institutions and Human Rights (ODIHR). Its roles are to coordinate election monitoring by international observers, serve as a central source of information for democratic institution building, and organize seminars on human dimension issues. All of the above-mentioned offices are located in the center of Europe and two are in former Warsaw Treaty Organization (WTO) states, partly for symbolic value. But because many functions of the different offices overlap or require close cooperation, decentralization results in poor communication and other inefficiencies, including higher costs. Additionally, the offices are severely understaffed.

b. Toward the Post-Cold War World: Oslo, Petersberg and Helsinki

The end of the Cold War called the previously understood rationales for the existence of the CSCE and NATO into question. Initially many observers believed that

1 Special meetings can be convened if a participating state undertakes significant maneuvers or other military action that violates CSBM or CFE commitments.

these two organizations, with the WEU and even the UN, would present Europe with competing security architectures. However, efforts are being made to avoid such confrontation, at least at the rhetorical level. CSCE, NATO and WEU representatives have recently recognized the need for "mutually reinforcing European and transatlantic organizations,"[2] as does the Washington Charter for American-Russian Partnership and Friendship. The CSCE Helsinki summit declared the CSCE a regional organization under Chapter VIII of the UN Charter.

The Helsinki Summit Declaration states that, "CSCE peacekeeping activities may be undertaken in cases of conflict within or among participating States to help maintain peace and stability in support of an ongoing effort at a political solution. In this respect, we are also prepared to seek, on a case-by-case basis, the support of international institutions and organizations, such as the EC, NATO and WEU, as well as other institutions and organizations, including the peacekeeping mechanism of the CIS."[3]

More concretely, according to a press communiqué issued in June 1991, leading NATO officials would prefer to leave responsibility for security guarantees east of where the Iron Curtain formerly bisected Europe mainly to the CSCE, preferring that the North Atlantic Cooperation Council (NACC)[4] remain primarily a consultative forum with former WTO countries.[5] Conflict prevention, crisis management and peacekeeping have been heralded as new purposes for the CSCE,[6] and the CSCE has begun to develop mechanisms intended to meet the demands of these roles.

---

2 *Petersberg Declaration of the WEU*, signed 23 June 1992 at Petersberg near Bonn. The final communique of the North Atlantic Council (NAC) Ministerial meeting in Oslo on 4 June 1992, declares that "[S]tability and security in the Euro-Atlantic area will increasingly be built on a framework of interlocking and mutually reinforcing institutions: NATO, the CSCE, the European Community, the WEU and the Council of Europe."

3 *Helsinki Summit Declaration*, July 10, 1992, Paragraph 20.

4 The North Atlantic Cooperation Council (NACC), inaugurated in Brussels on 20 December 1991, was developed to create a NATO forum that would include former WTO countries. In a Work Plan signed 10 March 1992, the group dedicated itself to two sets of activities: (1) consultations with the North Atlantic Council, the Military Committee and other specialized committees; and (2) cooperative activities including bi-monthly military staff talks and other exchanges, defence conversion cooperation and colloquia on economic and commercial relations.

5 Press communique, M-1 (91) 42 (6 June 1991): "But the new relationship [the NACC] was carefully couched as contributing to the achievement of the objectives of the CSCE ... while preserving its responsibilities and mechanisms." In short NATO's leaders have left the principal responsibility for stability and security in Central and Eastern Europe to other actors, most notably the CSCE: "We will seek to reinforce the CSCE's potential for conflict prevention, crisis management, and the peaceful settlement of disputes by appropriate means, such as creating a suitably structured emergency consultation mechanism and strengthening the Conflict Prevention Center [CPC]." Cited in James B. Steinberg, "The Role of European Institutions in Security after the Cold War: Some Lessons from Yugoslavia," *RAND Note* N-3445-FF, 1992, p. 2.

6 *The Economist*, July 18, 1992, p. 18.

c. Early Warning and Conflict Prevention

At the Moscow Human Dimension meeting (10 September-4 October 1991), a multilateral mechanism for monitoring human rights was established to help with early warning of instabilities that might lead to conflict. Under this mechanism, a written response to a request for human rights information must be provided by the member state as soon as possible and in a period not to exceed ten days. Member states may request a CSCE commission of experts to contribute to the resolution of human rights questions within their borders. A High Commissioner on National Minorities now heads the ODIHR in Warsaw, and can use panels of experts to investigate alleged abuses.[7]

The CSCE Emergency Mechanism proposed in Paris was established at the June 1991 Berlin meeting of the COM as a consultation procedure triggered by the request of one member state with the support of 12 others. As set out in the document produced at the Prague COM meeting of January 1992, the CPC/CC can alert the CSO concerning unusual military activities. Additionally, the recent Helsinki decisions provided that the CSO can be approached: by any state directly involved in a dispute; by a group of 11 states not directly involved; by the High Commissioner on National Minorities in situations where he/she finds that the scope of the conflict exceeds his/her authority; or through the use of the Human Dimension Mechanism or the Valletta Principles for dispute settlement and provisions for a CSCE procedure for Peaceful Settlement of Disputes.

Once the CSO is apprised of a simmering conflict, it is first supposed to try managing the crisis politically,[8] by recommending procedures for peaceful settlement. The CSO may establish a framework for a negotiated settlement, good offices or mediation. It may also refer to experts and set up fact-finding missions as instruments of conflict prevention and crisis management. The reports from these missions may be kept confidential if so requested by the states involved. Although confidentiality is likely to increase the concerned CSCE members' willingness to comply with a procedure to which they have already agreed, it reduces the potential impact of public opinion.[9]

---

7 The High Commissioner on National Minorities does *not* consider national minority issues in cases where organized terrorism is involved. If a *prima facie* risk of conflict is established the High Commissioner sends an early warning to the CSO via the Chairman-in-Office.

8 *Helsinki Decisions*, July 10, 1992, Chapter III, Paragraph 6.

9 CSCE charters, decisions and other agreements are not legally binding treaties under international law.

d. CSCE Peacekeeping[10]

The July 1992 Helsinki document states that peacekeeping constitutes an important complement to the political process of dispute settlement. CSCE peacekeeping follows the principles of Chapter VIII of the UN Charter,[11] which accepts the "principle of regionalism." Because the nature of regional organizations is not clearly defined in the UN Charter (see explanation of Article 52 under *"Meaning of Regional Arrangements"*), the CSCE is free to develop in any way "consistent with the Purposes and Principles of the United Nations" (Article 52, Paragraph 1). This gives CSCE leaders considerable freedom in developing structures and procedures for the organization. Article 52, Paragraph 2 of Chapter VIII states that, "The Members of the United Nations entering into such arrangements or constituting such agencies shall make every effort to achieve pacific settlement of local disputes [e.g. within the regional area] through such regional arrangements or by such regional agencies before referring them to the Security Council." Thus the CSCE would presumably be expected to act first to resolve conflicts within its area. Article 52, Paragraph 3 states that the UN Security Council may also call a regional organization's attention to disputes.[12]

For his part, UN Secretary-General Boutros Boutros-Ghali, saddled with substantial financial problems and proliferating regional crises that threaten to spread UN resources far too thin, claims that "the regional organizations are at the service of the United Nations, not that the United Nations is at the service of the regional organizations."[13] This can be taken to mean that regional organizations should act first. Therefore, if effective, the CSCE could provide some welcome relief to the Secretary-General, who in any case believes strongly that this relatively wealthy area of the world has the resources to solve its own problems.

---

10 See *Helsinki Decisions*, July 10, 1992, Chapter III, Paragraph 17ff.

11 See *Helsinki Decisions*, July 10, 1992, Chapter III: Early Warning, Conflict Prevention and Crisis Management (including Fact-Finding and Rapporteur Missions and CSCE Peacekeeping), Peaceful Settlement of Disputes, Paragraph 19.

12 The explaining text below Paragraph 3 clarifies the provision so that it remains harmonious with earlier provisions of the Charter: "This idea of reference of disputes by the Security Council to regional agencies seems to be a new one, not wholly in harmony with the procedures laid down in Chapter VI of the Charter. Under the Articles of Chapter VI the Security Council has only the power to recommend directly to the parties procedures to be followed in the settlement of their disputes, or the actual terms of settlement. It is, therefore, difficult to see how the Security Council can actually refer a dispute to a regional agency except upon the agreement of the parties concerned. What is apparently meant is that when the Security Council has before it a local dispute, which has been called to its attention under the provisions of Article 35, it is to refer the matter to the appropriate regional agency ... for such action as the agency in question is empowered to take."

13 Patrick E. Tyler, "U.N. Chief's Dispute With Council Boils Over," *The New York Times*, August 3, 1992, p. A1.

The recent Helsinki Decisions establish some procedures for peacekeeping. Requests for peacekeeping operations may be addressed through the Chairman-in-Office to the CSO by one or more participating states. The CSO then has authority to ask the CPC/CC to consider appropriate peacekeeping actions and submit recommendations to the CSO. The decision to initiate operations must come from a consensus in the COM or from the CSO acting as its agent.[14] Although the early warning procedures can lead to early awareness of a problem, the consensus requirement still hinders expeditious response.

CSCE peacekeeping operations may involve either civilian or military personnel. They may range from observer and monitor missions to larger deployments. Peacekeeping activities may include supervision of cease-fires and troop withdrawals, law and order maintenance, and medical and humanitarian aid to refugees.[15]

The Helsinki Decisions include several limitations and conditions for peacekeeping activities. They must be conducted impartially, they require the consent of the parties concerned, and they cannot involve enforcement.[16] Before a mission is dispatched, the CSO must establish both a clear mandate and cost projections.[17] The parties to the conflict must have established a cease-fire, and guarantees for the safety of peacekeeping personnel must be provided.[18]

All CSCE states pay for CSCE-authorized peacekeeping operations[19], within the limits of a ceiling established annually by the CSO. Beyond the ceiling, special arrangements are to be worked out and agreed by consensus. Finally, should CSCE not possess the resources or the competencies to carry out a given operation, the dispute should then be referred to the UN Security Council. The most costly and dangerous operations, therefore, may require UN Security Council consideration.

e. Use of New Mechanisms to Date

Many observers believe that the CSCE is today as weak as the UN was before the Security Council was formed, and that the prospects for solving the organization's decision making problems are bleak, largely because of the intractable issue of

---

14 *Helsinki Decisions*, July 10, 1992, Chapter III, Paragraphs 25-29.

15 Ibid., Paragraph 18.

16 Ibid., Paragraphs 22-24. In any case, Article 53, Paragraph 1 of Chapter VIII of the UN Charter stipulates that "[N]o enforcement action shall be taken under regional arrangements or by regional agencies without the authorization of the Security Council."

17 *Helsinki Decisions*, July 10, 1992, Chapter III, Paragraphs 32-33. Paragraph 47 states that, "Costs of CSCE peacekeeping activities will be borne by all CSCE participating States. At the beginning of each calendar year, the CSO will establish a reasonable ceiling for the cost of peacekeeping operations to which the CSCE scale of distribution will be applied. Beyond that limit, other special arrangements will be negotiated and agreed to by consensus. Full and timely payments will be required."

18 Ibid., Paragraph 30.

19 Ibid., Paragraphs 46-51.

consensus-based decision making.[20] In emergency cases, the CSCE currently facilitates decision making through use of the CPC/CC, or by formation of 11-12 member steering groups which make recommendations to the CSO, but can make no decisions themselves. Given the organization's broad membership, there is an indisputable need for a smaller body with authority to make decisions. But whereas World War II allowed for the formation of a small UN Security Council (including the nations with the most powerful armed forces), the end of the Cold War features no such exceptional circumstances. There is no accepted basis for building a steering group among sovereign equals that conforms with CSCE principles.

The aforementioned restrictions and requirements and the consensus rule[21] suggest that the CSCE is likely to be hamstrung in mounting timely conflict prevention and crisis responses. The Bosnian situation is a case in point. For purposes of crisis management, the Balkan situation was placed under permanent review by the CSO, and a human rights rapporteur and a monitoring mission were established. On 31 July 1992, the UN Secretary-General wrote to Chairman-in-Office Jozef Moravchik to request assistance in Balkan peacekeeping. The CSO responded with only "a vague promise of support." CSCE participating states are being canvassed to join in weapons monitoring in Bosnia, a mission arising out of an agreement reached by the EC peace conference which was then referred to the UN.[22] Clearly the Secretary-General would have liked the CSCE to take the lead in grappling with as many aspects of this conflict as possible.

But it appears impossible for the diverse participating states to approach Bosnia impartially. The months-long history of the conflict has demonstrated that cease-fires cannot hold and, because several of the parties to the conflict resist international intervention to stop "ethnic cleansing," any effective action would entail enforcement, for which the CSCE would have no authority to task NATO or the WEU. Thus the matter has been passed on to the UN Security Council, which will organize national troop contributions for the protection of humanitarian assistance convoys or other operations.

---

20 From an interview with Director François Heisbourg of the International Institute for Strategic Studies (IISS), August 18, 1992.

21 The requirement that all CSCE decisions be based on consensus has been relaxed to "consensus minus one" in order that a participating state judged to be in violation of CSCE principles may be removed from the decision making process in the treatment of a dispute in which it is involved. The rump state of Yugoslavia, the republics of Serbia and Montenegro, have accordingly been excluded from discussions of the Balkan crisis and suspended from the CSCE. The legalities are especially murky because if the two republics do not in fact constitute a bona fide successor state to the former Yugoslavia, then, some argue, they must go through the same process of scrutiny and be admitted to the CSCE as were the other former Yugoslav republics. See Annette Makino, "CSCE Prepares for Helsinki Summit," *BASIC Reports*, No. 23, June 26, 1992, p. 2.

22 David Shorr, "World Leaders Scramble for Response to Balkan Crisis," *BASIC Reports*, No. 24, August 17, 1992, p. 2.

The short record of CSCE conflict prevention and crisis management measures has not proven their effectiveness. Earlier this year, the CSCE decided to send a rapporteur mission to Nagorno-Karabakh, but the CSO failed to agree upon the terms of reference for the mission. Subsequently an 11-nation preparatory meeting in Rome for a peace conference on the matter fell apart at the end of June. Similar efforts to monitor tensions in Moldova have come to little.[23] However, the length and size of monitoring missions to the autonomous regions of Serbia, in countries bordering Serbia and Montenegro and those watching for cracks in the embargo have increased, from an average size of 3 to 6 people to missions of long duration possibly involving up to a few of hundred people. The CSO has asked the steering group on the former Yugoslavia to look into long-term missions to Kosovo, Vojvodina and Sandshak.[24]

Some caution that the CSCE is "still a child" and has been "unfairly damned" for failing to meet overblown expectations. They emphasize the fact that the CSCE is developing an authoritative voice on humanitarian issues, and that its capacity to deal with these issues and to promote the other principles of the CSCE in cooperation with other European institutions are strengths that should be developed into unique capacities.[25] The *Christian Science Monitor* concluded that "[w]ith the various new mechanisms of CSCE, its leaders have an impressive apparatus to help check the splintering of Europe; the question now is whether they will make use of it."[26] To breathe life into CSCE structures and to develop this linkage between principles and processes, it is first necessary to understand the perspectives of some of the actors that have shaped the CSCE.

3. Key Player Perspectives: Larger States

a. The USSR (pre-dissolution)

During the first decade of the Helsinki process, East and West opened slowly toward each other as the principles established by the CSCE allowed Western governments to speak out against human rights abuses in Eastern Europe while guaranteeing the sovereign integrity and accepting the political structures of the Warsaw Pact. Subsequently, Gorbachev saw the CSCE as a way to narrow the NATO-

---

23 Makino, "CSCE Prepares," p. 1.

24 Shorr, "World Leaders," pp. 2-3.

25 Comments from an interview with Christopher Cviic of the Royal Institute for International Affairs on 17 August 1992. CSCE Ambassabor John Kornblum expressed a similar opinion, saying that only earlier action on the nationality issue might have helped avert the bloody civil strife (see William Korey, "Helsinki's Uncertain Future: the CSCE at Twenty," *New Leader*, Vol. 75, March 9, 1992, p. 8).

26 David Shorr, "Plenty of Work Ahead for a Beefed-Up CSCE," *Christian Science Monitor*, March 3, 1992, p. 1.

Warsaw Pact divide once *glasnost* and *perestroika* had taken hold. But enthusiasm waned for a while as the surge of ethnic, religious and national tensions repressed under the Iron Curtain rushed to the surface, catalyzing unrest in many Soviet republics and neighbors. The principal concern of the former USSR was that the CSCE would use its human rights mandate in the Helsinki Final Act to meddle in Soviet internal affairs. In agreeing to the establishment of the emergency mechanism at the Berlin meeting of June 1991, Russia insisted that CSCE foreign ministers reiterate their commitment not to intervene in any nation's domestic concerns. This for a time weakened the principle in the Helsinki Final Act that human rights know no boundaries.[27]

However, once they recognized that the reunification of Germany was inevitable, the Soviets once again embraced the institutionalization of the CSCE and its synchronization with the "2 plus 4" talks, which included a series of agreements approved by the CSCE foreign ministers in New York during the fall of 1990.[28] The Gorbachev regime played an active role in promoting both new human rights norms[29] and development of conflict management institutions within the CSCE.

b. Russia

Following the break-up of the Soviet Union, Russian Prime Minister Boris Yeltsin saw the CSCE as a means of engaging with the United States and establishing a place for Russia at the international table. Russia softened its tone toward the CSCE in the Washington American-Russian Charter for Partnership and Friendship.[30] The CSCE may be helpful in protecting the Russian diaspora, which may well represent the largest and most difficult class of future problems in the post-Cold War CSCE. This problem will be discussed in more detail in Part Two. Like NATO and the WEU, CIS peacekeeping forces (now conducting operations in the

---

27 Steinberg, "The Role of European Institutions," pp. 3-4.

28 Adam Daniel Rotfeld, "New Security Structures in Europe: Concepts, Proposals and Decisions," *SIPRI Yearbook 1991: World Armaments and Disarmament* (Oxford: Oxford University Press, 1991), p. 595.

29 New democratic and human rights principles are enshrined in the Copenhagen Document. Just after the Iron Curtain was raised, the CSCE adopted rules for equality before the law, freedom to establish political parties, free elections and for elections monitoring by member states.

30 The Charter states that the United States and Russia "support the following initiatives: The creation of a CSCE special representative to help strengthen efforts to address ethnic antagonisms and the treatment of minorities; The strengthening of means within CSCE to provide for more effective international dispute prevention, management and settlement; The creation of a credible EuroAtlantic peacekeeping capability, based on CSCE political authority, which allows for the use of the capacities of the NACC, NATO and WEU to prepare, support, and manage operations for CSCE as well as allows for the contribution of forces and resources from any and all CSCE states." *American-Russian Charter for Partnership and Friendship*, June 17, 1992.

"Dniestr Republic" in Moldova and between Georgia and South Ossetia) have been made available for missions under CSCE auspices.

Yet, Russian cooperation in the CSCE and other European institutions should not be taken for granted. Indeed, Yeltsin's cooperation on Bosnia has been impressive in the face of public opposition. The Orthodox Church continues to foster sympathy with fellow orthodox Serbians helping justify Russia's repeated refusal to accept the expulsion of Serbia from the CSCE. The forces of reaction have begun to organize themselves in Russia. KGB members remain infiltrated in the Orthodox Church hierarchy; some in the Foreign Ministry denounce disarmament as a form of American espionage; and the Cossacks are emerging as nationalist defenders of Russia. More opposition has girded formation of the Cadet Party, which supports military-industrial interests at the expense of rapid progress toward capitalism. Because Yeltsin's position may grow more tenuous it is important that Western leaders be careful not to destabilize Russia by asking too much of its leadership.

c. France

The French, with the Germans, were initially among the staunchest supporters of the CSCE, which they hoped – in contrast to the United States – would evolve from a series of inter-governmental agreements to a body of treaty obligations. However, France's enthusiasm for the CSCE has waned because many believe that it has expanded beyond manageable proportions. Further, one apparent political objective of the French leadership is to decrease the American role in European affairs (while retaining an American security guarantee as a hedge against a descent into chaos in the East) now that the Cold War is over; one of the reasons behind French President Mitterrand's trip to Sarajevo was to make sure that "European" leaders took a visible lead in responding to the Balkan crisis. One suspects that the Gaullist perspective of a "Europe from the Atlantic to the Urals" (from the French, Spanish and Portuguese coastlines eastward across the Continent) and *sans* any more Anglo-Saxons than the British, remains. As in other European institutions such as the WEU, French leaders would like to be a bigger fish in a smaller and exclusively European pond – an expanded EC.

On the structural level, France does not believe that the problem of consensus can be solved without creating an elite group of states within the CSCE, but the idea that "some are more equal than others" in a *de jure* sense (the French strive to achieve this status in a *de facto* manner as leaders in the development of the EC) is repugnant to them, at least rhetorically. The French would prefer that multilateral approaches to peacekeeping be undertaken by the WEU, and that other measures for conflict prevention and crisis management be pursued under the mantle of the

EC's European Political Cooperation (EPC). Nevertheless, the French have been strongly supportive of building CSCE institutions, which, if properly structured and regularly used, could provide a stronger security community around the center of Europe without increasing US influence in European security affairs. France has been the leading proponent of the development of a CSCE conciliation court for the peaceful settlement of disputes.

d. Germany

For Germany, the CSCE has been viewed as the perfect vehicle for fulfilling the need to reduce apprehensions over unification while continuing to pursue a constructive *Ostpolitik*, and retaining the transatlantic link to the United States Former Foreign Minister Hans-Dietrich Genscher was the leading advocate of opening the CSCE to the East. In an early 1990 speech, he declared that, "The only element binding the whole of Europe at the present is the CSCE process. The efforts to intensify that process are ... indispensable contributions to stability in Europe."[31] German leaders strongly supported the declaration of CSCE as a regional organization under the UN. They want to strengthen the organization to play a larger role in peacekeeping.

The CSCE has been an important part of the active political debate in Germany over multilateral approaches to crisis response for some time. In early 1990, an editorial comment in *The Economist* described German supporters of the CSCE as "a curious alliance between Germany's anti-military left and its neo-nationalist right. The left, including a large part of the Social Democratic Party, wants as few soldiers in Germany as possible. The nationalist right wants Germany under as little foreign supervision as possible."[32] The article went on to assert that, for these groups, the CSCE was a better alternative to NATO. However, the authoritative *Die Zeit* concluded that in a re-emerging pluralistic Europe, "[a] uniform system that subordinates everything to a single organization is not suitable for the new Europe. Its security and welfare must instead be insured by a variety of organizations."

Germans are exploring the most efficient ways to transform the CSCE from a toothless organization based on consensus to an active conflict prevention and conflict management body. The Germans hope for a structural solution to the consensus problem. Before the Helsinki meeting in July 1992, Germans supported the concept of a more powerful steering committee to streamline the decision making

31 Hans-Dietrich Genscher, quoted in Francine S. Kiefer, "A New Europe Ponders Security: Some Say the Future Belongs to CSCE, but U.S. and Others See a Necessity for NATO," *The Christian Science Monitor*, April 16, 1990, p. 6.

32 "The Dream of Europax," *The Economist*, April 7, 1990, p. 14.

process.[33] What resulted from the meeting was the less powerful ad hoc steering group, mentioned above. Germany is also among the 16 nations that support the formation of an arbitration court.

However, popular support for the CSCE as a peacekeeping organization may not be strong. There is little public enthusiasm for military involvement in the Yugoslav conflicts. Legal wrangles over the constitutional limits on the use of the military have not been resolved and are likely to continue for some time. Nevertheless, in response to growing pressure both inside Germany and from the international community, the opposition Social Democratic Party (SPD) recently reversed two of its main stances: the SPD leadership announced in August 1992 that it no longer categorically opposes German participation in peacekeeping, but now favors restrictions on immigration. Current liberal immigration laws make Germany a destination for refugees; the conservative German leadership fully supported that policy (until recently) and pressured other European countries to liberalize their laws.

This *volte-face,* affecting even the opposition, reflects growing economic and social tension as Germany seeks to consolidate the unification process while maintaining a reputation as a benign power and a "good European." This rightward shift in the political spectrum is not unique to Germany. Other European powers as well are tempted to establish a "cultural cordon sanitaire" by limiting immigration – much of which EC members fear will pass through Germany into their countries.

e. United Kingdom

Like Canada and the United States, Britain places high value on the principles that the CSCE sets for its members. In February 1992, Douglas Hogg, British Minister of State in the Foreign Office, asserted that "the CSCE is...essentially a political institution using peer pressure to try and influence governments who are members. It is not a legal institution."[34] The British, like the Americans, strongly oppose the establishment of a CSCE conciliation court, preferring the greater flexibility of political dialogue.

The UK values the CSCE as a protector of human rights and as a monitor of military movements through CSBMs. But like the other countries discussed above (with the possible exception of France), the UK sees the value of having several interlocking institutions in Europe. *The Economist* argued in April 1990 that both

---

33 Francine S. Kiefer, "CSCE Seeks to Streamline Its Organization in Bid for More Decisive Role," *The Christian Science Monitor*, July 9, 1992, p. 1.

34 Francine S. Kiefer, "CSCE Seeks Role in Europe after Cold War," *The Christian Science Monitor*, February 3, 1992, p. 4.

the EC and NATO were essential to European security, and that neither could be replaced by a beefed-up CSCE. "Any European to think otherwise should ask himself how he would feel if the peace and safety of his continent depended solely on the United Nations. To dismantle the Atlantic Alliance and replace it with 'collective security' under CSCE, would be to rely upon a local version of the United Nations."[35] This reflects British skepticism about reliance on that form of collective security. The British would rather that the CSCE play a legitimizing role under the UN, while other organizations with smaller and more predictable membership command and carry out actual peacekeeping operations.

The British would like to see the CSCE become more active at the prevention than at the response stage. According to the British delegate to the Helsinki meeting, "There is a tendency to make the CSCE more active, especially in the early stages. We can't wait until a crisis is on our doorstep. We have a collective responsibility to ensure that the CSCE community is stable."[36]

Another factor is Britain's current occupation of the EC presidency and Prime Minister John Major's more conciliatory approach to European institutions following the deeply suspicious stance of his predecessor, Margaret Thatcher. The UK response to the Balkan crisis first came via the EC and CSCE and the now-moribund Carrington initiative. The failure of these attempts reinforced low British expectations for a direct CSCE role in peacekeeping. The British do not place a great deal of hope in the CSCE, but are willing to take it step by step to see if it can prove itself.[37]

f. United States

The American point of view is close to Britain's. One observer writes that, "New structures-according to US political philosophy – should be based on such Enlightenment ideals of universal applicability as individual political rights and economic liberty." The United States sees the CSCE as an important upholder of human rights and democratic principles; a forum for conflict prevention and for the establishment of more transparent military relations; and an organization that can help address the problem of proliferation-but by no means as a replacement for NATO.[38] At an April 1990 press conference, then Secretary of State James Baker commented, "I think we should go a bit slow with respect to the security basket of CSCE. There are some ways in which it can complement the NATO

35 "The Dream of Europax," *The Economist*, April 7, 1990, p. 15.

36 Makino, "CSCE Prepares," pp. 2-3.

37 Trevor Taylor, "La Position de la Grande Bretagne," in Yves Boyer, ed., *Les Européens Face aux Défis d'une Politique de Sécurité Commune, Les Cahiers du CREST*, No. 7, June 1992, p. 50.

38 Adam Daniel Rotfeld, "European Security Structures in Transition," *SIPRI Yearbook 1992*, p. 569.

alliance, but we do not want to in any way suggest the replacement of the functions of the NATO alliance by CSCE."[39]

The United States has in many cases been the main dissident in the strengthening of the CSCE, and is particularly opposed to making CSCE agreements into binding treaty obligations. This stems largely from US concerns – concerns shared to a degree by France and the UK – about the implications of supporting minority rights and the right to self-determination. The US philosophy, descended from the liberalism of John Stuart Mill, is that rights belong to individuals; according special privileges to a group could compromise the principle of equality before the law and frustrate efforts to integrate diverse populations into a single, coherent society. On a less abstract level, a deep-seated US apprehension is that CSCE principles could be invoked by minority groups, who would attempt to secede and form their own state under the right of self-determination.

The United States has also objected to giving CSCE institutions the capability to act without government intercession. Thus, a German proposal to allow the CPC to monitor and report on emerging conflicts was blocked, and this authority was given to the CSO instead.[40] As an alternative to the French proposal for a conciliation court, the United States proposed a voluntary "direct conciliation" mechanism, based on the Valletta dispute settlement mechanism. A three member Conciliation Committee would help parties to a conflict resolve the issue and outline terms of settlement. An American delegate commented, "It may be best just to pressure parties to abide by the Council of Ministers' recommendations. This would also let harebrained recommendations die a natural death."[41] Like the British, the Americans see the main value of the CSCE in its moral principles and ability to focus political pressure.

Although the United States would prefer that NATO remain the main military/operational organization in Europe, US leaders support the development of CSCE's capacity to take the political lead in conflict prevention and crisis management. The United States also sees the CSCE as a vehicle for remaining engaged in Europe should the NATO-WEU debate grow yet more intractable. The CSCE may serve US interests in maintaining a relationship with Europe in two possible ways. First, it allows the United States to remain engaged in a broad political dialogue as the relationship between NATO and the WEU and the positions of those two organizations is worked out. Second, because member states may choose whether or not to participate in the response to a given crisis, the United States

39 Francine S. Kiefer, "A New Europe Ponders Security: Some Say the Future Belongs to CSCE, but U.S. and Others See a Necessity for NATO," *The Christian Science Monitor*, April 16, 1990, p. 6.

40 Jonathan Dean, "The Conference on Security Cooperation in Europe: Can It Do the Job?," forthcoming journal article.

41 Makino, "CSCE Prepares," p. 2.

may opt out or select to play a more limited role in situations where its interests are not affected. Pressure for a prominent US role is thereby reduced.

4. Key Player Perspectives: Representative Smaller States

a. Greece

The Greeks value the CSCE because it gives them a place in a European security forum other than NATO.[42] But for Greece as for all countries facing ethnic and religious internal divisions, living up to CSCE principles may be difficult in practice. For the Mitsotakis government, these problems represent a many-headed Medusa, including Cyprus and now Macedonia, a problem of the previous century.

In its present form, the Macedonia issue today recalls the Greek civil war, which was won by the right – with foreign help. (International intervention in local affairs remains unwelcome in the eyes of many Greeks.) Following the war, much of the Slav-speaking minority emigrated to Macedonia. Besides a strong feeling that Macedonia is not only Greek but a cradle of Hellenic culture, a number of tensions threaten to create turmoil within Greece itself. There are now tensions with the Slav-speaking minority within Greece, Albanian and Macedonian reports of human rights abuses by Greek border troops, and mounting banditry within Greece by Albanians and Macedonians. The result is rising popular frustration with the Mitsotakis government for its inability to solve the "Macedonian problem."[43]

The Greeks have been able to lobby within the EC and the CSCE for non-recognition of a Macedonian state (the republic is now referred to as Skopje), even as the EC has fallen out of favor in Greece because of economic austerity measures imposed to fulfill obligations under the Single European Act and because of its anti-Serb stance in the Balkan crisis. Prior to the suspension of Serbia and Montenegro (with whom many Orthodox Greeks strongly sympathize), and if Macedonia were a member, the CSCE may have been a more attractive international forum for conciliation. Obligatory CSCE mediation on Macedonia – called for by a group of participating states – may have helped Mitsotakis straddle the fence between EC pressures to meet economic as well as democratic standards, and domestic pressures to react unilaterally.

---

42 Although it was expected that Greece would achieve full membrship in the WEU this summer, it remains an associate member.

43 For a cogent discussion of these issues see James Pettifer, "The New Macedonia," *International Affairs*, Vol. 68, No. 3, July 1992, p. 482.

b. Hungary

The Hungarians, like other Eastern European states, have been very supportive of strengthening the CSCE. Hungary has worked hard to meet the necessary standards for acceptance into the "Western club." The Hungarian perspective is both progressive and pragmatic, particularly on the issue of CSCE decision making. Like all small states, they are wary of arrangements that would reduce their role. The deputy head of Hungary's CSCE delegation, Zsuzsa Hargitai, stated that, "Small states don't want to see just another Security Council." Nevertheless, the Hungarians believe that more expedient decision making is needed to make the CSCE effective. "CSCE is not any longer about elaborating new commitments, it's about enforcing them."

Upholding minority ethnic rights outside of Hungary may be one area where the CSCE can help the Hungarian government. CSCE monitoring and reporting could help to ensure the rights of ethnic Hungarians living in Romania; if this were effective it could eliminate some of the pressure on the Hungarian government to adopt positions or policies that would strain relations with Romania.

c. Norway

Norway, like other neutrals and its fellow Scandinavian countries, is strongly supportive of CSCE norms and principles in the area of human rights. The Norwegians are deeply disturbed by the instabilities in the former East Bloc, and the Norwegian government would like to see the Helsinki decisions enabling CSCE to task peacekeeping forces applied in the Yugoslav conflict.[44] Norwegian leaders believe that a common European security policy is necessary to respond to this and other regional flashpoints. However, both the public and the political community are divided over EC membership and about the best architecture for European security.

In the political debate over the most suitable European security organization – the EC and WEU as opposed to the CSCE and NATO/NACC – Under Secretary of State Helga Hernes described the EC and the WEU as "the motive force for peace in Europe" while at the same time maintaining that transatlantic cooperation is not in conflict with the European dimension. "The CSCE cannot act as a collective defense organization, its chances of playing a decisive role in a crisis situation are limited. NATO has vigor, but unlike the EC, it is exclusively a military organization. The EC occupies a special place in the preservation of

44 "Security Cooperation Urged," *LD 1707130692 Hamburg DPA in German, 0952 GMT, 17 Jul, 1992*, FBIS-WEU-92-139, July 20, 1992, p. 29.

peace. This organization has more comprehensive and committed cooperation covering more areas than any other organization."[45]

The strongest supporters of the CSCE are now found in the Socialist Left Party (SV). Party leader Erik Solheim asserted that, "Security problems must be solved in organizations where the largest number of countries possible are members, and especially where the areas of conflict themselves are represented. That is why the CSCE and the NACC are important organizations."[46] Party spokesman for foreign and security policy Paul Chaffey believes that the broad membership of the CSCE is needed to legitimize peacekeeping operations in the East. "It would be unfortunate if a military alliance [NATO] at one end of Europe were to be responsible for resolving conflicts at the other end of Europe. But then it must be the United Nations or CSCE that approves the deployment of such a force."[47]

Another factor that shapes Norwegian opinion on European security is that Norway is less sure of the benign nature of the former Soviet Union in the post-Cold War world than some of its CSCE partners. Many Norwegians therefore see CSCE as a valuable forum to engage – or coopt – yesterday's enemy into today's Europe. Thus Norwegian perspectives combine the usual progressive Scandinavian attitudes about human rights, equal justice and international peace with local caution concerning the residual Russian menace.

5. Summary of National Attitudes

Several conclusions can be drawn from this selective discussion of national attitudes toward the CSCE. First, they highlight the diversity of CSCE membership, a diversity with historical roots extending back far beyond this century. Second, it is clear that differences between East and West are likely to linger and affect how far the CSCE can go in dealing with certain kinds of conflict. For example, most Western countries believe that they can accept the principle of sovereignty and the concept that human rights know no boundaries because these societies are based on the belief that a Social Contract à la Rousseau between people and government protects their individual rights. Therefore, the principle of sovereign equality of states should not come into conflict with the protection of human rights, based on the premise of the equality of individual rights; all individuals are fully enfranchised within the state. By contrast, "Of key importance for East European governments in the CSCE process were the principles of inviolability of frontiers

---

45 "EC's Security Role Noted," *PM 1008154292 Oslo AFTENPOSTEN in Norwegian, 31 Jul, 1992, p. 6*, FBIS-WEU-92-155, August 11, 1992, p. 22.

46 Ibid., pp. 22-23.

47 "Socialist Left Party Favors NATO Membership," *92EN0524A Oslo AFTENPOSTEN in Norwegian, 23 Jun 1992, p. 5*, FBIS-WEU-92-136, July 15, 1992, p. 45.

and territorial integrity, and non-intervention in domestic affairs, thus legitimizing one-party rule."[48]

The existence of disenfranchised groups in these societies is one of the major forces behind the rising ethno-nationalism in Europe today; there will be more Bosnias as self-described nations within present-day states call on history or cultural identity for national expression and demand control of their own destinies. These forces, currently challenging many national leaderships, are likely to be the main instabilities that the CSCE will confront. Thus the parallel treatment of security questions and the human dimension is important.

Another cautionary lesson is that the new Europe is fragile and unsure; even the development of the EC, pursued with such vigor on the Continent and viewed with such suspicion in North America over the last few years, has been threatened first by the Danish "no" to the Maastricht Treaty, followed by a very narrow margin of approval in France. The delicate fabric of relations in the new Europe cannot be stretched too far lest what progress has been made could unravel.

It may be tempting to look to the development of structures and procedures as an easy way of neutralizing the inevitable tensions that will arise in meeting these issues. "The desirability of making use of and adapting the existing organizations and structures in addressing new realities cannot be denied. It would be a misunderstanding, however, to look upon what is called 'security architecture' as a remedy for present and future challenges."[49] In order to explore the potential and limits to the new CSCE architecture, we now move to a discussion of conflict types and possible action under CSCE norms.

II. Applying Principles and Upholding Norms

1. CSCE Norms

In his address to the Moscow human dimension meeting,[50] then US Secretary of State James Baker identified "five fundamental principles" for admission into the CSCE. These are "democratic values and practices;" "respect [for] existing borders, internal and external," with changes to occur only by "peaceful and consensual means;" adherence to the "rule of law;" and "peaceful change" of government. CSCE member states must "safeguard human rights" and pledge "equal treatment of minorities" and respect international law and obligations, including the Helsinki Final Act and the Charter of Paris. Although Baker went somewhat beyond what has in fact been agreed, these norms include two principles, one based on the free-

48 Rotfeld, "European Security Structures," p. 569.

49 Ibid, p. 568.

50 The Moscow meeting was held in September 1991, at which time the Baltic states were admitted as members.

dom and rights of individuals and nations and the other on the sovereign equality of states, which are clearly in tension. Stated otherwise, the question is how the principle of inviolability of borders can be reconciled with the accepted right of self-determination; or, if they cannot be reconciled, which should be given precedence, and under which circumstances.

As the former Soviet Union breaks apart into smaller sovereign societies and the various groups seek to rediscover and reassert former national identities, CSCE principles that safeguard human rights have, over the past year, been strengthened. Although "[t]he tradition of democracy and human rights, the essence of the Helsinki process, is not very deep in most Western parts of the former USSR, and ... is even more tenuous in the six successor Moslem republics of Central Asia and the Caucasus,"[51] it was made clear in Moscow that these were fundamental conditions for participation in the CSCE. The CSCE delegates declared that human rights issues are of clear international concern "to all participating states and do not belong exclusively to the internal affairs of the state concerned."[52]

Thus, the human rights principles and the new mechanisms to alert the CSCE to abuses represent a legitimate basis for CSCE involvement in almost all cases. Different levels and types of conflict call for different CSCE responses; these are described below.

2. Types of Conflict

a. Internal and External Conflicts

Internal conflicts are those that arise wholly among groups within a single state and do not directly or necessarily involve foreign powers. In today's Europe, these may include collapse of democratic institutions due to failing economic reforms and disputes involving groups of outside or clearly different ethnic origin from the surrounding population but holding the citizenship of the state in question. Under present CSCE norms, such internal conflicts may be responded to with CSCE monitoring and fact-finding missions, or with mediation solicited by the state concerned.

As in Bosnia, action may be made possible if a group, expressing its self-ascribed right to self-determination, declares itself an autonomous state and the international community chooses to recognize it. In those circumstances, the fact of

51 Korey, "Helsinki's Uncertain Future," p. 10.

52 The idea of strengthening CSCE authority in this area was supported in the NATO Rome Declaration of 9 November 1991. Paragraph 14 calls for a greater push to augment CSCE ability to protect human rights, democracy and the rule of law in cases of clear, grave and uncorrected violations of CSCE commitments – *without consent* of the state concerned, if necessary.

recognition can turn the conflict into an international one. The principal problem for the CSCE is how to assure that internal disputes, or local ones, remain confined and do not grow into wider wars. Conflicts over territory normally bring to mind disputes over a state's external boundaries. It is established CSCE principle that alterations of present national boundaries achieved by force are not acceptable. There is, however, no established doctrine about internal frontiers, even when these purport to separate clearly diverse populations. Thus there is no agreed basis for establishing the territorial circumscription of threatened populations within recognized national territory. This situation requires CSCE or other would-be authorities to attempt resolution of disputes where there may be a basis to demand minority protection, but no agreed way to assure that minority any particular territorial claim.

3. Responses to Disputes

Before attempting to define how the CSCE could address such problems, it is useful to look at CSCE capacity to use established procedures. The CSCE crisis response mechanisms have been developed for progressive measures as the intensity of a conflict rises.

a. Conflict Prevention

Because human rights violations may be an early harbinger of larger conflict, a member state that finds itself faced with minority or human rights questions can invite CSCE mediators. If mediators are not invited, a second state can suggest their invitation and bring the problem to the attention of the CSO. With the support of five more member states, the intervening state can then approach the Secretariat for action. Possible measures include rapporteur and fact-finding missions and notification of the High Commissioner on Minorities by the CSO.[53] Such missions cannot be sent if they are not welcome by the sovereign authority, which paralyzes the process.

Prompt response procedures should include early formation of steering groups,[54] close coordination between the CSO, the High Commissioner on Nation-

---

53 In the July 1992 CSCE Helsinki Decisions, Chapter II, Paragraph 2 on the CSCE High Commissioner on National Minorities mandates that, "The High Commissioner will act under the aegis of the CSO and will thus be an instrument of conflict prevention at the earliest possible stage."

54 For a full discussion of the procedures for formation of *ad hoc* steering groups, see the July 1992 Helsinki Summit Decisions, Chapter I, Paragraphs 16-21. Briefly, such steering groups can be formed to assist the Chairman-in-Office in conflict prevention, crisis management and dispute resolution. They are composed of a restricted number of participating states, including the Troika (past, current and succeeding states to hold the chairmanship).

al Minorities and the CPC/CC, and early coordination with other international organizations such as NATO, the WEU, the EC, the Council of Europe, and the UN.

b. Crisis Management

In more urgent cases, the final recourse is to bypass or cease mediation efforts. This may occur in a state with a disenfranchised group that has taken to violence to redress grievances. With the support of nine other states, a concerned state can call for a rapporteur mission, as was requested for Nagorno-Karabakh. Subsequently, were a cease-fire actually established, the CSCE could task NATO or the WEU to send in forces to monitor weapons and keep the disputing parties separated. This is a straightforward matter where populations in conflict happen to occupy clearly defined territory (as was the case after 1974 when the Turkish and Greek Cypriots established a clear boundary between them), or where the internal parties agree to accept outside intervention to separate them. It is virtually impossible in cases such as Bosnia, whose opposing populations are interspersed.

Loss of life by NATO or WEU forces may also divide and weaken the CSCE. In such cases, keeping intervention to other means besides military options may be the only available choice. The best the CSCE may be able to achieve is to manage the external aspects – that is, to assure that all potential external parties avoid direct involvement. That means not only that CSCE members agree not to support the parties in conflict with volunteers, materiel or political pressure, but also that CSCE members undertake diplomatic campaigns to help assure that non-CSCE members refrain from any involvement.

c. Peacekeeping

Peacekeeping in fragmenting Eurasia is likely to be difficult. The international community's hesitations in Yugoslavia exemplify future CSCE trends, to the extent that these can be anticipated. Democratic states will be reluctant to risk lives of their own troops, especially conscripts, for purposes like preventing injury to faraway innocents, even when distant turmoil unleashes a flood of refugees.

Thus military authorities may be more willing to contemplate involvement that is of a lower intensity before a conflict has festered for too long. These ideas are supported by UN Secretary-General Boutros Ghali, who would like to develop a UN mechanism for "preventive diplomacy" to identify crises early on and possibly lead to "preventive deployment" of peacekeeping forces.

In a case which would involve actual peacekeeping operations, the CSCE will have to choose which organization – NATO, the WEU, CIS – it would approach to carry out operations. The criteria to be considered will be, first, which forces would be acceptable to the disputants. The Baltic states, for example, would not be likely to welcome CIS forces. Second, the CSO would have canvassed participating states to see which are interested in participating in the particular operation in question (this should be done as soon as there is enough warning to warrant discussion). One could speculate that if, for example, the United States did not wish to take part, the CSCE may look toward the WEU. However, if Turkey or Norway were strongly disposed to take part, the choice becomes more difficult. Such cases may justify NATO's development of variable geometry as suggested by Secretary-General Manfred Woerner: just as participating states in the CSCE can choose whether or not to take part in peacekeeping, so a similar system would be adopted by NATO. To choose effectively, the CSCE could call for force contributions on a national basis. In this manner significant interested parties would not be excluded, even if a particular institutional vehicle (e.g. the WEU) turned out to be the most effective structural vehicle.

Third, CSCE capacity to undertake and oversee actual missions should be considered. Under the new provisions in the Helsinki Summit Decisions, the Council/CSO assigns overall guidance to the Chairman-in-Office, who presides over an ad hoc group formed at the CPC. This group consists of the Troika (present, past and next Chairmen-in-Office) and of representatives from all participating states contributing to the operations. A Head of Mission nominated by the Chairman-in-Office has operational command in the mission area. Given this rather thin structure, the CSCE may be well advised to forfeit command to NATO, the WEU or other authorities. One of the fruits of early coordination with these organizations could be prompt establishment of rules of engagement and command arrangements. Without such coordination, there could be considerable difficulties in executing the peacekeeping mission.

4. CSCE as a Regional Authority

What seems clear from the foregoing is that the principles for CSCE action are widely accepted at the general theoretical level, but difficult to apply in particular cases. The result is that while considerable machinery for action has been developed in parallel with and in support of the growing amount of collective doctrine, consensus for its application in identifiable cases has not kept pace. Attempting to adapt procedures to overcome reluctance to act or to compel agreement will not work simply because parties negotiating procedural or structural changes are quick to recognize their implications. They will resist these changes for the same reasons that they resist direct action.

The central dilemma for the CSCE and for other security forums is the reluctance of governments to deal promptly and decisively with low level conflicts or with prospects of conflict. If they do not, Western governments, whether or not they are prepared, are very quickly forced to deal with the consequences of inaction (human suffering, refugees, international embarrassment and domestic political pressure once these are felt within the society). The failure of governments or security fora to establish clear rules, and to act on them, creates situations where the civilized community is forced to react at a disadvantage every time subnational grievants attempt to enrich or avenge themselves at the expense of their neighbors.

The CSCE as a community can alleviate and help manage, if not entirely resolve these dilemmas. This requires leadership, and manifest conviction about the potential utility of the CSCE process. Stated otherwise, no party to a decision will take the CSCE seriously enough to allow it to act until some prominent member identifies the CSCE process as the essential instrument of an obviously necessary purpose. That purpose is clear now, in both specific and general terms. It amounts to avoiding situations where the growing number of existing and potential ethnic conflicts within national states grow into conflicts between them, or worse, into conflagrations.

The generic issue for virtually all identifiable cases is how to keep conflicts that may attract the attention of governments in countries with consanguineous populations confined within national borders. Russia is perhaps the most immediate significant case with more than 30 million ethnic Russians outside its frontiers. Hungary, with almost three million Hungarians living outside its borders, is a close second, and similar situations abound.

Managing this class of problems in a way that reduces incentives for Moscow and other governments to act is as much in their interest as it is in the interest of the CSCE community. Such action would define the problem in a common and therefore more generally acceptable way. More importantly, it would identify the conditions under which the community would interfere to protect minorities and how it would do so. Even within the present constraints on enforcement action, the community can take several types of action either explicitly or informally. These measures include:

(1) Agreeing collectively not to interfere, or on who among them may interfere, and on the type and extent of such interference;
(2) Agreeing to act together to prevent parties outside the area from interfering;
(3) Embargoing goods traffic and weapons deliveries, and freezing the assets of belligerents;
(4) Collectively denying current and future recognition, credits, commerce and other rights of states in the international community until particular conditions are met;
(5) Interfering with external and internal communications with respect to the affected area;

(6) Monitoring individual acts with a view to subsequent trial and punishment;
(7) Agreeing collectively on the conditions under which refugees shall be accepted, on the accounting for refugee expenses and on which of the parties to the conflict is to be held accountable; and
(8) Identifying the facilities for mediation, separation of forces and other good offices which the community might offer the parties to the dispute.

Getting agreement on these types of measures may not be possible among the entire CSCE membership. Predictably, at least a dozen members may resist in each case, if only out of fear that a precedent may be established which could affect one or all in unpredictable ways. On the other hand, there is nothing to prevent some significant group of participating states from acting, even if they cannot formally act on behalf of the entire membership or on behalf of the CSCE as such. Were a significant group to do so, the remainder would either follow, quietly refrain from participation, protest, or drop out. None of these would be as ruinous for the CSCE as the present paralysis.

These measures may not be enough, or it may not be possible to get the necessary degree of consensus for them to be effective. In that case further action may be necessary. To recapitulate, the CSCE now has at its disposal a fairly complete crisis management apparatus, with most of the machinery it needs to address present problems, and similar foreseeable crises. If that machinery is not very robust, the structure to build on is there. On paper at least, the CSCE can investigate complaints and mount peacekeeping operations. Machinery notwithstanding, the CSCE, like the other security structures, has shown little progress so far; this does not bode well for the future. As Jonathan Dean has pointed out,[55] Japan aside, the CSCE represents virtually all of the world's richest and most powerful states. Given these resources, if the CSCE cannot make multilateral security work using the other institutions concerned with European security, then probably nothing or no one can or will. Unfortunately, such failure will have great impact elsewhere. Failure will damage the reputation, and therefore the possibilities of multilateral peacekeeping in other parts of the world.

Current examples like Bosnia and Nagorno-Karabakh, and prospects like Macedonia show clearly that if machinery is potentially useful, machinery alone is inadequate; present machinery is constraining; and consensus on the necessary measures may be impossible. Unless the minor modifications possible under plausible and acceptable consensus rules can make CSCE structures significantly more effective, then something more radical is required. One obvious way out of the current limits is actions by *participating states as participating states*; and, furthermore, compre-

55 Dean, "The Conference," p. 43.

hensive action that attempts to deal with the full range of issues both specifically and generically. Such action is perhaps easier to prescribe in general than in detail.

Very briefly, CSCE member states that are disposed to act in a particular crisis could choose to act together, as a self-designated CSCE caucus if necessary. Other CSCE members that did not wish to participate could stand aside, having first been invited to participate. The Caucus could call another Congress of Berlin, analogous to the one called together by Bismarck in 1878 as the Ottoman empire disintegrated in the Balkans, to which all interested parties could repair.[56] That Congress imposed order and frontiers on an unstable region for a considerable period. The job could usefully be done again. In its own name, the new Congress could suggest solutions to the parties concerned throughout the CSCE area, but concentrate on assuring the behavior of external parties; and on establishing sanctions against rogue states that are clear, long-lasting and universal so that offenders would be condemned to penury and pariah-hood. The Congress could also prescribe means of limiting the area of the conflict, so that disputants could continue fighting with lower risk to neighboring areas. Such measures could limit conflict duration, ascribe procedures for returning refugee populations or assess to belligerents the expense of their assimilation elsewhere. If such actions tilt the arguments between national sovereignty and human rights in favor of human rights, that may be a message worth broadcasting.

Such a Congress would inevitably raise questions of acceptability and fears of military intervention by dominant powers, especially among smaller CSCE participating states. Though, as the Hungarian delegate noted (see above), there is little that can be done to assure that no states seem to wield more power with the CSCE at any given time, there may be some basic guarantees and guidelines – based on what one American theorist calls "generalized organizing principles"[57] – that can be set down within CSCE documentation and provide a loose roadmap for the management of a Congress of this type.

The basic principles that apply today are very similar to those that were behind the nineteenth century Concert of Europe, when the five leading powers refrained from maximizing their own interests in order to maintain the "repose" of Europe. Military means were viewed as a last resort, but the five "were clearly of the opinion that force could be used individually or collectively for enforcing certain decisions and for coercing those who threatened the foundations of the order or the system of governance."[58] This restraint fits with the climate in Europe today; any

56 The authors are indebted to Christopher Cviic of Chatham House, London, for this concept. The elaborations, however, are entirely their own.

57 For a fuller discussion of this concept, see John Gerard Ruggie, "Multilateralism: The Anatomy of an Institution," *International Organization*, Vol. 46, No. 3, Summer 1992, pp. 561-598.

58 Kal Holsti, "Governance without Government: Modes of Coordinating, Managing and Controlling Politics in Nineteenth Century Europe," paper presented at the annual meeting of the Inter-

institution that did not incorporate it and inculcate it in its members would quickly be delegitimized. As a RAND analyst put it, "A future security model will be more stable if it accounts for basic political 'facts of life' in the U.S. and Europe. Whereas governments can lead, as well as be led by, public opinion, the viability of any arrangment must be judged in light of several important political trends ... [including] an interest in broader security frameworks in Europe, and a less 'military' approach to security."[59]

The main difference, and advantage, today is that the CSCE provides an institutional framework in which principles are embodied; because of this framework, the context is not only *multinational* but *multilateral.*[60] That is, participating states have agreed, in signing CSCE documents, to principles of non-discrimination. The challenge in making the Congress mechanism politically palatable within the CSCE context is to assure all members that these principles will continue to apply to states that take part in the suggested Congress. Possible points of departure include making sure that the Emergency Mechanism is applied early on, and that the Congress is called as a further step within this process. Secondly, parties to the conflict would have the right to prohibit nationals from certain states from entering disputed territory if the parties can demonstrate that these states have a clear bias. However, interested states would be allowed to provide financial support to the Congress if they so desired. Third, use of militaries would be strictly limited to containing the conflict, in consonance with the CSCE principle of impartiality. Finally, these and other basic rules and guidelines could be set down within CSCE documentation agreed to and signed by all participating states. This last step is likely to generate a great deal of debate, however. Thus, such "codification" is a long-term goal, and participating states may have to get there by responding responsibly to crises according to the above principles, legitimating the process *de facto* as they go.

5. Suggested Structural Reforms and Conclusions

Some structural adaptations in the CSCE process would help to make the above suggestion a viable possibility. Most of the following proposals advocate greater centralization of CSCE functions. For both communications and cost reasons, one main location should be established as "CSCE Headquarters," particularly as the

---

national Studies Association, Vancouver, Canada, March 1991, in Ruggie, "Multilateralism," p. 579.

59 Nannette Gantz and James B. Steinberg, "Five Models for European Security: Implications for the United States," *RAND Note* N-3446-A, 1992, p. 10.

60 Ruggie, "Multilateralism," p. 574. Ruggie explains that, "What distinguishes the multilateral form from other forms [of state interaction] is that it coodinates behavior of three or more states on the basis of generalized principles of conduct."

CSCE continues to define itself as a coherent institution. In the words of one observer, "The parallel activities of the CSCE senior officials in Prague and the CPC in Vienna contribute little except an element of confusion. The dispersal of CSCE institutions serves an important symbolic purpose in rewarding states that had contributed to the CSCE's new role, but these considerations are outweighed by the need to streamline CSCE functioning. The CSCE risks repeating ... the European Parliament's comic commuting between Brussels, Strasbourg, and the staff headquarters in Luxembourg."[61]

Increased coherence could be achieved first by increasing the role of the Chairman-in-Office so that he/she becomes a more visible figurehead along the lines of the UN Secretary-General. Second, the Emergency Mechanism should be merged with a much stronger CPC that is empowered to make recommendations to the COM, and is charged with establishment of steering groups and calling special meetings. The CPC, under CSO supervision, would oversee all mediation efforts so that all ongoing regional crises fall under the supervision of a single body.

Third, it is clear from the above discussion of conflict in the CSCE area that ethnic differences will be at the root of most, if not all, regional crises. Therefore coordination between the High Commissioner on National Minorities and the CPC should be institutionalized. The CPC needs to be alerted of building tensions as early on as possible in order to establish avenues for mediation that are acceptable to the parties to a dispute. These steps toward centralization should help avoid duplication of efforts or internal discord arising from perceptions that an initiative taken through one avenue was sacrificed for a parallel initiative pursued through a different CSCE mechanism.

Fourth, and most important, a means to circumvent the consensus requirement should be established to deal with clear emergencies. One potential avenue for accomplishing this would be for the CPC to advise the CSO that a situation had reached a level of urgency requiring prompt decisions. The CSO would then vote decision making power (within ascribed limits) to the steering group created to deal with the situation.

Finally, the diversity of participating states and their interests imply that limiting CSCE interventions to peacekeeping to the exclusion of enforcement action is necessary to avoid tearing the organization asunder. On the other hand, there is little benefit to assuring the continuing survival of a body which seems unable to carry forward the tasks for which it was allegedly designed, particularly containment of conflicts. Thus, if the adjustments suggested above, plus more robust staffing for the individual organs prove inadequate to deal with any of the ongoing or emerging crises, interested participating states could call the above-mentioned

61 Steinberg, "The Role of European Institutions," pp. 40-41.

Congress and welcome all CSCE members to take part. The combination of non-interference agreements among external parties, suggested solutions, powerful sanctions and the implicit threat of military action may be more powerful than the present Eunuch's chorus of meetings, resolutions, pious injunctions and bootless threats. An effective approach may be worth a little broken institutional crockery and a few bruises among the many conflicting grievants in the vast CSCE area.

10. NACC and the CSCE: A Contribution in the Context of the Concept of Interlocking Institutions*

John Barrett/Hans Jochen Peters

I. Introduction

With the establishment of the North Atlantic Cooperation Council (NACC)[1] another element was added to the already complex, indeed intricate, system of international political institutions and organizations in the Euro-Atlantic region. As against the great majority of older institutions and organizations, NACC does not owe its existence to the Cold War or to efforts aimed at overcoming the Cold War and the division of Europe by creating comprehensive institutions; NACC is a product of the end of the division of Europe, as some quite unusual attendant circumstances have illustrated at the inaugural session on 20th December 1991.[2]

NACC is therefore a very young organization, with little as yet clearly defined and much still in evolution, particularly in regard to procedures and competences, criteria for membership and, above all, its relationship to other institutions, not-

* The views represented in this article are those of the authors alone and not of NATO or NATO members.

1 NACC was inaugurated on 20th December 1991 at NATO Headquarters in Brussels. Foreign Ministers of the 16 NATO states, the former member states of the dissolved Warsaw Pact (Bulgaria, Czechoslovakia, Hungary, Poland, Romania, Soviet Union – represented by the Soviet Ambassador to Belgium) and the three Baltic states (Estonia, Latvia, Lithuania) participated in the inaugural session. Several months later, on 10th March 1992, the rest of the CIS states were invited to join the NACC. Georgia and Albania followed suit at the NACC meeting in Oslo on 5th June 1992. (On the same occasion, Finland, at its request, was granted observer status.) On 18th December 1992, NACC Foreign Ministers stated their readiness "to welcome the Czech Republic and the Slovak Republic as members of the North Atlantic Cooperation Council as of 1 January 1993." NACC thus currently consists of the following states: Albania, Armenia, Azerbaijan, Belarus, Belgium, Bulgaria, Canada, Czech Republic, Denmark, Estonia, France Georgia, Germany, Greece, Hungary, Iceland, Italy, Kazakhstan, Kyrgyzstan, Latvia, Lithuania, Luxembourg, Moldova, the Netherlands, Norway, Poland, Portugal, Romania, Russia, Slovak Republic, Spain, Tajikistan, Turkey, Turkmenistan, Ukraine, United Kingdom, United States of America, Uzbekistan. Observer: Finland.

2 In the course of the meeting, the Soviet Ambassador delivered a declaration concerning the successor states of the Soviet Union: "We proceed from the assumption that the agreement concerning the contacts in the framework of the North Atlantic Cooperation Council which is being created today are valid for the Sovereign States which are becoming legal successors of the Soviet Union." Subsequently, he stated: "In accordance with the latest instructions received from Moscow which result from the consultations between the sovereign states, we request that all references to the Soviet Union be excluded from the text of the Statement." As the North Atlantic Cooperation Council Statement on Dialogue, Partnership and Cooperation had already been adopted when this declaration was made, it was included in the text only as a footnote. Despite the Ambassador's declaration, the Russian Federation is considered a founding member of the Council – unlike the other CIS member states – and thus an official admission of Russia at a later date was not deemed necessary.

ably NATO and the Conference on Security and Cooperation in Europe (CSCE). What NACC will become and, in particular, whether it will be firmly established within the "system of interlocking and mutually reinforcing institutions" will presumably depend to a great extent on the evolution of NACC's relationship to NATO and to the CSCE process and its substructures.[3]

At the CSCE Helsinki Summit, the Heads of State and Government adopted on 19th July 1992 a Concluding Document, "The Challenges of Change." This document established, amongst other things, a new CSCE Forum for Security Cooperation (FSC) as an integral part of the CSCE. This Forum will be the site for further efforts of the CSCE states in three main areas: (1) arms control, disarmament and confidence- and security-building; (2) security cooperation; and (3) conflict prevention. In practice, this means further negotiations relating to new measures of arms control and disarmament (including CSBMs); consultation, "goal-oriented continuing dialogue" and cooperation in the field of security; and prevention of conflict through various techniques, such as cooperation in verification. The document also set out a fourteen-point Programme of Immediate Action to give concrete substance in the near term to these broad, general objectives.[4]

The question of duplication of work between the new CSCE Forum and the NACC does not arise in those areas of the Forum's Programme dealing with *negotiations*. As the NACC is perceived by most of its members as first and foremostly a consultative, not a negotiating, body, the possibility the FSC duplicating NACC does not arise. However, there are items of the FSC Programme (notably under the section entitled "Security Enhancement and Cooperation") which could indeed have much closer affinity with some activities already found in the NACC Work Plan, especially where these latter include consultations on security-related issues and the discussion of conceptual approaches to arms control.[5] Then there are the

---

3 It is not even certain whether all of the founding fathers would necessarily want NACC to survive for long, let alone evolve over time. A few might even secretly think of it as the moor for whom nobody has any further interest once he has served his purpose. On the other hand, the lack of established structures and of clarity concerning its competences is not necessarily a sign of weakness or lack of viability – certainly not in times of sweeping political change and institutional transformation in the NACC region. The implications of these and other possible reactions to the future of NACC are discussed subsequently in this paper.

4 For the objectives of the FSC, see: CSCE Helsinki Document 1992, *The Challenges of Change*, Chapter V, Paragraphs 11-25. The Programme for Immediate Action is set out in Paragraph 46. The FSC held its inaugural meeting in Vienna on 22nd September 1990.

5 *Work Plan for Dialogue, Partnership and Cooperation*, issued at the meeting of the North Atlantic Cooperation Council held at NATO Headquarters, Brussels, on 10th March 1992, published as Press Communiqué M-NACC-1(92)21 on 10th March 1992. The Work Plan identified two main categories of cooperation: (a) "intensified consultations on the part of the Central and Eastern European countries with the North Atlantic Council, NATO's various specialised committees, and the Military Committee," with all participants being expressly granted the right "to raise all political and security related issues of concern or interest to them;" and (b) a number of cooperation activities. Both categories focus on "security and related issues, such as defence

separate but related activities of the Ad Hoc Group on Defence Matters (GDM).[6] In particular, one might be forgiven if the GDM's programme relating to cooperation in defence-related areas with Central and East European partners appears to presage those put forward under sub-paragraphs 7, 8 and 10 in the CSCE Forum's Programme of Immediate Action.[7] Here, concern over duplication could be legitimate.

To some observers, this possible overlap between the work undertaken under the auspices of NACC (and the related Group on Defence Matters) and that developed subsequently for the CSCE's Forum for Security Cooperation may be a shining example of "interlocking institutions," where overlap is not only to be expected but fostered as a means of building a new European security architecture. Others, however, may take a less sanguine approach, seeing the potential for competition between these bodies arising as the inevitable result of political dynamics and differing security interests. To them, we might be sowing the seeds of interlocking but mutually competitive institutions. If they are right, the result will not be reinforcement of these institutions, nor enhancement of their efficacy in dealing with hard-edged security issues. Instead, there may be winners and losers.

In this paper, we will put forward three general scenarios which could emerge from the NACC process and consider what effect these could have on the CSCE in general. Before this is done, however, we need to look at, first, the security context at the time of the creation of NACC and the CSCE Forum for Security Coopera-

---

planning, conceptual approaches to arms control, democratic concepts of civilian-military relations, civil-military coordination of air traffic management, the conversion of defence production to civilian purposes and enhanced participation in NATO's "Third Dimension" scientific and environmental programmes as well as cooperation in the dissemination of information about NATO in the states of Central and Eastern Europe.

6 The Ad Hoc Group on Defence Matters was set up in the spring of 1992 by NATO defence ministers (minus France) and their counterparts from the Central and East European countries (with the exception of Georgia) to support the effort to deepen dialogue and promote cooperation on issues that fall within the competence of defence ministers. These would include, *inter alia*, issues of defence organization and planning; the role of armed forces in democratic societies; military strategies and their implementation; reform and restructuring of the armed forces; and, environmental clean-up of defence installations. The GDM is to become a kind of clearing house for proposals for cooperation in the defence field. The aim of the GDM is to make available to the new partners the expertise and experience of NATO members in defence-related areas.

7 For example, see Chapter V, Paragraph 46, sub-paragraph 7, which deals with Force Planning: "The elaboration of provisions to provide transparency about each CSCE participating States intentions in the medium to long term as regards the size, structure, training and equipment of its armed forces, as well as defence policy, doctrines and budgets related thereto." See also sub-paragraph 8: "The development of a programme of exchanges, cooperation and the sharing of expertise in the field of defence conversion." And sub-paragraph 10: "The development of a programme of military contacts, liaison arrangements, cooperation and exchanges, particularly in the fields of training and organization of armed forces."

tion, and then, the main features and objectives of the NACC, since these will define and limit the scenarios.

II. NACC and CSCE: The Security Context of the Early 1990s

The NACC emerged from the internal political revolutions in the Central and Eastern European countries, the collapse of the Warsaw Pact, the pending disintegration of the Soviet Union, and the dissolution of the security structure imposed on the eastern part of Europe after the Second World War. Freed at last from the ideological and physical shackles of the Warsaw Pact, these countries now, however, faced a security vacuum in their region. Given the precarious nature of the new political regimes – all aspiring towards variants of democracy or democratic nationalism – security of borders and regional stability became paramount concerns. The abortive coup in the Soviet Union in August 1991 further underlined the reality of anti-democratic reaction in that country. It showed their vulnerability to events beyond their boundaries: the possibility of unfettered civil conflict in the two largest republics of the then-USSR would have produced refugee displacement and spill-over which none of the smaller Central and East European (C+EE) republics could withstand alone. With Yugoslavia about to add to the turmoil with secessionist demands by some of its federated republics, the search was on for a guarantor of stability and security.

Allied states naturally had their own reasons to be alarmed at the growing potential for conflict and instability in this region. The growing concern felt by NATO members and other West European states over the situation to the east might not be addressed adequately through bilateral contacts and liaison established by them with the USSR and the former Warsaw Pact satellites. Should the Alliance be the chief forum for coordination on these and other security issues? It should be recalled that although the Treaty on Conventional Forces in Europe (CFE) had been signed in November 1990, it had not yet been ratified. With the break-up of the USSR came fresh concern over the location, disposition and control of Soviet tactical and strategic nuclear weapons. Were the political command and control structures and arrangements sufficiently robust and insulated to withstand the potential for nuclear proliferation, for illicit transfers of parts of the considerable Soviet nuclear arsenal?

The need for a pragmatic and quick response to such potential calamities brought forward the proposal for a means of extending both the hand of reassurance as well as the hand of friendship to the region. The creation of a new body or institution which would address this need would give Alliance members an instrument to help monitor and perhaps shape security developments in the C+EE region, in addition to the conduits provided by regular liaison and bilateral contact.

A consultative body, with no really operational powers, would be the most the Alliance could agree; yet that, despite its limitations, was better than nothing for those countries lying to the east of the Alliance. Thus the NACC was born – another addition to the network of "interlocking" institutions.

To some Alliance members, however, the NACC was not to be considered a new European security institution; it was neither an institution nor an adjunct to one. It certainly could not be compared with the Conference on Security and Co-operation in Europe. For the two years previous to the creation of the NACC, the Alliance had championed the CSCE as the emerging chief forum in Europe for the consideration of fundamental security issues. With the signing of the CFE Treaty simultaneously with the Charter of Paris in November 1990, all eyes turned to the next step in the development of the CSCE as a security institution – the 1992 Helsinki Follow-Up Meeting. Here the new CSCE Security Forum – a body originally proposed by Alliance members – was established. All security issues and negotiations on arms control and disarmament would find their new location in the Forum, which would ensure the participation now of all CSCE states. This lifting of perspective to the CSCE would be accompanied by a new term – cooperative security.

Much hope had been expressed in Alliance declarations and statements that the CSCE might develop into a viable collective security institution with a European and transatlantic reach. However, at the time of NACC's birth the CSCE was still in the process of evolution. The Charter of Paris had produced high-flown sentiments and expectations about the future of cooperative security in Europe; the Conflict Prevention Centre had been established in Vienna; and the forthcoming Helsinki Summit in July 1992 would make the CSCE into an effective security institution by improving and consolidating its conflict prevention and crisis management structures (in addition to creating the Forum for Security Cooperation).

Where the NACC would sit in relation to the CSCE was not readily apparent. Nor had some Alliance members yet made up their minds what they expected from NACC. Was it to be a long-term process, or confined to remaining a stop-gap measure, a response to the extraordinary circumstances and events of 1991? A detailed study of individual NACC members – both Allied and non-Allied – would be required to assess their current disposition towards the goals and objectives of the NACC. Such detail is beyond the scope of this paper. However, given the present state of uncertainty over the longer-term development of NACC, one might identify conceptually three possible outcomes. Each one of these yields different implications for the relationship between the NACC and the CSCE – indeed, these implications touch also on the future role of the Alliance. However, to get a clear perception of how these scenarios might develop, we first need to know exactly what NACC is at present.

III. The Main Features and Objectives of NACC

The aim of NACC, as laid down in its statement of 20th December 1991, is to "develop further the process of regular diplomatic liaison and to build genuine partnership among the North Atlantic Alliance and the countries of Central and Eastern Europe." In other words, its goal is to establish a genuine partnership – something which had so far not existed – and to enhance qualitatively the practice of regular diplomatic liaison between NATO and the individual Central and Eastern European states which had been, and continues to be, conducted on a bilateral basis.[8] Comparison with regular diplomatic liaison illustrates this point.

With the London Declaration on a transformed North Atlantic Alliance, issued on 6th July 1990, NATO had made a first response to the process of revolutionary changes in Central and Eastern Europe which was still in full swing. It extended the "hand of friendship" to its former adversaries in the Warsaw Pact. In this hand were three central offers: (a) the invitation to leading representatives of the C+EE states to address the North Atlantic Council; (b) the invitation to establish regular diplomatic liaison with NATO so that "our thinking and deliberations in this historic period of change" may be shared; and (c) the readiness to intensify military contacts between NATO and C+EE states as members of the still-existing Warsaw Pact.

What were the qualitatively new achievements that NACC has brought compared with the liaison launched by the London Declaration? The liaison proposed in the London Declaration and subsequently implemented was essentially a "confidence-building measure" in its broadest sense.[9] From NATO's perspective, the main objective of this liaison was to convey a true perception of the Alliance as a defensive security alliance to the governments and peoples in Central and Eastern Europe by showing them Western security conceptions, as well as the readiness of NATO to adapt to changed security situations.[10] It is also important to note that the liaison which emerged on the basis of the London Declaration was bilateral –

8 C+EE members of NACC will be referred to as "cooperation partners," in accordance with internal NATO usage.

9 Of course, NATO also used the liaison to exert a concrete influence on the policies of individual C+EE states. For example, in the spring of 1991, NATO Secretary General Wörner conveyed to the Soviet Ambassador to Belgium NATO's concern over Soviet military actions in the then-Soviet Baltic republics. The objective of this demarche was to bring pressure to bear on the Soviet government to show restraint.

10 The political message underlined in the London Declaration concerning the establishment of cooperative relations to the former potential adversary states was equally and perhaps even more so addressed to the public in NATO member states. It was intended to show that the Alliance continued to have a meaningful role to play in shaping the changing political and security environment in Europe.

i.e. between the Alliance and individual C+EE states.[11] In addition, it was supposed to be governed by the principle of "non-differentiation": anything offered to one liaison partner in the way of consultation and cooperation had also to be made available in principle to all others. The practical result, however, was a perception by some liaison partners that this principle was not observed consistently. This had a self-fulfilling effect. Fearful of being left behind, some liaison states deliberately sought differentiation from the others in their relations with NATO.

The bilateral character of the diplomatic liaison also meant that the substance of the dialogue on security matters remained limited. The liaison was an appropriate means of dismantling enemy images through dialogue and of assisting the C+EE states to cope with the difficult transition to "civil societies" through increasing technical cooperation. On the other hand, when it came to responding to the growing fears of the Central European states concerning the effects of the disintegration of the Soviet Union and to acquiring means for NATO to influence developments in this region, bilateral diplomatic liaison was not a very appropriate instrument. Furthermore, consultation and cooperation had been carried out almost exclusively on an ad-hoc basis. Cooperation requests of individual C+EE partners had often not been fulfilled, or not to the extent hoped for by them, and had usually been preceded by long and sometimes quite controversial discussion within the Alliance.

With the establishment of NACC, which was to supplement and not replace the "regular diplomatic liaison," these shortfalls have, to a large extent, been rectified. For example, the NACC member states elaborated and adopted in early 1992 a "Work Plan for Dialogue, Partnership and Cooperation." Although it was not possible to take up all the proposals of the cooperation partners – for instance, consensus within the Alliance could not be achieved on including the "Civil Emergency Planning" complex requested by some partner states – the Work Plan was, if compared with the "regular diplomatic liaison," a considerable qualitative leap forward. Cooperation partners could now become direct participants in the work of the Alliance through meetings with a number of important NATO committees, including, *inter alia*, the North Atlantic Council, the Senior Political Committee, the Political Committee and others.

The "Work Plan for Dialogue, Partnership and Cooperation 1993," adopted on the 18th December 1992 by the North Atlantic Cooperation Council, divided itself

11 On the Alliance side, the liaison was almost exclusively carried out by the International Staff or the International Military Staff. Direct contacts between liaison partners and the delegations of course existed. For instance, it became common practice for liaison partners' foreign ministers and political leaders, when visiting NATO, to meet not only with the Secretary General but also informally with members of the North Atlantic Council. It was nonetheless general practice that all day-to-day contacts were made through the International Staff, which thus acted as a kind of hinge in talks between the C+EE states and NATO.

into several discrete functional areas. These included: political and security-related matters; defence planning issues and military matters; defence conversion, economic issues; science; challenges of modern society; dissemination of information; policy planning consultations; and air traffic management. Among the topics listed under the rubric of political and security related matters was "conceptual and operational aspects related to peacekeeping." During the negotiation of the Work Plan a certain *frisson* arose over the precise nature of the activity that would be carried out to adress this topic. The result of protracted discussion was agreement on a clumsily worded phrase which sought to satisfy both ends of the spectrum – those who wished to see the NACC and its associated Work Plan activities remain solely at the *consultative* level and those who sought to seize on cooperation in peacekeeping as a means of extending the cooperation to embrace operational activities.[12]

The "brainstorming" at Ambassadorial level was duly held at the end of January 1993, followed by the establishment of a new working group devoted specifically to peacekeeping cooperation – the NACC Ad Hoc Group on Cooperation in Peacekeeping, chaired by the NATO Deputy Secretary General. The Ad Hoc Group met periodically during the Spring of 1993 and produced a "Report to Ministers," which was adopted on 11th June 1993 by the North Atlantic Cooperation Council at its ministerial session in Athens.

The report sets out a common understanding on conceptual approaches to peacekeeping, as well as a common programme for practical cooperation aimed at sharing information and experience, undertaking joint training and education and possibly conducting joint exercises.

The Ministers directed the Ad Hoc Group to "accelerate" its work in complementing this programme.

The Report of the Ad Hoc Group is interesting for a number of reasons. It is one of the first documents agreed by a substantial number of states belonging to the Euro-Atlantic and Euro-Asian security region that has sought to produce definitions, concepts and operational principles to guide their overall approach to international peacekeeping.[13] Further, it has produced a detailed programme for

12 The phrase reads: "Consultations on peacekeeping and related matters, starting in a brainstorming format at Ambassadorial level followed by ad hoc meetings of political-military experts, as agreed by Ambassadors, leading to cooperation among interested NACC members in preparation for peacekeeping activities, including: joint participation in peacekeeping training; and consideration of possible joint peacekeeping exercises."

13 Among the key agreed principles are that peacekeeping can only be carried out under the authority of the UN or CSCE; that the UN or CSCE must define arrangements for the conduct of peacekeeping; and that peacekeeping is undertaken in support of ongoing efforts to restore peace and stability through a political settlement. The definitions produced deal with conflict prevention, peacemaking, peacekeeping, peace-enforcement and peace-building.

practical cooperation among the states on international peacekeeping.[14] Thirdly – and more to the specific concerns of this article – it raises fresh questions about the possible eventual transition of NACC, from a consultative to a potentially operational body dealing with international security issues such as conflict prevention and peacekeeping.

A transition such as this, should it occur, would raise alarm bells in the CSCE, particularly among those who have sought to enhance the CSCE's own *operational* role in the security realm. The CSCE Helsinki Final Document 1992, with a whole chapter devoted to preventive diplomacy, crisis management and peacekeeping under the CSCE banner, bore testimony to the intentions of its authors – to provide the conglomeration of 50-odd states with its own effective operational mechanism for backing up its political declarations and directives. In the area of peacekeeping, at least, the dividing line between the CSCE and the NACC may thus be growing thinner with each NACC ministerial statement.[15] The CSCE is desperately trying to "operationalise" its declarations on CSCE peacekeeping, to give substance to political intention; the NACC is bereft at the moment of specific political direction to involve itself operationally in conflict settlement where peacekeeping activities may be required, and yet it is developing, nonetheless, a practical programme for cooperation in peacekeeping. The two separate CSCE and NACC tracks in this area may proceed in parallel, with a resulting duplication perhaps; alternatively they could collide – with implications that the scenarios set out in the Paragraphs below seek to describe.

Despite the seemingly positive prospects offered by NACC, a certain restraint or lack of enthusiasm on the part of some cooperation partners has been noticeable. For instance, Poland, Czechoslovakia and Hungary seem to feel that NACC may in fact thwart their long-term aim to become full members of NATO. This is all the more disappointing for them in the light of their history, geographic proximity, internal political development, and objective security concerns – all of which would add up at least to some preferential treatment. In their view, the creation of NACC, by virtue of its wide geographical reach and the lack of internal differentiation among its members, may, paradoxically, have put their goal even further off.

This lack of complete enthusiasm, or possible growing divergence over the objectives of NACC membership, leads one to consider whether there may be different ways in which NACC may develop or evolve over the next few years. Not only

---

14 Among the measures to advance practical cooperation are: cooperation in planning peacekeeping activities; exchange of national concepts and doctrines; possible development of a data base of available peacekeeping resources; a common technical base for cooperation in peacekeeping; and possible peacekeeping training, education and exercises.

15 A respresentative of the CSCE Chairman-in-Office attends as well. This observation is given even greater credence by the addition of Finland, Sweden and Austria as observers to the NACC Ad Hoc Group on Cooperation in Peacekeeping.

has the question of internal differentiation or "variable geometry" been raised, but there are other critical voices to be heard concerning the overall direction and purpose of NACC. For example, some Western non-NATO states have asked, with some irony, whether one had to have been a member of the Warsaw Pact in order to enjoy the close cooperation with NATO that NACC offers. Irony apart, they and perhaps others wonder what will eventually be the relation between NACC and other institutions. It is not just the NACC relation with NATO that is troubling them (and NATO member states), but also whether other institutions may suffer as a result. More to the point: any development of NACC in the direction of realizing its potential as a collective security system would pose a crucial question as to the relevance of the CSCE as the primary forum in which security issues in the CSCE region are addressed. To consider how and in what ways this could happen, three separate scenarios of NACC's evolution should be examined. Each of these would have different implications for the system of "interlocking" or "mutually reinforcing" institutions that is considered by many to be the basis of the emerging European security architecture.

1. The NACC as a Transitory Body

At the time of NACC's creation, the prevailing sense among most Allies appears to have been that it would be a transitional, and thus transitory, phenomenon. The maturation of the CSCE would supersede the NACC in the security realm once the new structures created by the Helsinki Summit were firmly in place. NACC was primarily designed to provide help and assistance to the newly independent and C+EE states during the period of transition to democratic societies. Once this goal was achieved, the raison d'être for NACC would disappear.

But there may be other reasons, apart from the pure logic of transcending itself through its own success or fulfilment of original goals, for some individual NACC members to emphasize the transitory nature of the body. *First*, as NACC is a hybrid organization, it offers to cooperation partners neither collective defence nor collective security, even though NATO could, through its Article II provisions, extend to cooperation partners an element of *collective security*. Absent any interest by Allies to do just that, then the element of security obtained through NACC participation may, to some of the partners, appear nugatory. *Second*, the NACC is doubtlessly viewed by some of the cooperation partners as not just unequal by view of the circumstances of its creation, but detrimentally so. In other words, it is a meeting held with cooperation partners under the aegis and at the behest of the North Atlantic Council. *Third*, because of its origins, it does not have any established mechanism for expanded membership, nor for the inclusion of others. *Finally*, and perhaps dramatically, some NATO and even non-NATO NACC member states may feel that the core functions of NATO as a collective defence organization may be hindered or indeed vitiated by the continued presence, expansion and/or deepening of the NACC.

However, it would not be accurate to assume that all NACC members would welcome this transitoriness. NACC gives to the geo-political region it embraces a special significance and political importance which other, non-NACC states in the CSCE region do not share. Not all NATO members would necessarily welcome the disappearance of NACC for a number of separate, though perhaps interrelated, reasons. *First*, the CSCE may never develop adequately or in line with one's own interests. NACC would thus serve as a hedge – that is, as an alternative, smaller "institution-in-waiting" which would already have a modicum of cooperative interaction, procedures and familiarity. *Secondly*, and perhaps more cynically to some, NACC acts as a partial diversion, a means of forestalling and/or evading the question of expanded NATO membership. Various means could be developed to grant an associate or similar status to the cooperation partners that would be interpreted as an elevation in their standing in the region. *Thirdly*, the fundamental objective of the transformation and continued relevance of NATO may partly, but significantly, be bound up in the continued existence of NACC. It is this very process of outreach to former adversaries that has characterized the changed NATO of the 1990s, where threats recede and risks are tempered by the stabilizing effect of a continuing practical and cooperative partnership. Membership need not thus be the ultimate goal; rather, an effective and real *modus vivendi*. In this latter sense, the NACC would in time gain enough strength in common purpose that it would indeed become, in the eyes of its proponents, part of the mutually reinforcing institutions of the new and evolving Eurasian security system. However, how it would then relate to other institutions (apart from NATO, of course) remains to be seen, and may prove a difficult endeavour.

2. NACC is Maintained

The Yugoslavian crisis has not convincingly demonstrated the viability of the CSCE in regional security affairs. This has been evident in the slow, tortuous response of the CSCE to Yugoslavian issues; the inability of the Conflict Prevention Centre to find any significant role to play; the restriction of the work of the CSCE Steering Group on Yugoslavia to largely "human dimension" issues; and the limited involvement of the CSCE (through its Troika alone) in the Steering Committee of the International Conference on Yugoslavia, co-chaired by the UN and the EC in Geneva. Ongoing crises and ethnic conflicts in other parts of the European region may similarly demonstrate an inability of the CSCE to do anything in the realm of conflict resolution, though it still may be able to develop viable structures and procedures for conflict prevention, early warning and confidence-building through the 1992 Vienna Document (VD 92). However, structures for crisis management and crisis resolution may prove more difficult to engineer.

What then would be the potential implications of the continuation of NACC beyond the transitory period suggested in its original justification? Could, for example, the NACC become a competitor to the CSCE in the security realm? Much would depend on the current and future development of the CSCE, as well as other developments in the security realm. For example, a prominent item on the Programme for Immediate Action of the new CSCE Security Forum is harmonization – that is, the entry into the CFE Treaty regime of those CSCE members not actually parties to the Treaty. How exactly this is to be done is still a matter for negotiation and cannot at this time be precisely documented. But one must recall that the CFE Treaty and the CFE IA document on personnel strengths of armed forces involve at this moment mainly NACC members.[16]

Thus, despite efforts to restrict the realm and scope of discussion and consultation in NACC, it would nevertheless become a powerful pole of attraction for non-NACC CSCE states, which would seek membership in it for that very reason. There may be, though, an internal dynamo which would force the NACC to evolve or disappear. Its ad hoc foundation means that NACC partners could still shape the dialogue and structure of NACC. By the same token, the fundamentally unequal nature of the NACC could provide the dynamo for either evolution or disappearance. If evolution occurs, then NACC would serve as a prelude to membership in NATO or some kind of associate status. It would then become a more intimate body dealing directly with areas of concern to most NATO members – a vehicle through which certain *influences* in the C+EE region especially may be preserved and perhaps refined/deepened. As such, it would circumvent to a certain extent the influence of other institutions in the region (or having a claim to the region).

The inability of the CSCE to go beyond normative postulations may lead some NATO countries to a different assessment of the potential for NACC to substitute for, or perhaps supplant entirely, the CSCE. NATO members – through the NACC process – would help the cooperation partners find solutions to (rather

16 Latvia, Lithuania, Estonia, Albania are not parties to the CFE Treaty, nor are they signatories to the CFE 1A document. Following the break-up of the Soviet Union, which created problems of apportionment of Treaty-Limited Elements (TLE) among the successor states and accession to the Treaty by them, a High Level Working Group (HLWG) was formed. It comprised NATO member states, East European members of the former Warsaw Pact, and newly independent republics whose territory was within the CFE Treaty's area of application (i.e. those former Soviet Union republics lying west of the Ural Mountains). Its sole purpose was to assist where possible in bringing the CFE Treaty into force without having to renegotiate the whole Treaty. It is particularly important to note that the HLWG, despite involving a number of NACC members, was *not* a subordinate body of NACC, although it is true that it was at the NACC Ministerial in December 1991 that the proposal for establishing the autonomous HLWG was first mooted.

than just discuss) the various problems that have been identified in the work plan process. Cooperation would therefore be viewed as an incremental process having no boundaries short of actual NATO membership. NACC would become regarded as an additional element of stability in Europe despite its limitations. Other attractions would be perceived concerning the fate of the Alliance itself: over time, NACC may be a more viable route for the de facto physical and political *preservation* of NATO as an entity. This would counter the decline of Alliance solidarity in the context of the CSCE. In NACC, the collective political and military weight of NATO can be brought to bear on an issue, whereas in the CSCE the NATO caucus is not so correspondingly strong in the face of a growing effort by EC countries to proceed on a common front.

In this scenario, the outcome would be one where the NACC would develop a legitimate role alongside the CSCE. However, the CSCE could in future stagnate or find its political impact on security issues attenuated or simply procedurally too unwieldy. This could result in the non-NACC CSCE countries pressing for membership in NACC, with the consequence that the CSCE itself could become undermined or weakened. The NACC would then become an alternative – perhaps an even more desirable – forum in which real security concerns would be addressed. By contrast, the CSCE Security Forum may never really develop, due to its own problems in handling anything more than dialogue at fifty-one. Or, it would become stunted by the evolution of the NACC.

For NATO, the chief concern would be: (a) offering a level of collective security short of the actual security guarantees that go with full NATO membership; (b) avoidance of being drawn into bilateral disputes between cooperation partners to be prevailed upon as an arbiter or used as a foil; and (c) being sympathetic to differentiation within the NACC as far as individual countries go, but stoping short of a so-called variable geometry, which would create different classes of NACC partners. Using the concept of interlocking institutions, NACC would thus find a place as a sub-unit in the CSCE region. This would, however, presuppose agreement on the limits of NACC development – which is absent at present and perhaps even unobtainable.

3. NACC Expands to Include the CSCE

A final consideration assumes that the move towards membership in the Alliance of all cooperation partners becomes unstoppable. As it is unlikely that Allies would extend the legally based security guarantee found in Article V of the Washington Treaty to the new members, the result would be a collective security rather than collective defence arrangement. Collective security institutions are debatable as to their effectiveness in providing real security.[17] Nevertheless, for non-NACC CSCE members a choice may be posed as to whether they could join NACC without fundamentally weakening the CSCE. This weakening effect would remain a consideration through the earlier stages of expansion, until a full overlap with the CSCE membership was obtained. At that point, it becomes moot whether NACC reinforces or rivals the CSCE. The likelihood is that the CSCE would split: the Council of Europe takes over human dimension; the NACC takes over security affairs; and the economic basket becomes irrelevant and disappears into the IMF, ERBD, EC and G-7.

However, before that stage is ever reached, the very process of expansion of Alliance membership under the NACC process would have fundamental implications for the Alliance. *First*, the US would reduce its military commitment in Europe. It would thus stand further apart politically from European security developments. *Second*, the WEU would become for its members the hard core of the European security structure. The result would be a fundamental shift in the balance of power within the framework of interlocking or mutually reinforcing institutions. *Third*, the NACC would become the body in which crisis management, conflict resolution and peacekeeping in the Eurasian space would be politically and practically exercised. If so, NACC could possibly become the military arm of the CSCE, as long as the latter was not entirely supplanted. *Fourth*, NACC would receive applications for membership from all CSCE participating states, and beyond (i.e., the Mediterranean, Middle and Near East, Asia). By then, however, NATO would be transformed to the point of becoming unrecognizable and eventually dissolving. At a minimum, the integrated military command would disappear. At a maximum, the present NATO members would leave the Alliance.

IV. Conclusion

The present relation of NACC to the CSCE has no formal standing and to all intents and purposes does not exist. Much will depend on the evolution of the CSCE in dealing with security affairs. Yet, the longer the NACC survives despite its "transitoriness," the sooner non-NACC CSCE states must weigh the benefits of joining NACC, in the event that its portfolio expands to deal with issues of direct concern to them. Straddling the NACC and the CSCE would, however, lead inexorably to a weakening of the CSCE – unless, of course, in the scenario where, by mutual consent, the NACC expands in one great leap its membership and role to become the military arm of the CSCE. Short of that, the effect on the CSCE becomes a self-

17 See on the efficacy of collective security institutions, Richard K. Betts, "Systems for Peace or Causes of War? Collective Security, Arms Control, and the New Europe," *International Security* (Cambridge, MA), Vol. 17, No. 1, Summer 1992, pp. 5-43.

fulfilling prophecy: the whole CSCE process either dissipates or simply reaches the natural boundaries of its effectiveness. But CSCE effectiveness is a matter of the collective and concerted political will of its individual participating states. Until one knows the natural limits of both NACC and the CSCE, then the nature of the relationship between the two cannot be accurately forecast. We are in the realm of the *politics* of interlocking institutions. Their mutual reinforcement – that is, if NACC evolves or aspires to an institutional status – may not take place. At least, given the foregoing arguments, this non-reinforcement should not be precluded as we move further into the post-Helsinki, post-Cold War period.

11. Russia's Interests and Approaches towards the System of Interlocking European Institutions

Grigoriy J. Chudakov/Dmitriy A. Danilov/Sergei A. Karaganov/ Pavel T. Podlesnyi

Russia's approaches towards the system of European security institutions are currently in the process of shaping and there are several reasons for this. The main reason is still a rather unclear understanding by Russian elites of their national interests within their new political, economic and ethno-cultural borders. Weakness in bureaucratic and state structures including those involved in the formation of foreign, defense and security policy also hinders the process. Nevertheless, Russia's policy approaches are very actively being formed. It is not difficult to foresee the final results of this process, if we thoroughly analyze the objective challenges and threats which Russia faces.

I. Challenges

1. In a broader sense, the main challenge to Russian security and that of other states of the former Soviet Union, is embodied in the very process of establishing new states, which, as a rule, have weak historical, geographical and even ethno-cultural legitimation. Throughout history, such processes were almost inevitably accompanied by wars and conflict, due to border disputes, violation of minorities' rights, control over resources, emergence of new balances of power, fragmentation of new state entities, etc. The present situation is being aggravated by the disintegration of Yugoslavia and Czechoslovakia. These could yield dangerous prospects for undermining stability in the whole region. At any rate, the formation of a more or less stable balance of power will take many years.

2. Political conflicts due to ethnic differences in different regions of the former USSR (i.e. Karabakh, Ossetia, Abkhazia, Transdniestria and Tajikistan) present the main immediate danger to Russia. Additionally, the number of such conflicts is steadily and perhaps irreversibly growing. There is a constant risk of direct Russian involvement in those conflicts, especially when political groups using "power politics" defending "national interests" increase their influence within the society. Pressure from these groups has already forced Russian authorities to reject the idea of isolation from conflicts and to begin active peacekeeping policies in Transdniestria, Ossetia, Abkhazia, for example. However, there are no firm guarantees that Russia will succeed under any circumstances in not crossing the fragile border between displaying a degree of necessary responsibility and sliding towards attempting to impose a neo-imperial will. The consequences of such attempts

would be quite clear: sharpening of relations with other CIS states, even probable wars between them; involvement of neighboring European and Asian countries in CIS conflicts; and the probable failure of economic reforms. Consequently, avoidance of wars and peaceful conflict resolution on the territory of the former USSR are the main tasks of Russia's foreign and defense policy in the coming years.

3. Another serious challenge to Russia's security is the possibility of a further deepening of the economic crisis, which is fraught with social unrest. A continuing combination of price rises, production decline and growth in unemployment, especially in big cities, could make such a dangerous trend in the internal affairs of the Russian Federation a reality.

However, it does not necessarily mean that radical right-wing groups would come to power. In Russian society there are influential political forces of centrist orientation who support changes in the current policy of economic reforms to prevent further industrial decline and demand improvements in social security. But the destitution of the absolute majority of the population, high rates of crime and violence, large-scale corruption in state institutes, crisis in the democracy movement and growing distrust of the government enlarge the potential social base for radical political groups. If they come to power they could push the Russian state to pursue an adventurous foreign policy, thus severely furthering the process of Russia's disintegration.

4. Political disintegration in Russia is being stimulated by a number of factors. Autonomous republics (i.e. Tatarstan and the Chechen, Bashkir and Tuva republics) aspire toward a greater degree of independence. There is also a separatist trend in such purely Russian regions as Siberia, the Far East and Sakhalin. These regions are trying to use their own resources to survive the period of painful economic reform. The Federal authorities avoided for a very long time a demonstration of their determination not to allow any disintegration in Russia or proclaiming all nationalist movements unlawfull, which threaten the territorial integrity of Russia. Passive reaction of authorities regarding some ethnic conflicts also played a negative role (i.e. the delayed reaction to the conflict in Abkhazia).

This tendency towards political disintegration is being stimulated by certain mistakes in government economic policy, including: artificial cash deficits, problems with money turnover and shifting social spending to local authorities. Political disintegration in Russia could unleash a stagnant civil war and/or lead to the emergence of authoritarian, if not totalitarian rule. In sliding in this direction Russia would face internal and external catastrophes. The West has not lost its ability to quickly restore its system of deterrence, but in relation to the present political-military situation, even more tough and qualitatively less favorable to Russia. The line of confrontation would be not in the center of Europe, but rather on the borders of the Russian Federation. The isolation would be even more complete then in the 1920s-1930s or 1940s-1950s. For the first time in its history Russia would find itself in a situation of terrible military weakness and without any possibilities to bridge the military and technological gap. Disintegration would open Russia for all kinds of interventions (i.e. in order to prevent accidents with weapons of mass destruction), and would end Russian statehood.

5. The problem of preserving the rights of Russian and Russian-speaking minorities is going to be more and more acute in some of the CIS states and in certain Autonomies of the Russian Federation, where Russians face discrimination and forceful emigration (i.e. the Baltic states, Central Asia, Azerbaijan, Moldova and the Chechen republic). In 1991-1992, 2 million refugees came to Russia, mostly from the Central Asian states. According to expert estimates, migration from the CIS states in the period up to 1996, could reach the level of 3 million Russians and approximately 1,5 million other nationalities. At the same time the possible level of migration from Russia itself is estimated at 3-3,5 million people. These figures could grow rapidly in the case of a serious deterioration of the situation within some of the CIS states or in relations among them. Massive migration would undermine the internal stability not only in Russia and would form a social base for radical movements and provoke inter-ethnic conflicts. But, the question is not limited to the problem of Russian-speaking minorities as the majority of the former Soviet republics are multinational states.

6. A special security challenge is presented by the situation in the armed forces: the chain of command and subordination is in a very poor condition in practically all the CIS states; the level of political control is lower then ever; and the degree of political and social discontent is extremely high. It is not clear whether the recent changes in the top echelons of the Russian Defense Ministry will improve the situation. Within the CIS, unauthorized militarization in unstable regions is occurring because the weaponry of the regiments of the former Soviet Army are being transferred to local authorities. This policy has already provoked escalation of a number of conflicts and its continuation in the Central Asian region could lead to catastrophic consequences for stability.

7. Crisis in the armed forces, economic problems and political instability help deteriorate the nuclear weapons control system. Still some countries (first of all, Ukraine) aspire toward control over the nuclear forces on their territory. An increase in the risk of the unsanctioned launch of nuclear missiles is not the only dangerous consequence of such developments. Authorities of the country which acquired control over nuclear weapons would almost inevitably hold more radical political positions.

8. The situation in the military-industrial complex also presents a number of difficult problems. There is no consistent policy of its adjustment toward the new realities. Enterprises and population connected with the military-industrial com-

plex are separated from changes in the economic and political environment and have very little opportunity for cooperation with foreign countries. The policy of conversion still faces a lot of drawbacks with a general lack of investment and long-term credit with low interest rates.

9. The general situation in Russia is being severely aggravated by a relatively high degree of incompetence at different levels of Russia's bureaucracy, and its poor control over political and economic processes. The situation in other CIS states is even worse.

10. Russia faces new long-term challenges in the external world. Above all, the challenges are connected with not very optimistic prospects for Russia's relations with the main centers of economic and political power in the contemporary world.

Notwithstanding all of its problems, Western Europe continues the process of formation of the European Union, which in a 8-15 year period would be transformed into a semi-federal state entity with common economic, foreign/defense and even, perhaps, financial policies. All European countries with the exception of the former Soviet republics, some republics of former Yugoslavia, Albania and Romania, would join the European Union or one of its associated circles. Only catastrophic events in Eastern Europe could hinder the formation of the Union. Russia in coming decades should build up a basis for rapprochement and partnership with the Union, otherwise Moscow will not be able to avoid isolation and a weakening of its position. The formation of the Union will absorb all the resources and political energy of Western Europe. The same policy of self-concentration will characterize the situation in Germany in a short-term perspective. This will impede economic and other assistance from Europe. Exclusive orientation on Europe ("Eurocentrism") will turn out to be untenable, as will premature fears of German hegemony in Europe.

A growing tendency toward neo-isolationism and concentration on internal problems in the US also limit long-term opportunities for active US participation in Russia's economic recovery. This means that exclusive orientation on the US would also be unwise.

11. The relative decline of Russia in comparison with the former USSR and its protracted economic crisis also change the political calculus of Russian-Chinese relations. China surpasses Russia in GNP two-fold and in population eight-fold. In a nationalist perspective, China could enter a period of instability or begin a policy of territorial and economic expansion. Prevention of such negative developments through only political means and conventional deterrence may prove insufficient. The Chinese factor forces Russia to continue to rely on nuclear deterrence and toward a strategic alliance with the West. Russia is also faced with the process of rapid transformation of Japanese economic power into political initiatives. At the same time Japan demonstrates a rather low interest toward economic cooperation

with Russia. It is not difficult to foresee the Japanese capability in establishing substantial military potential in the long-term. The combination of rapid economic growth and a political vacuum opens prospects for drastic political and military changes in the Asian-Pacific region.

12. Radical changes in the correlation of military forces have not lead toward any increased military threat from the West. Presently, this threat is estimated to be as minimal as ever. It is being reduced by new kinds of political relations; the emergence in Central Europe of a circle of non-offensive states, not belonging to the Western security system; and a reduction of Western military efforts, although compensated for by technological advancement. The powerful nuclear potential of Russia should compensate for all kinds of technological breakthroughs for the foreseeable future (10 years). Although further arms reductions and the construction of an effective global anti-ballistic missile (ABM) system could reduce the role of nuclear arms, thus allowing other potential threats to emerge.

Nevertheless, there is a growing anxiety in Russian society regarding military weakness and alleged vulnerability of the new geo-political position of Russia. If such anxieties can not be neutralized, then "the Weimar syndrome" in Russia will gain momentum.

13. Russia also faces the threat of semi-isolation. Economic cooperation with foreign countries is declining. The severe crisis in the oil industry is fraught with a further deterioration of the situation. The geo-strategic separation of Russia from Europe and decline of its economic and political weight reduce Western interest in cooperation with Russia. It is one of the main reasons of weakening of ties with Germany. It becomes clear that in the coming years prospects of Western economic expansion and involvement in Russian economic affairs are seriously limited. Threat of Russia's disintegration also restrains activities of potential partners. The spreading of Western security institutions' guarantees (NATO and the WEU) to East-Central Europe, excluding Russia, would deepen possible isolationist tendencies in Russia.

However, neo-isolation is not inevitable, if Russia pursues a policy of effective reforms it should not slide toward authoritarian rule. In the case of sliding toward neo-fascism or disintegration complete hostile isolation would be the inevitable outcome.

14. To the South of the former USSR a zone of relatively powerful, though unstable states, is being formed. The interests and policies of those states are very similar to the interests and policies of the European countries in the late 19th and early 20th centuries. They are trying to exert greater influence in international affairs, thus supporting some kind of repartition of the world. If the conduct of international relations in general is now moving away from power politics, in this Southern region everything is opposite. Challenges from this region could be

seriously aggravated by instability, security vacuums and a growth of Muslim fundamentalism in the former Soviet Central Asia. Although dangers of fundamentalism in Central Asia are very often overstated.

In sum, Southern challenges to Russia are unclear and have not as yet formed. Military-political containment of these challenges demands extremely flexible use of force in order to support diplomacy through peacekeeping operations, preferably agreed within the framework of the Euro-Atlantic community. At the same time, promotion of cooperation with some of the Asian states could also be useful (India, China, Pakistan, Turkey, Saudi Arabia, Syria and Israel).

Recent changes in relations between Russia and the outside world have in general had a rather favorable character due to the real reduction in external threats and pressure. Russia now enjoys the status as the main USSR successor state and could neutralize new challenges through a well developed policy. But Russia's international influence has been reduced, and opportunities for Moscow's leadership to use foreign assistance in domestic reforms are also rather limited.

15. Challenges to Russia's security have a continental character. Further deterioration in the political-military and socio-economic situation on the vast territory of the former USSR would threaten to "export" internal instability to neighboring countries. However, the territory of the former USSR is the main, but not the only source of conflict and instability in Europe. The conflict in the former Yugoslavia continues and could spread. Thus, there is the possibility of 30-40 years of instability in Europe, threatening to ruin all the achievements in enhancing peace and security during the last decades.

II. Current Problems of Pan-European Institutions: A View from Moscow

After the collapse of bloc confrontation new challenges to European security emerged. They urgently demand restructuring the already existing security institutions and establishing new mechanisms for conflict settlement. Recent events vividly demonstrate that intensive transformation of the modern institutionalized system of European security gives no adequate answer to increasing instability, closely connected with the disintegration of the USSR and with the permanent worsening of the political, military and socio-economic situation in the former Soviet region and in Russia as well.

Europe still has no effective mechanisms for crisis prevention and management. Major security institutions act without any predetermined strategies. They can only respond to events, but their responses are inconsistent and fragmented from each other and their interaction is on a very low level. All these problems are illustrated in the protracted conflict in Yugoslavia, which in parallel with the further ineffectiveness of international peace efforts could be a prologue and model of a more large-scale crisis in Eastern Europe, especially Russia.

The Conference on Security and Cooperation in Europe (CSCE), the only pan-European security arrangement, from the very beginning participated in attempts to settle the crisis in the Balkans, but failed to succeed.

Military conflicts during 1991-1992, on the territory of the former Yugoslavian Federation, Transdniestria, Southern Ossetia and Karabakh met very passive reaction in the CSCE. This situation provokes a question: how adequate to the existing challenges to security and stability in the Euro-Asian region are the CSCE principles and procedures, its institutions and mechanisms? The collapse of Yugoslavia and the USSR revealed sharp contradictions between the principles of inviolability of post-war borders, non-interference into domestic affairs and self-determination of peoples. But the CSCE in its present form will hardly settle these contradictions.

Fast growth in the number of CSCE members urgently dictates a necessity to reform the principle of voting by consensus (its transformation into "consensus minus one" is insufficient). The Yugoslavian crisis put the problem of coordination between the CSCE permanent structures (Committee of Senior Officials, Conflict Prevention Center and Secretariat) and operational management of their activities on the agenda. The procedures of CSCE mechanisms for peaceful settlement of disputes and for extraordinary situations turned out to be very slow, complicated and bureaucratic. Decisions adopted within the framework of these mechanisms are not mandatory for member states. This is the main drawback of the CSCE; it still remains an institution without an established basis in international law and faces lack of political, judicial, economic and military means of implementing its own decisions.

A similar comment can be made on the subject of ethnic problems. The CSCE in 1990-1991, failed to properly evaluate the threats of inter-ethnic clashes to European security and to elaborate any real method of settling such conflicts. Missions of rapporteurs and observers, the only instrument for crisis management under the CSCE, are ineffective and yield poor results. Another drawback of the CSCE is an absence of official relations with other international organizations in Europe, above of all with leading security institutions of the West (the only structures able to render real assistance to the CSCE in crisis management).

The ineffectiveness of pan-European security mechanisms, as steadily revealed in the increasing instability in the East, compels Western countries to strengthen their own security arrangements. At the same time it is clear that the main task of Western structures – maintaining security for a limited number of member states – prevent them from meeting current security challenges, which have a pan-European scale.[1] At present, the most dangerous threats come not from confrontation between European states, but rather from internal ethnic conflicts. That is why radical restructuring of Western military institutions seems to be a necessary response to the revolutionary changes in Europe of the late 1980s and early 1990s, but not a reliable guarantee against future crises.

Unfortunately, it is also difficult to characterize as sufficient the changes in political activity in the Western institutions. The policy of dialogue and partnership with Eastern Europe, proclaimed by NATO and the WEU; recognition of the CSCE as a necessary and important element in the system of European security; and a readiness to consolidate its structures do not lead to shaping new effective mechanisms of crisis management. The policy of NATO and the WEU related to the institutionalized structures of the European security system is still concentrated on eliminating disproportions, inherited from decades of confrontation.

NATO initiated the establishment of the North Atlantic Cooperation Council (NACC), which opened good prospects for discussing political-military aspects of East-West relations. The NACC proved its effectiveness in settling complicated questions of arms control, for example in eliminating problems connected with ratification of the CFE Treaty. Still, the direction of NACC's further evolution is rather unclear.

On the one hand, serious growth in its members will hardly allow the NACC to play a decisive role in solving the problems of disarmament and of institutional transformations of a European security system in the future. On the other hand, the NACC's image as a forum for East-West dialogue will also lose its attractiveness for member states. Quantitative growth in the NACC sharpened differences of opinion and proportional political weight among its members. Now the NACC is very similar to other pan-European forums, where East-West dialogue has been conducted for many years.

The readiness of NATO to interact with the CSCE and share resources and experience of the Alliance during peacekeeping operations opens good prospects for cooperation among European security institutions in managing and settling conflicts. But the potential for cooperation will hardly be realized unless concrete mechanisms of NATO-CSCE interaction are institutionalized. The main obstacle to developing such mechanisms is the necessity to ensure consensus within the

1 NATO's latest documents take into account the pan-European character of security challenges and security's indivisibility in modern Europe. The communiqué from NATO's Council session in Oslo (4.7.1992) states, that the security of NATO's countries is inseparably connected to the security of all other European states, and that a fundamental task of the Atlantic alliance is not only to maintain security for its members, but also to contribute through dialogue, partnership and cooperation to the construction of a new peaceful order in Europe. The communiqué speaks to NATO's ability to play a more essential role in crisis management on a pan-European scale.

CSCE on the question of whether to use military instruments for conflict settlement. NATO's military activity beyond its area of responsibility could also be blocked by some participants in the Alliance (i.e. Denmark or Iceland).

Even more doubts arise in relation to attempts of WEU countries not only to establish their own military structure with the French-German (European) corps as its nucleus,[2] but also regarding plans to use the French-German corps both in NATO's area of responsibility and in peacekeeping operations and humanitarian missions conducted under the auspices of the UN and the CSCE.

In the first place, use of the French-German corps as a regional instrument for crisis management contradicts the German constitution. Although reform of the constitution is on the current legislative agenda, partners of France and Germany have to consider today's realities. "Pan-European" prospects of a French-German corps are rather unclear, and this situation prevents other West European nations from joining the corps. There is another major obstacle for "Europeanization" of the French-German corps – France doesn't participate in NATO's integrated military command. Thus, the most probable option for the French-German corps' insertion into the Western defense system is NATO's operational control, and not the corps' direct subordination to NATO's command structures. Giving the same status to military regiments of other WEU countries, if they were to join the French-German corps, would inevitably weaken the military organization of NATO. The idea of "double hatting," already put forward, could hardly be implemented.

It is possible to state that separating responsibility between NATO and the EC/WEU in the process of Western security institutions' transformation will provoke unnecessary competition in the political and military dimensions of their activity. Such competition is not necessarily antagonistic, but any serious discord on the "Western pole of stability" would stimulate uncertainty in the whole system of European security, at a time when other countries, including Russia, are deeply interested in keeping the West European security system as stable and solid as possible. European states, facing the failure of their security structures to settle conflicts, have no other choice, but to apply traditional instruments (i.e. the United Nations). It was the UN, which turned out to be the most active, though ineffective, in managing the Balkan crisis. However, the study of the UN's possible role in preventing and settling European conflicts goes beyond the scope of this paper.

Meanwhile it is necessary to underline the limited effectiveness of the UN in preventing conflicts. Additionally, if the UN takes responsibility for settling a growing number of European conflicts, it will have less resources to maintain sta-

---

2 *WEU: The Operational Organization*. Report submitted on behalf of the Defence Committee by Sir Dudley Smith, Chairman and Rapporteur, Assembly of Western European Union (38th Ordinary session, First part), Doc. 1307, May 13, 1992, p. 10.

bility and peace in other regions, which have no comprehensive system of their own security institutions. At the same time, taking into account the inadequacy of the present structures, it seems to be useful to give the CSCE status as a UN "regional organization."

III. The European System: Scenarios of Development, Institutional Responses

At present, we see three main scenarios for transformation of the European security system.

1. The process of its evolution, on one hand, would be relatively slow, but, on the other, the situation in the East could quickly worsen. Events in Yugoslavia demonstrate that insufficient activity and ineffectiveness of international institutions at the beginning of a crisis ruin any possibility to control the situation later. A Russian drift toward a Yugoslavian scenario (sharpening ethnic and territorial problems in Southern Russia and the Tatar region, escalation of conflicts in the republics of the CIS, or involvement of Russia in these conflicts) could be put under some control only in its initial stages. If the international community fails to establish working mechanisms for coping with CIS problems, the whole system of international crisis management could collapse.

The serious danger of a growing inadequacy of European security structures is connected not only to the possible worsening of the situation in Eastern Europe, but also to a certain increase of instability in the West. Failures of European institutions in crisis management or trends toward isolation from Eastern conflicts by either NATO or EC/WEU will force some Western countries (especially Germany and France) to look for their own instruments of crisis management and possible promotion of national interests. This would mean a slackening of Western security institutions and would stimulate the process of re-nationalization of security policy. That is why Russia is deeply interested in maintaining and strengthening Western institutions as a stabilizing element in the European security system, even though Russia itself in a short-term perspective will hardly have any chance to enter these institutions.

2. Growing uncertainty in the East, especially in the region of the former USSR, would steadily push the West to concentrate efforts on providing security solely through the use of its own institutions. Apprehension of Western countries to become involved in conflicts in the East could compel them to distance themselves from those conflicts; this would mean de-facto isolation form Russia and other CIS states. Such developments could also lead to a resurgence of political-military confrontation in Europe. But, if the post-war bloc system was more or less strategically balanced and therefore relatively stable, a new confrontation under the conditions of instability in the East could be dangerously explosive. The process of spreading

Western security guarantees to East European states would only strengthen the above mentioned negative trends; because (1) it will leave Russia without allies and political partners, (2) it will tend to undermine the cohesion of the West. Thus, the combination of instability and a new divide in Europe would repeat the situation of the inter-war years, but on a qualitatively much higher level of consequences.

3. The third and most preferable scenario suggests activity aimed at establishing effective mechanisms for preventing and managing conflicts. At present, many in the Russian political elite understand that the only way to avoid Russian isolation is to strengthen its own security and European security as well, and to eliminate old approaches toward European institutions as competing structures. The new idea of a system of interlocking security institutions should be implemented.

Even the most optimistic scenario would show certain limits for rapprochement between Russia and Western security institutions. That is why Russia is deeply interested in advancing and strengthening CSCE structures to form a basis of reliable mechanisms for crisis management. Weaknesses of CSCE would deprive Russia from participating in solving the problems of European security and would hinder Moscow from occupying the status of an influential political power.

Russia, acting in the CSCE as the main successor to the USSR, has a special interest in its development: the CSCE is one of the few international organizations where Russian diplomacy really enjoys equal rights with other nations. Active participation in pan-European dialogue within the CSCE will allow Russia to solve the following problems in its foreign policy:

- Providing the political and judicial basis for maintaining the inviolability of Russian borders; protection of rights of Russian and other national minorities in all former Soviet republics; reforming internal legislation with special attention toward human rights and democratic development of state institutions;
- Developing institutionalized multilateral interaction with countries of East-Central Europe; using the CSCE as an opportunity for promoting intensive political dialogue with all states in this region; settling of certain aspects of political relations between Russia and other CIS states;
- Opening the only channel of institutionalized interaction with the West on the broad agenda of European problems; the possible cooperation between the CSCE and NATO-EC/WEU probably means an additional channel of interaction with Western institutions. It is especially urgent because Russia could make a serious contribution to developing procedural rules, regulating cooperation between the CSCE and NATO-EC/WEU;
- Negotiating within the framework of the CSCE new approaches toward the problem of conventional disarmament, implementation of the 1990 CFE Treaty and further agreements, signed during "Helsinki-2;"

- Establishing and developing within the CSCE collective mechanisms; on one hand, that will provide international support and legitimation to Russia's efforts in maintaining security in the area of the former USSR and on the other, these mechanisms would mean direct participation for Russia in discussing all items on the pan-European agenda.

The Prague session of the Council of Foreign Ministers (January 1992) granted full membership in the CSCE to Kazakhstan, the Caucasus and Central Asian states. Such "Eastern-oriented" enlargement of the CSCE was supported by Russia, above all because it saw in the Prague decision an attempt to legitimate international participation in preventing and regulating conflicts on the territory of the former USSR.

At the same time many people in Russia share the fear that such quantitative growth of the CSCE could "bury" the whole process under the burden of already new organizational and procedural problems. The Prague decision has a philosophical aspect: the CSCE faces the situation, where its new members do not follow the fundamental European values on human rights. The CSCE pays surprisingly little attention to massive violations of human rights in the Baltic states, in the Caucasus, in Central Asia, and even in Russia. It seems also, that many CSCE member states approached the process of adopting new members in a very formal way. The West has little desire to be involved in the settlement of sharp ethnic and political problems in South-Eastern Europe, Central Asia and the Caucasus. Under such circumstances the CSCE has poor chances of influencing in real terms the situation in those regions.[3] Participation of the CIS states in the CSCE and in the NACC seems to be the maximum desired level of Western political involvement in the internal affairs of the former USSR. The maximum level of desired Western economic involvement also seems to be the membership of the CIS states in the IMF, the World Bank, EBRD and Western humanitarian and technical assistance.

Russia, due to its role in preserving stability within the CIS is deeply interested in developing the CSCE mechanism for prevention and settlement of conflicts which was established during the "Helsinki-2" follow-up conference. The Helsinki decision about possible peacekeeping operations under the CSCE "umbrella," which allows the CSCE to apply for assistance not only to NATO and EC/WEU, but also to the CIS peacekeeping mechanism, may be evaluated as a multilateral de-facto legitimation of Russia's role in the CIS region.

---

3 This could be illustrated by the silence of foreign ministers in Helsinki (March 1992). They were reluctant to discuss the fact of war between two CSCE members (Armenia and Azerbaijan), conflicts in Transdniestria and Ossetia. Involvement of the CSCE in the conflict in Karabakh has a very formal character.

At the same time, from any point of view any attempts of Western states to compensate for the drawbacks of the CSCE by expanding their own security guarantees could only hamper further progress of the CSCE. The above-mentioned situation may be avoided by using the potential of NATO and the WEU for establishing military and political-military pillars in the CSCE. Western institutions would find in the CSCE a firm political basis for their own activity in the conflict zones of the East. Legitimation of Western security institutions' activity in the East not through direct extension of their responsibility, but rather through the formation of new international mechanisms with advanced frameworks for military instruments could be more preferable to the West, too. In this case Western countries, not limiting themselves with rigid commitments, will acquire a channel of effective control over the situation in the East.

Closer interaction between Western institutions and the CSCE will open Russia to better prospects for deepening cooperation with NATO and EC/WEU within the CSCE framework. This is necessary for legitimation of Russia's role in crisis management in the CIS zone and also for putting this role under international control within a multilateral framework.

A mechanism for political consultation between Russia and leading Western countries, which could exist without formal links under the CSCE or other European institutions, could also be helpful. Its main task would be discussing general problems of conflict prevention and stability in the region of the former USSR. Formation of such a mechanism would gain political support of Russia and recognize its role and responsibilities within the CIS. Moscow's efforts in conflict settlement would receive additional political weight. This mechanism would also provide the West with a leverage over Russian behavior in such conflicts.

The first step necessary to provide real interaction between the main elements of the European security system (CSCE, NATO and EC/WEU) is the establishment of formal relations between these institutions. Any practical achievements in their cooperation would improve the degree of openness of Western institutions and limit isolationist tendencies (so vivid in the WEU's relationship with Russia) within them. Cooperation with the CSCE would accelerate the transformation of Western institutions into pan-European structures.

IV. Prospects for the CSCE

Development of CSCE structures is one of the most important conditions in the process of strengthening the European security system on the basis of interaction and interdependency of its institutionalized elements. In this endeavor the CSCE should solve three main problems.

The first one embraces the disarmament dimension of the CSCE. Apart from the implementation of the CFE Treaty, ratification of the Vienna CSBM Document, Open Skies Treaty and the Final Document of the "Vienna-2" negotiations it is necessary to realize the provision in the "Helsinki-2" Final Document on the establishment of the Forum for Cooperation in the Sphere of Security, to elaborate strict procedural rules for its Special and Consultative Committees, and to give its decisions a legal foundation.

The second problem is connected with the formation of the political-military dimension of the CSCE. The political-military dimension should consist of mechanisms for extraordinary situations and for the peaceful settlement of disputes; other procedures for conflict prevention; and should enrich the CSCE with means of political, judicial and military influence on conflicting parties. Only such facets could provide mechanisms and give meaning to cooperation with NATO and EC/WEU.

The third problem concerns the question of procedure (decision making mechanisms, distribution of power and coordination between CSCE structures, and the legal foundation of CSCE decisions). Quantitative growth in the CSCE makes it very difficult to develop decisions, even when there are no serious political disagreements, due to obstacles of a technical and bureaucratic nature. Especially acute is the problem of how to reform the rule of consensus (or "consensus minus one"), while voting on crisis situations. The only way to strengthen CSCE structures is to introduce voting by a qualified majority. The sphere of majority voting should be strictly limited, because this decision making procedure clearly undermines the principle of equal rights of all CSCE members in favor of great powers.

Many of the CSCE organizational and procedural deadlocks could be overcome with the formation of a CSCE Security Council. This idea was widely circulated in the Fall 1991, but received little support among European states. Nevertheless, the idea deserves additional consideration.

(1) A CSCE Security Council is badly needed for arranging cooperation between CSCE and other European institutions (other levels of the CSCE hierarchy are either "overcrowded" or have no legal authority).

(2) A CSCE Security Council seems to be a structure necessary for successful formation of a possible political-military dimension to the CSCE.

(3) A CSCE Security Council allows reforming and simplifying the highly bureaucratic and ineffective decision making process of the CSCE, which otherwise may lead the whole pan-European process to a deadlock. Some decisions and documents developed by the Security Council later could be "ratified" by qualified majority voting in other CSCE structures. Such procedures could help to avoid slow and unproductive diplomatic bargaining involving all CSCE members.

(4) A CSCE Security Council, while including leading European powers, would improve Russia's status and responsibilities in the sphere of European security. In the same way it would strengthen the US position, thus reducing fears of a rapid decline of America's military and political role in European affairs. Occupying a place at the Security Council, Germany would further restore its influence in Europe, eliminating the remnants of all postwar political limitations. Membership in the CSCE Security Council would allow neutral and non-aligned states and other countries, not present in NATO and EC/WEU, to assume a more solid place in the interlocking system of European security institutions.

(5) Cooperation within the framework of a CSCE Security Council between Russia and leading Western nations could form a basis for their long-term strategic alliance as a cornerstone of stability and security not only in Europe, but in a more broader area – from Vancouver to Tokyo.

New institutions and mechanisms should help fill the security vacuum in Eastern Europe. Armed conflicts on the territory of the former USSR and growing instability within the Russian Federation and on its borders present the main danger to the security of Russia and Europe as a whole. But, as of yet there have been no real attempts to cope with this danger through collective measures by European countries. However, now such steps have better chances to be successful due to a number of new factors.

(1) A one-year period of uncertainty in Russian foreign policy in relation to the former Soviet republics should come to its end. In recent months Russia actively participated in settling crisis situations in the CIS region.

(2) The combination of Russia's political efforts (mediation) with activity of the CIS peacekeeping forces (also de-facto Russian) allowed the extinguishing over a short span of time of conflicts in Ossetia and Transdniestria, thus opening the way for their political settlement. Russian policy can be interpreted here as its first attempt in forming crisis management mechanisms on the territory of the former USSR.

(3) Settlement of these two conflicts greatly helped to improve the prestige of Russia within the CIS. Now newly independent republics involved in different conflicts strive, more than in the past toward constructive interaction with Russia in the sphere of crisis management.[4]

(4) The implementation of the idea of national independence and the high costs of disintegration have led members of the CIS toward closer relations with

---

4 The plenipotentiary representative of Azerbaijan in Moscow, Mr. Khikmet Gadji-Zade, for example, characterized Russia's role in Karabakh in the following way: "In perspective it is impossible to imagine peaceful efforts without Russia's participation. Obviously nobody could influence the settlement of conflict as greatly as Russia could." *Izvestija*, 5.9.1992.

Russia. Under current circumstances, there is an opportunity for the establishment of effective alliances between Russia, Belarus and Kazakhstan forming the necessary skeleton of the CIS and promoting activity aimed at prevention and containment of conflicts.

The political weight of Russia within the former Soviet region ensures Moscow's hope to meet the increased political support of the West. Such support seems to be crucial, if not for the legitimation of Russia's role in crisis management within the CIS, then for its de-facto recognition. As mentioned above, this aim also may be reached through the formation of a special institute for political consultations and interaction in the security sphere between Russia and the West. Such a step appears quite logical especially after the Munich summit "seven plus one."

V. Conclusion

Probably the best way to regulate inevitable conflicts on the territory of the former USSR would be the serious involvement of international institutions, procedures and legal norms. That was one of the main reasons why some analysts and politicians in the USSR and Russia, foreseeing this inevitability, insisted on the speedy build-up of the CSCE and its powers. But for various reasons this build-up has been too slow and clearly lagging behind demand. It is also relatively clear by now, at least for these authors, that Western countries have proved to be unwilling to involve themselves deeply in the prevention and management of conflicts on the territory of the former USSR. A very similar unwillingness by the USSR and Russian governments has proved to be dangerously counterproductive. The most obvious case is the Karabakh conflict, which could have been avoided in its early stages. Gorbachev's administration stayed away and now Armenia is living through a national catastrophy, while the whole Caucasus has been "lebanized" and the dynamic spreads to the territory of Russia. Similar *laissez-faire* approaches toward Central Asia could prove to be even more devastating.

Under these circumstances one of the few, if not the only, solution could be (along with strengthening European institutions and capabilities) assigning to Russia and the CIS of a special role in managing conflicts on most of the territory of the former USSR. But this special role should become part and parcel of an all-European policy of general CSCE efforts under its supervision and within its legal framework. One could think of a creation of two or more regional CSCE substructures, obviously an "Eastern" and "Western" one. In the first one, Russia and the CIS would play a leading role under the general CSCE auspices and supervision. In the second, this role could be performed by NATO and the WEU. These two substructures should not be clearly deliniated, they should remain interlocked both in geographic and political terms. One could and, indeed, should envisage cooperation in peacekeeping forces, exchange of observers, and mutual economic and logistical support of peacekeeping operations.

This idea is imperfect, has obvious weaknesses, and smacks of zones of influence. However, the alternative is either a deepening security vacuum and expansion of zones of instability on the territory of the former Soviet Union, almost inevitably bringing ultra-nationalist and militarist forces to power in Russia, and/or Russia trying to control instability unilaterally, outside of a European framework. Under such a scenario regression toward neo-imperialism or excessive violence seems more likely. The inevitable ostracism could then push Russian leadership along a Serbian path.

Clearly the situation lacks easy solutions. However, a solution along the proposed lines (together with the continous build-up of CSCE and related structures) could, if properly handled, provide instruments for curtailment of the spread of Yugoslavian type situations to the territory of the former Soviet Union. If it spreads, the whole European structure will probably begin to come unraveled.

12. Das Zusammenwirken multinationaler Institutionen: Neue Optionen für kollektive Verteidigung und internationale Friedensmissionen?

Uwe Nerlich

I. Der Wandel des Multilateralismus in der postkonfrontativen Ära

1. Der Triumph des Jahres 1990 im Rückblick

Das Jahr 1990 war einer jener "seltenen Augenblicke der Geschichte", von denen Henry Kissinger an einer anderen politischen Zäsur festgehalten hat, daß sie politischen Führern ermögliche, sich "substantiell neuen und kreativen Aufgaben der Diplomatie zuzuwenden. Die Lasten der Vergangenheit waren überwunden, das internationale Umfeld im Fluß, wie es nur einmal in einer Generation geschieht – bereit, neu formiert zu werden".[1] 1972 war dieses Resümee verfrüht: Auf die internationalen Umwälzungen, die mit dem Ende des Vietnamkriegs ihr Ende gefunden hatten, folgte Watergate und damit eine mühselige Verlangsamung *der* Prozesse, für deren Erfolg die Weltpolitik in wichtigen Regionen ohnehin noch nicht reif war. Hätte die Diplomatie 1972 ihren freien Lauf gehabt, so wäre eine frühere Beendigung der Konfrontation denkbar gewesen, aber auf einer völlig anderen Grundlage und mit einer ebenso anderen Struktur der resultierenden internationalen Verhältnisse.

Was 1990 Gestalt gewann, war durch viele Umstände – Zufälle der Geschichte – bedingt, aber *daß* es zum Umbruch internationaler Verhältnisse kam, war das Ergebnis langfristiger Entwicklungen. Dies charakterisiert, warum 1990 als Ende einer Ära von der hoffnungsvollen Erwartung fortschreitender internationaler Neuordnung begleitet war und doch sehr rasch die Ungewißheit darüber hinzukam, ob mit der Beseitigung von Antagonismen schon tragfähige Grundlagen dafür gegeben waren, die destruktiven Kräfte, die mit der Stabilität der Ost-West-Beziehungen gebannt waren, und die Aufbauaufgaben, die mit der Ausweitung von Demokratie und Marktwirtschaft gegeben waren, in eine geordnete Entwicklung einzubeziehen.

Die irakische Aggression mit der Perspektive grundlegend veränderter Kontrolle über zwei Drittel der Erdölproduktion der OPEC stellte die erste Interferenz dar. Der zunehmend sichtbare Zerfall der UdSSR, die eben zugleich Antagonist und Stabilitätsträger war und seit 1990 vor allem in der letzteren Rolle gesehen wurde, machte vollends klar, daß die Situation Anfang der 90er Jahre jener nach 1945 in der dramatischen Verbindung von Triumph und Ungewißheit über den

---

1 Henry A. *Kissinger*, White House Years, Boston/Toronto 1979, S. 1471.

weiteren Fortgang glich. Die Neuordnung nach 1945 hat einige Jahre gedauert, aber in jenen Jahren ging es um die zentrale Frage, ob die Vereinigten Staaten ihr gewaltiges Potential in die Gestaltung der Nachkriegsverhältnisse einbringen würden oder nicht. Dies war lange ungewiß. Das internationale Engagement der USA hat den weiteren Gang der Entwicklung auf allen Ebenen internationaler Strukturbildung entscheidend geprägt.

Nach 1990 stehen große Teile der nördlichen Hemisphäre wiederum vor der Aufgabe der Neuordnung. Die UdSSR, die während eines langwierigen Transformationsprozesses schließlich zum Stabilitätsträger und darin zum Partner der USA geworden war, zerbrach letztlich folgerichtig, wenn auch in kaum zu erwartender Weise gewaltfrei, an der Logik eben dieser Transformation und stellt gegenwärtig die größte Herausforderung für jeden Versuch internationaler Neuordnung dar. Mit dem Bilateralismus der beiden Weltmächte der Nachkriegszeit schwand zudem die Kraft der USA, eine "neue Weltordnung" maßgeblich zu gestalten. Der Golfkrieg hatte schon die engen Grenzen der amerikanischen Führungsrolle deutlich gemacht. Der politische Niedergang des 41. Präsidenten der USA signalisierte den Wandel amerikanischer Prioritäten, die Hinwendung zur Agenda innerer Erneuerung. Das ist der entscheidende Unterschied zu 1945. Diese Erneuerung ist Voraussetzung für eine erneute internationale Führungsrolle der USA, aber sie reduziert die internationale Ordnungsfähigkeit der USA in der Übergangszeit, in der sie – nach der Analogie von 1945 – am stärksten gefordert wäre. Der amerikanisch-sowjetische Bilateralismus hat sich – Ironie der Geschichte – vor allem auf das Management *der* Zerstörungsmittel reduziert, in deren Schatten die gemeinsame Stabilitätsträgerschaft der USA und der UdSSR entstanden war.

2. Perspektive eines organischen Zusammenwirkens multinationaler Institutionen

Die künftige Rolle multinationaler Sicherheitsinstitutionen ist in der Perspektive dieser veränderten Weltlage zu sehen. Dem Ende der UdSSR ging das Ende der von ihr instituierten multinationalen Organisationen voraus – vor allem des Warschauer Pakts. Der Umbruch der Jahre 1990/91 hat seine relativ ruhigen Bahnen ohne Zweifel darin gefunden, daß einige westliche und gesamteuropäische Institutionen von unterschiedlichen Teilnehmern am Prozeß, die auch zu völlig auseinanderstrebenden politischen Vorgehensweisen disponiert waren, als Strukturen akzeptiert und genutzt wurden, die eine Verträglichkeit von Interessen und eine Verminderung von Ungewißheiten ermöglichten.

Die Londoner Erklärung vom 5./6. Juli 1990 signalisierte der UdSSR, daß die NATO eine Form der Einbindung eines vereinigten Deutschlands und der Perpetuierung des amerikanischen Engagements in Europa gewährleisten kann, die auch aus sowjetischer Sicht als stabilisierend verstanden werden konnte – ein Prozeß freilich, der bei den mittelosteuropäischen Staaten rasch die Hoffnung auf Einbeziehung in das Bündnis mit den USA, bei der UdSSR die Sorge vor völliger Ausgrenzung auslöste.

Die Pariser KSZE-Konferenz mit der Charta vom 21. November 1990 versprach in der Art, wie sie die deutsche Wiedervereinigung im Rahmen der bestehenden westlichen Institutionen sanktionierte, "neue Strukturen und Institutionen des KSZE-Prozesses" zu ermöglichen.[2] Die KSZE erschien als der Rahmen, in dem auf der Grundlage einer rückversichernden NATO und unter den relativ stabilen Bedingungen, wie sie das VKSE-Abkommen in Aussicht stellte, Stabilitätspartnerschaft auf dem eurasischen Kontinent gestaltet werden konnte.

Soweit solche Entwicklung Dynamik gewinnen konnte, wurde diese vor allem von der EG erwartet. Folgerichtig wurden am 14. Dezember 1990 die beiden Regierungskonferenzen mit dem Ziel der Bildung einer Europäischen Union aufgenommen – mit dem schließlichen Ergebnis des Maastricht-Vertrages. Es bahnte sich eine Entwicklung an, in der die EG (verstärkt durch den G-7-Prozeß, die G-24 u.a.) der maßgebende Motor gesamteuropäischer Stabilisierung als Resultat innerer Reformen und neuer internationaler Kooperationsformen ist, die KSZE den absichernden Rahmen für Stabilitätspartnerschaft und fortschreitende Wertegemeinschaft bildet und die NATO der Rückhalt für beides sein könnte: durch Einbindung der USA, durch Entlastung des europäischen Integrationsprozesses von zu frühen Festlegungen in der Frage gemeinsamer Verteidigung innerhalb einer EU und als Garantie für den Fall postsowjetischer Fehlentwicklungen.

Diese europäische Sicherheitsarchitektur hätte vermutlich organisch entstehen können. In der Tat kam es im Spätherbst 1990 zu mehrseitigen Konsultationen zwischen dem NATO-Generalsekretariat, der EG-Kommission und dem WEU-Generalsekretariat, mit der Aussicht auch auf Sondierungen mit der KSZE (nach Konstituierung des Ausschusses der Hohen Beamten) und den Vereinten Nationen. Das Ziel war es, ein zweckmäßiges Zusammenwirken der wichtigen Sicherheitsinstitutionen zu erreichen und konkurrierende nationale Präferenzen hinsichtlich der künftigen Rolle einzelner Institutionen frühzeitig einzufangen. Im NATO-Generalsekretariat war mit dieser Zielsetzung die Konzeption eines *framework of interlocking institutions* entwickelt worden.[3]

---

2 Charta von Paris vom 21.11.1990.

3 Dieses Konzept ging auf Überlegungen der SWP zurück, die auf dem 2nd NATO-Review in Ebenhausen vom 9. bis zum 11.3.1990 vorgestellt worden waren (vgl. Das Atlantische Bündnis am Scheideweg. Mögliche politische und militärische Funktionen in einem sich verändernden Europa, unveröffemtlichtes Manuskript, Stiftung Wissenschaft und Politik, Ebenhausen, Juli 1990, S. 47f). Sie sind vom damaligen Beigeordneten Stellvertretenden Generalsekretär, Hans-Henning Wegener, ausgestaltet worden. Initiator dieser mehrseitigen Konsultationen zwischen den wichtigen Institutionen war denn auch das NATO-Generalsekretariat.

3. Interferierende Entwicklungen

Zu einer solchen organischen Entwicklung ist es im weiteren Verlauf bekanntlich nicht gekommen:

- Der *Golfkrieg* hatte mehrere Wirkungen: Er demonstrierte eine bis dahin beispiellose Instrumentalität der Vereinten Nationen bei der Ermöglichung der Ad-hoc-Koalition gegen den Irak, die die VN als wichtige Sicherheitsinstitution in der postkonfrontativen Ära erscheinen ließ. Zugleich veränderte er die NATO-Agenda des Londoner Gipfels vor allem im britischen Sinne, indem der kollektive Verteidigungszweck der NATO noch im Vorfeld des Pariser KSZE-Gipfels wieder in den Vordergrund rückte. Die NATO erwies auch während der Operationen Desert Shield und Desert Storm ihren Nutzen dank ihrer vielfältigen Unterstützungsfunktionen. Zugleich hat der Golfkrieg den Abzug amerikanischer Streitkräfte aus Westeuropa und vor allem der Bundesrepublik beschleunigt, der den kollektiven Verteidigungszweck der NATO wiederum zurücktreten läßt.
- Die *postjugoslawischen Konflikte* offenbarten zunehmend, daß die drei Institutionen, die vor allem auf militärische Sicherheit in Europa spezialisiert sind, nämlich die NATO, die WEU und die KSZE, von wichtigen Mitgliedstaaten aus unterschiedlichen Interessen jeweils am Wahrnehmen wichtiger Aufgaben gehindert werden und wohl auch von vornherein für derartige Konflikte – die ersten europäischen Kriege seit 1945 – nicht eingerichtet sind. Statt dessen kam zunächst die EG als Sicherheitsakteur ins Spiel, die für solche Rollen bis dahin nicht vorgesehen war, und schließlich wurden – abgesehen vom Zypern-Konflikt – erstmals die VN in europäische Konflikte eingeschaltet.

  Dies hätte eine erweiterte Konzertierung des Zusammenwirkens multinationaler Institutionen aufgrund konzertierter Politik wichtiger Mitgliedstaaten eröffnen können. Aber genau diese Konzertierung oder, allgemeiner, eine *gemeinsame Konzeption für den kollektiven Umgang mit derartigen Konflikten und* die *Rolle der einzelnen multinationalen Institutionen dabei* kam nicht zustande und wurde letztlich auch gar nicht angestrebt oder für möglich gehalten.

  Diese weitgehende Indifferenz der Institutionen und ihrer wichtigsten Träger hat zwar Bemühungen um die funktionale Verknüpfung multinationaler Institutionen nicht verhindert, auf die noch einzugehen ist. Sie hat aber bis auf weiteres die Perspektive eines "framework of interlocking institutions" verstellt, also eines gemeinsamen konzeptionellen und organisatorischen Rahmens für das jeweils zweckmäßige Zusammenwirken in einer Situation, zu dem die NATO in ihrer Erklärung von Rom immerhin festgestellt hat, daß künftig keine einzelne Institution ausreicht, um internationale Konflikte zu bewältigen.
- Die dritte Entwicklung, die einen organischen Verlauf in Richtung einer multiinstitutionellen Sicherheitsarchitektur verhindert oder zumindest verlangsamt

und kompliziert hat, ist der *Zerfall der UdSSR.* Mit ihr ist der gerade etablierte östliche Stabilitätspartner innerhalb der KSZE verlorengegangen. Die Anfang 1992 in Prag erfolgte Ausweitung der KSZE auf alle Republiken der ehemaligen UdSSR nahm der KSZE zugleich viel von ihrem besonderen Charakter als einer Normen- und Wertegemeinschaft, die auf längere Sicht eine Sicherheitskultur sui generis würde hervorbringen können. Sie war damit eine noch unzureichend institutionalisierte Gruppierung ohne klar definierte und akzeptierte Trägernationen, mit einem "Multilateralismus der großen Zahlen"[4] und ohne wirksame Handlungsmöglichkeiten in einer wachsenden Anzahl vor allem postsowjetischer Konflikte. Das Entwicklungspotential der KSZE, das dieser 1990 noch zugemessen worden war, erscheint so gegenwärtig blockiert.

Die institutionelle Perspektive der KSZE wurde durch eine weitere Auswirkung des Zerfalls der UdSSR noch kompliziert: Die im Ansatz sinnvolle Konzeption eines Nordatlantikkooperationsrats (NAKR/NAAC) für die Zusammenarbeit zwischen der NATO und den Staaten Osteuropas, mit denen eine besondere sicherheitspolitische Liaison zu erwarten war oder sich schon abzeichnete, wurde schließlich auf alle Republiken der GUS ausgeweitet, also, wie bei der KSZE, auch auf die nichtslawischen Republiken, deren Zugehörigkeit den Bezug zu einer entstehenden europäischen Sicherheitskultur weiter schwächen mußte. Paradoxerweise waren es vor allem die USA, die konsequent vor einer Verdoppelung von NATO-Aufgaben durch die WEU gewarnt hatten, die nun eine Duplikation zumindest potentieller KSZE-Aufgaben durch die NATO in Gestalt des NACC herbeiführten.

Der Zerfall der UdSSR veränderte aber auch die Zweckbestimmung und das Selbstverständnis der NATO. Trotz der in russischer Hand verbleibenden militärischen Fähigkeiten ließ sich die NATO in ihrer reformierten Gestalt nicht mehr auf die kontinentale Balance mit einer östlichen militärischen Großmacht als Hauptzweck ausrichten: Fehlende politische Strukturen und militärische Kohäsion, die nochmals vergrößerte geostrategische Distanzierung von Westeuropa mit der Ukraine als zusätzlichem Puffer sowie der wachsende Zeitbedarf für eine Rekonstitution des russischen Offensivpotentials wirken hier zusammen.

Mit der schwindenden militärischen Funktion der NATO und dem entsprechend nachlassenden sicherheitspolitischen Engagement der USA in Europa, das in der Entwicklung von der amerikanischen Demarche vom 21. Februar 1991 bis zur Indifferenz gegenüber den postjugoslawischen Konflikten Ausdruck fand und sich in weiteren Truppenreduzierungen fortsetzen wird, gelangt die WEU nach ihrer jahrzehntelangen institutionellen Scheinexistenz und nach

---

4 Miles *Kahler*, Multilateralism with Small and Large Numbers, in: International Organization, 46 (Sommer 1992) 3, S. 708.

der Schwebelage, in die sie der Kompromiß von Maastricht versetzt hat, in ein Stadium, in dem sie wirklich zum Rahmen westeuropäischer Verteidigungskooperation werden kann, und zwar mit dem absehbaren Resultat, daß sich ihre institutionelle Eigenständigkeit im Maße ihrer Einbeziehung in die entstehende EU wieder verlieren wird.

Schließlich hat der Zerfall der UdSSR auch die dynamische Rolle der EG vermindert: Die Dimensionen der gesamteuropäischen Stabilisierungsaufgabe haben sich mit dem Zerfall so vergrößert, daß die EG vor zwei gleichermaßen unpraktikablen Alternativen steht, nämlich entweder die GUS aus der Stabilisierung auszugrenzen oder Grenzen der Machbarkeit und die damit gegebenen Ungewißheiten hinzunehmen. Die Rolle der Bundesrepublik als Dynamo der EG ist durch den Wegfall der östlichen Märkte der neuen Bundesländer zusätzlich geschwächt worden. Zugleich wird eine fortschreitende Vergemeinschaftung bei gleichzeitiger Wahrnehmung der Stabilisierungsaufgabe und schrittweiser Einbeziehung mittelosteuropäischer Länder immer schwieriger harmonisierbar. Die zunehmend diffusen Prioritäten der Gemeinschaft haben überdies einen politischen Diskurs in den Mitliedstaaten erschwert, der den evolutionären Charakter des Maastricht-Projekts für die Bevölkerung mitvollziehbar macht.

Auswirkungen hat der Zerfall der UdSSR im übrigen auch auf die VN, die während des Golfkrieges gerade ihre Renaissance erlebt zu haben schienen. Ein Rußland, das nicht nur von autoritären Entwicklungen, sondern selbst wieder vom Zerfall bedroht ist und interne Konflikte zunehmend unter Inanspruchnahme der VN wie der KSZE zu lösen bzw. eigenes Vorgehen auf diese Weise zu legitimieren sucht, und das im übrigen – ein wichtiger Teilaspekt – als einer der drei Depositarstaaten des NV-Vertrages die Kontrolle über ein ungeheures Nuklearwaffenpotential zu verlieren droht, wird kaum als Stabilitätsträger im VN-Rahmen akzeptiert werden. Drohende und tatsächliche Konflikte mit anderen ehemaligen Republiken der UdSSR, die inzwischen Mitglied den VN sind, machen die Stellung Rußlands in den VN zusätzlich kontrovers. Mit der östlichen Gegenmacht ist aber auch die amerikanische Stellung in den VN und, allgemeiner, weltpolitisch verändert worden. Mit einem geschwächten Rußland wird keine Reziprozität im bilateralen Verhältnis entstehen. Dies wird den stärker werdenden Hang der USA zum offenen Unilateralismus und damit zugleich die Ambivalenz einer amerikanischen Position als einziger verbliebener Weltmacht noch deutlicher hervortreten lassen: Als Ordnungsträger – auch spezifisch der VN – sind die USA unverzichtbar, was Sorge vor einer eher kontinentalen Orientierung amerikanischer Politik aufkommen läßt, wie sie in hochgesteckten Erwartungen an die Nordamerikanische Freihandelszone NAFTA sichtbar werden. Zugleich wird eine Vormachtstellung der USA ohne Gegenmacht zunehmend auf Ablehnung stoßen, was eine amerikanische Abwendung vom globalen Geschehen verstärken könnte.

4. Die Krise des Multilateralismus

Betrachtet man die Kerninstitutionen im Lichte der Erwartungen der Jahre 1990/91, so läßt sich für die Europäische Union wie die WEU, für NATO und NACC, für die KSZE und die VN feststellen, daß die weitere institutionelle Evolution in allen Fällen unsicher ist. Alle befinden sich in einem Prozeß der Veränderung. Es gibt in keinem Fall einen stabilen Status quo. Aber für alle ist auch zu sagen, daß *Entwicklungsziel und Zweckbestimmung ungewiß* und in der Sicht von Hauptträgern strittig sind, daß die Größe des Mitgliederkreises und teilweise auch seine Qualität die Wirksamkeit der Institutionen vermindern oder sogar die gemeinsamen Grundlagen in Frage stellen, daß das *Rollenverständnis im Verhältnis zu anderen Institutionen an Profil verliert* oder sich verschiebt und daß die instrumentellen Interessen der hauptbeteiligten Trägernationen nicht mehr von einem zielgerichteten und kooperationsorientierten Impuls dominiert sind.

Die Alternative einer stärkeren Renationalisierung mag überwiegend als weniger attraktiv – unter Umständen aber dennoch unausweichlich – angesehen werden. Aber die eher schwindenden Aussichten für das Gelingen der gesamteuropäischen Stabilisierungsaufgabe und die zunehmenden Probleme und Beschränkungen eines multinationalen Konfliktmanagements rücken evolutionäre Zielsetzungen im Sinne fortschreitender Integration und kooperativer Strukturbildung aus dem Blickfeld pragmatischer Politik.

Vor allem seit dem Winter 1991/92 und dem Frühjahr 1992 ist der evolutionäre Elan multinationaler Institutionen deutlich schwächer geworden. Die *Europäische Unionsbildung* ist angesichts der fraglichen politischen Zustimmung in den meisten Mitglieds- und Beitrittsländern in ihrer Finalität und Entwicklungsfähigkeit in Frage gestellt, wobei das eigentlich beunruhigende nicht die unklare Zukunft des Vertrages von Maastricht ist, sondern der absehbare Verlust *jeder* evolutionären Perspektive für Europa im Falle der Ablehnung. Mit dieser zögernden Konsensbildung verbindet sich der geringe Erfolg in der praktischen Zusammenarbeit der Mitglieder, zum Beispiel der GASP.[5]

Die *Reform der NATO* ist bisher kaum über die Beschlüsse von Rom im Dezember 1991 hinausgegangen. Zwar hat die NATO auf ihrer Ministertagung in Oslo am 4. Juni 1992 wiederholt, daß die Sicherheit "im euro-atlantischen Raum sich zunehmend auf einem Geflecht ineinandergreifender, sich gegenseitig verstärkender

5 Zu den wenigen eher positiven Entwicklungen, wenn auch begleitet von einer im übrigen ineffektiven Politik der EG in den postjugoslawischen Konflikten, gehört die Rolle, die die EG neben den VN bei der Genfer Jugoslawien-Konferenz einnimmt.

Institutionen aufbauen" wird.[6] Zu diesem Zweck nahm sie in Oslo teilweise den seit dem Herbst 1991 von Generalsekretär Wörner vertretenen Vorschlag auf, "von Fall zu Fall, in Übereinstimmung mit unseren eigenen Verfahren, friedenserhaltende Aktivitäten der KSZE einschließlich der Bereitstellung von Ressourcen und Fachwissen des Bündnisses zu unterstützen".[7]

Derzeit gilt jedoch in der Praxis weiter, daß "bisher der NATO noch kein konkreter Platz im Rahmen des angestrebten Systems 'ineinandergreifender Institutionen' zugewiesen" ist.[8] Der Fall einer kollektiven Beistandspflicht wird unter künftigen Umständen kaum noch eintreten, wenngleich Frankreich die NATO nach Möglichkeit darauf zu beschränken suchte. Andererseits fehlt es bei nahezu allen NATO-Mitgliedern an Vorstellungen für erweiterte Sicherheit zugunsten der mittelosteuropäischen Staaten, die über eine Mitgliedschaft im NACC – auf einer Ebene mit Rußland und allen übrigen ehemaligen Republiken der UdSSR – hinausgehen. Hier hilft gegenwärtig auch die *Konzeption mandatierter NATO-Aktivitäten* nicht weiter, zumal sie bisher auf die Unterstützung friedenserhaltender Maßnahmen begrenzt geblieben ist.

Die *KSZE* hat zwar in Helsinki eine Klarstellung ihres Verhältnisses zu den VN vorgenommen, indem sie sich als "umfassenden regionalen Zusammenschluß im Sinne des Kapitels VIII der Charta" definiert und "als solcher ein bedeutendes Bindeglied zwischen europäischer und globaler Sicherheit darstellt",[9] was den Vorstel-

---

6 Kommuniqué der Ministertagung des Nordatlantikrates vom 4.6.1992, in: Bulletin des Presse- und Informationsamts der Bundesregierung (Bonn), 12.6.1992, S. 613. Schon in der Erklärung von Rom war konstatiert worden, daß künftig keine Institution mehr allein ausreiche und deshalb ein "framework of interlocking institutions" erforderlich sei. Die NATO arbeite daher auf eine neue Architektur hin, in der sich NATO, KSZE, die Europäische Gemeinschaft, die WEU und der Europarat gegenseitig ergänzen (§ 3 der Erklärung von Rom).

7 § 11 der Erklärung von Oslo, S. 615. Zu dieser Zeit waren die Vorschläge von Manfred Wörner bereits wesentlich weiter gegangen. So hat er im Februar weitreichende und detaillierte Vorschläge für eine Rollen- und Arbeitsteilung der KSZE, der EG/WEU und der NATO unterbreitet. Sein Dreistufenplan für die Entwicklung des Zusammenwirkens von NATO und KSZE sah für die zweite Stufe vor, daß "NATO will support future CSCE peace keeping and peace enforcement activities ... NATO could offer it support in areas such as logistics, transport, intelligence and close air support ... The military relationships that the Alliance is currently developing with the Central and Eastern European countries will facilitate such a back-up and support role". In einer dritten Phase würde die KSZE schließlich zur "overarching organization" werden, die konkrete Ausführung aber an bestehende Organisationen delegieren. Das Bündnis würde "accept reponsibility for ... assuming jointly with the WEU peace keeping and peace making functions" (Remarks by the Secretary General at the North Atlantic Assembly's Conference on CSCE Matters, 12 February, 1992, S. 12f).

8 So zwei Mitglieder der Policy Planning Section des NATO-Generalsekretariats. Siehe David *Law*/Michael *Rühle*, Die NATO und das "Out-of-area"-Problem, in: Europa-Archiv, 47 (1992) 15/16, S. 439.

9 KSZE-Helsinki-Dokument 1992: Herausforderung des Wandels, 8.7.1992, S. 28. Vgl. dazu Winrich *Kühne*, Völkerrecht und Friedenssicherung in einer turbulenten Welt: Eine analytische Zusammenfassung der Grundprobleme und Entwicklungsperspektiven, in: *ders.* (Hrsg.), Blauhelme in einer turbulenten Welt. Beiträge internationaler Experten zur Fortentwicklung des Völ-

lungen des VN-Generalsekretärs entgegenkommt, gegenwärtig aber ohne praktische Konsequenz bleibt. Hingegen wiederholt das in Helsinki beschlossene Dokument, "Herausforderung des Wandels", in bezug auf ein Zusammenwirken mit europäischen Institutionen nur die Feststellung des Prager Dokuments, daß eine Vielfalt von Organisationen und Institutionen zu Veranstaltungen der KSZE eingeladen werden kann, "Beiträge zu leisten"[10]. Die unzureichende Institutionalisierung der KSZE und die fehlende Kollokation ihrer Organe erschweren ein Zusammenwirken mit der KSZE bei Krisenprävention und Konfliktmanagement gegenwärtig ohnehin schwierig. Die vorherrschende Tendenz wichtiger westlicher Teilnehmerstaaten scheint es daher auch zu sein, einer Überforderung der KSZE vorzubeugen.[11]

Die *Vereinten Nationen* machen zwar im kleinen wichtige Fortschritte, aber die hohen Erwartungen nach dem Golfkrieg haben sich lange verflüchtigt. Die Konstellation, die zur Koalition im Golf führte, wird als schwer wiederholbar angesehen. Reformen der VN bleiben auf kleine Teilbereiche beschränkt, und alle Reformen, die Satzungsänderungen erfordern, werden vorerst vertagt, obwohl eine ausreichende Wirksamkeit der VN ohne sie kaum zu erwarten sein wird. Eine Ausweitung der VN-Aktivitäten im Rahmen des derzeit Möglichen stößt rasch auf finanzielle Grenzen, was bei einem breiteren Aufgabenspektrum einen neuen Finanzierungsmodus notwendig machen würde. Unter diesen Umständen ist die Tendenz des VN-Generalsekretärs, Aufgaben an regionale Organisationen zu delegieren, im Sinne einer Entlastung der VN folgerichtig.[12] In diesem Kontext fällt auf, daß die Bereitschaft in den VN, sich auf Organisationen wie die NATO abzustützen, gegenwärtig klarer erkennbar ist als auf seiten der KSZE.

---

kerrechts und der Vereinten Nationen, Baden-Baden 1993, S. 17-100, sowie Tom *Farer*, The Role of Regional Organizations in International Peace-making and Peace-keeping: Legal, Political and Military Problems, ebd., S. 275-292, und Helmut *Freudenschuss*, The Changing Role of the U.N. Security Council: Trends and Perspectives, ebd., S. 151-176.

10 Herausforderung des Wandels, S. 28. Eine erheblich weitergehende Feststellung des KSZE-Ministerrats im "Summary of Conclusions" der Prager Konferenz blieb im Helsinki- wie schon im Prager Dokument unberücksichtigt. Darin hieß es immerhin: "The Ministers stressed that the CSCE also has a prominent role to play in the evolving European architecture and that the challenges facing Europe call for multi-faceted forms of cooperation and a close relationship among European, transatlantic and other international institutions and organizations" (Summary of Conclusions, 1.2.1992, Abschnitt vi.10, S. 3).

11 Vgl. Bernard *von Plate*, Ost- und Mittosteleuropa: Eine Herausforderung für KSZE und NATO, S. 71-94 in diesem Band.

12 Statt dessen ist ein neues Problem des "interlocking" zwischen den VN (bzw. ihrer Special Commission für den Irak) und der IAEA aufgetreten, das für die Zukunft des NV-Regimes weitreichende Bedeutung haben kann. Vgl. Wolf *Häfele*, Supranationalität als Element künftiger Nichtverbreitungspolitik, in: Joachim *Krause* (Hrsg.), Kernwaffenverbreitung und internationaler Systemwandel – Neue Risiken und Gestaltungsmöglichkeiten, Baden-Baden 1993, S. 529-538.

Die einzige Sicherheitsinstitution in Europa, die gegenwärtig günstigere Perspektiven hat als 1990, ist die *Westeuropäische Union*, und zwar nicht so sehr aufgrund der kleinen Fortschritte bei der weiteren Institutionalisierung (Sekretariat nach Brüssel, Bildung der Planungszelle u.a.), sondern weil die Erwartung weiterer amerikanischer Truppenabzüge aus Europa der Verteidigungskooperation Westeuropas neue Dringlichkeit verleiht. Dafür ist die WEU zumindest für die nächsten Formationsschritte der geeignete Rahmen, allerdings, wie gesagt, ohne eigene Finalität: Die ist nur bei fortschreitender Unionsbildung im Rahmen einer *Politischen Union* vorstellbar.

Da sich alle Institutionen in einem Prozeß der Veränderung befinden und keine zur Zeit ein klares oder unstrittiges Aufgaben- und Entwicklungsprofil hat, kann es kaum erstaunen, daß das Zusammenwirken multinationaler Sicherheitsinstitutionen bisher über Anfänge nicht hinausgekommen ist, sofern nicht überhaupt der alte Zustand des institutionellen Nebeneinanders wieder eingetreten ist oder gar präferiert wird. Dabei war der entscheidende Gedanke, der dem "interlocking of institutions" zugrunde lag, nicht, daß es zwischen verschiedenen Institutionen und Organisationen funktionale Verbindungen und Arbeitsteilungen geben kann. Das ist in anderen zwischenstaatlichen Bereichen ebenso Praxis wie in der Organisation von Firmenkonglomeraten. Vielmehr ging es darum, *ohne Hierarchie und entsprechende Institutionalisierung einen konzeptionellen und verfahrensmäßigen Bezugsrahmen herzustellen, in dem verschiedene Institutionen unbeschadet anderer spezifischer Aufgaben auf gemeinsame Zwecke hin arbeitsteilig zusammenwirken.* Zu einem solchen Bezugsrahmen (dem "framework") ist es bisher nicht einmal in Ansätzen gekommen, obwohl die Zunahme internationaler Konflikte, für deren internationale Regelung keine etablierten und wirksamen Verfahren existieren, eben dies heute noch dringlicher macht als 1990. Das Fehlen eines solchen Bezugsrahmens weist auf die Krise und begrenzte Handlungsfähigkeit der einzelnen Institutionen, letztlich aber der einzelnen Handlungsträger, also der nationalen Regierungen hin.

Die Krise des Multilateralismus resultiert vordergründig aus institutionellen Egoismen bzw. unzureichender Institutionalisierung und aus nationalen Interessenunterschieden. Erwartungen an institutionelle Evolution und ein zweckmäßiges Zusammenwirken verschiedener multinationaler Institutionen müssen jedoch von tieferliegenden Ursachen geleitet sein. Sie liegen sowohl auf der Seite der Staaten wie des Multilateralismus.

Auf seiten der Staaten resultiert sie in der postkommunistischen Welt vor allem aus der fehlenden staatlichen Souveränität und Handlungsfähigkeit als den Voraussetzungen für internationale Kooperation. Darin ist die Heterogenität von Mitgliedstaaten gerade in den multinationalen Organisationen begründet, die gegenüber kollektiven Verteidigungsorganisationen mit im wesentlichen homogener demokratischer Staatlichkeit und Umständen legitimationsstiftend wirken sollen. Mit der Ausweitung der KSZE auf alle ehemaligen Republiken der UdSSR ist dies besonders augenfällig geworden. Aber auch bei westlichen Demokratien beginnt sich in der Kombination von schwindender Handlungsfähigkeit aufgrund innerer Reformnotwendigkeiten und Anforderungen und zunehmend gefordertem Souveränitätsverzicht eine Krise der Staatlichkeit abzuzeichnen. In Westeuropa wird sie im Verlauf fortschreitender Integration dadurch verschärft, daß die Mitgliedstaaten nur noch bedingt über die Qualität ihrer Staatlichkeit entscheiden können, da sie den Integrationsprozeß nur noch bedingt beeinflussen können.

5. Exkurs: Kritik am Multilateralismus der Nachkriegsära

Es handelt sich also um mehrere Krisen von Staatlichkeit. Sie liegen dem derzeitigen Zustand des Multilateralismus zugrunde, dessen Krise aber letztlich ebenso daraus resultiert, daß mit dem Ende der Ost-West-Konfrontation die Grenzen eines seit Jahrzehnten vorherrschenden Multilateralismus deutlich wurden.

In neueren Untersuchungen zum Multilateralismus sind sie so zusammengefaßt worden: "Um das Selbstverständliche zu unterstreichen, haben die Vereinigten Staaten formale internationale Organisationen nicht mit extensiven unabhängigen Befugnissen auszustatten versucht. Das war nicht die multilateralistische Agenda der USA."[13] Entsprechend war die NATO eine "sonderbare Mischung. Als eine formale Institution war die NATO während der längsten Zeit ihrer Geschichte ausdrücklich nichtmultilateral, wobei die USA zum großen Teil die Entscheidungsgewalt und Verantwortung innehatten. Zugleich hat die NATO ihren Mitgliedstaaten auf eine Weise Sicherheit gegeben, in der multilaterale Prinzipien starken Ausdruck fanden."[14] Als allgemeine Folgerung aus Untersuchungen zu multilateralen Organisationen der Nachkriegszeit wird konstatiert, daß die kollektiven Handlungsprobleme multilateraler Regierungsweise meist über "minilaterale Zusammenarbeit großer Mächte" angegangen worden sind, die durch "multilaterale Institutionen und Beeinträchtigung multilateraler Prinzipien in Gestalt beständiger Bilateralismen und Regionalismen kaschiert war".[15]

---

13 John Gerard *Ruggie*, Multilateralisms: The Anatomy of an Institution, in: International Organization, 46 (Sommer 1992) 3, S. 590.

14 Steve *Weber*, Shaping the Postwar Balance of Power: Multilateralism in NATO, ebd., S. 633. Im einzelnen werden *drei multilaterale Prinzipien* unterschieden: "Security was *indivisible*. It was based on a *general organizing principle*, the principle that the external boundaries of alliance territory were completely inviolable and that an attack on any border was an attack on all. *Diffuse reciprocity* was the norm" (ebd., Hervorhebung des Verfassers). In diesem Sinne heißt es: "NATO has generally scored low as a multilateral organisation but high as an institution of multilateralism" (ebd., S. 634).

15 *Kahler*, Multilateralismus, S. 707.

Es ist offenkundig, daß zwar Formen eines solchen "Minilateralismus" auf absehbare Zeit immer wiederkehren werden, aber es ist kaum vorstellbar, daß in der weiteren internationalen Entwicklung die Art von Multilateralismus, die unter konfrontativen Bedingungen im Interesse vieler Staaten dominierte, der vorherrschende Typus bleibt. Wie beschrieben, hat schon in den letzten zwei Jahren ein tiefgehender Wandel eingesetzt. Minilateralismus als dominierende Form multinationaler Zusammenarbeit entspricht dem stationären Modell, das gegenwärtig als instabil anzusehen ist. Er würde in der gegebenen Situation regressive Tendenzen stärken und multinationale Zusammenarbeit und deren institutionalisierte Formen überhaupt schwächen.

6. Zusammenwirken multinationaler Sicherheitsinstitutionen: Funktionale Vorkehrungen oder neue Form des Multilateralismus?

Im gegenwärtigen politischen Diskurs laufen zwei Tendenzen weitgehend ohne Kopplungen:

- Die Konzeption der "ineinandergreifenden Institutionen" wird mit Skepsis aufgenommen oder verworfen.
- Grundlegende interinstitutionelle Zuordnungsfragen kommen einer Klärung näher oder stehen als dringend an.

Auf dem Hintergrund der bisherigen Analyse kann das nicht überraschen. Das Zusammenwirken von Sicherheitsinstitutionen wird entweder als technisch-funktionale Vorkehrung oder als eine neue Form des Multilateralismus verstanden, bei der staatliche Souveränität und Handlungsfähigkeit anders als bisher zur Disposition stehen.

Als organisatorische Vorkehrung wird das "interlocking" vor allem unter drei Aspekten betrachtet:

- vom Selbstverständnis einzelner Institutionen her,[16]
- vom gegebenen Entwicklungsstand der Institutionen her,
- als Vernetzung unter sehr allgemeinen Zielsetzungen, das heißt vieler Organisationen mit unspezifischen Verknüpfungen (z.B. Prager Dokument der KSZE).

In diesem Sinne gibt es eine Praxis des Zusammenwirkens, die aber für die Legitimität bzw. Effizienz einzelner Institutionen nicht konstitutiv ist und keinen

16 In der Praxis haben hier sogar funktionale Gesichtspunkte oft nur eine untergeordnete Rolle gespielt. Vielmehr ging es meist in statischer Betrachtung um neue Rollenabsicherung durch Herunterspielen konkurrierender Zielsetzungen wichtiger Mitgliedstaaten bzw. institutioneller Egoismen, um Architekturbildung mit Rollendifferenzierung, um Zuständigkeits- und Kompetenzklärung ("jede Institution für das, wofür sie am besten geeignet ist"), um Komplementarität (etwa durch Aufgabenteilung zwischen NATO und WEU) oder um abstrakt beschriebene konstitutive Wechselbeziehungen, bei denen es dann aber eben gerade um die Konkretion geht (Beispiel: Mandatierung und Implementierung).

übergreifenden Bezugsrahmen erfordert. Sie ist ohnehin per se nicht an institutionellen Entwicklungszielen orientiert. Da aber alle multinationalen Sicherheitsinstitutionen in einer Funktionskrise sind, die Organisationsprinzipien in der neuen politisch-strategischen Gesamtlage nicht mehr wie bisher anwendbar sind,[17] und die Führungsmächte, die bisher Minilateralismus ermöglicht haben, weder ausreichend handlungsfähig, noch hinreichend akzeptiert sind, reicht die bisherige Praxis des institutionellen Zusammenwirkens jedenfalls nicht aus, um regressiven Tendenzen entgegenzuwirken bzw. evolutionäre entscheidend zu fördern.

Die internationale Entwicklung befindet sich gegenwärtig am Scheideweg, und dies wird nicht zufällig gerade in der Frage des Zusammenwirkens multinationaler Institutionen sichtbar. Soweit es hier um mehr als technisch-funktionale Vorkehrungen, nämlich um neue Formen des Multilateralismus geht, ist dies von konstellativen Bedingungen abhängig, die durch eine verbreitete Zielsetzung eines der neuen Lage angemessenen institutionellen Zusammenwirkens begünstigt werden, so wie diese Zielsetzung nur bei dominanten Evolutionstendenzen erreichbar wird.

Als neue Form des Multilateralismus ist das Zusammenwirken multinationaler Institutionen zu gemeinsamen Zwecken der Mehrheit ihrer Träger eine *multilaterale Regierungsweise*, die *nicht* mehr im herkömmlichen Sinne *zwischenstaatlich* ist, sich aber auch *von supranationaler Regierungsweise unterscheidet*, weil eine hierarchische Ordnung gerade nicht besteht. "In dieser neuen Welt der multilateralen Regierungsweise ... werden die Institutionen für kollektives Handeln zunehmend wichtig. Solche Institutionen werden eine Struktur erfordern, die es ermöglicht, zwischen der Effizienz und Legitimität von Entscheidungsabläufen jene schwierige Balance zu finden, die nötig ist, für einen erfolgreichen Multilateralismus mit großen Zahlen."[18]

II. Institutionelles Zusammenwirken zu Zwecken kollektiver Sicherheit und Verteidigung

1. Aufgaben und institutionelle Erfordernisse

Die faktische Unwirksamkeit bestehender Sicherheitsinstitutionen bei zunehmend dominanten Konflikttypen, die entsprechenden sicherheitspolitischen Aufgaben und die institutionellen Voraussetzungen, die dafür geschaffen werden müßten, verbinden sich zur Leitfrage in bezug auf ein institutionelles Zusammenwirken, sofern dieses nicht nur pragmatisch angestrebt, sondern längerfristig konzipiert wird.

---

17 Für kollektive Verteidigungsorganisationen wie die NATO wird dies etwa am Beispiel der Nichtverletzbarkeit der territorialen Bündnisintegrität deutlich, die nicht mehr als Organisationsprinzip ausreicht, da es künftig gerade um erweiterte Sicherheit, unter Umständen aber auch nur um sektorale Beistandspflicht geht.

18 *Kahler*, Multilateralismus, S. 708.

Den vorausgegangenen Teilstudien ist zu entnehmen, daß schon für die traditionellen Aufgaben der Friedensmissionen und kollektiven Selbstverteidigung erweiterte Optionen, Grundlagen und institutionelle Voraussetzungen erforderlich werden. Darüber hinaus zeichnen sich inzwischen vier neue Arten von Aufgaben ab:

- die *Internationalisierung von Konflikten*, die von friedensbrechenden Konfliktparteien als innere Angelegenheit betrachtet werden,[19]
- die Erweiterung kollektiver Beistandsverpflichtungen der NATO-Mitglieder im Sinne *kollektiver Stabilitätsverpflichtungen* gegenüber bestimmten Staaten,[20]
- die *Eindämmung* aggressiver Vorbereitungen während *langer Konfliktvorläufe*,
- die *Sanktionierung* von bzw. *Vergeltung* gegen Friedensbruch mit Massenvernichtungswaffen (vor allem Nuklearwaffen).

Bestehende Institutionen sind für keinen dieser Zwecke eingerichtet. Aber sie sind, wie gesagt, auch für traditionelle Aufgaben unter den neuen Bedingungen nicht mehr ausreichend organisiert. VN, KSZE, NATO, WEU, EU und IAEA weisen sämtlich gravierende institutionelle Defizite auf.

Unter evolutionären konstellativen Bedingungen dürften sich mehrere Zwecke am besten im Zusammenhang verfolgen lassen:

- die Bewältigung staatlicher und institutioneller Probleme des Multilateralismus,
- der Schaffung eines wirksamen Systems der Konfliktbeherrschung,
- die Verankerung neuartiger Aufgaben kollektiver Sicherheit und Verteidigung darin,
- eine zweckgerichtete Reform aller bestehenden multinationalen Institutionen,
- die Entwicklung neuer Formen intergouvernementaler Koordinierung und Orchestrierung,
- ein organisches Zusammenwirken von Institutionen im Sinne der jeweiligen Aufgabe.

Mit anderen Worten, das "interlocking of institutions" tritt nicht als ergänzende Vorkehrung zu etablierten Aufgaben und Institutionen hinzu, sondern die Zielsetzung eines organischen institutionellen Zusammenwirkens in bezug auf neue Aufgaben stellt den optimalen Rahmen für den Umgang mit der Krise des Multilateralismus, für die weitere Entwicklung der einzelnen Institutionen und für das Schaffen aufgabengerechter Handlungsoptionen dar. Es geht um eine neue Form des multilateralen Regierens, die im übrigen nicht auf kollektive Sicherheit und Verteidigung beschränkt ist, sondern vor allem bei der Organisation des Welthandels und der Energieversorgung und bei neuartigen ökologischen oder intersozialen Herausforderungen zunehmend ihre Entsprechung haben wird. In diesem Sin-

19 Vgl. dazu *Kühne*, Völkerrecht und Friedenssicherung, und *von Plate*, Ost- und Mittelosteuropa.

20 Dies wäre eine mittlere Ebene unterhalb der NATO-Mitgliedschaft und oberhalb der pragmatischen Zusammenarbeit und der NAAC-Mitgliedschaft.

ne ist ein institutionelles Zusammenwirken zu Zwecken kollektiver Sicherheit und Verteidigung nicht nur eine Entwicklungsaufgabe, sondern es wird in weitem Maße davon bestimmt sein, ob es innerhalb eines gemeinsamen Bezugsrahmens entsteht, der vor allem auch Ausdruck einer gemeinsamen Sicherheitskultur ist.[21] Umgekehrt formuliert kann ein organisches und aufgabengerechtes institutionelles Zusammenwirken nur zustande kommen, wenn die einzelnen Institutionen auf spezifische Aufgaben hin reformiert oder ausgebaut werden, was in manchen Fällen auch die Einbeziehung und Integration anderer Institutionen (z.B. NACC bei KSZE oder WEU bei EU) bedeuten kann. Unter dem einen wie dem anderen Aspekt ist wesentlich, daß es in bezug auf spezifische Aufgaben *konstitutive interinstitutionelle Beziehungen* geben kann, die insoweit von technisch-funktionalen bzw. organisatorischen Vorkehrungen zu unterscheiden sind.

2. Elemente eines Systems institutionellen Zusammenwirkens

Die gegenwärtige Situation zeigt widerstrebende Tendenzen sowohl im Bereich kollektiver Verteidigung wie kollektiver Sicherheit. In beiden Bereichen geht dies zurück auf die Gegenläufigkeit, die sich in der Sicht nationaler Handlungsträger zwischen der wiederkehrenden und durch Umstände begünstigten Neigung zu nationaler Interessenorientierung der Sicherheitspolitik und den objektiven Erfordernissen neuer internationaler Strukturbildung darstellt. Wahrscheinlich wird dies weder zu einem ausgeprägten neuen Multilateralismus, noch zu einer vollen Renationalisierung der Sicherheitspolitik führen, sondern sich in suboptimalen Mischformen ausprägen.

Ein System institutionellen Zusammenwirkens sollte dabei trotz aller Rückschläge, wie sie zur Zeit vor allem in Bosnien eintreten, leitende Vorstellung sein. Es wird indessen nur in dem Maße möglich werden, in dem sowohl kollektive Verteidigung wie kollektive Sicherheit über den traditionellen, an nationaler Souveränität und territorialem Schutz orientierten Rahmen hinauswachsen: Kollektive Verteidigung muß sich dahin erweitern, daß sie auf den Schutz solcher Länder ausgedehnt wird, deren Gefährdung eine Gefährdung auch des NATO-Territoriums erwarten läßt und mit denen eine entsprechende Verteidigungskooperation unterhalb der Ebene der NATO-Mitgliedschaft möglich ist ("kollektive Stabilitätsverpflichtungen" der NATO). Kollektive Sicherheit muß über den Schutz von Souveränität und territorialer Unversehrtheit hinaus dahin erweitert werden, daß eingreifendes Handeln aufgrund entsprechender Mandate auch dort möglich wird, wo eine Konfliktpartei dies als innere Angelegenheit betrachtet: Es muß – und dahin

---

21 Vgl. Michael *Staack*, Eine europäische Sicherheitskultur: Aussichten für eine regionalspezifische Normen- und Regimebildung, S. 187-208 in diesem Band.

weisen die Erfahrungen der letzten zwei Jahre – ein erweitertes Spektrum von Fällen von Friedensbruch im Sinne der VN-Satzung geben.

Die bisher – und im Sinne vorrangig nationalstaatlicher Orientierung folgerichtig – kategorial unterschiedenen Konzeptionen kollektiver Verteidigung und kollektiver Sicherheit wachsen in dem Maße mit dem Resultat zunehmender operativer Verknüpfung aufeinander zu, in dem jede sich in diesem Sinne erweitert. Die Verknüpfung erfolgt einerseits über die Mandatierung von kollektiven Verteidigungsorganisationen wie der NATO durch kollektive Sicherheitsorganisationen, vor allem die VN. Andererseits ist sie in der zunehmend erkannten Notwendigkeit begründet, bei begrenzten mandatierten Maßnahmen den primären Verhandlungsvorgang durch eine Konzeption möglicher militärischer Steigerungen zu ergänzen und abzustützen. Andernfalls würde sonst die Begrenzung der Maßnahmen wie im Fall Bosniens darin resultieren, daß sich das Verhandlungsziel ständig im Sinne fortschreitender militärischer Erfolge der stärkeren Seite verändert bzw. auf den schließlichen Status quo beschränkt.

Im Sinne so erweiterter Konzeptionen für kollektive Sicherheit wie kollektive Verteidigung lassen sich entsprechende Institutionen, institutionelle Zwecke, konstitutive Beziehungen bzw. Auftragsstrukturen zwischen Institutionen darstellen. Dieser Zustand ist in allgemeiner Form als dritte Stufe eines Stufenplans zu verstehen, der über die bisherige zwischenstaatliche Praxis hinausgeht, aber unterhalb der Ebene supranationaler Strukturbildung bleibt. Die gleichen Akteure bleiben im Prinzip die Träger kollektiver Sicherheits- wie Verteidigungsinstitutionen, wenngleich sie im einen und im anderen Bereich aus unterschiedlichen Gründen unterschiedliche Arten von Souveränitätsverzicht üben.

Dem entspricht, daß Ad-hoc-Koalitionen wie formale Bündnisse sowohl für kollektive Sicherheits- als auch für kollektive Verteidigungszwecke in Anspruch genommen werden können. Den Aufgaben der kollektiven Stabilitätsverpflichtung, der kollektiven Beistandspflicht, der Rekonstitution und der Vergeltung auf seiten der kollektiven Selbstverteidigung stehen die verschiedenen Friedensmissionen, mandatierte Formen der kollektiven Selbstverteidigung sowie punitive Sanktionen auf seiten der kollektiven Sicherheit gegenüber.

Der kategoriale Unterschied zwischen den beiden Formen kollektiven Handelns zu Sicherheitszwecken besteht darin, daß *Maßnahmen der kollektiven Sicherheit der Autorisierung und Legitimierung bedürfen*, während *Maßnahmen der kollektiven Selbstverteidigung aus inhärentem Recht ausgeführt* werden können, wenngleich begrenzt durch die Anwendbarkeit autorisierter Maßnahmen kollektiver Verteidigung. Der Stufenplan impliziert eine *evolutionäre Logik*, nach der sich in der Praxis der *Anwendungsbereich kollektiver Sicherheit erweitert, der kollektiver Selbstverteidigung* (trotz erweiterter Aufgaben) *verringert.*

Für die kollektive Verteidigung wird angenommen, daß dies die wichtigen Institutionen sind:

- flexible Ad-hoc-Koalitionen,
- eine Europäische Union, in der die WEU aufgegangen ist,
- eine NATO als euro-atlantisches Bündnis (EU plus Rekonstitutionsfähigkeit),
- eine Organisation für Abwehr und Vergeltung im Falle von Gefährdungen mit Massenvernichtungswaffen (vor allem nuklearen Waffen).[22]

Bei der institutionellen Entwicklung der Einrichtungen für kollektive Sicherheit werden vergleichbare Fortschritte unterstellt:

- ein erweiterter VN-Sicherheitsrat mit ausreichenden Unterstützungsfunktionen und einer durch Vetorecht nicht gehemmten Fähigkeit zur Autorisierung von Maßnahmen,
- einer KSZE, die mit eigener Legitimierungsfunktion, entsprechenden Entscheidungsstrukturen, Kollokation der unterstützenden Funktionen, Übernahme von NACC-Funktionen und -Strukturen ausgestattet ist,
- eine Funktionserweiterung der IAEA bei klarer Zuordnung zum VN-Sicherheitsrat,
- eine flexible Fähigkeit zur Mandatierung und Koalitionsbildung.

---

22 Vgl. zu möglichen Maßnahmen Joachim *Krause*, Ausbau, Erhaltung und Schutz von Nichtverbreitungsregimen, in: *ders.*, Kernwaffenverbreitung und internationaler Systemwandel, S. 265-286, sowie Lewis A. *Dunn*, Containing Nuclear Proliferation: The Role of Military Options, ebd., S. 373-396. Dort bleibt allerdings die Frage der zweckmäßigen Institutionalisierung ausgeklammert. Sie ist vor allem deshalb wichtig, weil nukleare und vergleichbare Bedrohungen von P-5-Mächten ausgehen können. Sollte eine Reform des VN-Sicherheitsrat zur Abschaffung oder Qualifizierung des Vetorechts führen, würden sich Voraussetzungen für die Organisation zu Zwecken kollektiver Selbstverteidigung in dieser Kategorie verändern. Als Lösung kommen im Extremfall einerseits Souveränitätsreservate für Nuklearwaffen in Betracht, andererseits die Beibehaltung nuklearer Abschreckung im Rahmen kollektiver Verteidigungsorganisationen wie der NATO. Ersteres liefe eindeutig der allgemeinen Tendenz zur Souveränitätsbeschränkung zuwider, und entsprechende Souveränitätsverzichte sollten konstitutiver Bestandteil eines ebenfalls für die dritte Stufe in Aussicht genommenen Regimes für Nuklearwaffen und Nichtverbreitung sein. Letzteres wird bei schwindender Teilhabemöglichkeit (als Resultat geringer Zahlen, Diversifizierung und Stationierungsoptionen) zum klassischen Beispiel für "minilateralism".
Denkbar wäre ein kollektives System der Minimalabschreckung (in Europa oder global), wie es 1989 von sowjetischer Seite vorgeschlagen worden ist (vor allem mit Frankreich als Adressaten). Eine solche Lösung würde aber ebenfalls einen Sonderstatus der Nuklearwaffenstaaten festschreiben, der mit der Gesamtentwicklung schwer vereinbar ist. Sinnvoll wäre eine *gemischtes System von Nuklearwaffen- und hauptbetroffenen Schwellenstaaten*, das im *engen institutionellen Zusammenwirken (interlocking) mit Europäischer Union und/oder euro-atlantischem Bündnis fungieren* würde. Es wird hier als Multilaterale Abschreckungsstruktur bezeichnet. Einzelheiten des Konzepts sollen an dieser Stelle ausgespart bleiben.
Bei Konsens auf seiten des VN-Sicherheitsrat (die KSZE kommt hier als legitimierende Instanz kaum in Betracht) kann bei ähnlicher Ausführung oder Androhung aus Vergeltung punitive Sanktion werden, wobei der IAEA (wiederum im institutionellen Zusammenwirken) eine spezielle Funktion bei der Anforderung punitiver Sanktionen zukommen kann.

3. Zwecke, die multiinstitutionelles Zusammenwirken erfordern

Es lassen sich so sieben Zwecke kollektiver Sicherheit bzw. Verteidigung unterscheiden: auf seiten der kollektiven Sicherheit mandatierte kollektive Selbstverteidigung, Friedensmissionen und punitive Maßen, auf seiten der kollektiven Verteidigung Maßnahmen im Sinne kollektiver Stabilitätsverpflichtung, kollektiver Beistand, Rekonstitution in Krisenfällen und Vergeltung. Auch unter den angenommenen institutionellen Bedingungen lassen die Strukturen in der Regel keine einfachen Entscheidungen zu. Im Bereich *kollektiver Verteidigung* handelt es sich in drei Fällen um *institutionenspezifische Zwecke*, während im vierten der *Konsens der Betroffenen* in bezug auf das Erfordernis kollektiver Selbstverteidigung nötig ist. Formal ist der Beistandsfall der EU am einfachsten. Hier kommen die anderen, vor allem nichtmilitärischen Funktionen der Europäischen Union ins Spiel. Aber außer bei massiver Rekonstitution einer Bedrohung bzw. einer Bedrohung durch nukleare oder vergleichbare Waffen handelte es sich hier um einen relativ autonomen Fall. Bei kollektiven Beistandsverpflichtungen oder aber bei massiveren Gefährdungen wären ein partieller *Transfer von Aufgaben und Funktionen* und ein entsprechendes Zusammenwirken von Institutionen erforderlich.

Im Bereich *kollektiver Sicherheit* liegt der primäre Grund für institutionelles Zusammenwirken in der *Trennung von Legitimation und Implementierung* von Maßnahmen kollektiver Sicherheit. Dies wird jedenfalls zweckmäßig und der Regelfall sein. Die *Legitimationsautorität* liegt beim VN-Sicherheitsrat, kann aber an Institutionen wie eine institutionell entwickelte KSZE *delegiert* werden. Bei Handlungsunfähigkeit des VN-Sicherheitsrat bzw. in bezug auf eine spezifisch europäische normative Berufungsgrundlage sollte die KSZE überdies auch eigene Legitimationsautorität haben (in beiden Fällen: als Rückfallposition und aufgrund einer spezifischen Eingriffsautorität). VN-Sicherheitsrat und KSZE können insoweit *Mandate* erteilen, das heißt Mandatsträger autorisieren, definierte kollektive Sicherheitsmaßnahmen auszuführen. Zwischen autorisierender und implementierender Institution bestehen also zweckbezogen *konstitutive Beziehungen.*

Mandatsträger können Ad-hoc-Koalitionen oder formale Bündnisse sein. Letztere können auch die Durchführung von Mandaten durch Koalitionen mit Informationen, Kommunikationsmitteln, Transportmitteln, Infrastruktur, militärischem Gerät unter anderem *unterstützen.* Solche Unterstützung kann Teil eines Mandats sein oder aus dem Konsens der Mitgliedstaaten resultieren. Insoweit kann es im Bereich der Implementierung zwischen verschiedenen Organisationen zu funktionalem Zusammenwirken kommen.

Die bemerkenswerteste Neuerung gegenüber der traditionellen Sicherheitspolitik bestünde darin, daß *Verteidigungsorganisationen neben ihrem inhärenten Zweck auch Mandatsträger* sein können. Das gilt für formale Bündnisse, aber für beide Zwecke kommen auch Koalitionen in Betracht. Wenn dieser *institutionelle Doppel-*

zweck seine entsprechende konzeptionelle und strukturelle Ausgestaltung erfahren hat, wird dies die Dichotomie zwischen kollektiver Sicherheit und kollektiver Verteidigung relativieren: Es wird die internationale Sicherheitsarchitektur verändern.

Der doppelte institutionelle Zweck bildet den Kern eines Systems der "interlocking institutions". *Transfer* im einen, *Delegation, Mandatierung* und *Implementierung* (einschließlich *Unterstützung* von Mandatsträgern) im anderen Bereich stellen die wesentlichen *interinstitutionellen Beziehungen* in einem solchen System dar, das für Krisen- und Konfliktlagen durch vielfältige *technisch-organisatorische Vorkehrungen* für das Zusammenwirken verschiedener Organisationen (z.B. Intelligence-Unterstützung der VN durch die NATO), für Krisenprävention und Konfliktmanagement durch konzertierten Einsatz *nichtmilitärischer Mittel* ergänzt werden kann und in der Regel muß.

Die Notwendigkeit institutionellen Zusammenwirkens ergibt sich aus den sicherheitspolitischen Zwecken. Seine Verwirklichung erfordert, daß die wichtigen Akteure bzw. Entscheidungsträger für diese Zwecke in Grenzen gemeinsam eintreten und zu einer entsprechend orchestrierten Nutzung institutioneller Optionen und Mittel bereit sind. Dies wird um so eher gelingen, je mehr sicherheitspolitisches Handeln im Kontext einer gemeinsamen Sicherheitskultur, also eines normen-, werte- und erfahrungsbezogenen Bezugssystems erfolgt. Eine solche Sicherheitskultur wird vor allem europäisch bzw. euro-atlantisch sein.[23]

Gemeinsames Handeln wichtiger Akteure wird institutionell präformiert sein: Es gibt weit mehr Anlässe und Optionen. Andererseits sind handelnde Mächte bei einem entwickelten System institutionellen Zusammenwirkens und entsprechendem Souveränitätsverzicht bzw. -transfer auch in ein System intergouvernementalen Handelns eingebunden, das zwar flexibler ist als zu Zeiten der Konfrontation, aber die Akteure eben auch stärker auf individuelles Handeln festlegt. *Gemeinsame Sicherheitskultur ist eine wesentliche Voraussetzung für Kollektivität sicherheitspolitischen Handeln.*

Unter diesen Gegebenheiten kommen eine Reihe von Mechanismen dazu, die institutionelles Zusammenwirken stärken können:

- Es lassen sich informelle Formen *intergouvernementaler Koordinierung* entwikkeln, die der Vorbereitung kollektiven Handelns dienen können.[24]

---

23 Vgl. dazu Uwe *Nerlich*, Europäische Sicherheitskultur: Das Ziel und der Weg, in: Albrecht *Zunker* (Hrsg.), Weltordnung oder Chaos? Beiträge zur internationalen Politik. Festschrift zum 75. Geburtstag von Professor Dr. Klaus Ritter, Baden-Baden 1993, S. 21-36.

24 Vgl. dazu Robert D. *Blackwill*, Requirements to Coordinate National Security Policies as a Precondition for Effective Multiinstitutional Crisis Management: The Role of Informal Structures, S. 305-314 in diesem Band.

- Es sind formelle oder informelle *Exekutivstrukturen* innerhalb multinationaler Institutionen möglich; am Beispiel der KSZE würde ein Europäischer Sicherheitsrat die eine, ein "Konzert der Mächte"[25] die andere Option illustrieren.
- Informelle *Führungsgruppierungen* können auch *außerhalb* formaler Strukturen organisiert werden wie beispielsweise die G-7 oder die unter anderem von japanischer Seite vorgeschlagene P-5/G-7-Kombination.
- Institutionelles Zusammenwirken kann durch *Mitgliedschaft* wichtiger Akteure in möglichst *vielen* der betroffenen multinationalen *Institutionen* erleichtert (oder auch blockiert) werden, wenngleich dieselben Staaten in verschiedenen Institutionen nicht durchweg die gleiche Politik verfolgen.[26]
- Ein "interlocking" ist auch durch *korporative Mitgliedschaft* einer Institution in einer anderen möglich.[27]
- Eine wichtige Option ist schließlich die Möglichkeit *vorgeschalteter Konsultationen* (etwa nach dem Modell der EPZ in den VN) bzw. eine systematische *Caucus-Bildung* etwa der EU oder der euro-atlantischen Allianz in der KSZE bzw. den VN.

4. Nutzen eines Stufenkonzepts

Die hier erläuterte Architektur ist an die Möglichkeit einer evolutionären Konstellation gebunden und würde diese umgekehrt im Maße ihres Erfolges stabilisieren. Aber selbst unter solchen Umständen können sich Sicherheitsstrukturen anders entwickeln. Sie können sich auch stärker asynchron entwickeln, was die Möglichkeit institutionellen Zusammenwirkens beschränken würde.

Die hier vorgestellte Architektur geht aus von den antizipierbaren sicherheitspolitischen Zwecken, von den evolutionären Perspektiven, die längerfristig für die einzelnen Sicherheitsinstitutionen beschrieben worden sind, sowie von einer möglichen Optimierung der einzelnen Institutionen bzw. Instrumente durch aufgabengerechtes institutionelles Zusammenwirken auf gemeinsame Zwecke hin.

Bei einigen zusätzlichen Annahmen, etwa über weitgehende amerikanische Truppenabzüge und eine nachfolgende Beschleunigung der Vergemeinschaftung westeuropäischer Verteidigung, kann man für alle in europäischen Institutionen bis zum Jahr 2000 eine weit fortgeschrittene Entwicklung im vorgeschlagenen Sin-

---

25 Vgl. Bernard *von Plate*, Die innerstaatliche Funktion der KSZE, S. 209-217 in diesem Band, sowie Anne M. *Dixon*/Thomas J. *Hirschfeld*, Adapting CSCE to Modern Problems: Limits and Opportunities, S. 219-247 in diesem Band.

26 Unter Konfrontationsbedingungen hat Dulles diese Möglichkeit beim Aufbau des Systems regionaler Beistandspakte besonders genutzt: Außer den USA und in einigen Fällen Großbritannien gehörten keine weiteren Mitgliedstaaten gleichzeitig mehreren Bündnissystemen an.

27 Diese Idee hatte Adenauer schon mit dem Vorschlag einer EVG-Mitgliedschaft in der NATO verfolgt.

ne annehmen. Sie wird in allen Fällen in Stufen erreichbar sein.[28] Pragmatischer Inkrementalismus würde zur Regression tendieren. Diese Stufen bei Teilentwicklungen sollten aufeinander abgestimmt werden, wenngleich förmliche Paketvorschläge kontraproduktiv werden könnten.

Die Konzeption einer so oder ähnlich beschreibbaren Struktur ist aber wichtig, um Regierungen vor allem handlungsrelevanter Staaten zu intergouvernementaler Koordination zu bewegen. In diesem Sinne ist das System institutionellen Zusammenwirkens eine regulative Idee europäischer Sicherheitspolitik, die über die dissoziativen Risiken einer auf das Management des Übergangs beschränkten Politik hinwegführen kann. Es ist eine Konzeption, zu der sich zumindest Alternativen in langfristiger Perspektive formulieren lassen. Der Test ist offen.

---

28 Vgl. etwa den Dreistufenplan Manfred Wörners für die Gestaltung des Verhältnisses von NATO und KSZE (s.o. Anm. 7).

13. Requirements to Coordinate National Security Policies as a Precondition for Effective Multiinstitutional Crisis Management: The Role of Informal Structures

Robert D. Blackwill

As the world has shifted dramatically on its geopolitical axis in the past three years, Western governments, some of which brilliantly managed the end of the Cold War, have so far fumbled the challenge of producing stable patterns of cooperation and new structures to deal with the consequences of both the end of superpower global confrontation and the division of Europe. Aside from the extraordinarily successful diplomatic and military policies by the international coalition immediately before and during the Gulf War, the litany of confused and divided Western policies in the past eighteen months is familiar:

- Lack of a coherent, coordinated and consistently active approach by the West to the successive and increasingly violent crises in the former Yugoslavia;
- Insufficient Western political and diplomatic involvement, resource transfer and international organizational creativity directed at the struggling democracies of Eastern and Central Europe;
- Deeply inadequate financial and especially technical assistance by Western governments to the nations of the former Soviet Union, and particularly to Russia and Ukraine; and
- Pervasive hesitancy if not lethargy by and among most Western dominated international institutions (EC, WEU, G-7, IMF, World Bank, and, to a lesser degree, NATO) in dealing with these revolutionary circumstances and their strategic effects; only the United Nations, even with its many structural and budgetary problems, has undertaken a comprehensive effort led by the Secretary-General to deal within its competencies with the new world.

In short, nowhere in the industrial democracies does one see even faint signs of the emergence of a Western strategy (Gesamtkonzept) to influence the political, economic, military and moral content of Europe, not to say the globe, after the collapse of communism.

Many excuses are offered in Western capitals for this sorry performance. The United States, as occurs every four years, fights its Presidential campaign partly at the expense of its role in the world and incessantly examines its significant internal ills. Germany concerns itself with its monumental task of building a functioning society in the five eastern Länder. France suffers from its President's failing grip and intermittent attention to matters of French foreign policy. Britain remains uncomfortable with its European vocation. Italy struggles to avoid political and economic chaos. Financial markets undermine Western currencies and business confidence. Possible failure in the GATT talks threatens the very foundations of the international trading system. The European Community reaches new heights of self-involvement about its future after the Danish referendum and the narrow vote in France, and fails in important ways to concert its foreign policy vis-a-vis the East. NATO strives to reconcile familiar and sometimes bitter differences between Washington and Paris regarding the Alliance's future directions. The WEU at best takes baby steps. The G-7 fails to build an organizational infrastructure that would support a more active mission. Almost everywhere in the industrial democracies, faltering domestic economies sap national political wills and focus prime public attention on internal rather than external preoccupations. Finally, in Eastern and Central Europe and the former Soviet Union, feeble and disorganized governments, frail democratic political structures, mammoth social dislocations and ethnic conflicts confound already insufficient Western efforts to help.

What to do? First, no more excuses from governments in the West. The new Europe is being formed yesterday, today and tomorrow. Truman and Acheson would know what to do now as they did then. Western policymakers must ask of themselves the same sweep of aspiration and imagination that produced the Marshall Plan and the North Atlantic Alliance, if not an equal genius of execution. To persist with domestic engrossment among nations in the West, to continue with confused and often conflicting individual Western policies toward the East, to proceed with no agreed strategy among the advanced democracies to ease the challenges on the other side of the Oder, will certainly ensure an increasingly bloody Europe and consequently an ever more violent world. Eventually none of the countries of the West will be safe.

Thus far, much of the Western analytic community's attention concerning these trials east of Germany has concentrated on the relationship between and among the major international institutions which potentially could help ameliorate the many difficulties being generated and experienced by the former countries of the Warsaw Pact. It is hard to imagine a sustained and successful Western effort to deal with the problems in the East if these international institutional capacities and objectives remain, as at present, largely uncoordinated or worse – not interlocking but interblocking as Uwe Nerlich has cogently put it. At some point, the organizational alphabet soup regarding European security broadly defined must systematically be put through a conceptual and practical sieve to separate out mutually reinforcing missions.

At the same time, however, it is unrealistic to expect such a fruitful and comprehensive meshing of the capacities of international organizations without first developing and then assiduously maintaining intensified efforts and increased means to coordinate national security policies. If profound systemic deterioration in the international security environment is to be averted, *major* Western nations must urgently reach fundamental strategic agreements that would define the challenges to the new world and especially those in Europe, examine the array of policy options and actions that might be applied to these challenges, and then hammer out macro and micro implementation plans toward the East and other impending or nascent regional crises. In the absence of such an agreed Western strategy, arguments about abstractions like a European defense identity, security initiatives like the Eurocorps, or trade disputes regarding agricultural subsidies are likely to dominate the intra-European and Transatlantic agendas.

The question arises of what means and mechanisms, formal and/or informal, should be utilized to attempt a harmonization of national security policies. The North Atlantic Alliance naturally comes to mind first. NATO, after all, is the dominant Western security organization. It has considerable institutional capacity for this sort of strategic inquiry. Its membership contains most of the relevant countries which should participate in such an exercise. And, the Alliance could certainly use the added legitimization which would result from being the locus of the effort to produce a new Western strategy to replace containment.

Unfortunately, NATO suffers disabling drawbacks with regard to this endeavor. Its area of competence, although presently under constant conceptual review and argument, is too limited both geographically and functionally to capture all the current international problems facing the West, or even many of those confined to Europe. The Alliance is obviously not the forum to deal with matters of political economy that are now more important than ever in fashioning a global Western strategy, and clearly closely interrelated to the security dimensions of any overall Western approach to post-Cold War conditions. In addition, the North Atlantic Council is both too large and too "public" to permit the frankness and focus required by major national governments to complete this enterprise of strategic conceptualization and intense practical implementation.

Moreover, debates in the Council on this acutely controversial subject would likely bring forth traditional French reservations about American dominance of NATO. And, of course, Japan would not be present at these Alliance deliberations, an entirely unsatisfactory circumstance in the 1990s. Finally, given the gravity and domestic political sensitivity of the substance at hand in such an exercise, only senior officials from capitals would have the authority and immediate proximity to crucial policymakers at home, including heads of government, to speak candidly and authoritatively. For all these reasons, NATO is not the place in the first instance to attempt to coordinate national security policies to cope with the new world order/disorder.

Many of these same limitations apply to using US-EC consultative mechanisms for this purpose. That forum would be too large and transparent. Its institutional rigidity on the EC side would preclude fluid Transatlantic give and take. It would allow too little security substance in the deliberations. Even more, in this forum France would seek to constrain the level and quality of exchanges with the United States on such a pivotal subject. And, again, Japan would be excluded entirely. So, as in the case of NATO, the US-EC consultative channel is not appropriate to undertake the tasks under discussion in this paper. (One does, however, need to stress that both NATO and the European Community, as well as many other international organizations, would certainly be responsible for various implementing actions which would flow from a generalized Western strategy agreed elsewhere.)

Because of the decisive limitations indicated above with respect to the Alliance and the EC, the possible organizing role of the G-7 in this strategic examination comes to the fore. This forum is far less formal than either of the other two organizations. It exists and thus would not have to be created. Its conceptual and policy writ is geographically global in character. Indeed, it is the center of Western efforts to manage international financial affairs. Especially in the last decade, the G-7 has extended its area of interest and public statements to issues of trade, drugs, the environment, international stability, and even on occasion arms control. And, Japan is a founding member of the group.

Despite these advantages, the G-7 also has serious liabilities in coordinating national security policies in the period ahead. First, although Foreign Ministries sometimes play an important role in G-7 deliberations, especially in the case of the United States, Treasury Departments most often have the organizing lead in the forum's substantive work. (Representatives from Defense Ministries are nowhere to be seen in these exchanges). This inevitably means that the particular and narrow perspective of Treasuries has a critical impact on the general context in which the G-7 considers issues, including those generated by the dramatic changes in the European and international landscapes. Put simply, and hopefully not too bluntly, experts on international finance are not the best representatives from capitals to take the lead in concerting Western national security policies. They are not the ones to examine and formulate an integrated diplomatic, economic and security approach to the radically changed geopolitical situation.

Nonetheless, any attempt to alter this long time financial emphasis on the part of the G-7 and replace Treasuries as lead agencies within the group would probably both weaken its indispensable contribution to international financial stability, and leave buckets of blood all over bureaucratic floors of every one of its members. Another enduring problem with this organizational alternative is that France resists, as a matter of principle, any fundamental shift of the G-7's traditional substantive focus and any serious institutionalization of its work.

If NATO, the EC and the G-7 are not the bodies to tackle the urgent task of organizing a comprehensive Western strategy as well as implementing means to deal with current and prospective crises, who then? The place to begin with is the quality of bilateral relations between major Western nations. Unless these respective bilateral bonds are strong over time, it seems quite unlikely that the industrial democracies will succeed in coordinating national security policies or in producing an agreed strategy.

For reasons of space, this essay will dwell only on US-French and US-German relations. Nevertheless, it is also true that with the exception of Franco-German ties which remain robust despite occasional and usually passing problems, most bilateral links among the major industrial countries are in need of considerable repair. This is decidedly the case with Japan's relationship with the United States and with virtually all of Tokyo's European trading competitors, and with Franco-British and UK-German relations.

Although all these bilateral ties are important, arguably the critical variable regarding the success or failure of a Western strategic exercise is the US-French relationship, a sometimes very troubled partnership. In the period 1989-90, cooperation between Washington and Paris, and particularly between Presidents Bush and Mitterrand, was a crucial ingredient in the West's consummate management of the Cold War's end game. After serious doubts at the outset, France finally accepted in the spring of 1990 the reality of German unification and acquiesced gracefully to American leadership in the international dimensions of the issue and to US primacy in the management of 'the Gorbachev factor' in the equation. In addition, during this twelve-month period one saw unusual flexibility from Paris concerning a variety of US-inspired arms control and institutional reform initiatives within the Alliance.

The high tide of this US-French harmony was reached somewhat before the July 1990 NATO summit in London. At that meeting, the French including President Mitterrand felt they had been rolled over by the American juggernaut and shortly thereafter US-French collaboration regarding European security went into decline. (Cooperation in the Gulf to defeat Saddam Hussein was, of course, another matter.) As communication between the White House and the Elysee continued to deteriorate, the permanent bureaucracies in the two governments became more important in the relationship, reverted to form and began incessantly sniping at each other. The affair of the Franco-German Corps triggered months of trench warfare between the State Department and the Quai d'Orsay. Bitter bilateral disputes arose over teleological issues related to the establishment of a European defense identity, practical questions arising out of the relationship between Franco-German Eurocorps command arrangements and NATO practices in peace and war, and the effect on the quality and speed of Alliance deliberations on the creation of an EC caucus within NATO.

Meanwhile, US-French trade policies came into ever sharper conflict over agricultural subsidies. Presidents Bush and Mitterrand became increasingly preoccupied with their accelerating domestic political problems. Although progress was made on US-French disagreements on security questions at a series of high level NATO meetings in 1991/92, bilateral relations between the two countries remained uneasy at best and not of a kind likely to facilitate strategic accord.

What is the problem here and how can it be fixed? Both nations have yet to digest the implications for their bilateral relationship brought on by the end of the Cold War. Bureaucrats in each capital fight battles of the past with the other while the European and international security environments degenerate.

Here are three rules of thumb to get US-French national security policies back on reinforcing tracks:

- Keep policy control of security and economic discussions between the two sides at the White House and the Elysee;
- Washington should accept that European defense cooperation through the EC and WEU will grow at some expense to current NATO practices and procedures; the challenge is to manage the transition to a new Trans-Atlantic security and institutional balance and bargain without disrupting the Alliance's capacity to act in a near-term crisis; and
- Paris should stop voicing its self-defeating litany that the United States is about to withdraw its troop commitment and central security involvement on the Continent, and sincerely welcome America's role as a European power in the broadest sense.

Recent problems in the US-German relationship are more difficult to explain. After the historic feat of together managing the peaceful unification of Germany within Western security structures, Bonn and Washington seemed to have lost some geopolitical perspective as bilateral disputes have arisen over the former Yugoslavia, the Eurocorps and that perennial, German interest rates. Again, parallel to the US-French case, this is importantly the result of the White House and the Chancellery becoming consumed by domestic problems, thereby allowing splintered and parochial agencies in the two capitals to act as if the only issue each cared about – be it former Yugoslavia, agricultural trade, interest rates, European defense, and so forth – was the *only* substantive matter of consequence between the two nations. Henry Kissinger warned twenty years ago of the dangers of such policy compartmentalization on both sides of the Atlantic and counseled strong political control at the top to mute the inevitable braying by bureaucratic special interests. For not the first time, Kissinger's advice should be heeded as Bonn and Washington seek to revive some degree of the policy intimacy of their 1989-90 collaboration. Again, a few fundamental principles:

- As in the US-French case and that of Washington's exchanges on this subject with London and Tokyo, coordination of US-German national security policies and bilateral discussion of an integrated Western diplomatic, economic and security strategy to deal with the new world should be done quietly, informally, intensively, in small groups, and at very senior political levels; keep the bureaucratic hordes away from both the specific preparation for and participation in these acutely sensitive meetings;

- Washington should digest the profound implications of the fact that Germany (and Russia) will be the two nations in Europe that will most determine the Continent's future and America's interests therein; the US bilateral relationship with Bonn should therefore be treated in Washington with the utmost gravity and sense of strategic purpose. In particular, the United States should accept that Germany will be largely preoccupied with the problems of unification for some time to come; show sensitivity to Bonn's refusal to be trapped between US-French policy disputes, and its deeply held desire to establish the closest possible links with Paris; demonstrate patience as Germany slowly works its way through formidable psychological barriers to redefine its security role in Europe and beyond; and understand that German interest rates will be tied in the most primary way to Germany's past and not be especially subject to external influence;
- For its part, Bonn must decide how important it is for Germany that the United States remain deeply engaged in Europe's future, and calibrate the Federal Republic's diplomatic, financial and trade, and security policies accordingly; the ways in which Germany interacts on policy matters with Washington in the 1990s will have a decisive impact on how US Administrations, the policy community over here and ordinary citizens will view the pros and cons of America continuing an intense involvement across the Atlantic.

Consequential as these bilateral conversations on national security policies could be, they are necessary but not sufficient to construct a coordinated Western strategy to address the manifold tests of Europe and the rest of the globe in this decade. In the end, the leading industrial democracies must meet and *decide together* on these matters. Only in this way can comprehensive regional threat assessments be developed, alternative approaches to an integrated diplomatic, economic and security strategy generated, decisions made at the highest political levels regarding the essential elements of a preferred strategy, and a detailed, equitable and functioning division of labor developed among the participating states. As indicated earlier in this paper, such an endeavor cannot be undertaken in any existing formal consultative structure. All those bodies are either too large, too open, too geographically restricted, too substantively narrow, too exclusively Atlanticist in membership, or all of the above.

Rather, *a new and informal collaborative intergovernmental structure* should be created to manage this decade's tumultuous and dangerous international environment. Of course, the first issue which arises is the proposed membership of such a new grouping. The group must be small to facilitate easy exchange and to reduce the likelihood that its discussions would continually appear in the press. It must include the principal industrial countries whose collaborative analyses, concerted strategies and implementing actions are a precondition to a productive treatment of the problems of the 1990s. It is these few predominant nations that have the size and/or the population, the political stability, the governmental capacities, the economic resources, the diplomatic influence, the military capability – in short, the *power* both present and potential – to deal in the first instance with the challenges of the new world. (Whether they would have the political will to do what is necessary would remain to be seen.)

Here is a circumstance in which many would wish to be called and few would be chosen. Such an informal grouping could include the United States, Germany, France, Britain and Japan. A few comments on the selection. After the United States, begin with the most notable innovation, the inclusion of Japan. This is not simply because Japan is a potential source of large capital to address problems of political economy and its effects on national and regional crises, both immediate and prospective. In addition to that oft stated hope on the part of Japan's Western partners, international peace and stability needs an active Japanese presence in the attempt to lessen local tensions around the world. It needs a Japan which continues to broaden its strategic perspective beyond the search for commercial advantage. It needs a Japan willing to take a more forward role in coping with the evolution of China and the rest of East Asia. Indeed, Japan's membership in this informal structure is so important that the directorate could not perform its daunting tasks in an effective way without Tokyo's active participation.

As stated above, Germany is becoming the most powerful and influential nation in democratic Europe. France must be included because of its intrinsic merits including permanent membership in the UN Security Council, and because Paris would undoubtedly try to sabotage any directorate of which it was not a part. Britain, too, holds the influence of the UNSC, is a bridge to North America, will retain considerable military capability, and exercises probably the finest diplomacy over the years in the West.

Again, it should be emphasized that this informal directorate should not, could not do everything itself. Far from it. After this informal and private structure had reached its initial conclusions and courses of action, naturally members would seek to involve all other appropriate national and international organizational assets (individual countries, NATO, the EC, the WEU, the G-7, the EBRD, the IMF, the World Bank, the United Nations, regional security organizations and political groupings and so forth).

As time passed, there would be need of many mid-course corrections on the part of this new informal coordinating mechanism, and perhaps even a change of strategy brought on by decisive external events. Thus, this group would meet as discreetly as possible and frequently, certainly at the outset not less than once a month. Its national makeup (no more than four individuals per side, hopefully less) would include experts on economic, diplomatic and security issues. Over time, subgroups could be developed if circumstances warranted and more detailed time and expertise were required to deal with a particular issue or crisis. Each of the five teams would be led by a representative from the senior political level back home, an indispensable element in success.

Some will certainly argue that the creation of such an informal structure to coordinate national security policies is too difficult to accomplish. If the endeavor became public, as it probably would eventually, some Western nations would undoubtedly complain vigorously about their exclusion. Italy comes to mind. Canada would likely wish to use its US connection to get a place at the table, although the withdrawal of Canadian troops from Europe reduces the persuasiveness of Ottawa's possible claim. The EC Commission could mount arguments that it should be present. A representative of the UN Secretary-General might also like to attend. And perhaps Russia, too, might believe it deserved a part in such central discussions on the future of global security and its European and Northeast Asian manifestations. The question is where one draws the line and still maintains the integrity and effectiveness of the directorate. The five countries named earlier seem right for the job.

Another criticism of this idea might be that these core nations would simply be unable informally to orchestrate their national security policies in the context of an agreed grand strategy. At the moment, all these governments are politically weak and economically troubled at home to one degree or another. This leads them to concentrate on internal developments, and tends to make them myopic in the face of the great international changes and challenges going on around them. Moreover, differences among these five countries in geography, natural resources, historical experiences, military capability including its possible use, and social cohesion also militate against successful accord. Finally, vision, or even the wish to acquire and then employ one, is not now readily noticeable in any of these capitals. In the US case, the 18-month Presidential election campaign is nearly over with no discussion beyond banalities of America's proper role in the world in this decade and into the next century. So, the obstacles to creating and utilizing this proposed five nation informal structure are considerable.

Yet, what are the alternatives to the courses of action recommended in this paper? A continuation of the present Western strategic drift will surely increase the likelihood of ever more violence and chaos in Europe, and around the globe. If that happens, the renationalization of Western security policies is likely to ensue, especially in Europe, as each country seeks behavioral lessons in its past and endeavors to protect its interests at least partially at the expense of its traditional friends and allies. One shutters at thoughts of where that might lead.

The time for endless excuses by leading Western governments has passed. Too much is at stake for the long-term health of the industrial democracies not to act quickly, decisively and on behalf of a concerted strategy. There may well be better ideas than the ones outlined in this paper to coordinate Western national security policies through informal structures as a precondition for effective multiinstitutional crisis management. If that is the case, let them by all means be put forward. But please, no more endless bureaucratic complaints and petty squabbling. No more pervasive political paralysis in democratic capitals. No more everpresent Western tactical argument and confusion. In sum, no more fragmented, often conflicting, and entirely inadequate policies and actions by main Western governments. History will sit in judgment of the responses by these major Western nations to the challenges of the post-Cold War geopolitical environment. If things do not change and change rapidly, History's verdict will be harsh for those who are present at this creation.

Anhang

1. Abkürzungen

AFCENT	Allied Forces Central Europe
AHB	Ausschuß Hoher Beamter
AIRCENT	Allied Command Air Forces Central Europe
ATAF	Allied Tactical Air Force
BDIMR	Büro für Demokratische Institutionen und Menschenrechte
C+EE	Central and East European (Republics)
CFE	(Conference on) Conventional Armed Forces in Europe
CFSP	Common Foreign and Security Policy
CINCCHAN	Commander in Chief Channel Command
CIS	Community of Independent States
CMEA	Council on Mutual Economic Assistance
CNA	Center for Naval Analyses
COM	Council of Ministers
CPC	Conflict Prevention Center
CPC/CC	Conflict Prevention Center Consultative Committee
CSBM	Confidence- and Security-Building Measure
CSCE	Conference on Security and Cooperation in Europe
CSO	Committee of Senior Officials
EBRD	European Bank for Reconstruction and Development
EBWE	Europäische Bank für Wiederaufbau und Entwicklung
EC	European Community
ECE	Economic Commission for Europe (UN)
ECMM	European Community Monitoring Missions
EFTA	European Free Trade Association
EG	Europäische Gemeinschaften
EPC	European Political Cooperation
EU	European Union / Europäische Union
FAZ	Frankfurter Allgemeine Zeitung
FR	Frankfurter Rundschau
FSC	Forum for Security Cooperation
G-7	Group of Seven / Gruppe der Sieben (die sieben führenden westlichen Industrieländer)
G-24	Gruppe der 24 Staaten (Mitgliedstaaten der OECD)

GASP	Gemeinsame Außen- und Sicherheitspolitik
GDM	Group on Defence Matters
GNP	Gross National Product
HCM	High Commissioner for National Minorities / Hoher Kommissar für nationale Minderheiten
HLWG	High Level Working Group
IAEA	International Atomic Energy Agency
IEPG	Independent European Program Group
IGH	Internationaler Gerichtshof
IISS	The International Institute for Strategic Studies
IKRK	Internationales Komitee vom Roten Kreuz
IMF	International Monetary Fund
IRA	Irish Republican Army
IWF	Internationaler Währungsfonds
JVA	Jugoslawische Volksarmee
KSE	Konventionelle Streitkräfte in Europa
KSZE	Konferenz über Sicherheit und Zusammenarbeit in Europa
KVAE	Konferenz über Vertrauensbildende Maßnahmen und Abrüstung in Europa
KVZ	Konfliktverhütungszentrum
LANDCENT	Allied Command Land Forces Central Europe
MBFR	Mutual and Balanced Force Reductions
MC	Military Committee
MOE	Mittelosteuropa
N+N	Neutrale und Nichtpaktgebundene (Staaten)
NACC	North Atlantic Cooperation Council
NAFTA	North American Free Trade Association
NAKR	Nordatlantischer Kooperationsrat
NV	Nicht(weiter)verbreitung
NZZ	Neue Zürcher Zeitung
OAS	Organization of American States
OAU	Organization of African Unity
ODIHR	Office for Democratic Institutions and Human Rights
OECD	Organization for Economic Cooperation and Development
OEEC	Organization of European Economic Cooperation
ÖIIP	Österreichisches Institut für Internationale Politik
OFE	Office for Free Elections

P-5	Permanent Five / Die fünf ständigen Sicherheitsratsmitglieder der Vereinten Nationen
PKK	Partîya Karkerên Kurdistan (Arbeiterpartei Kurdistans)
RGW	Rat für Gegenseitige Wirtschaftshilfe
SAMCOMM	Sanctions Assistance Mission Communications
SEATO	South-East Asia Treaty Organization
SZ	Süddeutsche Zeitung
TLE	Treaty-Limited Elements
UN	United Nations
UNHCR	United Nations High Commissioner for Refugees
VBM	Vertrauensbildende Maßnahmen
VN	Vereinte Nationen
VSBM	Vertrauens- und Sicherheitsbildende Maßnahmen
VVSBM	Verhandlungen über Vertrauens- und Sicherheitsbildende Maßnahmen
WEU	Western European Union / Westeuropäische Union
WTO	Warsaw Treaty Organization
WVO	Warschauer Vertragsorganisation

2. Die Autoren

John *Barrett*, Dr., ist Mitarbeiter der Political Affairs Division, NATO, International Staff.

Robert D. *Blackwill* ist Professor an der John F. Kennedy School of Government der Harvard University.

Grigoriy J. *Chudakov* ist wissenschaftlicher Mitarbeiter am Europa-Institut der Russischen Akademie der Wissenschaften in Moskau.

Dmitriy A. *Danilov*, Dr., ist wissenschaftlicher Mitarbeiter am Europa-Institut der Russischen Akademie der Wissenschaften in Moskau.

Anne M. *Dixon* ist wissenschaftliche Mitarbeiterin am Center for Naval Analyses in Alexandria, Virginia.

Wim F. *van Eekelen* ist Generalsekretär der Westeuropäischen Union (WEU) in Brüssel.

Thomas J. *Hirschfeld* ist wissenschaftlicher Mitarbeiter und Projektdirektor am Center for Naval Analyses in Alexandria, Virginia.

Johan Jørgen *Holst* ist Außenminister Norwegens.

Sergei A. *Karaganov*, Dr., ist stellvertretender Direktor des Europa-Instituts der Russischen Akademie der Wissenschaften in Moskau.

Uwe *Nerlich* ist Mitglied der Institutsleitung der Stiftung Wissenschaft und Politik (SWP) in Ebenhausen bei München.

Hans Jochen *Peters* ist Head der Central and Eastern Europe and Liaison Section, NATO International Staff.

Ingo *Peters*, Dr., ist Akademischer Rat an der Arbeitsstelle Transatlantische Außen- und Sicherheitspolitik am Fachbereich Politische Wissenschaft der Freien Universität (FU) Berlin.

Bernard *von Plate* ist wissenschaftlicher Mitarbeiter der Stiftung Wissenschaft und Politik (SWP) in Ebenhausen bei München.

Pavel T. *Podlesnyi*, Dr., ist Abteilungsleiter am Europa-Institut der Russischen Akademie der Wissenschaften in Moskau.

Michael *Staack*, Dr., ist wissenschaftlicher Assistent und Leiter der KSZE-Arbeitsgruppe an der Arbeitsstelle Transatlantische Außen- und Sicherheitspolitik am Fachbereich Politische Wissenschaft der Freien Universität (FU) Berlin.

James B. *Steinberg*, Dr., ist wissenschaftlicher Mitarbeiter der RAND Corporation in Santa Monica, Kalifornien.

Heinz *Vetschera*, Dr., Dr., ist Universitätslektor für Internationale Politik an der Universität Wien und derzeit Assistent des Direktors des KSZE-Konfliktverhütungszentrums in Wien.

Helmut Handzik

Politische Bedingungen sowjetischer Truppenabzüge 1925–1958

Die Rückführung der letzten noch auf fremdem Territorium stationierten früheren sowjetischen Truppen soll Mitte der 90er Jahre abgeschlossen werden. Gleichwohl wurden bereits vor Beginn der Ära Gorbatschow mehr als ein Dutzend Länder oder Regionen von sowjetischen Streitkräften geräumt. Welches waren die politischen Bedingungen dieser Abzüge, welche Ursachen und Intentionen lagen zugrunde? Diesen Fragen wird in einer Reihe von Fallstudien nachgegangen. Nachgezeichnet wird die Mehrzahl der sowjetischen Truppenrückführungen aus europäischen und asiatischen Ländern zwischen 1925 und 1958.

Nach dem Präzedenzfall der Invasion und politischen Gleichschaltung der Äußeren Mongolei Anfang der 20er Jahre wurde die Rote Armee während des Zweiten Weltkrieges und unmittelbar danach systematisch als Instrument zur Erreichung kommunistischer Regime in den besetzten Gebieten eingesetzt. Die Mitte der 50er Jahre eingeleitete Serie von Truppenabzügen war Ausdruck einer Neubewertung der strategischen Situation der UdSSR, aber auch der Erkenntnis, welche wirtschaftlichen und politischen Kosten der Sowjetunion aus der langfristigen Stationierung von Streitkräften auf fremdem Territorium erwuchsen.

1993, 320 S., geb., 48,– DM, 338,50 öS, 43,50 sFr,
ISBN 3-7890-3033-3
(Internationale Politik und Sicherheit, Bd. 34)